INSIGHT GUIDES

RUSSIA
BELARUS & UKRAINE

D1051618

Discovery
CHANNEL

APA PUBLICATIONS
Part of the Langenscheidt Publishing Group

INSIGHT GUIDE
RUSSIA
BeLaRUS & UKRaine

Editorial
Project Editor
Jane Hutchings
Managing Editor
Clare Griffiths
Editorial Director
Brian Bell

UK & Ireland
GeoCenter International Ltd
The Viables Centre, Harrow Way
Basingstoke, Hants RG22 4BJ
Fax: (44) 1256 817988
United States
Langenscheidt Publishers, Inc.
36–36 33rd Street 4th Floor
Long Island City, NY 11106
Fax: 1 (718) 784 0640
Canada
Thomas Allen & Son Ltd
390 Steelcase Road East
Markham, Ontario L3R 1G2
Fax: (1) 905 475 6747
Australia
Universal Publishers
1 Waterloo Road
Macquarie Park, NSW 2113
Fax: (61) 2 9888 9074
New Zealand
Hema Maps New Zealand Ltd (HNZ)
Unit D, 24 Ra ORA Drive
East Tamaki, Auckland
Fax: (64) 9 273 6479
Worldwide
**Apa Publications GmbH & Co.
Verlag KG (Singapore branch)**
38 Joo Koon Road, Singapore 628990
Tel: (65) 6865 1600. Fax: (65) 6861 6438

Printing
Insight Print Services (Pte) Ltd
38 Joo Koon Road, Singapore 628990
Tel: (65) 6865 1600. Fax: (65) 6861 6438

©2005 Apa Publications GmbH & Co.
Verlag KG (Singapore branch)
All Rights Reserved
First Edition 1990
Third Edition 1999
Updated 2005

CONTACTING THE EDITORS
We would appreciate it if readers
would alert us to errors or out-
dated information by writing to:
**Insight Guides, P.O. Box 7910,
London SE1 1WE, England.
Fax: (44) 20 7403 0290.
insight@apaguide.co.uk**

www.insightguides.com

ABOUT THIS BOOK

This guidebook combines the interests and enthusiasms of two of the world's best known information providers: Insight Guides, whose titles have set the standard for visual travel guides since 1970, and Discovery Channel, the world's premier source of non-fiction television programming.

The editors of Insight Guides provide both practical advice and general understanding about a destination's history, culture, insti-tutions and people. Discovery Channel and its popular website, www.discovery.com, help millions of viewers to explore the world from the comfort of their home and also encourage them to explore it first-hand.

How to use this book
◆ The **Features** sec-tion, with a yellow colour

bar, covers the area's history and culture in lively authoritative essays written by specialists.
◆ The **Places** section, with a blue bar, provides full details of all the sights and areas worth seeing. The chief places of interest are coordinated by number with spe-cially drawn maps.
◆ The **Travel Tips** listings section, with an orange bar, at the back of the book, gives information on travel, accommodation, restau-rants and other practical aspects.

The contributors
This new edition of *Insight Guide: Russia, Belarus & Ukraine*, which builds on the previous edition edited by **Anna Benn**, was edited by **Jane Hutch-ings**, assisted by manag-ing editor **Clare Griffiths** Hutchings, a former Lon-don *Sunday Times Maga*

Discovery
CHANNEL

zine journalist and freelance editor, has worked on a number of Insight titles.

The book's main contributor, **Jonathan Bastable**, offered invaluable advice throughout the project and wrote the chapters on *Land and Climate*, *Windows on the West*, *The Emperors*, *The Rise and Fall of the Soviet Empire* and picture stories on the Moscow Metro and the Trans-Siberian Railway. Bastable lived in Russia for many years and is writing a book on the Cathedral of Christ in Moscow.

Russian graduate **Esther Wolff** wrote the feature on *Life Today*, while *Insight on the Hermitage* was written by art historian **Catherine Phillips**, who also revised **Ivan Samarine**'s chapter on art. Phillips' chapter *The European North* was updated for this edition by writer and St

Petersburg Times journalist **John Varoli**. Varoli also worked on the chapters on St Petersburg and the European South (originally written by **Vladimir Brodetsky**) and wrote new pieces on the Russian media and film.

The feature on *Women in Russia* is by **Olga Lipovskaya** while credit for the updating of the music chapter goes to **Iosif Raiskin**. **Rowlinson Carter's** chapter on religion has been updated by Moscow-based **Robin Minney**. **Marc Bennetts** updated the chapter on Moscow, originally written by **Anne Lavelle**. **Kirill Koriukin** wrote the story on the mafia. **Iain Law** revised the chapter on food and wrote the *Insight on Lake Baikal*. **Charmaine Bickley** wrote the chapter on The Southwest.

The feature essays on Belarus and Ukraine and the Crimea picture story were written by **Tim Gould**, a political and economic analyst who first moved to Kiev in 1993 and revised by **Marc Bennetts**, who also extensively revised the Belarus and Ukraine chapters by **Joanne Levine** and **Albert Lantuch**. **Claire Bigg** made a significant contribution to this edition by updating several chapters and writing the chapter, *The Golden Ring*.

Many of the book's striking images are by **Cathleen Naundorf**, **Jim Holmes** and **Tony Perrottet**. Picture research was by **Susannah Stone**. **Sylvia Suddes**, **Alyse Dar** and **Richard Carmichael** all made significant editorial contributions to this edition and the index was compiled by **Penny Phenix**.

Map Legend

—‥—	International Boundary
—•—	National Park/Reserve
----	Ferry Route
Ⓜ	Metro
✈ ✈	Airport: International/Regional
🚌	Bus Station
🅿	Parking
❶	Tourist Information
✉	Post Office
⛪ † ⛪	Church/Ruins
†	Monastery
☪	Mosque
✡	Synagogue
🏰	Castle/Ruins
∴	Archaeological Site
⋂	Cave
🗿	Statue/Monument
★	Place of Interest

The main places of interest in the Places section are coordinated by number with a full-colour map (e.g. ❶), and a symbol at the top of every right-hand page tells you where to find the map.

Insight Guide

RUSSIA
Belarus & Ukraine

Maps

Russia **136**

Moscow **138**

Central Moscow **142**

The Golden Ring **174**

St Petersburg **182**

European Russia **212**

Novgorod **220**

Along the Volga **230**

Astrakahn **235**

The Urals **240**

Yekaterinburg **242**

The European South **250**

Sochi **252**

Siberia & the Far East **260**

Belarus **302**

Minsk **304**

Ukraine **310**

Kiev **312**

Odessa **322**

Kiev Metro **343**

Minsk Metro **344**

Inside front cover: Russia
Inside back cover: Moscow
and St Petersburg metros

CONTENTS

Introduction

The Riddle of Russia **15**
A Boundless Land **17**

History

Decisive Dates **24**
Beginnings **27**
The Mongol Yoke...................**33**
The First of the Tsars.............**37**
Windows on the West **41**
Five Emperors.......................**47**

The Rise and Fall of the
  Soviet Empire **53**

Features

Life Today **65**
Women of Russia **75**
Russia's Mafia **78**
Food......................................**82**
The Religious Revival **89**
Art and Inspiration.................**97**
Literature **109**
The Music Makers **116**

The magnificent
exterior of The
Catherine
Palace, St
Petersburg

Travel Tips

Getting Acquainted **330**

Planning the Trip **332**

Practical Tips **335**

Getting Around **342**

Where to Stay **346**

Where to Eat **353**

Nightlife **359**

Shopping **360**

Language **362**

Further Reading **367**

◆Full Travel Tips index
 is on page 329

Insight on ...

Trans-Siberian Railway **124**

Moscow Metro......................**168**

Highlights of the Hermitage ...**206**

Lake Baikal **272**

Crimea...............................**326**

Information panels

Freedom of Speech **73**

Russian Cinema **123**

Places

Introduction **133**

Moscow **141**

The Golden Ring **173**

St Petersburg **185**

The European North.............**211**

The Southwest **226**

Along the Volga **229**

The Urals **239**

The European South **249**

Siberia and the Far East........**259**

Belarus and Ukraine:

Introduction **279**

Belarus and Ukraine: History **283**

Life Today in Belarus
    and Ukraine **291**

Belarus: The Sights **301**

Ukraine: The Sights **309**

THE RIDDLE OF RUSSIA

Everything about the country is monumental: its turbulent
history, its cultural achievements and, above all, its size

> *Russia cannot be understood*
> *With the mind,*
> *Nor can she be measured*
> *By a common yardstick.*
> *A special character she has:*
> *In Russia one can only have faith.*
> —Fyodor Tyutchev, 19th-century poet

Such understanding has never come easily to outsiders. "Russia is impenetrable," wrote the American historian Henry Adams in 1895, "and any intelligent man will deal with her better, the less closely he knows her." Sir Winston Churchill, trying to predict Russia's behaviour in 1939, coined the masterly description: "a riddle wrapped in a mystery inside an enigma."

Such mystery always fascinates, and since the raising of the Iron Curtain at the end of the 1980s, curious tourists have poured into Russia, many of them venturing beyond the cities of St Petersburg and Moscow to find out what provincial and rural Russia is like. Just as Russians are discovering that foreigners are not, in the words of the poet Yevgeny Yevtushenko, "all spies with cameras in their buttons, radio transmitters in the heels of their shoes, and pockets full of Colorado beetles", so Westerners are having their own preconceived ideas overturned. Siberia, for example, is shedding its *Gulag Archipelago* image and revealing itself as a stunningly beautiful and diverse land so vast that a pocket of Old Believers – a branch of the Orthodox Church – was unaware of the fall of the tsar when it was stumbled upon in the 1980s.

Meanwhile, Russia's pre-Revolution culture has emerged from cold storage. Religion has resumed its important role in society, and art, music and literature are rediscovering their pre- and immediate post-Revolutionary vigour. Added to these is the explosive energy of Russia's "New Culture", in which young Muscovites and St Petersburgers are experimenting with new modes of expression – and not all of them copied from the West. There is a darker side, too: the gap between rich and poor has widened alarmingly, while economic uncertainty and organised crime have had a destabilising effect.

While much of this book focuses on Russia, sections are dedicated to the fully independent states of Belarus and Ukraine; they are included because of their cultural and historical links with Russia. Minsk and Kiev, the capitals of Belarus and Ukraine respectively, are alluring tourist destinations and the countryside of both states offers much of interest, along with the sunshine resorts of the Black Sea. ❑

PRECEDING PAGES: Kuzma Minin and Dmitry Pozharsky monument, Moscow; ceiling panel, Moscow Metro station; painting the Church of St Saviour's Blood, St Petersburg; octopus ice sculpture in Moscow's Gorky Park. **LEFT:** Space Obelisk, Moscow.

A BOUNDLESS LAND

*To make sense of the immensity of Russia, its varied and dramatic scenery
and its diverse climate, one must begin with the land itself*

The vastness of the Russian land is hard for Westerners to grasp. The territories of the Eastern Slavonic peoples – the Russian Federation, Ukraine and Belarus taken together – cover around 18 million sq km (7 million sq. miles). This is twice the size of the United States, and more than 73 times the size of Britain. Russia ranges across 11 time zones. When citizens in westerly Kaliningrad are getting up in the morning, their fellow countrymen on the Pacific seaboard are home from work and thinking about going to bed. Train journeys in this country are measured in days rather than hours.

Russia reaches well into the Arctic Circle. The world's largest polar city is Murmansk, built on the uppermost fringe of the Kola peninsula at the point where the warm Gulf Stream licks the coast. Because it takes advantage of this geographical accident, Murmansk is Russia's only ice-free seaport in the north. But in the south, Russian territory extends into the balmy climes of the Black Sea. Here, around the coast to the west, is the Crimea. Once the Soviet Riviera, this sun-washed peninsula is now the jewel of independent Ukraine. In better times this was a wine-making region. It is still fertile land, sheltered by the tall, sharp crags of the Caucasus.

White nights of June

Russia's landmass is shaped like a great wedge, which has its point in the west. (This geopolitical fact alone helps to explain 500 years of Russian foreign policy: the further west Russia's borders lie, the shorter is its frontier and so the easier to defend.) The Eurasian, fatter, end of the wedge extends to the north and east for 10,460 km (6,500 miles). Moscow is roughly on the same latitude as Glasgow in Scotland or Edmonton, Alberta, in Canada. Consequently the days are long in summer and short in winter. Murmansk is in darkness round the clock from

LEFT: young worker in the fields of Siberia.
RIGHT: long, cold winters are a feature of the climate.

November to March, while St Petersburg has made an annual festival of its "white nights", a month-long celebration in June and July when the city is bathed in an eerie, nocturnal translucence, which makes it difficult to sleep.

The climate across Russia is continental: that is, short hot summers with long cold winters.

Ukraine has briefer, milder winters due to its more southerly location. Temperatures of minus 20°C (minus 4°F) are not unusual in Moscow in January, and the winters in Siberia are cold beyond description. The coldest inhabited place on earth is Oimyakon, in the diamond-rich uplands of Yakutia, where daytime temperatures of minus 70°C (minus 94°F) have been recorded.

East-west divide

Only one geographical feature interrupts the great, level Eurasian plain between the Carpathians and the Far Eastern highlands. Like the spine of a book laid open on its face, the

Urals run in a straight line for 1,930 km (1,200 miles) from the Barents Sea in the north almost to the Caspian Sea in the south. These low mountains are the official boundary between Europe and Asia, and between European Russia and Siberia. But they are not a formidable natural barrier, and no invader was ever stopped by the Urals.

To the west of the Urals lies the most populous part of Russia, and Belarus and Ukraine. Belarus is landlocked; its terrain is hilly in places, and about a third of it is forested, but the glacial soil is rich. The traditional crops are rye, buckwheat and potatoes, which are the staples of the diet throughout the region. Peat is harvested in the flat marshes south of Minsk, and used in power stations; Belarus has no fossil fuels on its territory.

Ukraine is richer. It has unexploited reserves of coal and another form of black gold, the *chernozem* or "black earth" which covers two-thirds of the land. It is this rich, fertile earth, together with the relatively mild climate, which made Ukraine the traditional "breadbasket of Europe".

In the summer the Ukrainian countryside resembles its blue-and-yellow national flag: all the eye can see is a thick ribbon of ripe yellow

TOXIC EARTH AND POISONED SEAS

For all its natural beauty, the former Soviet Union is a land of ecological nightmares. The Chernobyl disaster of 1985 is symbolic of the dangers, but even that catastrophe pales next to the environmental damage that was done in earlier Soviet times. The nuclear installation at Chelyabinsk-65 in Siberia is a kind of serial Chernobyl. It has had several massive accidents, the worst in 1957. It is still spewing nuclear waste into Lake Karachai, officially the most radioactive spot on Earth. An hour's exposure on the lake's shoreline can be fatal. Nuclear contamination is only part of the picture. Much of the pollution is the result of the Stalinist drive to industrialise at any cost. Lake Baikal, the largest body of fresh water on the planet, is in grave danger of irreversible poisoning from the paper-pulping plants on its shore. The acid rain which falls on the Kola peninsula, and has devastated thousands of hectares of forest, is the result of the gases released from nickel refineries. And in Dzerzhinsk, the centre of Russia's chlorine and pesticide industries, almost the entire population is ill, and the life expectancy for adults has dropped into the forties. These are just a few examples: there are hundreds of equally grave problems. And the future is bleak. According to one American study, by the year 2015 only 20 percent of Russian babies will be born healthy.

wheat under a blue band of sky. The same good land underlies much of the Russian south. Here the main crop is winter wheat, sown in the autumn and protected from the cold by a layer of snow. Further to the north, all kinds of farming are to be found in the cleared expanses between the ancient forests: dairy, pigs and poultry, oats, root crops, flax and potatoes.

Tundra, taiga, steppe and forest

A satellite's-eye view of the Russian plateau would show that, east of the Urals especially, it is divided east to west into four broad vegetational zones. Three of these zones are so dis-

of snow melts, the moss and lichen burst forth and the ground is carpeted with bright and hardy flowers. Later in the year migratory birds pass through, and regiments of furry animals – silver foxes, wolves, ermine, ferrets and lemmings – emerge from the southern forests. But as winter and darkness draw in again, the only animals that can survive the tundra are polar bears and seals.

The tundra gives way to the taiga, a gigantic and almost impenetrable belt which accounts for about a third of the world's forest. This zone is about 5,000 km (3,000 miles) long and 1,000 km (600 miles) wide. The insulating effect of

tinctive that they are known to geographers by their Russian names: the tundra, taiga and steppe. The fourth zone is the great swathe of mixed forest which has fed hunters and hindered farmers for generations.

The tundra is the northernmost belt. At its most extreme, in the Arctic, it is a cold, white, lifeless desert. A little further south a few stunted trees grow, but their roots are shallow because they cannot penetrate the eternal permafrost. In spring, when the uppermost layer

LEFT: steppe landscape in the Orenburg Region of the southern Urals.
ABOVE: a European beaver at the water's edge.

such a density of trees means that in its deepest pockets the snow almost never melts and even the permafrost persists.

The result is a "drunken forest" where overtall spruce tilt at tipsy angles in the shallow top soil. The species of tree vary from region to region over this wooded ocean: there are pine, larch and, in the southern reaches of Siberia, the archetypal Russian birch. This dark kingdom is the habitat of the sable, prized for its fur above all other animals, as well as of Russian bears, lynx, and in Siberia elks and maral deers. In summer black swarms of bloodthirsty gnats and midges make the area of the taiga almost uninhabitable for humans.

The taiga shades gently into a variegated stripe of mixed forest, where the trees are deciduous, such as oak, ash and maple. In European areas the trees have been systematically cleared for agriculture, but chestnuts abound in the Ukraine, where they are considered a national tree, as the birch is for Russia. East of the Urals the mixed forest covers an area far beyond Russia's borders. There are few animal species unique to this zone, though the last European bison are to be found living in conservation areas.

South of the forest is a relatively narrow strip of open grassland running from Romania to

China. This area is known as the steppe. It is easily traversed, and as such has served as the main highway for nomadic peoples travelling from Asia to Europe. The soil here is prone to erosion by the freezing winds of winter and the thunderstorms of summer.

In the Siberian steppe there is a sense of emptiness and desolation which is increased by the fact that much of the native fauna – antelopes and wild horses – has been hunted by man to extinction. But in the air, the magnificent steppe eagle is still in evidence, and underfoot there is a variety of small and exotic rodents such as the bobak marmot, the five-toed jerboa and Chinese striped hamster.

Rivers and other riches

These four bands are criss-crossed by great, meandering rivers. In Siberia they flow from south to north. The longest of the Siberian waterways, at 5,700 km (3,360 miles), is the Ob, though the Yenisei and the Lena are both more than 3,200 km (2,000 miles) long.

In the Brezhnev era of the 1970s there was an ill-conceived plan to reverse the flow of Siberian rivers to irrigate the cotton fields of central Asia and save the Aral Sea. The plan was abandoned, and the Aral is now a desert of poisonous dust, with some 200,000 tonnes of salt and sand swirling around daily on a radius of 300 km (186 miles), affecting the health of people, animals and plants.

Before it was destroyed by overuse and chemical pollution the Aral ranked as the fourth-biggest inland sea in the world; the biggest is the Caspian Sea on Russia's southern flank. In Siberia, near the Mongolian border, is the world's biggest freshwater reserve and also the deepest freshwater lake, Baikal. Drawn on a map the lake looks tiny, but it holds more water than the entire Baltic Sea, and is home to 960 species of animal found nowhere else in the world.

Untapped mineral wealth

Beneath all this variety is a buried treasure chest of mineral riches. Western Siberia has vast untapped deposits of coal, iron ore and natural gas. The Urals are studded with emeralds, rubies, malachite, jasper and gold. The diamond deposits in Yakutia are immense – enough to unbalance the world market if their mining and sale are not carefully controlled.

Beyond the highlands of Yakutia and the now-abandoned Gulag zone of Kolyma is the eastern seaboard, where Russia is washed by the waters of the Pacific. The Kamchatka peninsula, a strange proboscis on Russia's eastward-looking face which is dotted with active volcanoes, is located here. Here, too, is the Chukotsky peninsula, on the tip of which is Cape Dezhnev. This is where Russia's territory runs out. It is the country's easternmost point. On a clear day you can stand on the shore of the Bering Strait and wave across to America. ❏

LEFT: in Siberia the summer months are warm enough for trekking and other outdoor activities.
RIGHT: a wild elk majestically surveys his territory.

Decisive Dates

THE FIRST RUSSIANS

The Moskva and Volga rivers region was settled from pre-historic times by Finno-Ugrians, Indo-Europeans and Germanic tribes. Scythians inhabited the steppes.
AD 400–600 Eastern Slavs migrate into what is now Ukraine and western Russia.
800–900 Swedish Varangians (Vikings) under Prince Rurik advance southwest along the rivers establishing strongholds at Novgorod and Kiev, "the mother of Russian cities". Polotsk on the Dvina River forms the nucleus for Belarus.

900–1240 Kiev becomes the centre of the Russian empire; trade flourishes with Byzantium.
988 Christianity is introduced from Constantinople.

THE MONGOL YOKE

1200–1300 While Alexander Nevsky defends Russia's western borders from Swedish attack, Batu Khan, grandson of Genghis Khan, invades from the east, conquers Moscow (1238) and sacks Kiev (1240). For the next 250 years, Russian princes are forced to pay tribute to the Golden Horde (Mongols).
1300–1400 Poland captures Belarus and Ukraine.
1328 Ivan Kalita ("Moneybags") is designated Grand Prince by the Khan. He moves from Vladimir to Moscow, where he builds his kremlin (fortress).

1380 Grand Prince Dmitry, grandson of "Moneybags", challenges the Mongols in the Battle of Kulikovo but cannot prevent them from sacking Moscow. The city recovers to become a symbol of Russian unity. The power of the Mongols begins to wane.
1462–1500 Ivan III, "Grand Prince of Moscow and All Russia", refuses to pay Moscow's tribute to the Mongols, whose domination comes to an end. Russia succeeds Byzantium as the "Third Rome".

THE RULE OF THE TSARS

1547–84 Ivan IV (the Terrible), is crowned Tsar of All Russia. He defeats the Tatars in Kazan (and builds St Basil's Cathedral in celebration) and Astrakhan, colonises Siberia, reduces the power of the wealthy boyars (nobles) and sows the seeds of serfdom.
1584–1613 Anarchy and civil war prevail; Boris Godunov presides over The Time of Troubles.
1613 Tsar Mikhail Romanov restores stability.
1648 Bogdan Khmelnitsky launches the Ukrainian offensive that drives out the Poles. The Pereyaslav agreement of 1654, which grants autonomy to Ukraine, is soon undermined: east Ukraine falls under Russian control following a Cossack revolt, 1667; west Ukraine and Belarus come under Polish rule.

A WINDOW ON THE WEST

1682–1725 The widely-travelled tsar, Peter the Great, son of Alexei Romanov, introduces Western ways, reforms the civil service and army, and builds a modern navy. He recaptures the Baltic coast from the Swedes and starts building his new city, St Petersburg, at the mouth of the River Neva. In 1724 St Petersburg becomes the official capital of Russia.
1725–62 Under Peter's heirs the court becomes Westernised and alienated from the people.
1763–96 Catherine II (the Great) ushers in a period of enlightenment. She reforms local government, liberalises the penal code, founds hospitals and invites leading architects to St Petersburg who give the city its classical look. Belarus and Ukraine are recaptured from Poland, Crimea is conquered and the mineral wealth of Siberia is exploited.

THE EMPERORS

1796–1825 Catherine's son, the military dictator Paul I, is assassinated in 1801. He is succeeded by the more liberal Alexander I.
1812 Napoleon invades and occupies Moscow. The inhabitants set fire to the city. Napoleon withdraws.
1825–55 Decembrist Rising in St Petersburg is crushed by Nicholas I in 1825. He rules with obsessive attention to detail, but lacks initiative to deal with the

big issues, such as food and clothing for the Russian army in the Crimean War (1853–56).

1855–81 Alexander II liberates the serfs, 1861. He is assassinated by revolutionaries, 1 March 1881.

1881–94 Rapid industrialisation under the repressive rule of Alexander III leads to a huge increase in the size of the urban working class.

ABDICATION AND REVOLUTION

1894–1917 The last tsar, Nicholas II, is unable to contain the groundswell of revolutionary activity.

1898 Vladimir Lenin forms Social Democratic Party.

1905 Bloody Sunday (9 January): 140,000 workers march to the Winter Palace.Troops open fire; 100 marchers are killed, hundreds wounded. The Tsar agrees to establish the Duma (State Assembly).

1914 Russia enters World War I against Germany.

1917 Russia is on the brink of economic and political catastrophe. Tsar Nicholas II abdicates. A provisional government is set up. On 25 October the Bolshevik Central Committee, under Lenin's leadership, seizes power in the Great Socialist Revolution. Lenin nationalises industries and radically reforms agriculture.

1918 Treaty of Brest–Litovsk ends war with Germany. The Tsar and family are murdered. Civil war rages until 1922 when Lev Trotsky's Red Army declares victory.

COMMUNISTS TAKE CONTROL

1922 Lenin declares the Union of Soviet Socialist Republics (USSR); Moscow becomes the official capital. Lenin dies in 1924 and Petrograd is renamed Leningrad in his honour. Joseph Stalin wins power struggle and starts the first Five Year Plan of industrialisation and agricultural collectivisation backed up by a purge in which millions either die or are deported.

1941–45 Adolf Hitler invades the USSR around 25 million citizens die in the Great Patriotic War. Victory over Germany is declared on 9 May 1945.

1953 Stalin dies. Nikita Khrushchev emerges as leader. A cultural thaw ensues.

1955 Eastern Bloc countries sign the Warsaw Pact declaring a military alliance.

1956 Russia invades Hungary.

1964–82 Leonid Brezhnev partially reverses Khrushchev's reforms and imposes a regime of censorship. He intervenes in Czechoslovakia (1968) in the name of protecting socialism, and invades Afghanistan (1979). The Cold War with the West and arms race with the US continue until *détente* and the Strategic Arms Limitation Talks (SALT) of the late 1970s.

PRECEDING PAGES: the Time of Troubles, Moscow.
LEFT: Catherine the Great. **RIGHT:** Vladimir Lenin.

THE DAWN OF DEMOCRACY

1985 Mikhail Gorbachev introduces reforms based on restructuring, openness, democratisation and a market economy. Satellite states agitate for independence.

1991 A failed coup d'état by hardline communists leads to the eclipse of Gorbachev, the collapse of communism and the disintegration of the USSR. A fragile federation of the republics, the Commonwealth of Independent States, takes its place. Russia under Boris Yeltsin becomes successor state to USSR.

1993 Political struggle between president and parliament turns violent. Street battles in Moscow. Yeltsin uses tanks to shell the parliament building. In the aftermath, the presidency is granted sweeping powers.

1996 Boris Yeltsin wins a second term as president.

1998 The rouble is devalued. Yeltsin appoints Yevgeni Primakov as prime minister to restore stability.

2000 Vladimir Putin wins presidential election.

2001 Putin offers immediate support to the US after the 11 September attacks and sanctions the stationing of US troops on former Soviet territory in central Asian states bordering Afghanistan.

2002 Over 100 people die in siege of Moscow theatre.

2003 St Petersburgh hosts tri-centenary celebrations, featuring restored buildings and world leaders.

2004 Putin is re-elected to a second term. Over 330 people, many of them children, die in a school siege in Beslan (Russian Caucasus), the world's worst hostage crisis. ❏

BEGINNINGS

Of all the migratory groups to cross Russia in the Dark Ages, the Slavs and the Vikings were the most influential

The 9th-century Viking conquest of hitherto stateless Slavs scattered across modern Russia, Ukraine and Belarus was traditionally made to sound like an act of high-minded charity. "Our land is great and rich but there is no order in it," the Slavs are reputed to have cried. "Come and rule over us." Prince Rurik of South Jutland in Denmark was ready to oblige. He made himself master of Novgorod, the most northwesterly Slav settlement, and within three years of his death in 879 his successors, who came to be known as Varangians, had extended their rule to include Smolensk and Kiev.

The invitation – such as it was – fitted in perfectly with the Varangian desire to monopolise the lucrative trade route between the Baltic and the Black Sea, which happened to pass through the allegedly rich but disorderly land in question. The main artery of this largely river-borne trade was the Dnieper (Dnipro) River, and of the settlements which the Varangians deigned to rule over, Kiev was the most valuable strategically. It was accordingly declared "the Mother of Russian cities".

Kiev was only one, but by far the grandest, in a network of embryonic city-states which various Varangian princes established and fought over among themselves. The estate of Yuri Dolgoruky of Suzdal was the beginning of Moscow while Prince of Polotsk's settlement on the Dvina River was the nucleus of Belarus.

It was not until the Mongol invasions of the 13th century that the focus of Russia moved away from Kiev to the north. Viewed from the forests, the depopulated area around Kiev was seen as "Ukraine", meaning the borderland.

Ukraine was also referred to as "Black" land because of its dark rich soil, but it was common land on which the semi-nomadic population had the right to roam on payment of a kind of licence fee to the ruling prince, and "Black" became synonymous with these property rights.

"White Russia", on the other hand – the translation of "Belarus" – drew attention to the fact that the territory was not common land but subject to the feudal tenure which applied while it was, as we shall see, under Polish administration. The people living on it were tied serfs.

Three Russias therefore came about, even if

the dividing lines were historically and geographically fluid: Great Russia, born of Muscovy and these days simply called Russia; Ukraine, which picked up yet another name, Little Russia; and White Russia (Belarus).

Cultural melting pot

To begin with, there were no ethnic or cultural divisions. Migration across the northern plain from Central Asia into Europe had long been taking place before Rurik and his Vikings sailed south. The Slavs who supposedly invited the Vikings to come and rule over them were relatively recent arrivals, mostly 5th and 6th century, who spoke kindred Slavonic languages.

LEFT: an ancient hero of Rus defends his kingdom.
RIGHT: Rurik, the legendary 9th-century Viking prince who was invited by the Slavs to rule over them.

They followed in the wake of Finno-Ugrians who ended up in Finland and Estonia, Indo-Europeans who became Lithuanians and Latvians, and a host of Germanic tribes who, one way or another, became not only Germans but French and Anglo-Saxon English, which helps to explain why even into this century Russians were inclined to describe all non-Slavic Europeans as "Germans".

There was a high degree of fusion between the newly arrived Slavs and earlier inhabitants. The Lithuanians were spread across the plains and forests until, under pressure from the Slavs, they retreated to the marshy Baltic shores. The

high cheekbones, darkish complexion and broad nose typical of the Great Russian are attributed to the Finno-Ugrians, obviously a far cry from notions of fair-haired, blue-eyed Scandinavians, a different group altogether.

The Varangians did fit the Scandinavian model, but they were only a military elite and it was a case common throughout history of conquerors being assimilated by the numerically superior conquered. It is unrealistic to think of the Varangians as being anything other than bona fide Slavs quite soon after their conquest.

Cultural comparisons between modern Russians and the tribes who roamed the northern plain long before the Slavs are irresistible. Rus-

sians cheerfully admit to being a trifle xenophobic and, according to Herodotus, the ancient Greek historian, the Scythians, who inhabited the steppes in the 5th century BC, had "an extreme hatred of all foreign customs". Herodotus was sceptical about Scythian descriptions of people living even farther north. According to them, they had goats' feet, could turn themselves into wolves if the occasion arose, and slept for six months at a time like hibernating animals. He did not doubt, however, that the northern winters were so cold that the inhabitants could drive wagons across frozen rivers and lakes and if necessary make war on them. "The ground is frozen iron-hard, so that to turn earth into mud requires not water but fire."

The Empire moves east

The Scythians eventually had to make room for new migrants arriving from Central Asia, and it was the overflow of these northern tribes – notably Huns, Goths, Visigoths and Vandals – across the Danube that spelt the end of the Roman Empire in the West. With repeated sackings of Rome, the Empire was moved from west to east, specifically to the ancient Greek colony of Byzantium, nicely positioned at the narrow Bosphorus crossing to control what was becoming the greatest trade route in the world, the one between Europe and the East.

The Mediterranean provided the obvious connection between Byzantium and Western Europe, but it was plagued by pirates. In any case, Northern Europe had something special to offer the markets of Byzantium: amber from the Baltic shore, furs and honey from the Russian forests and fair-skinned slaves. It was this trade via the Dnieper and to some extent the Volga that attracted the Varangians.

By the time the Slavs had settled along the Dnieper, the transplanted Roman Empire had made Constantinople, the Christianised capital of the East, the richest and most glamourous city on earth, Greek in flavour rather than Roman. Rome was degenerating into a run-down dump on a dirty river.

The Slavs arrived at the tail-end of the transition from Rome to Constantinople. They drifted in different directions on reaching Europe and later assumed regional characteristics on either side of considerable natural boundaries like the Carpathian mountains, or because they were split by alien invaders such as the Finno-Ugrian Magyars, the founders of Hungary. The Slavs in the Balkans came to be recognised as Southern Slavs, or "Yugoslavs", while those in the West took on the national identities of Poles, Czechs and Slovaks. The future Great, Little and White Russians were lumped together as Eastern Slavs. The first split in the homogeneity of the Eastern Slavs was between those who elected to remain on the steppes, which were reminiscent of the grasslands they had left behind in Central Asia, and

SAILING TO BYZANTIUM

Every spring a flotilla would sail down the Dnieper to the great city of Constantinople with its cargo of furs, honey and luckless slaves, in order to return with gold, silk, wines and spices.

Vikings needed to trade with Constantinople.

In 957 Princess Olga of Kiev joined the Dnieper River traders to see the fabled sights of Constantinople and was so impressed that she defied powerful pagan traditions to be baptised as an Eastern Orthodox Christian. This was a most portentous development. The Christian world was then torn by a contest between the Eastern and Western Churches for converts among the heathen hordes of Europe, the forces of Rome being led by the German-

those who ventured into the northern forests. The plain-dwellers grew rye and barley and kept a few cattle on the side.

The main drawback to living on the plain was exposure to new and invariably hostile migrants arriving from Asia. The forests, on the other hand, were relatively safe. Furthermore, the natural products of the forest, notably furs, honey and wax, were so plentiful that the forest-dwellers generally had surpluses available for trade. It was their surplus wealth which the

LEFT: a Finno-Ugrian tribeswoman.
ABOVE: Prince Vladimir, who converted to Christianity in 988 and adopted Eastern Orthodoxy.

dominated Holy Roman Empire founded by Charlemagne in 800. The Western Church was then doing well, having won over the kings of Poland and Norway among others. The most notable Orthodox success had been with the formidable Bulgarian Empire.

Princess Olga tried to persuade her son, Svyatoslav, to follow her example but he was more interested in a military campaign which in due course added the Volga region to Kievan Rus. The question of the religious allegiance of the Eastern Slavs was passed on to his successor, Prince Vladimir, and he was not to be rushed either. Vladimir wished to hear not only from advocates of Byzantium and Rome but also those of Islam and Judaism. They were invited to state their cases, the lead being given to the Jewish representatives. Both they and the Muslims who followed made a poor impression by mentioning circumcision and abstention from pork and alcohol.

The Pope's emissaries were able to guarantee flexibility on the issues of circumcision, pork and alcohol, but they were obliged to add that a certain amount of fasting was required. Vladimir's response to the prospect of fasting was unambiguous: "Depart hence!"

Forewarned, the Byzantine Greeks launched into a history of the world, saving until last a

painting which showed in terrifying detail just what an infidel could expect come the Day of Judgement. Vladimir was unsettled by this revelation, but reserved final judgement until emissaries could visit Constantinople and confirm that joining the Eastern Church would bring material benefits. They returned to say that the city was so magnificent they had wondered whether they were in heaven.

Vladimir's alignment with Byzantium was formalised by his baptism at Kherson in 990 and cemented by marriage to Anna, the Byzantine emperor's sister. This illustrious marriage brought up a point of principle which had so far been overlooked. Vladimir was already

married several times over and had a harem that he had no intention of giving up. The Orthodox authorities and his brother-in-law quietly conceded the point. Vladimir was truly, says the chronicle recounting these events, a *"fornicator immensus et crudelis"*.

The rise and fall of Kiev

Kiev acquired a cathedral, named after and modelled on St Sophia's in Constantinople, and numerous churches. It was more emphatically than ever the outstanding Russian city of the age, but not for long. The eastern Mediterranean, long closed to traders by pirates and the Arabs who had taken over the Levant, was reopened by the success of the early Crusades. The sea route to northern Europe through the Strait of Gibraltar was longer, but it could take ships of any size and eliminated porterage. The value of the Dnieper route dwindled and so did Kiev's profits from it.

The Varangian princes were inclined to move north. Prince Yuri Dolgoruky, founder of Moscow, also acquired Kiev only to be told the city had become virtually worthless. "Here, father, we have nothing," his son said, "let us depart to Suzdal while it is still warm." The same son inherited Suzdal, and in 1169 he proved his point by sacking Kiev and casually tossing the princedom to a younger brother.

In both trade and religion, Russia's orientation had been towards Constantinople, but in 1204 the Fourth Crusade abandoned its avowed purpose of fighting the infidel Turk in the Holy Land in order to ransack Constantinople and put a hostile "Latin Emperor" on the throne of Byzantium. Baldwin, the emperor in question, was not long in office, but the reprieve became meaningless in the light of what was developing unseen thousands of miles away.

While Alexander Nevsky ("of the Neva") defended Russia's western borders from Sweden, a different threat was gathering force in the east, where Temuchin Bagatur, the chief of a Mongol tribe, had conquered China in nine years, a victory which prompted him to assume the name of Genghis Khan, "Ruler of the World". He meant to make that boast good by finding out what lay west of the Ural mountains and conquering it as well. ❑

THE MONGOL YOKE

The Mongols – or Tatars – descended on Russia like a whirlwind,
and the reign of terror they imposed lasted for hundreds of years

The Tatar onslaught took the Russian people by complete surprise. It was a vicious, bloody bolt from the blue. Even now, the folk memory of the Tatars' bloody rule is an indelible scar on the national psyche. Russian mothers can still be heard invoking the name of a long-dead Tatar commander to frighten naughty children. "Eat up your greens," they say, "Or Mamai will get you."

The Russians' first encounter with these fearsome aliens on horseback came in 1223, when an army was smashed at the Kalka River by a Tatar detachment which then melted back into the steppe. News of this strange catastrophe rippled through to the cities of Russia, but no more was heard of the dangerous horsemen from the east, and Russia fell back into its usual complacency.

The Kalka outriders were no more than an advance guard, sent by the Mongol Emperor Genghis Khan to investigate the rich pickings to the west. The real invasion came in 1236, under the command of Genghis Khan's own grandson Batu Khan, and this time it was utterly devastating.

Tatar onslaught

The Tatars were the most awesome fighting force the world had seen, not excluding their contemporaries, the Crusader knights. They were undeterred by the Russian winter, and in fact preferred to campaign when the earth and the rivers were frozen. The frost and the ice provided a hard surface for their ponies, which were trained to dig through snow to find grass.

Every Mongol warrior kept two or three ponies in tow, and this gave them remarkable speed and endurance. They never went into battle without first erecting dressing stations. Soldiers wore an undershirt of raw silk next to their skin. This light vest sank in under the impact of an arrow, enabling the barbed head to be drawn

out without aggravating the wound. Their small bows had a range far longer than the English long-bows used at the Battle of Crécy (1346), and could be fired from the saddle at a gallop.

The Tatars' preferred method was to pick off enemy strongholds one at at a time and let the news of their victory travel ahead to weaken

the resolve of the next target. The city of Ryazan, a small vassal state of Suzdal, was one of the first to fall.

Grand Prince Yuri of Ryazan tried to buy off Batu Khan with gifts, but laughed at the Khan's suggestion that he hand over his own wife as part of the tribute. Khan was not joking; he put the Grand Prince to death on the spot.

The Khan then laid siege to the city, breaching its defences just before Christmas 1237. "The pagans entered the cathedral church of the Most Holy Mother of God," recount the chronicles, "And there they put Yuri's mother, Grand Princess Agrippina, and her daughters-in-law and the other princesses to the sword.

LEFT: the Mongols acquired a bloodthirsty reputation.
RIGHT: Genghis Khan, the Mongol emperor, who sent an advance guard to survey all that lay to the west.

They consigned the bishops and the clergy to the flames and burned them in the holy church. They spilt much blood on the sacred altars. Not one man was left alive in the city. All lay dead together. And all this came to pass because of our sins."

Moscow and, to the northeast, Suzdal and Vladimir were subdued in similar fashion. Novgorod was the next prize on the Tatars' path, but the city was spared by an unseasonal thaw. Novgorod became an island in

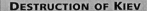

DESTRUCTION OF KIEV

Following the sacking of Vladimir in 1240 the Mongols moved south to mount a devastating attack on Kiev, sparing only St Sophia's Cathedral and a few houses. A visitor to the scene five years later reported that skulls and bones still littered the streets.

a vast sea of mud, and the Tatars chose to turn back rather than attempt to wade through it.

Under the yoke

By 1241, the Tatars had conquered most of Hungary, Romania and Poland, and it seemed that nothing could stop them. But just as Europe lay within his grasp, Batu Khan learned that his uncle, the Emperor Ogedei, had died in the Tatar capital of Karakorum. Batu Khan decided to go home and fight his corner in the domestic power struggle.

This timely death, and the snap decision it drew from Batu Khan, saved Western European civilisation from a second Dark Age. But it was

already too late for Russia. The country was now condemned to the Tatar yoke, cut off from all the great advances of the Renaissance which were destined to take place in Western Europe over the next centuries. All of subsequent Russian history – the frantic westernising of Peter, the agonies of serfdom and emancipation, the wily wartime machinations of Stalin, the uncritical embrace of capitalism in today's Russia – can be read as an attempt by the Russian state to catch up with all that it missed out on during this period, to win recognition from the West for Russia having borne the Tatar yoke alone, for having absorbed the killer blow on behalf of all Europe.

But this is to run ahead. When Batu Khan rushed home in 1241, he left his Russian domains in the charge of a detachment whose base, Sarai (encampment), was near the site of the present-day city of Volgograd. This particular detachment was known as the Golden Horde, and in time their name became synonymous with the Tatar regime.

The rise of Moscow

That regime, once its dominion was established, revolved around the business of tax-collecting. The Tatars were not interested in imposing their culture, and while only too happy to burn down churches to encourage prompt payment of tribute, they did not interfere with the religion of their subject peoples. Consequently, the Russian church became a focus of Russian nationhood, and the local vassal princes of cities such as Moscow found that they could still wield a good deal of power, just so long as they made sure they paid their tribute to the Golden Horde at Sarai.

All this time, no one in the West had the smallest idea, or expressed any interest in, what had become of Russia. Only cities such as Novgorod and Pskov, which lay beyond the Mongol orbit, retained links with the Baltic cities and the world beyond.

Behind this medieval Iron Curtain the insignificant but strategically placed city of Moscow (which together with its lands is known to history as Muscovy) was growing strong. Successive grand princes of Muscovy had gained favour with their absentee landlords, the khans of the Golden Horde, and in 1328 a prince named Ivan was put in charge of collecting and delivering all taxes and tributes. This dubious honour earned him the nickname "Kalita" ("Moneybags").

Moreover, troops of the Muscovy principality were used to crush revolts against the Tatars instigated by lesser princes. In this way the Moscow state slowly took on both the political authority and the methods of the Golden Horde.

A PRICE TO PAY

Moscow's annual tribute to the coffers of the Golden Horde was 4,000 roubles compared with the more important city of Vladimir, which paid 85,000 roubles.

"Dmitry of the Don"). The Tatars came back and wreaked vengeful havoc on Moscow in 1382, but the story of the 100 years that followed is one of gradual decline for the Golden Horde.

The Tatar yoke ended in anticlimax in 1480. Ivan III, the incumbent Grand Prince of Muscovy, had been withholding tribute for 20 years. However, when it came to a Kulikovo-style showdown, neither side had much of a stomach for the fight.

The Mongols turned their backs and retreat-

LEFT: a 16th-century miniature depicting combat between Russians and Tatars in 1238.
ABOVE: 13th-century encampment of invading Tatars.

Russian princes retaliate

Ivan Kalita's grandson, Grand Prince Dmitry, was the first Muscovite prince to feel strong enough to challenge the Tatars's demands in battle. In 1380 he met the Mongol host at the Field of Kulikovo on the River Don and, sensationally, he defeated them.

This battle was Russia's Agincourt, a pivotal moment in the country's history. Dmitry's victory shattered forever the myth of Tatar invincibility (he was afterwards dubbed "Donskoi",

ed, and Ivan let them go. The Golden Horde decamped to the area south of the Don, and established a state of its own, the Khanate of Astrakhan, which survived until it was conquered by Ivan the Terrible.

The Tatars' legacy in Russia is immense. It is there in the language; it is there in the casual ease with which centuries of leaders have been prepared to spill blood; it is there in the very faces of the people. The high cheekbones and slightly Asiatic features characteristic of many Russians are a legacy of the Tatars: a Tatar provenance is clearly visible, for example, in the face (and indeed in the ruthless politics) of Vladimir Ilyich Lenin. ❑

THE FIRST OF THE TSARS

The new caesars ruled Russia with an iron hand,
persecuting treacherous nobles and laying the foundations of serfdom

A wandering German knight ventured into Muscovy some six years after Khan Ahmed had meekly brought 250 years of Mongol overlordship to an end. The report he made to the Holy Roman Emperor, Frederick III, was full of strange and fascinating things.

The title which anyone addressing the Grand Prince of Muscovy was required to know by heart was a measure of recent military successes. He was "Ivan, by the grace of God, Sovereign of all Rus, and grand prince of Vladimir and of Moscow and of Novgorod and of Pskov and of Tver and of Yugria and of Vyatka and of Perm and of Bolgary and of others".

Frederick was impressed and sent word that as Holy Roman Emperor he was prepared to bestow on Ivan the title of king. "We have been sovereign in our land from our earliest forefathers," came the reply, "and our sovereignty we hold from God." Ivan III, who had played an important role in consolidating the Muscovite state, was in fact using the title tsar, a derivation of caesar, because the Orthodox Church had proclaimed Moscow the third Rome after Byzantium. His son, Ivan IV, was crowned Tsar of all Russia in 1547.

Reports filtering through to the West of Italian architects and engineers engaged in strengthening Moscow's defences and building churches and cathedrals aroused enormous curiosity. In 1553 Sir Richard Chancellor, an English seaman, was looking for a northern sea route to China when storms forced him to land near Archangel in the White Sea. Local fishermen informed him that he had wandered into the realm of Ivan Vassilievich.

Chancellor travelled inland with a view to meeting this king, a journey which he described as colder and more uncomfortable than anything he had ever experienced at sea. It was only after "much ado" that he came to Moscow, "the chief city of the kingdom and the seat of

the king". The 12 days Chancellor spent waiting for an audience were an eye-opener. Moscow was larger than London, he thought, but "rude and without order". The nine churches in the Kremlin he considered "not altogether unhandsome" but he did not think the royal palace compared with "the beauty and elegance of the

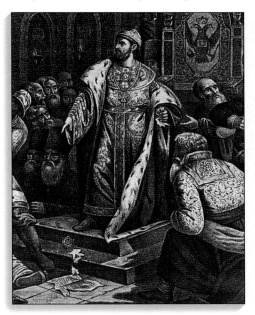

houses of the kings of England". The king, Ivan IV, he learned, commanded an army of more than 200,000 mounted archers, and what he heard about the system of government sounded like tyranny.

Chancellor was dazzled by the splendour of the court when at last he got to see it. A hundred courtiers were dressed in gold down to their ankles. The king himself, Chancellor reported, was not only dressed in gold but had a gold crown on his head and a gold sceptre inlaid with precious stones. All the tableware at the state banquet he attended was gold. He dined on roast swan and other dishes accompanied by copious quantities of mead which had to be

LEFT: the crowning of Mikhail Romanov in 1613 marked the end of the Time of Troubles.
RIGHT: Ivan III unifies Moscow in the 15th century.

drained to the last drop. Ivan was clearly impressed by what Chancellor told him of England, so much so that he decided there and then that he wished to marry the English queen, the redoubtable Elizabeth I. Chancellor secured a favourable trade agreement for English merchants and said he would forward the proposal.

Ivan the Terrible

Chancellor's suspicions of tyranny at work were well-founded. Ivan IV (1530–84) came to be known in his own lifetime as "Ivan the

Terrible", although it should be noted that "Awe-inspiring" is a more apt translation of the Russian. Ivan IV succeeded to the throne when he was only three, and owed his early survival to the clever machinations of his mother and regent, the Polish Princess Elena Glinskaya. She was eventually poisoned by the lesser nobles (boyars). Instead of murdering the young tsar at the same time, it suited the boyars to let him be. Ivan continued to live in the palace, but the boyars used it as a kind of play-ground, helping themselves to anything that caught their fancy, Ivan's toys included.

These experiences fired in Ivan a desire for revenge, but to begin with he participated lustily

A TRAVELLER'S VIEW

Russia, observed the English seaman Sir Richard Chancellor in 1553, was "a very large and spacious country, every way bounded by divers nations".

in the unbridled licence of palace life. He is reputed to have rollicked in the company of several hundred women before his 16th birthday, when it was thought he ought to get married. He chose Anastasia for his wife, the daughter of a minor noble family named Romanov.

Ivan's foreign policy was to win the remaining fragments of the Mongol Empire. He conquered the Kazan khanate on the Upper Volga in 1552, a victory he celebrated by building St Basil's Cathedral in Moscow. The capture of Astrakhan four years later made him master of the Volga from Moscow to the Caspian. These victories opened the way to the conquest of Siberia, a task entrusted to the Stroganov family of merchant-adventurers protected by the Cossack hero Yermak and his men.

With the Stroganovs energetically at work, Ivan looked west towards the Baltic, especially as the Turkish conquest of Constantinople in 1453 had made the Varangian trade routes down the Dnieper and Volga redundant. Ivan's Baltic ambitions ran into stiff opposition. The Teutonic Order of Knights had dug themselves into Estonia and were in possession of Narva, the port which was Russia's most obvious Baltic outlet. Neither Denmark nor Sweden were inclined to sit back and let the Russians encroach, and farther south Poland and Lithuania had united to become a powerful force.

At home Ivan reformed the legal codes and introduced local self-government. He grew increasingly ruthless in his determination to reduce the powers of the boyars. He confiscated boyars' estates, and installed his own placemen, called *pomeshchiki*, to run them. He ensured that the *pomeshchiki* had the labour they needed by confining the peasants to the land, thus laying the cornerstone of Russian serfdom. Peasants who risked the death penalty by running away often headed south to the steppes where they joined the growing number of footloose adventurers and fugitive slaves who together constituted the Cossacks.

To enforce his repressive measures Ivan instituted the *oprichnina*, a kind of cross between a Spanish inquisition and a palace guard. They were the first incarnation of Russia's secret police, and they set a precedent for many of Ivan's successors up to and including Stalin. The *oprichnina* wore black, rode black horses and on their saddles they carried a broom and a severed dog's head to symbolise their role as purifiers of the state and their ferocious loyalty to the tsar.

The worst example of Ivan's terror resulted from his conviction that Novgorod was seething with treachery. In 1570 he sentenced the entire population to death and thousands of inhabitants were killed in the space of five weeks. As Russia braced itself for his next move, Ivan died.

CHECKMATE

Ivan the Terrible liked to play chess, but only according to his own rules. These eliminated the king from the board, so that the king could never be checked.

treason. In so doing he invoked the wrath of the boyars, and when a young man arrived with a Polish army swelled with Russians and Cossacks and claiming to be Dmitry, half-brother of Fyodor (who had died in mysterious circumstances in 1591), the nobles believed him. Following Godunov's death, the false Dmitry was installed as tsar.

The troubles finally came to an end with the advent of the Romanovs: Mikhail Romanov was elected tsar in 1613, mainly on the strength of his family's connec-

Time of Troubles

Ivan's heir was his second son, the simple-minded Fyodor (he had accidentally killed his eldest son in a fit of anger) and so began Russia's "Time of Troubles", a bleak period of anarchy, civil war and invasion. Fyodor's regent and successor as tsar was Boris Godunov (1551–1605). While Godunov reformed the justice system and encouraged trade with Western Europe, he, too, had a ruthless nature and was swift to persecute anyone suspected of

LEFT: Ivan the Terrible, tyranny at large.
ABOVE: Tsar Boris Godunov in troubled times.
RIGHT: the False Dmitry, mysterious interloper.

tion by marriage to Ivan the Terrible. He was followed by his son Alexei, who began to open Russia to Western influences and so lay the foundations for the momentous reign of his son, Peter the Great.

Meanwhile, restrictions on the free movement of serfs imposed in the mid-17th century led to a number of peasant rebellions. In 1670 Stepan (known as Stenka) Razin and his force of 7,000 Cossacks captured the Volga-Don region, including the towns of Tsaritsyn, Astrakhan and Saratov. Razin was finally defeated by the tsar's Western-trained army and was executed in Moscow's Red Square. He lives on as a folk hero, immortalised in songs and stories. ❑

WINDOWS ON THE WEST

Peter and Catherine both looked to the West for ideas that would

transform Russia into a progressive nation

Peter was in every sense a giant of a man: not just in stature – though at 2 metres (6ft 7in) he towered above his fellow countrymen – but also in his titanic energy and appetites, in his vast breadth of interests, in his capacity for kingly generosity and in his bloodthirsty rages. But the biggest thing about Peter was the scale of his ambition and the size of his achievement. He set himself the task of hauling Russia out of the thick mud of medievalism and onto the paved highway of European civilisation. He wanted his Russia to be a modern state and a great power, and he did not care what it cost.

The child tsar

Peter was born in the Moscow Kremlin in 1672. His mother, Natalya Naryshkina, was Tsar Alexei's second wife. At the age of 10, in 1682, he was proclaimed tsar along with his sickly elder half-brother, Ivan. But his ambitious and wilful half-sister Sophia chose this moment to foment a revolt among the Streltsy, the palace guard, against the Naryshkin faction at court. The coup turned into a frenzied bloodbath.

The boy Peter was spared, but many of his relatives and courtiers were hacked to death before his eyes. It is hard to imagine the impression this made on the 10-year-old prince, but by all accounts Peter showed no emotion as he watched the butchery.

Sophia was installed as regent and Peter, still co-tsar, was sent into semi-exile to Preobraz-henskoye, a hunting lodge near Moscow. Here, in the country, Peter was left largely to his own devices. Guided by his own insatiable curiosity, he set up a "toy regiment" with his young play-mates. This game of soldiers soon became deadly serious: Preobrazhenskoye was trans-formed into a barracks where Peter drilled and trained with a small army of teenage men-at-

arms, fully equipped with artillery, dark-green uniforms and tricorn hats. Out of Peter's ado-lescent experiments grew the Preobrazhensky regiment, for 200 years the proudest and most elite unit in the Russian army.

Preobrazhenskoye also happened to be near the "foreign suburb", the home of Western

merchants and specialists, many of whom had come to Russia in the reign of Peter's father. Peter spent days in this Little Europe, and saw that the foreigners had all sorts of knowledge that was new to him and to Russia. One of these foreigners, a Dutchman, taught Peter to sail a Western-style boat on the River Moskva. Peter, already an accomplished carpenter, resolved to learn the art of boat-building. Now the three passions of his life were in place: a fascination with the West; a gift for waging war; a desire to build a navy.

As soon as he was old enough to do so, Peter put an end to the regency. After a brief power struggle, Sophia was confined to Moscow's

LEFT: Peter the Great, mastermind behind the westernisation of Russia in the 18th century.
RIGHT: Catherine I, wife of Peter the Great.

Novodevichy monastery and Peter came back to the city. He continued to rule jointly with Ivan until the latter's death in 1696.

Peter's "year out"

As soon as he was sole and undisputed tsar, Peter did something so unprecedented, so radical, that it was perceived by many of his subjects as a downright blasphemy. He went abroad. No Russian tsar had ever left the country, but for more than a year Peter travelled round Western Europe. This was no ordinary diplomatic progress. Peter's aims were practical: he went to lectures on anatomy, made

tion in which Peter personally took part. Red Square ran with the blood of the mutineers, and their corpses hung on the Kremlin walls for months after. Peter's vengeance for the massacre of his mother's family was complete.

Peter had come back from the West inspired to build a modern navy. To achieve this he needed a port, and so he spent most of his reign in a protracted war with Sweden to win a stretch of Baltic coastline.

Building St Petersburg

Peter finally wrested the province of Karelia from Swedish control, and on this marshy

shoes, visited cannon foundries, but chiefly spent his days working as an apprentice in the shipyards of Holland and England under the transparent incognito of Peter Mikhailov. He felt that the way to learn any subject was to immerse oneself in the basics, and he applied this principle to his new civil service and remodelled army: everyone started at the lowest rank and worked their way up.

Peter's travels were cut short by the news that the Streltsy had once again risen against him. The revolt had been put down by the time Peter got back to Moscow, but he was determined to deal with the rebels once and for all. There was an orgy of torture and public execu-

desolate piece of land, at the mouth of the River Neva, he built his seaport. The human cost of the construction is incalculable – thousands died of disease or mishap – but Peter got what he wanted: a modern city, a "window on the West", and a shop window in which the West might admire his achievements. He equipped it with the trappings of a civilised society: Western style palaces and ministries, a university, a library, museums. To symbolise the break

ABOVE: *Peter the Great at Deptford Dock*, by Daniel Maclise.
RIGHT AND FAR RIGHT: two of Catherine the Great's lovers, Count Potemkin (left) and Alexis Orlov.

with the old Byzantine ways of Moscow, he designated the new city the capital of Russia and named it Petersburg (Peter's city).

Meanwhile Peter sent hundreds of young Russians west to learn the technologies and skills which Russia lacked. He also invited a range of Western specialists to Russia. More radically still, he insisted that Russians adopt Western dress and manners, hence the tax on beards, which was Peter's way of declaring that the Westernising reforms were not just a passing whim.

By the time Peter died in 1725, at the age of 53, Russia had indeed changed irreversibly. No lesser personality could have shaken Russia out of its age-old slumber. Peter's successors could not turn the clock back, and some, notably Catherine the Great, made it their business to carry on the work of this remarkable man.

Six monarchs reigned over the next 37 years: Peter's wife Catherine I, his grandson Peter II, then his niece Anna, followed by Ivan VI, Elizabeth and Peter III (ineffectual great-grandson of his namesake). During this period, some of Peter's achievements were eroded or corrupted. The court became Westernised to the extent that it was completely cut off from the world of the peasant masses, almost an alien ruling class;

THE LOVERS OF CATHERINE THE GREAT

Catherine was no great beauty, but she possessed an ability – part womanly instinct, part cold calculation – to inspire loyalty as well as passion in the men who wooed her. There were many such men in the course of her life, and for this her enemies dubbed her "the Messalina of the North". Among the first was Grigory Orlov, a leader of the coup that brought Catherine to power and the murderer of her demented husband. But before that, while Peter III was Emperor, she secretly had a son by Orlov. The infant was smuggled from the Winter Palace in the pelt of a beaver – *bobr* in Russian. In memory of this, the boy was named Alexei Bobritsky, and his descendants are still one of the proudest families in Russia. Before Orlov, there had been an assignation with Stanislaus Poniatowski, a Polish count. When Catherine tired of him she installed him as King of Poland, a typically Catherinesque conjunction of political and emotional convenience. But the great romance of her life came when she was 51. This was Grigory Potemkin, a shaggy, one-eyed giant of a man who conquered the Crimea for the love of his Empress. Catherine, for her part, was glad to surrender to so grand and untamed a personality. He was not her last love – she continued to take lovers into her sixties – but he was the one she always came back to, like a prodigal wife.

the nobility found ways round Peter's merito-cratic rules, and reasserted its ancient privi-leges; the God-fearing lower classes began to forget the impossibly tall Antichrist who made them shave their chins.

Catherine the Great

Peter III was deposed by his young German wife Catherine. In the coup that brought her to power Catherine showed the skills she was to exhibit throughout her life: a politician's instincts, a lack of sentimentality, an appetite for personal glory, and a habit of making her lovers her closest advisers and political allies.

Catherine's reign began in the spirit of the Enlightenment. As a Westerner herself, she was aware of the backwardness of her adopted land and, like Peter, she was determined to impose change for the better. She liberalised the penal code, introduced plans for primary education, reformed local government, founded hospitals and orphanages, expressed the view (in her cor-respondence with Voltaire as well as to her advisers) that rulers were called to serve the state. She invited the leading architects of the day to Russia, and it was during her reign that Petersburg first acquired its cool, classical char-acter. These are some of the achievements that merit her title "the Great". Catherine was also

possessed of an imperial acquisitiveness which would have made Peter proud. In her reign the Crimea was conquered, and Russia thus gained a port on the Black Sea at last. And at her behest, the vast riches of Siberia – the furs, the forests and the minerals – were exploited.

A turning-point in Catherine's reign was a peasant revolt of such scope and fury that it nearly tore the Russian state apart. The leader of the revolt was a Cossack, deserter Emelian Pugachev. In 1773 he appeared on the south-ern fringe of the Empire making the unlikely claim that he was Peter III, Catherine's mur-dered husband. Enough people chose to believe him – outlaws, disaffected Cossacks and Old Believers, Muslim Kalmuks and Tatars – for him to raise a ragbag army. Serfs flocked to him in their thousands: for what did they have to lose? Pugachev captured the city of Kazan and put it to the torch. The serfs of Nizhny Novgorod rose up and laid waste the entire region. As Pugachev's confidence grew, so did his ferocity. His shabby juggernaut rolled on, murdering and raping as it went.

A loyal army, hurriedly recalled from the war with the Turks, headed Pugachev off when he marched on Moscow. Pugachev turned south, and this retreat damaged his prestige. He was betrayed by his own lieutenants and handed over to Catherine's forces, who paraded him through the desolate provinces in a cage. He was put to a cruel death in Moscow.

After Pugachev, Catherine's rule slowly took on a darker hue. Her early intentions to abolish serfdom were abandoned, and in fact by the end of her reign the serfs were more numerous and more tightly bound than ever, the human prop-erty of the landowners.

Catherine's youthful plans and mature achievements were diminished still further after her death in 1796. Her son, the new Tsar Paul I, hated his mother, and set about undoing her legacy the moment he came to the throne. He introduced a Prussian-style military dictatorship, and heaped scorn on his mother's memory and accomplishments. But it did not last long. He was assassinated in 1801, strangled with his own nightshirt by supporters of his dreamy son Alexander. Russia's 19th century had begun as it was to continue: in bloodshed and turmoil. ❏

LEFT: Catherine the Great in her prime.
RIGHT: Catherine in later years at Tsarskoe Selo.

FIVE EMPERORS

The last five Russian autocrats were unable to control their wayward land.

For a century the country zigzagged between repression and reform

Russia began the 19th century in hopeful mood. Mad Paul was dead and the new tsar, his son Alexander, was a man of known liberal views. One of Alexander I's first acts as tsar was to abolish the secret police (they were soon reinstated).

These years were dominated for Russia, as for all Europe, by the problem of Napoleon. Alexander chose to make peace with the French Emperor at Tilsit in 1807. But a treaty did not put an end to the aggressor's ambitions, it merely bought a little time: France invaded Russia in 1812.

The war with Napoleon was one of those occasions when Russia was roused from lethargy to awesome heights of righteous fury. Ancient class enmities were forgotten as the nation rallied to the flag. When the French took the old capital, Muscovites put the city to the torch and rendered it uninhabitable. Napoleon had no choice but to turn back. His army was harried all the way by partisans, regular troops – and by "General January and General February", the merciless Russian winter. Of the 450,000 French troops who crossed the Niemen into Russia, barely 100,000 completed the long march home.

After the defeat of Napoleon, Alexander became increasingly distracted. He had always been weak and indecisive (the writer Alexander Herzen famously described him as "Hamlet crowned") and now he indulged his growing interest in religious mysticism, leaving the country in the hands of the deeply reactionary minister Count Arakcheyev.

The Decembrist uprising

Alexander died unexpectedly in 1825, and his death provoked a constitutional crisis which set the tone of Russian history for a century to come. A group of officers had been planning a coup against the tsar. They were all acquainted with life in the West – many had fought the French all the way to Paris – and they were convinced that Russia could take her place in the European family of nations if the autocracy were abolished and replaced with a constitutional republic. Alexander's death provided them with their opportunity.

On the day the army was due to take its oath of allegiance to the new tsar, Alexander's brother Nicholas, they led their troops onto Senate Square in St Petersburg, and faced up to the ranks of loyal guardsmen ranged on the far side. It was a freezing December morning, and for most of the day the two sets of troops stood eyeing each other in the cold and confusion. Most of the soldiers under the command of the plotters had no idea that they were the pawns in a revolt.

While negotiators rode back and forth across the square, the builders who were then working on the new St Isaac's Cathedral threw a few bricks from the scaffolding at the massed

LEFT: the liberally inclined Tsar Alexander I.
RIGHT: Alexander I meets the French Emperor, Napoleon, at Tilsit in 1807 to discuss peace terms.

troops. As evening fell, there was a brief and bloody exchange of cannon fire, and then the revolt simply fizzled out.

All the plotters were arrested and some were interrogated by Nicholas personally. The ringleaders were executed and others were sent to Siberia. The incident became known as the Decembrist uprising after the month when it took place. It left Nicholas with a pathological dread of revolution which he passed on to his successors like a hereditary illness. Nicholas's own

BLACK LOOKS

Nicholas I was renowned for his intolerance: he ordered imperial guardsmen to wear only black moustaches; other colours, he decreed, had to be painted black.

dress, decided which university students should be awarded prizes, designed the buttons for bandsmen's uniforms, suggested changes to Pushkin's poems. The inadequacy of Nicholas's regime was exposed by the Crimean war. It was ironic that an empire run on strict military lines could not win a war on its own soil. It was a matter of intense humiliation for Nicholas personally that the British and French troops, with supply lines running halfway round the world, were better armed and fed than the Russians fight-

treatment for the revolutionary disease was to put the patient on ice.

For the 30 years of his rule, Nicholas was the cold, cold leader of a frozen country. He inaugurated a government department called the Third Section, the function of which was to extinguish any spark of dissent, indeed any sign of original thought. This department was headed by Count Benckendorff, another of those ideological policemen that Russia so often produces. Nicholas himself functioned as a kind of supreme government inspector, taking a minute interest in the day-to-day running of his unhappy empire – especially in matters of discipline. He sacked civil servants for scruffy

ing in their own back yard. Nicholas died – one might almost say he died of shame – before the war was declared at an end.

Alexander II frees the serfs

His son Alexander II came to the throne convinced of the need for reform. The national disaster of the Crimea, he understood, was due to the backwardness of Russia, and in particular to the iniquitous institution of serfdom. Alexander signalled his good intentions by releasing

LEFT: Nicholas I lived in fear of revolution.
RIGHT: the 1905 Bloody Sunday massacre in which hundreds of workers died when guards opened fire.

the last surviving Decembrists from exile, and then set about the complex task of liberating his nation of peasant slaves. The emancipation of the serfs came in 1861, not without terrible problems and injustices, but nevertheless it came: no more would Russians sell their fellow Russians like cattle.

Despite the changes for the better, or more likely because of them, revolutionary groups were more active than ever during the reign of the Tsar Liberator. These men (and women) were a different breed from the well-intentioned aristocrats and reformers of the past. They were anarchists and extremists, firm believers in assassination as a political weapon. Their chief target was, naturally, the tsar himself: there were many attempts on his life: a bomb in his train, another in the Winter Palace, a lone gunman who chased the emperor down the street. Each attempt on his life led to a crackdown which in turn justified the next murderous attempt. And in the end they got him. On 1 March 1881, Alexander's legs were blown off by a suicide bomber as he rode in his carriage through St Petersburg. He bled to death in the Winter Palace. Later that day, he had been due to issue a promulgation granting Russia a limited constituent assembly. The announcement was cancelled.

Return to repression

And so, in the now familiar rhythm, the pendulum swung back towards repression. The first days of the reign of Alexander III were especially brutal, marked by widespread semi-official pogroms against the Jews. In the years that followed, national minorities were forcibly Russianised, censorship was tightened, and access to education was restricted for the working classes. At the same time, the working classes were swelling as a result of the policies of Alexander's chief minister, Sergei Witte, who instituted an astonishingly rapid process of industrialisation. Thousands of miles of railway were laid (the Trans-Siberian railway was begun in 1891), a vast coal industry was founded in the Don basin, and foreigners queued up to invest in this new Russia. The process continued under the last tsar and his prime minister Peter Stolypin. But the combination of political repression and a large urban

STOLYPIN – TSARISM'S LAST HOPE

After 1905, Peter Stolypin was Russia's last hope of avoiding the catastrophe of revolution. He said he needed 20 years of stability to rescue Russia – he got five years of chaos. He was made prime minister in 1906, at a time when government officials were being murdered by terrorists at a rate of more than 100 a month. Stolypin answered violence with violence. He set up court-martials which tried and executed assassins so swiftly that they were often in their graves before their victims. Having crushed the revolution, Stolypin passed laws to liberate peasants from the rustic tyranny of the commune and from feudal practises such as strip farming. Peasants were invited to buy land, sow whatever crops they chose, and employ workers. (The able peasants who seized this opportunity were annihilated as kulaks, or exploiters, under Stalin.) Stolypin also presided over an industrial boom which made Russia an emergent economic superpower. He tried to work with the fractious Duma, but was hamstrung by the disapproval of the weak and stubborn tsar. Yet given more time and luck, Stolypin might just have steered the Russian state out of the path of disaster. His luck ran out in 1911: he was assassinated at the Kiev Opera in full view of his Imperial employer. His successors were well-meaning nonentities, and Russia blundered on into the abyss.

proletariat was dangerous: the revolutionary brew was beginning to bubble again.

In 1894 Alexander III died in his bed – by now no mean achievement for a tsar. He was succeeded by his son, Nicholas, a devoted family man of limited intelligence and imagination.

The last tsar

The accession of Nicholas II was marred by a dreadful accident which set the tone for his entire reign. A crowd of half a million gathered to celebrate

at Khodynka Field near Moscow, where they were plied with free beer from coronation mugs. At some point in the afternoon an urgent rumour circulated among the crowd that the beer was running out. There followed a drunken stampede for the booths, and thousands of people, mostly women and children, were crushed to death.

Khodynka was not the last pointless loss of life in Nicholas's reign. Far worse was to come. In January 1905, in the midst of war with Japan, a priest named Father Gapon led a demonstration of aggrieved workers to the Winter Palace. It was a huge but loyal gathering – many of the workers were carrying icons and portraits of the tsar. But when they reached Palace Square they were met by mounted guards, who panicked at the sight of so large a crowd and opened fire. The carnage was terrible, and it sparked a full-scale revolution. Within days the entire country was on strike. A new kind of workers' committee, dubbed a soviet, sprang up in the capital and other cities. The leader of the Petersburg soviet was a fiery young man named Lev Trotsky.

The 1905 revolution, which Lenin later referred to as the "dress rehearsal", was put down by a mixed policy of repression and concession. A kind of pale parliament, called the Duma, was set up to advise the tsar. But it was heavily weighted in favour of the land-owning gentry and deeply resented by Nicholas, who saw it as an affront to his God-given right to rule. It was, in any case, too late for parliamentary democracy.

By 1905 the autocracy was unreformable. The revolutionaries bided their time in foreign exile, and Nicholas gradually retired into the bosom of his beautiful family. The scandalous symptom of the rottenness of the regime was that Nicholas allowed a profoundly sinister peasant healer, Grigory Rasputin, to dominate his wife and dictate to his ministers.

Riot and revolution

The collapse of the autocracy, when it came, was an anti-climax. On a February day in 1917, hungry people queueing for bread began to riot. The troops who were routinely sent to disperse them were themselves peasant conscripts, and they joined the rioters. The rule of law simply evaporated in a moment.

Revolution spread through the land just as it had done in 1905, only this time nothing short of the tsar's abdication would placate the angry, tired masses. Nicholas gave in. With a weary flourish of his pen, he put an end to 304 years of rule by his family. Eighteen months later came the Romanov dynasty's mournful postscript: gunsmoke, blood and bayonets in a far-flung Siberian basement. ❑

LEFT: the infamous Rasputin, whose domination of the tsarina led to his assassination by a group of nobles.
RIGHT: Nicholas II and his family at Peterhof, 1901.

THE RISE AND FALL OF THE SOVIET EMPIRE

Russia's communist experiment is a central fact of 20th-century history and its consequences will endure well into the 21st century

The fall of the Romanov dynasty in March 1917 was greeted with relief and jubilation, but it did not solve Russia's political crisis. The war with Germany raged on, and at home the many fragmented political factions – Mensheviks, Socialist Revolutionaries, Constitutional Democrats, Liberals, Bolsheviks, Monarchists – were at each other's throats. A provisional government was established, but in the cities food was scarce, and the chance of popular unrest high. In the midst of the chaos and the infighting Lenin, the exiled leader of the Bolshevik faction, arrived back in Petrograd (St Petersburg).

Vladimir Lenin (1870–1924) had been a professional revolutionary all his life. After the usual apprenticeship – expulsion from university followed by a string of terms in tsarist prisons – he had escaped to the West, where he spent his middle years organising congresses, publishing clandestine newspapers and writing theoretical pamphlets.

The October revolution

Lenin's grand theory, the core idea of Bolshevism, was that the coming revolution must be led by a small band of dedicated activists, otherwise it was bound to become watered down into mere social reform. Lenin expounded this view with all the power of his great intellect. He possessed self-discipline to an awesome degree, and he devoted every waking moment to the cause (his only personal pleasure was chess, at which he was unbeatable). Yet he never expected to get the chance to put his ideas into practice. The March revolution took him, as it did everybody, by surprise.

Now that the revolutionary opportunity was there, the single-minded Bolsheviks were best placed to make the most of it. They struck in

LEFT: poster of Lenin directing the Revolution.
RIGHT: a commander of the Red Army wears his heart on his sleeve.

the autumn, seizing control of key institutions around Petrograd and arresting the provisional government in one night. It is this coup, not the popular uprising of the previous spring, which was for 74 years celebrated in Russia as the

pivotal event in modern history, the Great October Socialist Revolution.

In the months that followed the Bolshevik putsch, the Cheka, the new secret police, began the long work of rooting out "counter-revolutionaries". Meanwhile Lenin withdrew unilaterally from the war with Germany. But peace did not come to Russia, as the country was plunged into a civil war. For three years the Bolshevik regime tottered, but did not fall.

By 1921 the country was, once again, in a state of utter ruin. At this moment Lenin made a bold move: he announced concessions allowing for a partial return to a market economy. Peasants were to be permitted to sell their produce for a profit; city-dwellers were to set up and own businesses. Moscow and Petrograd filled up with Art Deco restaurants where jazz-age Russian yuppies celebrated the fact that the good times were back.

Many Bolsheviks in Lenin's own government were horrified by this "New Economic Policy" (NEP). For them, any kind of trade was un-Marxist and bound to lead down a slippery slope to petty-bourgeois capitalism. But Lenin saw it as an essential tactical retreat. The old devil of the profit motive was the only thing which could get the economy moving again. When the time came, they would stuff the devil

back in its sack. It is not clear how long Lenin intended NEP to last. It was in full swing when he died in January 1924, having been incapacitated by a stroke more than a year before. The power struggle that followed was in the oldest Kremlin tradition. It lasted four years and was won by the rank outsider, Joseph Stalin.

Stalin's brutal regime

Stalin, unlike most of the top-ranking Bolsheviks, was not a middle-class intellectual: He was the son of a Georgian cobbler, and made his name in the revolutionary underground by leading "expropriations" – bank robberies – in

THE REVOLUTION'S SPURNED GENIUS

Lev Trotsky (1879–1940) was the haughty ringmaster of the Russian Revolution. He was the only thinker in the movement who could argue on equal terms with Lenin, and he was a writer of such polemical brilliance that he was known as "the Pen". As Menshevik chairman of the St Petersburg soviet (workers' committee) he played a leading role in the 1905 uprising, and this practical experience of revolution gave him huge authority. In 1917 he defected to Lenin's Bolsheviks, consigning his former Menshevik allies to the "dustbin of history". He garnered yet more influence as architect of the victorious Red Army in the civil war, and was seen as the natural successor to Lenin. But

after Lenin's death, his ancient feuds with the leader were disinterred and made to look like disloyalty. Moreover, his intellectual conceit did not make him a popular figure, and his long years as a Menshevik were held against him: the Bolsheviks were deeply snobbish about party pedigree. In 1927, Stalin expelled him from the party, then from the country. In exile, Trotsky railed eloquently but impotently against "the gravedigger of the revolution", while his own achievements – his very name – were expunged from Soviet history. Stalin had him murdered in Mexico City in 1940. Trotsky's books include *History of the Russian Revolution*, *Stalin* and *Diary in Exile*.

the Caucasus. He played a very minor role in the October Revolution, but had since established himself as a good organiser. At the time of Lenin's death, he occupied the key post of general secretary, which meant that he controlled appointments within the party. It was through this office that he levered himself into power, out-manoeuvring factions led by high-profile leaders such as Trotsky.

Once swathed in Lenin's mantle, Stalin drawing on massive support among rank and file

DESERTING HIS POST

At the start of the war with Germany, Stalin locked himself away. It seems he had a nervous breakdown. Foreign minister Vyacheslav Molotov announced the news of war to the Russian people.

tal. He effectively declared war on the countryside. Millions were branded as *kulaks* (peasant exploiters) and herded into the burgeoning gulag; millions more died in artificially engineered famines, particularly in the Ukraine. Stalin said he was "liquidating the *kulaks* as a class".

The Great Terror

These measures were backed up by a purge of indescribable horror. The secret police, now renamed the NKVD, swept through the country their task to

Party members brought NEP to a halt and launched the first Five-Year Plan, a massive programme of state-led industrialisation intended to transform the Soviet Union into a modern power.

The parallel collectivisation of agriculture aimed to harness the country's productivity and bring it under state control. But the mass of peasants refused to be herded into collective farms; many killed their cows and sheep rather than hand them over. Stalin's response was bru-

LEFT: Trotsky as Commissar of Defence.
ABOVE: Khrushchev extolling the virtues of maize.
RIGHT: Leonid Brezhnev, guardian of the Cold War.

arrest "enemies of the people". It was as if the vicious, pathological personality of Stalin had been magnified and unleashed against the entire nation. In blind terror, arrestees denounced everybody they could think of, thereby providing new crops of pseudo-enemies to be harvested. Others denounced neighbours and workmates out of sheer ideological zeal.

The Great Terror of the 1930s was a silent slaughter of millions upon millions of people; later entire nationalities such as the Chechens were deported. And through it all, in factories and schools, happy workers and their children sang the Stalinist anthem: "I know no other country where a man can breathe so free..."

After the Terror it was almost a relief for some when, in 1941, Hitler invaded the Soviet Union. Here, at least, was an enemy one could speak about openly and hit back at. The Soviet people threw themselves into the fray, and yet more millions died in what Russians have called the Great Patriotic War. There were countless acts of epic heroism, particularly in Leningrad (Petrograd had been renamed to commemorate Lenin in 1924), which was besieged for 1,000 days but did not surrender.

As with the Mongol invasion centuries before, Russians felt that they had taken the full force of barbaric onslaught upon themselves,

Terror. He declared the nightmare to be over, and it is a measure of his success that when he was subsequently deposed it was not thought necessary to liquidate him physically.

In the cultural thaw that accompanied "de-Stalinisation" Russians had a tiny intoxicating taste of freedom: to read, to speak, to criticise. It was not much – and as the tanks on the streets of Budapest in 1956 proved, it had very definite limits – but it was never forgotten.

Nikita Khrushchev is fondly remembered in Russia for other reasons too. He increased state pensions, was fanatical about planting maize (during the Khrushchev years, Soviet

thereby saving the West from submission. The defeat of Germany in 1945 left Russian troops in the heart of Europe. In a way, this was a fulfilment of Peter the Great's dream: a Russian state at the heart of Europe, respected and even feared by its Western neighbours. Stalin's final years in office saw renewed mass paranoia. A grand purge aimed at Jews was in the pipeline when he died in 1953. His successor, after a power struggle, was Nikita Khrushchev.

Cultural thaw

Khrushchev's great achievement, the act for which he will forever have the gratitude of the Russian people, was to denounce Stalin's

shops overflowed with cornflakes and popcorn), and he launched a massive and much-needed housing programme: the five-storey apartment blocks which abound in the suburbs of most Soviet cities are known in his memory as *khrushchevki*.

But Khrushchev made some terrible blunders: he brought the world to the brink of nuclear war by provoking the Cuban missile crisis; he quarrelled with China and so divided the world communist movement; he clowned around on the world stage, thumping tables at the UN with his shoe. It was to put a stop to these alarming and embarrassing escapades that he was removed by a conspiracy of cautious, faceless Party men.

The grip tightens

One of these Communist careerists – Leonid Brezhnev – replaced him. Brezhnev's tenure represented a return to a mild form of Stalinism. A monstrously bloated cult of personality grew up around this unappealing man, who unblushingly awarded himself high honours, including even the Lenin Prize for Literature. On the international stage, Brezhnev was a monumental disaster for his country. In 1968, he crushed the Prague Spring, Czechoslovakia's experiment

> ### TWO SIDES OF THE MAN
>
> Khrushchev's tombstone in Novodevichy cemetery is a bust of his head, one side of which is black, the other white. This symbolises his personality and achievements: part good, part bad.

and rushed to a shop where, it was rumoured, there had been a shoe delivery. The black market became endemic, and was in fact the only efficient part of the economy.

This decrepitude was covered in a thick blanket of lies. Brave individuals who spoke out were silenced, or worse, declared insane as psychiatry became a weapon of the KGB (secret police). Christians were oppressed; Jews were persecuted, but refused permission to leave for Israel or the USA; the people were paralysed by cynicism.

with liberal socialism; and in 1979 he sent Soviet forces into Afghanistan, committing his country to an unwinnable war.

Under Khrushchev and Brezhnev the USSR became deeply embroiled in the Cold War. The arms race against America drained a Soviet economy crippled by the age-old sicknesses of indolence and absenteeism. Consumer goods were scarce, and became practically non-existent by the end of the 1970s. People queued for hours to buy frozen chicken, or left work

FAR LEFT: Gorbachev wins popularity on the streets.
LEFT: Boris Yeltsin, following a Congress meeting.
ABOVE: the Baltic States call for independence.

The dawn of perestroika

This was the situation inherited by Mikhail Gorbachev in 1985. Gorbachev believed passionately in the communist ideal, but saw that the whole system was in need of a drastic overhaul; this project was given the slogan *perestroika*, restructuring (or "retuning", as of a sound but neglected piano). He knew he needed the genuine support of the people, and decided that the way to win it was to be honest about the country's problems. This part of the plan was called *glasnost*, usually rendered "openness", though a more accurate translation would be "frankness", because the Russian word implies owning up to what is already clear.

Perestroika was not intended to make the USSR more Western, still less to dismantle the communist system. It was all done under the banner of a "return to Leninist principles". At the same time, Gorbachev was careful to endear himself to the West: he put an end to some of the grossest human rights abuses of his predecessors (for example, he released the dissident physicist Andrei Sakharov from internal exile); he allowed the satellite states to pursue *glasnost* locally, though several of them such as Czechoslovakia and the GDR were deeply opposed to the policy; he talked seriously about disarmament, and he cleverly made this look

as though he was merely doing the world a favour; and all the while he used his vast personal charm to win dollar support for his reforms.

But Gorbachev had sown the seeds of his own downfall. The spotlight he turned on the Soviet system only revealed that it was rotten beyond repair. The limited debate under *glasnost* soon broadened into a discussion of the legitimacy of the entire regime. The peoples of East Europe, who had always viewed communism as the oppressors' tool, turned on their Communist leaders. In 1989, the Soviet sphere in Europe fell apart in a series of popular revolts from Berlin to Bucharest. Gorbachev, to his credit, just let it happen. The USSR tottered on for two years. An

attempted coup against Gorbachev in the summer of 1991 was the regime's death rattle. Gorbachev was sidelined: president of a geopolitical entity that was about to disappear. Power devolved to the new President: Boris Yeltsin.

Capitalism arrives

The new man in the Kremlin was master of a much-reduced domain. Russia was suddenly a smaller state than it had been at any time since Catherine the Great and free of the responsibilities of Empire and of ideological constraints of communism. Yeltsin threw open the doors and invited capitalism in. Within a year Russia had all the trappings of a free market economy: a stock market, hyperinflation, robber millionaires, homelessness, food in the shops, mafia cartels.

The market economy was never given the chance to stabilise. Yeltsin constantly changed tack, throwing out the government and its policies by presidential decree.

When the reactionary parliament opposed him he sent tanks into Moscow and shelled their stronghold; he used similar strong-arm tactics, on a much bloodier scale, against the separatist republic of Chechnya. In his second term, as his democratic credentials wore thin, he looked less like a Westernising reformer in the tradition of Peter the Great (which is how he saw himself), and more like a sad repeat of Leonid Brezhnev: unaware, drunk and helpless.

On the final day of the 20th century, in a move that surprised the world, Yeltsin resigned from office and named Prime Minister Vladimir Putin as acting president. A former KGB officer, Putin rode a wave of patriotic fervour after the renewal of the military campaign in Chechnya. He was elected president in 2000 and won a second term in 2004.

Despite Putin's promises, the country remains corrupt from the top down, with bribes seen as an everyday part of life. The Chechen war continues, with almost daily losses on both sides. The violence from this war again reached Moscow in October 2002, when Chechen separatists took hundreds hostage in a theatre; 129 people died after special forces used nerve gas to take out the terrorists. In September 2004, over 330 people died after Chechen separatists seized a school in Beslan, southern Russia. ❑

LEFT: destroying Communist Party membership cards.
RIGHT: a mural shows the way to a bright new future.

LIFE TODAY

Capitalism has brought with it unexpected hardships,
yet the Russian people remain remarkably resourceful in their ability to survive

French intellectual and writer Joseph de Maistre (1753–1821) summed up the Russian character thus: "Scratch the Russian and you will find the Tatar." Situated at the crossroads between Europe and Asia, Russia is a country of incredible ethnic diversity. Apart from the dominant Slavic group, which makes up some 82 percent of the population of the Russian Federation, there are an estimated 85 native peoples, groups of vastly varying number, culture and origin. From the Tofalars in Central Asia to the Chukchi in the far north, each of these peoples has its own language, none of which is related to Russian. Many of these languages and cultures are now threatened, mainly as a result of Soviet policies which intruded on traditional ways of life.

Soviet influence

The Soviet era left its imprint on the Russian majority, too, both materially and culturally. More than a decade after Communism began to crumble, it is still visible not only in the country's general state of decay but in people's mentalities. Just as physical remnants of the old regime linger – Lenin's Mausoleum, certain place-names, the occasional statue – so the effect of seven decades of stifling dictatorship is only slowly wearing off.

Communism taught people not to take the initiative in case they were blamed for mistakes. Factory workers grew lazy because they knew they would be paid regardless of the rate of production. A complex culture of subordination coupled with defiance has developed, and the capitalist reforms are having to fight the established tradition of deceiving Big Brother and looking after your own.

As a result, Russia is developing its own extreme breed of capitalism. Businesses are springing up all over the place, but the service

PRECEDING PAGES: newlyweds by Peter the Great's statue, St Petersburg; Russian biker at Moscow rally.
LEFT: a young Russian.
RIGHT: storing potatoes for winter.

is still appalling; the idea of free trade has taken off, but that of paying taxes has not yet caught on. Trying to do business in Russia today is a colossal undertaking: even sending a fax seems to take a whole day.

Endless delays are caused by government departments, which can take months to issue

any kind of permit; indeed, many of the committees in charge of reviewing cases have not even been set up yet. Many offices close, without warning, for "cleaning days" once a month or so; an application can be faulted on virtually any grounds, such as the whim of the clerk processing it.

Split personalities

The Russian is famous for having "two faces": that of the man or woman on the street, and that of the man or woman at home.

It is striking that Russians are relentlessly rude and unpleasant when you meet them in any formal public situation, yet delightfully warm and generous in personal relationships. Clerks at the railway station will shout at you if you queue at the wrong desk – or even at the right one. Shop assistants will sit sulkily filing their nails or reading a book as you try to catch their attention; when you finally succeed, you are greeted with a surly "What?"

But in private life, these same clerks and shop assistants are transformed into big-hearted individuals for whom friends and family – not to mention friends of friends and family – are

really know a man until you've eaten a sack of salt with him". Above all, Russians' unyielding bluntness may well find its roots in their country's long history of being a peasant nation.

Peasant roots

It should not be forgotten that until the middle of the 20th century Russia was inhabited almost entirely by peasants. During the 1930s the country was transformed, within a single generation, from a nation of illiterate agricultural workers

everything. The "Russian spirit" is a great stereotype, but it is certainly true that Russians are very emotional and loyal towards those they love. Another celebrated feature of the Russians is their hospitality. An invitation to dinner will entail not only elaborate and abundant *zakuski* (starters), a large main course and a sugary dessert, but also numerous toasts with the best vodka, to "friendship", "reunions" and "health".

The dichotomy between public and private life is difficult for outsiders to understand. There is probably no single explanation, but it is likely that years of Communist corruption have taught Russians not to trust anyone they don't know. As the proverb goes, "You don't

to an educated proletariat, thanks to Stalin's massive industrialisation drive which was radical on many fronts: politically, economically and socially.

This incredibly rapid change has meant that people's peasant roots are still fairly strong, and are reflected in their clan-like tendencies: firm loyalty and boundless generosity towards those they know, severe mistrust and hostility towards those they don't.

A manifestation of this mentality is found in Russians' fierce patriotism, which applies not only to Russia but to the whole of the former Soviet Union. A Soviet census conducted in 1989 found that nearly 25 million Russians lived outside Russia, while according to one survey, almost as many considered themselves to be Soviet as to be Russian.

Russians' attachment to their country reminds one of a child's relationship with its parent: the parent can be stern, severe, even harsh, but is still adored by the child. A Russian will refer to Russia as "our" country, in the collective, conjuring up a real sense of a united people, history and culture; equally, they will refer to peoples of the former USSR as "our".

THINKING TIME

Before setting out on a journey, Russians traditionally assemble their suitcases in the hallway and sit on them together for a moment to collect their thoughts.

purges, and the whirlwind of capitalism with its accompanying hardships.

Yet it is questionable whether this capacity to withstand harsh and lengthy ordeals is not itself part of the problem. The Communist tradition of building for the future, of suffering today so that the next generation can enjoy tomorrow, has instilled an almost boundless patience in the Russian people. They await change, they do not demand it. Only in 1998, after months without pay and years on or below the poverty

Nowhere is this patriotism expressed more starkly than in Russians' defence of the "motherland", time and time again. The degree to which Russians have suffered for their country is remarkable, and perhaps unsurpassed by any other nation – you need only to reflect that the period of the "Great Patriotic War" of 1941–45 saw the deaths of some 27 million people. Their tremendous resilience has served them well, under Tsarism and serfdom, revolution, civil war, Stalin's

LEFT: newly-weds pay homage to Russia's past at the Tomb of the Unknown Soldier.
ABOVE: guess what's for dinner at Goritsky.

line, did miners on the far eastern island of Sakhalin begin to register their dissatisfaction with the Yeltsin administration through strikes. Ominously, a survey conducted in August 1998 found that some 65 percent of respondents believed the government "can no longer count on people's patience".

Attitudes to change

Psychological adjustment to the break-up of the USSR has been very difficult for Russians, many of whom considered its entire expanse to be their homeland. The entry of Latvia, Lithuania and Estonia into the European Union in May 2004, and the presence of US troops in the former Soviet central Asian republics evoke mixed feelings to put it mildly. Despite the fact that Russia is still the world's largest country, and although it was widely recognised that the Soviet Union could not have survived unchanged indefinitely, the Russian people feel impoverished by the loss of their empire, an enormous, and enormously powerful union of which they were extremely proud.

By the same token, Russians have mixed feelings towards the period that has followed the union's collapse. The majority supported President Yeltsin in his reform movement, reasoning that the gains of free speech, information, politics and religion have compensated for the loss of stability and material security. Yet a significant minority – as represented by the strength of the Communist Party in the Duma (the Russian parliament) – maintains that "*ranshe bylo luche*" ("things were better before"). This view is not difficult to understand, especially when one considers that it is held largely by the poor and the old, who have lost most through all the turmoil and upheaval.

What is of concern to democrats, though, is that President Putin appears to be adopting authoritarian practices reminiscent of the old days. Witness the recent attacks on the inde

THE DARK SIDE OF REFORM

Ironically, the freedom of information brought by Yeltsin's reforms may yet work against the reformers. Russians are now more aware of social problems which, although long-standing, were hidden by the dark secrecy of the Communist culture. Today's Communist Party has also profited from the fact that the past is almost inevitably seen through rose-tinted glasses, particularly by pensioners remembering their youth. However, the backlash against the reform movement also stems from real worries, such as rising crime, unemployment and poverty. During the 1990s, 37 percent of the population was living below the officially defined poverty line.

pendent media or the measures taken by Putin in the aftermath of the Beslan hostage tragedy that extended the Kremlin's power over the regions.

The initial heady thrill of consumerism, of new freedoms and opportunities, is beginning to wear off; the drunken festivities have given way to thumping hangovers. To be sure, food, clothes and foreign travel can all now be bought – but at a price few can afford. It remains to be seen whether Putin's efforts to bring growth and stability to the economy can be sustained in the long term.

The old Communist hierarchy based on position has not, after all, disappeared, it has merely been replaced by one based on money.

Furthermore, the new elite strongly resembles the old, composed largely of former Party bosses and their hangers-on. As before, those who get on do so through contacts rather than merit. The corruption found in Russia's government is a prime example of the old system masquerading as the new.

Putin himself was a KGB operative. However, in 2003, things suddenly changed. Mikhail Khodorkovsky (the founder of the oil and gas company YUKOS and Russia's richest man) and his top associate Platon Lebeder, were arrested and jailed for fraud. Although oligarchs tend to have made their fortunes in

currently on the rise). The country has a high proportion of professionals such as doctors, scientists and academics, despite the fact that these careers have never been well-rewarded financially: Russians have been taught to labour for the joy of intellectual satisfaction alone.

The Russian education system relies heavily on rote learning and can be criticised for its rigidity. Certainly there is little room for independent thought, but it does leave its children with a thorough knowledge of their town or region's history, of literature, music and ballet. What is more, the range of opportunities on offer – with specialised dancing, music, sports

shady privatisations in the 1990s, Khodorkovsky's arrest is seen by many as a crackdown on the super-rich and a punishment for his political ambitions.

Education, training and leisure

As a rule, Russians are highly trained and the nation's biggest asset at the moment is its human capital. It is in danger of losing this, however, if people cannot afford to study (although, interestingly, student numbers are

---

LEFT: demonstrators in search of stability and order demand a return to Communism.
ABOVE: vodka, salad and conviviality at the *banya*.

RUSSIAN BANYAS

A *banya* is the Russian equivalent of the Finnish sauna, the main difference being that the heat is wet rather than dry. Every town has its *banya* and the cities have several. During the long winter nothing gets the circulation going better than exposing the body to steaming heat followed by the shock of the icy plunge pool (or, if you're visiting a *banya* in the countryside, a quick roll in the snow). More invigorating still is the tradition of first covering the body in honey to smooth the skin, then beating it with a *venik*, a bunch of birch twigs. It is inadvisable to eat during a *banya*, but Russians quench their thirst with beer (never vodka), as it is believed to prevent dehydration.

and foreign-language schools – is astounding. It is not uncommon for chess, karate and skating to be part of the everyday school curriculum.

Westernisation creeps in

The pursuit of these interests was encouraged by the Communist policy of making theatre, ballet and classical music affordable for all. Every large city had its own companies, and an evening at the opera was as commonplace as a trip to the cinema. Books, too, were extremely cheap to buy.

As prices rise, however, live entertainment is gradually being usurped by television, show-ing tacky South American soap operas which have Russian audiences gripped. In the cities, nightclubs and bars have mushroomed, and cater for all tastes in music from garage to jazz. Many attract a trendy clientele. Most young Russians are fashion-conscious and women especially are always smartly turned-out and carefully made-up.

Outdoor recreation is widely enjoyed, as Russians love nothing better than an excursion to their *dacha* (country cottage) to pick wild berries or mushrooms. *Babushki* (grandmoth-ers) returning to the cities with loaded baskets are a common sight, as *dachas* and their

New Year is the high point of Russia's annual festivals; 10 days later, the "old New Year" celebrations begin, in accordance with the Julian calendar. Victory Day comes a close second (9 May), followed by International Women's Day (8 March). There are days for each of the professions, such as "policemen's day". Revolution Day, celebrated for decades, was cancelled by Putin and replaced with People's Unity Day on 4 November, marking the day Polish troops exited Moscow in 1612. In the religious calendar, Orthodox Easter overshadows Christmas, which is barely acknowledged as everyone is anticipating the arrival of New Year.

vegetable plots have become a vital source of subsistence for many. Winter sports include sledging and cross-country skiing, at which most Russians are quite accomplished. Those who are brave enough (nicknamed "walruses") even swim, cutting holes in the ice for a quick winter dip.

Russians adore animals and transport their dogs out to the *dacha* for some exercise at weekends. It is prohibited to take them on the Metro, however, so they hide them in zip-up bags or blanket-covered baskets. Cats tend to be left at home, but their owners will often bring back some twigs from the country as a present to their housebound pets.

High-rise homes

The vast majority of city-dwellers in Russia live in tiny flats in enormous high-rise blocks. Indeed, in some parts of the country, entire cities are made up of row upon row of these bleak dispiriting buildings. While Westerners may associate such structures with crime, poverty and misery, in Russia they do not carry the same connotations. In true Communist spirit, they are inhabited by representatives from every social stratum. By any

> **LIVING SPACE**
>
> The average living area for each person in Russia is 16.4 sq metres (20 sq yards) as opposed to 60 sq metres (71 sq yards) in the United States; 5.5 million people live in *komunalki* (communal flats).

things are starting to change. Increasingly, *komunalki* are being bought up by the affluent "new Russians" who convert them into generously-sized "Euro-standard" apartments.

The cost of living

The phenomenon of the extended family, largely eroded in the West, is one of Russia's most valuable resources: rent is cheaper if the flat is registered in a pensioner's name, and grandparents provide free childcare for working parents. The

standards, Russian living conditions are extremely cramped: many flats have only one room besides the kitchen and bathroom, and larger flats invariably house a substantial extended family.

A fair number of *komunalki* (communal flats) still exist, too. Made famous by the novelist Fyodor Dostoyevsky, these are reserved for the very poorest. Whole families live in a single room, sharing the kitchen and bathroom with their fellow tenants. Admittedly, however,

LEFT: a pampered pet, evidence that the Russians are great animal-lovers.
ABOVE: high-rise apartments in St Petersburg.

young and the old have a special place in Russian society (not least inasmuch as they are both given priority for seats in the Metro). Children are adored and utterly spoilt, while pensioners and war veterans are treated with great respect.

One of the most attractive aspects of Russian society is its supportive and generous social networks, which go a long way to explain how millions of Russians today are managing to get by on what appear to be impossibly small sums of money.

Whereas prices of food and clothing are starting to parallel those in the West, wages and state benefits remain at a staggeringly low level. It is almost impossible to conceive that the average teacher's salary, for example, is approximately one-fortieth of that of his or her counterpart in the West, while a Russian doctor earns less in a month than most doctors in the West earn in a day. Similarly, the ordinary pension is at least 20 times lower, while the student grant is disappearing altogether. Add to this the fact that many workers in the public sector have not been paid for months, or else are paid in tins of fish or bags of wheat, and it seems miraculous that Russians survive at all.

Rent, heating, water and telephone calls are all subsidised by the state, yet these bills still swallow up a substantial part of Russians' mea-

gre wages. People happily chat on the telephone for hours: calls within cities are free (a fixed rate is payable each month).

Withdrawing subsidies

From the point of view of economic efficiency, the withdrawal of subsidies can only be a good thing. Yet for Russians already bewildered by the roller-coaster of rocketing prices, revaluation and, most recently, devaluation that has characterised the post-Communist period so far, these adjustments are very hard indeed. Unsurprisingly, the tradition of dependency on the state combined with the instability of the financial markets means that Russians have a rather

different attitude to money from Westerners. The concepts of saving and investment have not really caught on, mainly because most people can't afford to save money anyway.

The capitalist system has undoubtedly been set back still further by the events of 1998, whereby those who put their faith in it saw their life savings wiped out overnight by the devaluation of the rouble.

In the last couple of years there have been more hopeful signs. In 2000 the economy grew by 9 percent, in 2001 and 2002 by 5 percent. Nevertheless, Russians remain sceptical that the good times can be sustained.

New Russians

As a result of this uncertainty, many people spend what they have when they have it, because who knows what it will all be worth tomorrow? Those who can summon the cash splash out on trips abroad (Turkey and Egypt are popular holiday destinations) and other luxuries, or even "invest" it by stocking up on cabbages or cucumbers to pickle, in anticipation of a hike in prices during the long winter. The visible wealth on the streets of the big cities – in the form of fast cars and furs – belongs to the emerging class of so-called "New Russians": young, rich and flashy *biznesmeny* with money to burn.

"New Russians" are different from the Russia's mafia *(see page 78)*, although there is some overlap. While the latter are associated with guns and violence, the former are akin to wheeler-dealers with sharp minds and a nose for business. Both break the law inasmuch as they dodge their taxes, but that is hardly surprising, given that any law-abiding businessman would find himself giving away 90 percent of his income to the state. Indeed, the absurdly complicated taxation system makes it difficult for even the most upright citizens to work out what they owe.

There has been some progress on tax collection by Putin, but the problem persists. One of the most pressing issues for the Russian Government today must surely be to unravel this tangle, as it cannot hope to fuel its reforms as long as the payment and collection of taxes remains unworkable. ❑

LEFT: counting the roubles – ice cream is popular whatever the weather.

Freedom of Speech

One of the most obvious and important changes from the totalitarian days of Soviet rule has been the dismantling of the Communist Party's monopoly over the media. In recent years, however, and particularly under the rule of President Putin, it has become increasingly clear that early hopes for a free, competitive media along western lines have been somewhat disappointed. In the 1990s, most of the concerns about the independence and objectivity of the Russian media centred on the control exercised over it by a small band of "oligarchs". In the new millennium, however, Russians are increasingly concerned by the more familiar problem of interference from powerful politicians, apparently determined to prevent criticism being aired on major television channels.

Nevertheless, the profound political changes arising out of the fall of communism have led to a proliferation of newspapers, television networks, foreign media and magazines. Russian *Cosmopolitan* is one of the most successful in the world. Political magazines such as *The Economist* and *Newsweek* are available on newsstands in the major cities. CNN and BBC World are widely watched. English language newspapers such as *The Moscow Times* and *St Petersburg Times* are also available. Although there was liberalisation under Mikhail Gorbachev's policy of Glasnost in the late 1980s, this represents a huge change.

But since President Putin came to power in 2000, the television media in particular has been brought under increasing control from the centre. Some of the biggest and most powerful oligarchs of the 1990s, such as Boris Berezovsky and Vladimir Gusinsky, have been dispossessed and forced into exile with large parts of their media empires being taken over by big, Kremlin-friendly businesses such as Gazprom and Lukoil. Though few were happy with the dominance of the oligarchs, it is grudgingly accepted by many that they did at least provide for a multiplicity of views in the country's most powerful media outlets. The trend under Putin towards centralisation is a source of grave concern to western governments and human rights organisations, and, of course, Russia's own, liberal opposition.

However, political interference may not be the only problem facing Russia's newly liberated media.

RIGHT: competing financial and political interests have resulted in a lively press.

As with other countries in the post-communist world, journalists are inexperienced in investigative reporting. Many citizens are still uncomfortable with the idea of hostile questioning of their leaders. Others, brought up in a communist system where news and propaganda were synonymous, simply do not trust journalists to tell the truth. In the regions outside Moscow and St Petersburg, there is generally less choice and more political control.

It is not all gloom and doom of course. The educated and multi-lingual have easy access to domestic and foreign news outlets. Though the thirst for news is less obvious than in the days of Gorbachev's policy of openness, Russians are as avid

readers of newspapers as their western counterparts. Vladimir Potanin, one of the oligarchs who remains in favour, controls the most popular daily tabloid, *Komsomolskaya Pravda*. He also owns *Izvestia* as part of his powerful Interros group. Alexander Smolensky's Kommersant publishing house produces some of Russia's most authoritative publications, such as *Kommersant*, Russia's answer to the UK's *Financial Times*. And of course, Russia's young people are well versed in using the Internet. While observers are concerned about recent developments, it is agreed that the media is now a much healthier and multifaceted animal than the one that Russians lived under from 1917 to the end of communist rule. ❏

THE WOMEN OF RUSSIA

The concept of motherhood has always been central to Russian culture, yet women still have some way to go to achieve an equal status in society

The name "Russia" has a feminine gender in the Russian language and according to Russian tradition the country itself has a feminine soul. The myth of "mother Russia", deriving from the divinity of "mother earth" is central to the history of Russian culture from pre-Christian times to the present day. This is reflected in Russian fairytales, folklore, art and social structures.

Until the 13th century many Russian women had a certain status, power and even equality in some spheres of life, including military affairs. The situation changed when the central government moved from Kiev to Moscow. With the introduction and growing influence of Byzantine religion and the militarisation of Muscovite society, particularly during the Tatar invasion, the status of women diminished and the Christian doctrine of "female impurity" spread to Russia. Women from the upper classes were confined to the realm of domestic life and their status there was the lowest.

In rural areas, in peasant communities, women continued to have some freedom and power. They worked in the fields with the men, and often ruled the roost at home, particularly if their husbands were serving in the army. They could even become *starosta*, the head of a rural community.

Female achievers

Russian history is full of outstanding women who played key roles in the political, cultural and social life of the country.

Catherine the Great, who ruled Russia from 1762 to 1796, extended the territories of the country, introduced new liberal laws and improved educational institutions. Her foreign policy made Russia one of the greatest European countries. Her friend Catherine Dashkov (born Vorontsova) was the first woman in the world to become the head of an Academy of Sciences, an institution which she herself founded, together with the Russian Academy of Arts.

Other outstanding figures include Vassilisa Kozhina, who led the peasant army during the Napoleonic War, and Sofia Kovalevskaya, a mathematician, astronomer, physicist and

writer. The first female astronaut, Valentina Tereshkova, was also Russian.

In the 19th century, Russian women were more prominent as instigators of social and political change than women anywhere else in Europe. They campaigned for equal education of the sexes, organised charity fairs for women from a lower social background and worked as nurses in the Crimean War. They fought for social justice and equality on the barricades of the Paris Commune and in the underground terrorist groups in St Petersburg.

Many of them were educated in Europe. Thousands of women belonging to *Narodniki* (Going to the People) walked down muddy

LEFT: images of womanhood – *Traktoristka* (the Tractor Driver), by Georgy Gurianov.
RIGHT: "Emancipated Women Build Socialism".

country tracks to take literacy and social consciousness to the peasants. Equality of the sexes was a popular concept, particularly among the urban intelligentsia. The women who supported the cause were known as *Ravnopravki* (women for equal rights). They organised small ventures, providing jobs for other women, and published newsletters and journals.

Opportunities open

In 1917 feminist ideas were swallowed up by socialist ideology. However, a decade later, Russian women again achieved a certain equality and social status. Besides the right to vote

of mother, Soviet women were also expected to work in factories and collective farms, as well as in professional spheres.

During World War II women fought alongside men on the battlefields, serving as doctors, surgeons and nurses. There were women pilots and women snipers in both the artillery and among the marine troops. Women formed the overall majority of the workforce in the plants and factories producing arms and military equipment, and constituted the bulk of labour in the collective farms.

During the Soviet period Russian women enjoyed increased success in professional

which was guaranteed by the new Soviet Constitution, the state provided a child daycare system, free abortion and a new marital law which made husbands provide child support in cases of divorce. Marriage and divorce became very easy and the ideas of free love were expressed and supported by a prominent Bolshevik and feminist leader, Alexandra Kollontai.

Stalinist industrialisation and militarisation of the Soviet state put a new demand on women to produce more soldiers and workers for the Motherland. A special tax for childless families was introduced and abortion became illegal in 1936. Divorce procedure in court became far more complicated. As well as fulfilling the role

spheres. In 1988, 52 per cent of the labour force were women, and the same percentage applied to those who possessed higher education, such as university teachers, doctors and lawyers. But since the family tradition was and still is very patriarchal, women were also supposed to carry the double burden of domestic chores and childcare. Equality was harder to achieve in reality than on paper.

The Soviet period, marked by the declining economy of the state, was especially hard on Russian women. Poor household equipment (lack of washing machines, vacuum cleaners and the nonexistence of dishwashers), a poor (though cheap) system of childcare, and a deteriorating medical service, made Soviet women resent the achievements of "emancipation".

Perestroika ushered in new aspirations for social and political change. However, it didn't improve the position of women. If anything, their situation has become worse than before. In the preceding period women were guaranteed 33–34 per cent of parliamentary seats. The first election in the democratic period left women with 5–6 per cent of seats in the Russian parliament and in all local governing bodies.

Growing unemployment has hit women particularly badly. Statistics for Moscow and St Petersburg estimated that up to 75 or 80 per cent of the unemployed are women, most of them professionals with higher education.

The return of the sex-object

Today, the social and cultural climate is even more conservative than before. The growing power of the Orthodox Church, overwhelmingly dominated by men, and a popular obsession with the mythological past have produced a new concept of womanhood in Russian society. The idea of equality is illogically associated with the rejected ideas of Communism, and therefore considered misguided and wrong. The former concept of woman-comrade, and woman-friend, is being replaced by woman-wife and woman-mother. A new phenomenon, prompted by the Westernisation of Russian society through advertisements and films, is the image of woman as a sex-object.

Women's response to this development is not simple. Some believe that their place is in the home as wives, mothers and caretakers. Others are struggling for the economic survival of their children and themselves in a difficult economic reality. Those who are active socially and politically are operating in a changed society.

The experience of building a civil society is new to Russia, but women are actively bringing it about. They have formed various political, social, environmental and cultural groups, associations of women in business, single mothers

---

LEFT: women labourers on site.
RIGHT: the proliferation of Western culture has brought with it a demand for glamour.

WOMEN IN FOLKLORE

Among the fairytale images of feminine strength are *Rusalki*, the virgin mermaids with powers of witchcraft; *Baba Yaga*, a witch with a wooden leg, and *Vassilisa Premudraya* (Vassilisa the Wisest), a woman who is far wiser and cleverer than any of the men.

and widows. There are professional unions of women writers, women journalists and university-educated women. Freedom of the press has produced many new women's journals and newspapers.

Despite their differences in content and purpose, these publications indicate a growing desire of women to express themselves. Like their 19th-century predecessors, they are striving to maintain and improve their social and political status and are reluctant to give

in to conservatism. Despite the hardship of everyday life, Russian women still form the majority among the producers and consumers of cultural values. In museums and theatres, in libraries and exhibitions you will see far more women than men.

In cities and villages it is the women who do the shopping and take care of the children, it is the women who help the poor, and it is the women who perform the duties of social workers. The battle to achieve real equality and status for women in Russian society might be long, but the evidence of Russian history, the strength and great abilities of the women themselves, are proof that it will be won. ❑

RUSSIA'S MAFIA

The mafia is assiduously at work in Russia, but it is the activities
of the street thugs that could catch the visitor unaware

The Moroccan track and field star Hicham El Guerrouj was among some 50 athletes who, in late 1998, balked at coming to the Grand Prix Final in Moscow, asking for a "more serene venue". He changed his mind at the last moment, and, before going home with a chunk of a US$1 million jackpot, said, "I was told Rus-

sia is a criminal country, but after I came here, I could see it's a nice and beautiful country and Russian people were very kind to me." Guerrouj had no way of knowing that while he was racing his way to victory a police task force was storming a private mansion in Odessa, Ukraine, where top mafia ringleaders from all over the former Soviet Union were gathered to discuss a grave financial problem. They had made the blunder of investing much of their "mutual benefit fund" in state securities, on which the government had defaulted the month before.

In fact, the mafia having problems on such a scale is the reason why a foreign athlete, tourist or exchange student will never be threatened by it or even feel its presence. It's of minor league thugs that foreign visitors must beware.

Russia is indeed a criminal country. To get an idea of the extent to which Russia's powers-that-be are laced together with the mafia, one only has to look at figure such as Boris Berezovsky, one of the most notorious of the country's "oligarchs" in the 1990s. Admittedly, the entrepreneur raised funds for and organised Boris Yeltsin's successful 1996 re-election campaign as well as for Putin in 2000.

Berezovsky was also believed to have been behind the government reshuffles in the 1990s and now lives in exile in London accused of financing terrorists in Chechnya. For his part, Berezovsky accuses the FSB, the successor to the KGB, of blowing up apartment blocks in Moscow in 1999 to justify the reopening of the war in Chechnya – a move which led to a surge in popularity for Vladimir Putin.

In 1996, *Forbes Magazine* linked Berezovsky to the assassinations of several men who stood in the way of his conquest of Russia and branded him "the Godfather of the Kremlin". Berezovsky denied the allegations, took *Forbes* to court in the UK and lost.

The most high-profile murder the Russian state was trying to pin on him was that of Vladislav Listyev, a popular television host and head of ORT who attempted to break up an advertising monopoly at the channel run by an associate of Berezovsky. Listyev was gunned down at his apartment door in 1995, and Berezovsky was one of the first people to be interrogated in the case, which remains unsolved to this day. Berezovsky was also interrogated after the editor of Russia's *Forbes* magazine, Paul Klebnikov, was gunned down in Moscow in 2004. The case remains unsolved.

Guns for hire

The visitor to Russia, however, doesn't need to worry about Berezovsky and his ilk. If you were to meet them, you would probably find them refined and amiable men. Consider instead Dmitry Kashnitsky, a 23-year-old unemployed St Petersburg resident who recently placed an advertisement in a local publication that read: "Seeking any kind of one-time-only, dangerous work." He soon found a client. A man who tried to get a St Petersburg residence permit through an arranged marriage hired Kashnitsky for US$6,000 to get rid of his wife and her mother after they discovered his real motives were less than romantic.

"Life here has reached the point where people look for killers in the newspapers," an investigator in the case told a local newspaper. One St Petersburg reporter said this was the 13th case of a contract killer found through a newspaper advertisement in the past few years.

Life in Moscow is even more violent and the city has the highest murder rate in the industrialised world after Washington DC.

Spot the gangsters

You will easily spot the generic mafia specimen in a casino or a night club – or driving his Mercedes 600 or Jeep Grand Cherokee down Moscow's Tverskaya. These are known as "New Russians". Whoever coined the term in the early *perestroika* years meant the fledgling Russian middle class. However, it soon became a byword for thieves.

People once referred to mobsters as "Robin Jackets". They indeed used to sport brightly coloured jackets, as well as Adidas sweat pants a few years ago. Most have long since donned Pierre Cardin suits, but you can't miss the thick gold bracelets and chains with crosses around their necks. The gangsters' cars often have a blue flashing light on top to amplify the don't-mess-with-me message. (By law, only top officials are allowed flashing lights.)

At the bottom of the mafia food chain are small-time bosses who control drug and prostitution rackets as well as street confidence tricksters. Their operations enjoy a steady supply of cheap labour from the provinces; they also have full co-operation from the local police. The venality of law-enforcement officers at all levels is a scourge.

The small-time *mafiosi* consider foreigners easy game. They approach visitors on the street offering the most lucrative dollar exchange rates, but the temptation should be avoided. Count on these guys to vanish in the middle of the negotiation with both your dollars and their roubles. Even Muscovites fall victim of the "exchangers", and can tell you about their experience of being cheated out of dollars on the street.

The *mafiosi* peddle Bolshoi tickets outside the theatre for twice the booking-office price

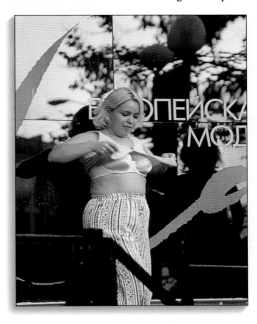

and sell fake icons. They will send a prostitute to a tourist's hotel room door armed with barbiturates with which to lace the client's drink so that she can clean out his room while he sleeps peacefully. Even gypsies begging for money in central Moscow are controlled by local gangs. Beware of gypsies hanging round railway stations and the Kremlin – while little children stretch out their hands begging for a piece of bread, older ones will steal the unsuspecting visitor's wallet and camera.

In other words, be relaxed but on your guard, if you're street wise, you'll find the cities of Moscow and St Petersburg are generally safe places to visit. ❑

LEFT: meeting a violent end on the streets.
RIGHT: prostitutes are often linked to mafia gangs and may drug their clients before robbing them.

A TASTE OF RUSSIA

Traditional cuisine is making a comeback as Russian
restaurants compete for custom alongside multinational chains

The popular belief that Russians survive on a diet of potatoes and beetroot alone, with a healthy portion of *ogurtsi* (small cucumbers) and vodka to aid the digestion is not actually that far from the truth. These are indeed national favourites. However, with a little less prejudice and a desire to discover the truth,

your stay in Russia can be enriched and your palate educated by the wealth of cuisines on offer. From the Ukrainsky *borshch*, that infamous but delicious beetroot soup, normally served in a *gorshok* (deep clay pot) with *petrushka* and *smetana* (fresh parsley and sour cream), to the *sibirskie pelmeny*, a small boiled pastry parcel of meat, mushrooms or potatoes, the national cookbook is as comprehensive as the country is big.

The years since *perestroika* have seen a renewal of the European influence in every walk of Russian life, including the kitchen. The sunny summer streets of towns buzz with café-life, and with trendy bars below street level. In

addition to the foreign fads, there is a noticeable revival of traditional Russian restaurants catering for every pocket from the modest student stipend to the extravagant, no-holds-barred, *novy-Russky* (new-Russian) cash-filled handbags for men.

In the 19th century, Russia was in thrall to all things French, and borrowed from Paris not only its food, but also its theatre, poetry, architecture and fashion in hats. The French influence is felt in the penchant for thick sauces for meat, in the love of complicated salads, and in the huge variety of cream-filled tortes to be eaten at the end of the meal with *chai* (tea). One such cake is the *piteechiy moloko* (bird's milk), so called because it is supposed to be so fine that it cannot possibly be created by humans.

Tempted by *zakuski*

The glory of Russian cuisine is the genuine desire of the host to see his or her guests fed and watered to capacity – a desire that springs from the quintessence of the Russian soul: generosity and pride. It is the tradition to load the dinner table in advance with a vast variety of *zakuski* (hors d'oeuvres).

The *zakuski* plays an important role in the process of dining in Russia, and can save the inexperienced from certain disaster when drinking with the locals. Russians may have a big heart, but their capacity to consume alcohol is tremendous. As a guest in a private home you will be treated in style to the best your host has to offer. However, don't expect any leniency when it comes to drinking, you will have to imbibe your share. Toasting is as important, and here, too, you won't be let off the hook with a moderate "cheers". Toasts can last for minutes and are a science of their own. The formula to remember is your host, the women present and the spread in front of you.

In fact, the *zakuski* are the main event of the meal, and it is an experience as daunting as it is appetising to look on a table laden with red and black caviar, a selection of cold meats, garlic sausage, smoked sturgeon, salmon, the array of potato salads, mushrooms in sour cream, pickled cabbage, beetroot vinaigrette, goat's cheese, as well as the usual liquid ensemble of deep-chilled vodka, *shampanskoye*, and fruity Georgian wines.

Every hostess will confide in you her secret recipes and claim that nobody beats hers. Popular favourites include *seledka pod shuboi*, literally, "salted herring in a fur coat", which is a delicious combination of fish, beetroot, boiled (and grated) egg and mayonnaise, and *domashni*

MOSCOW TAKEAWAY

In competition with McDonalds, Mayor Luzhkov initiated a chain of Russian cafés in Moscow known as Russkoye Bistro, serving local fast food: *piroshki* (pies), sweet and savoury, with *kvas* and *chai* to wash them down.

tan – which make liberal use of typical Asian ingredients such as coriander leaf, fruit and meat together, walnuts, vine leaves, chillies, beans and flavoured breads – can be found in the Russian home as well as on the menu in restaurants. Meat in these Asian countries will more often than not be boiled – with the tasty exception of *shashlik*, which is normally made from sheep and pork and grilled over hot charcoal. This favoured dish is known throughout the CIS, and

piroshki (homemade pies), which can be stuffed with cabbage, meat, mushrooms or apricots. By the time the second course arrives, most diners are already too replete to lift a fork.

Asian specialities

Russians can also call on the spicy southern, almost Mediterranean traditions in food. The cuisines of Armenia, Georgia and Azerbaijan, as well as Uzbekistan, Kazakhstan and Kygizs-

the chef, normally the man of the house, will be passionate about the preparation and cooking of what some may simply call a barbecue.

The *pelmeny* puts in an appearance wherever you are in the CIS: you'll find it smaller than usual in Siberia – but made in vast quantities for the winter; it comes large, flat, fried and known as *cheburek* throughout Central Asia and the Transcaucasus, or *manti* in Kazakhstan; the more wholesome version in Georgia is known as the *khinkali*.

All of these are found on the *zakuski* section of the menu, and the most expensive restaurants will have them waiting on the table when clients arrive. Other *zakuski* include *zhulien*

PRECEDING PAGES: seafood restaurant window.
LEFT: *solianka* (stew) and *borshch*.
ABOVE: celebratory pie.
RIGHT: barbecue time.

(julienne), slices of smoked and non-smoked red and white sturgeon and *kolbasa* (salami-like sausages). *Salat* (salad) is often simply tomatoes and cucumbers, but green salads comprise *travky* (literally, "grasses") which in reality can be a refreshing plate of fresh basil, dill and other green herbs.

Traditional dishes

The Russian cookbook may now be as cosmopolitan as any other, but the traditional meals as eaten during the reign of the tsars would have been very different. *Kisel* (blancmange), made from oatmeal, was the basis of most

meals and was eaten with savoury and sweet foods alike. *Shchi*, a soup made from *kislaya kapusta* (sauerkraut) and meat or fish, would probably feature in every main meal of the day.

The fruits of Russia's abundant forests have long been harvested. Berries such as *brusnika*, *chernika*, *klyukva*, *zemlinika*, *golubika*, *malina*, and *yeshevika* (foxberry, bilberry, cranberry, wild strawberry, blueberry, raspberry and blackberry) were gathered and used to make preserves, jams, desserts and drinks – as indeed they are still today. Vegetables such as *brukva*, (swede) *redka*, (radish) *markov* (carrot) and *chesnok* (garlic) were staple foods, too.

What remains traditional today is the *blin* (pancake), which is eaten both as a savoury and sweet dish. *Bliny* with lots of honey, *smetana* and red caviar are natural choices of filling for hungry Russians.

Bliny are most prominently eaten at *Maslinitsa*, the week leading up to the *veliki post* (great fast of seven weeks) before Easter, which in turn is celebrated at the end with a *kulich*, a light, Easter cake similar to the Italian Christmas *panettone*. A delicious sweet dish, *paskha*, synonymous with the celebration of Easter is prepared from *tvorog* (curds) with dried fruits and sugar.

The upper echelons of society would have known a different menu, one which shocked many visiting dignitaries with its richness and quality. Carp in *smetana*, baked *osyotr* (sturgeon) and *okorok* of ham (baked leg of ham in pastry with fruit and spices) were some of the dishes served to important visitors and the ruling class. Great pies of fish and meat, *zapikanky* (bakes) of rice, *smetana*, eggs and sugar and *kulebyaki* (more pies) with fillings of cabbage,

---

VODKA IS NOT THE ONLY DRINK

Russians are great *chai* (tea) drinkers and make as much fuss over their *chai* as the British. Before the onslaught of imported flavoured teas, Russians would eagerly add mint, cherry and currant leaves to their brew. Piping hot green tea is a favourite on a summer's day to cool the brow. Other *napitki* (drinks) include *kvas*, made from rye bread, currants and spices, and *medovuka*, a mixture of honey, spices and water; both are experiencing a comeback, thanks in part to Moscow's Mayor Luzhkov's challenge to McDonald's and Coca-Cola. *Sbiten* – *medovuka* with alcohol – is one of the many *nastoiki* and *nalivki* that are considered national drinks. *Nastoika* tends to be bitter and made from berries

and herbs and, on occasion, chilli peppers; *nalivka* is sweet and aromatic. The common element is vodka – no less than 40 percent! Armenian cognac should be taken chilled with slices of lemon to complement the rich, smooth flavour. *Kindzmariuli* and *Khvachkara* are Georgian sweet red wines not to be missed, while *Mukuzani* and *Saperavi* are red and dry. Stalin was reputed to prefer the young, dry and white Tsinindali and *Yereti* wines. *Shampanskoye* (champagne) should be *polusukhoye* or *polsladkoye* (semi-dry or semi-sweet). Try *Sovietskoye*, *Nadezhda* or *Novi Svet*. *Pivo* (beer) has improved dramatically and varieties of Baltica can be found in European Russia, and even abroad.

mushrooms and meat, or fish, were common for those that could afford it. *Khren* (horseradish sauce) was often the only addition to the natural juices that the dish was cooked in. *Kholodets*, or aspic is another favourite method of preparing meat and fish.

Welcome treats

Possibly the greatest sign of respect that can be shown to a guest is the giving of *karavai*, an intricately decorated bread shaped like a cake, which is presented, normally at the border of a village or as the guest

CAVIAR ON THE MENU

Beluga, osetrina and *sevruga* are translated as one, "sturgeon", and produce black caviar. Red caviar comes from salmon.

The *grib* (mushroom) is at the heart of a national pastime: whole families spend their weekends together in the country gathering mushrooms to preserve for the rest of the year in various concoctions of vinegar, spices and herbs. The culture of mushroom-gathering is one instilled from an early, age and most Russians will be able to recite a lengthy list of edible, and deadly, sorts.

The marinading of *griby* and *ogurtsi* (mushrooms and cucumbers) is another passion of the Russians, and one of the few occasions when

enters the house, and is accompanied by a small pot of salt. This ritual symbolises the wealth of the village, or host. One is expected to break off a corner, dip it in the salt and taste it before advancing. As bread was eaten with every meal and was what people survived on during the harder times, it was seen as dear to life and therefore a sign of readiness to welcome newcomers. It is a tradition often observed at weddings, when the two newly related mothers prepare the *karavai* for the newly-weds' return.

LEFT: vodka is available in both plain and flavoured varieties, including lemon and pepper.
ABOVE: Caucasians enjoy the local produce.

Russian men will glady role up their sleeves and help out in the kitchen.

A real treat when visiting Russia is tasting the *ikra* (caviar) which comes in *chornaya* and *krasnaya* (black and red) and is sold by the kilo to the rich and in little tins to the tourists. Be sure to check the date stamped on the packaging before making your purchase.

Red caviar is best eaten on white bread spread with a generous layer of butter, and black caviar from little egg-baskets (made from the white of hard-boiled eggs, carefully cut into a basket form). Despite being significantly cheaper than at home, black caviar in a restaurant can still push up your bill dramatically. ❑

THE RELIGIOUS REVIVAL

The relationship between Church and State has not been an easy one

and even today the renaissance in open worship has its opponents

The gradual rehabilitation of churches since the late 1980s, together with the congregations they attract and the growing number of novices entering the priesthood, constitutes something of a religious revival in Russia. Some see it as a triumphant repudiation of the propaganda drummed into Russians over four generations by State organs such as the Society of the Militant Godless. Others draw comparisons with the rise of Islamic fundamentalism in the Asian republics of the former Soviet Union, a manifestation of confused societies dredging through their past for some kind of cultural anchor.

Religion in Russia should not be equated with, say, Roman Catholicism in Poland, itself undergoing a renaissance. The latter is a more political and intellectual force at loggerheads with everything atheistic Communism represented. Russian Orthodoxy, on the other hand, was never intellectualised as Christianity in the West was by the likes of Thomas Aquinas in the 13th century. The Russian faith was and is rooted in worship, not scholastic theology, and it is not inconceivable that it could have contrived a *modus vivendi* with Communism as it did with tsarist absolutism.

Who goes to church

Visitors to a Russian Orthodox service will be struck by the highly orchestrated ritual. There are no books in evidence, but almost everyone seems to know the procedure. Even those who don't can cross themselves and bow at almost any time. The air is thick with incense, the richly coloured icons hold pride of place, and there is close interaction between clergy and congregation, communicating with one another through the medium of splendidly sonorous chant. Anyone familiar with the Greek Orthodox liturgy can see their common Byzantine source.

Anyone who visited Russia in Communist times will be struck not only by the large num-

ber of churches open, especially in Moscow and St Petersburg, but also by the age range of the worshippers. One or two Moscow churches even provide a carpet and toys for children. Even in less accommodating churches, people feel free to come and go. Closer acquaintance will reveal that nearly all middle-aged and

younger Christians, at least in the cities, are well-educated, while poorer, working-class people are to be found only in the few churches that undertake serious social involvement, such as prison visiting and distribution of food and clothing. In addition, there are the sometimes bossy *babushkas* (grandmothers) and other elderly people who have been faithful through the decades of persecution.

Of course, the enthusiasm for getting baptised, a craze which started in the late 1980s, has produced many nominal Christians who no longer go to church; some of these, in particular, are inclined to look back to times before Bolshevism, with a view to reliving past glories

---

PRECEDING PAGES: Orthodox iconostasis.
LEFT: Church of the Resurrection, St Petersburg.
RIGHT: a baby is baptised.

of the Russian Empire. Russian culture is closely interwoven with Orthodox values and symbols, and even Communism could not conceal this. But nostalgic fantasy can lead to alarming ideas. One of these is a desire to restore an absolutist monarchy. A small minority of Orthodox church-goers are monarchists.

The role of Church and State

The Russian Church had a peculiar role in society, because it never went through the process which eventually separated Church and State to varying degrees in the West. Ivan the Terrible directed arbitrary horrors against the church in

the 16th century (for which he undertook exaggerated penances), but the Church was not subjugated until the early 18th century, as part of the Westernising reforms of Peter the Great. Peter abolished the office of patriarch, replacing it with the Holy Synod. The synod was an organ of the State, presided over by a government official who had power to appoint and move bishops, and parish priests were even required to report to the police things heard in private confessions. When their time came, the Russian Communists regarded themselves as the ultimate spiritual authority, in exactly the same way as they assumed command of the armed forces.

The messianic manner in which the Bolsheviks presumed to convert the whole world to Communism was uncannily reminiscent of the phenomenon of Moscow as "the Third Rome". (Constantinople became "the Second Rome" after Rome was overrun by barbarians in the early 5th century.) Although the Russian Church had progressively distanced itself from its Greek origins by adopting Old Slavonic for liturgical purposes (the Cyrillic alphabet was invented specifically to facilitate the translation of Byzantine Greek texts into Slavonic languages) and replacing its Greek bishops with native Russians, the bonds remained close, if only to counter the hostility of Western Christianity to the Eastern rites as a whole.

The fall of Constantinople to the Turks in 1453, just as Russia had emerged from the Mongol yoke, was therefore a devastating blow to the Russian Church, and Ivan III decided it was Moscow's sacred duty to become "the Third Rome", the beacon of the True Faith. This mission ultimately led to what were in large part religious wars with Roman Catholic Poland in which the latter was no less determined to win Russia for the Pope and Rome.

Old Believers

In the mid-17th century Russia was plunged into a religious dispute, which, unlike the Reformation, was about ritual rather than doctrine. Nikon, a peasant monk who was a close friend of the Romanov Tsar Alexei Mikhailovich, became patriarch in 1652. He decided to bring Church ritual into conformity with contemporary Byzantine practice. In effect this meant people crossing themselves with three fingers rather than two and a few changes in verbal formulae. These proposals were opposed by conservatives within the Russian Church who came to be known as "Old Believers".

Nikon was an authoritarian and uncompromising character, and persecution was fierce and even cruel in some places. It continued into the reign of Peter the Great when the Old Believers refused to surrender their beards in the interest of bringing Russian society into line with Western Europe, where men were in the habit of shaving. Old Believers fled to remote areas.

Colonies of Old Believers exist to this day, and have at least two active churches in Moscow. When official persecution ceased, many Old Believers chose to remain in their remote colonies. They became famous for their hospitality, although if the visitors were not Old Believers any plates or glasses they used had to be smashed afterwards. Guests were expected to leave money for replacements.

Monasticism

Russian monks could claim much of the credit for opening up vast tracts of the Russian interior. Taking after the desert fathers of Syria and Egypt, they went deep into virgin forests to find sites for secluded monasteries. The tireless energy with which they made these remote areas habitable was their undoing because they were trailed by peasants pleased to exchange their labour for the right to settle on the monastic lands as tenants. These arrangements were preferable to serfdom, and led to the monasteries becoming the biggest and richest landowners in Russia. Many monks were content to capitalise on their enterprise and become landlords, but others preferred to push the frontiers ever outwards and start all over again. The cycle repeated itself until monasteries ringed the White Sea and encroached on the fringes of Siberia.

St Sergius of Radonezh (14th century) is the best known and most popular of the monks who simultaneously Christianised and colonised Russia. His tomb is revered at Sergeyev Posad Monastery, 50 km (30 miles) outside Moscow, probably the holiest shrine in the country. It resembles a walled fortress and contains seven churches and one of the Orthodox Church's theological seminaries. There is also provision for visitors, with a museum and shops.

LEFT: women sit in quiet contemplation at Moscow's Victory Park Church.
RIGHT: a monk reads from an ancient text.

The Church under Communism

The Tsar's abdication in February 1917 was welcomed by the Church which saw its opportunity to break free from State control and to restore the office of patriarch after a gap of two centuries. Patriarch Tikhon, who had been metropolitan archbishop in North America, was elected. Some people welcomed the Bolshevik revolution and Lenin's decree of 23 January 1918 which separated Church from State and schools from Church. This separation turned out to be rather one-sided, as the State took over all Church property, and placed obstacles in the way of free association and travel.

This was before serious persecution began. The famine of 1921–23 persuaded Patriarch Tikhon to hand over much of the Church's gold and silver plate, stipulating only that sacred vessels be melted down by Church authorities and handed over in the form of bullion. This was done, raising enormous sums, but accounts show that all the money went into Party funds, and none, apparently, to the famine victims. The Party, or often just local officials, wanted to take everything. Tikhon issued an appeal to resist the theft of Church property, and the result was 1,500 "bloody conflicts", followed by exile to Siberia or execution for the culprits. Tikhon was also arrested and ecclesiastical

Communist sympathisers usurped his position. They declared the patriarchate void and called on "every faithful churchman…to fight with all his might together with the Soviet authority for the realisation of the Kingdom of God upon earth…and to use all means to realise in life that grand principle of the October Revolution."

The faithful proved to be unmoved by the call and stayed loyal to the patriarchate rather than the alternative "Living Church" offered to them. The Living Church derived from sincere moves for reforms within the Church dating back to the 1880s. There was a general desire for change, but little agreement on detail. Var-

ious groups amalgamated and the Communists saw this as an opportunity to split the Church. They favoured the Living Church with privileges, including free travel, while restricting everyone else. Gradually, believers saw through this trap and deserted the group, unfortunately leaving to this day the suspicion that moves for change are tainted with Bolshevism.

Tikhon was arrested and urged to repent in order to resume his duties. "I was filled with hostility against the Soviet authorities," he said on his release in 1923. "I repent of all my actions directed against the government." Tikhon's confession reaffirmed the traditional solidarity of Church and State.

The Church moves underground

More serious was the statement made by Tikhon's successor, Patriarch Sergei in 1927, although the content was very similar to that of Tikhon, his predecessor. Assuming that both these confessions had been made under duress, elements of the Church went underground. Taking their cue from the Communist cell system, they used passwords to make themselves known to one another. Priests in plain clothes would pop up unannounced in villages, administer to the faithful, and as suddenly disappear.

In 1927, the year in which the first Five-Year Plan commenced, intellectuals and Christians were denounced as enemies of the revolution. Over the next 15 years historians estimate that hundreds of thousands of church priests, monks and nuns were killed. Tax collectors swooped on churches and, if the sum demanded was not met, they were boarded up. Teaching religion to children under 18 was forbidden except in private houses and to groups of no more than three children at a time.

Stalin relaxed the ban on Church activities during World War II in an attempt to lift morale. The Germans were allowing churches to open in territories they occupied, and after they withdrew the churches remained open by popular demand. When the war was over, however, controls were reimposed in the form of intense anti-religion propaganda in schools and general intimidation of anyone who aired religious convictions.

Under Khrushchev and Brezhnev, many believers served terms in prison for holding prayer meetings or conducting baptisms – not because they were crimes as such, but because they constituted anti-Soviet agitation. The few officially registered places of worship were infested with KGB informers. Bibles and other religious texts were unavailable except on the black market. Persecution intensified in the early 1960s, and more churches were closed under Khrushchev than had been under Stalin. The Communist state went to great lengths to discourage religious observance. For example, at Easter, the high point of the Orthodox calendar, state television would schedule a rare night of rock music. Those who went to midnight mass would encounter police whose job was to stop anyone under 40 from entering the church. They were not forbidden to enter, but it was made clear that names of those attending "cult events" would be noted by the authorities.

When Gorbachev introduced *perestroika* in the 1980s, Christians of all denominations sensed freedom, and took every opportunity to come into the open. The millennium celebration of Russian Christianity, held in 1988, was a big international event. The present Russian constitution makes an official separation between Church and State, but today's politicians like to appear in public from time to time with the patriarch or an archbishop somewhere in the background.

20TH-CENTURY SAINT

A statue was unveiled in London's Westminster Abbey in 1998 to commemorate St Elizabeth Feodorovna, one of Russia's most famous martyrs of the Communist era of religious persecution.

easy to control from Moscow. There are Buddhists too, and a pre-1917 Buddhist temple in St Petersburg. Today, there are Pentecostal churches in many parts of Russia, and missions from Mormons and other sects.

The scale of this theological invasion has begun to alarm both the Orthodox Church and some politicians. Under pressure from right-wing nationalists, and with some support from the patriarchate, Boris Yeltsin passed laws which curb the religious activity of sects such as Aum Shinrikyo

Other faiths and denominations

All religions suffered repression and persecution under Communism. The Baptists, an active (though not numerous) union of Protestants who trace their origins in Russia to 1870, were in turn tolerated and persecuted like the members of the Orthodox Church. Roman Catholics, who were granted freedom by Peter The Great, were totally suppressed. Islam had a marginally easier time because most Russian Muslims live in communities that are ethnically not Russian, and less

LEFT: a nun pictured in 1908.
ABOVE: religious freedom allows an Orthodox ceremony to take place outdoors.

(which gassed the Tokyo metro in 1995). Fears that the laws would damage established denominations such as Roman Catholics and Baptists have so far been unfounded. Nevertheless, the pendulum is swinging back towards intolerance and persecution of religious minorities as "Orthodoxy" is accepted as the *de facto* State religion. For instance, the government actively interferes in property conflicts, solving the problem in favour of the Orthodox Church, while it smothers other Christian denominations with bureaucracy. The patriarch has amassed enormous power and influence over Putin, say some sources, because the president sees the church as a foundation for the nation. ❑

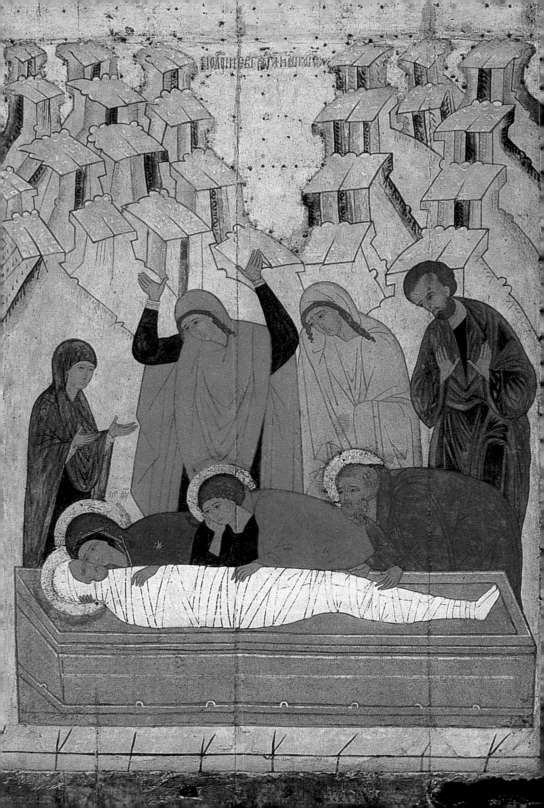

ART AND INSPIRATION

Early Russian icon painting was to have a profound influence
on the avant-garde work of the 20th century

Russia's art and culture was for 700 years – from the official adoption of the Orthodox faith in 988 until the time of Peter the Great – largely derived from Byzantium. After the Roman Emperor Constantine, the first Christian emperor, moved the capital from Rome to Constantinople, now Istanbul, in 323, civilisation and Christianity prospered in this new Byzantine Empire for a millennium.

Soon after the Turks captured Constantinople in 1453, Moscow became "the Third Rome", the presumed heir to Rome and Byzantium. All art produced in Russia served the one ideal of a Christian, theocentric view of the universe. Byzantine art – and hence Russian art – was subject to strict rules regarding what could be depicted and how, in keeping with the dogma of the Orthodox religion. We should not seek to apply Western humanistic criticism to icon painting: in doing so we are seeing things that were not necessarily intended and not seeing other things that were. The austere spiritual power that radiates from icons is a reflection of a universe with God at its centre. Their painterly language and use of colour and line are powerfully expressive; so much so that icon painting was to exert profound influence on the avant-garde at the beginning of the 20th century, and in turn have a vital effect on 20th-century painting worldwide.

Pre-15th century

Both wall paintings and icons survive from before the 15th century, but most painters at this time were either Greek masters invited to Russia, or their Russian pupils working faithfully in the Byzantine tradition. The most famous, and probably one of the last of these Greek painters to make his career in Russia, was Theofan, called "the Greek", who arrived in Veliky Novgorod around 1380. Few works have survived which can be positively attrib-

PRECEDING PAGES: *The Apparition of Christ to the People* by Alexander Ivanov.
LEFT: *The Entombment* (anon.).
RIGHT: *The Rider* by Karl Bryullov.

uted to him. A panel showing the Transfiguration in the Tretyakov Gallery in Moscow is probably by him or a pupil.

In 1240 the fire-worshipping Tatars took Kiev, and there followed a period of occupation which lasted well into the 15th century. Only the far north of Russia, including the merchant

city state of Novgorod, remained unaffected by the Tatars. Cut off from Constantinople until the late 14th century, the icon painting of Veliky Novgorod and the northern monasteries, to which learned Slavs from much of occupied Russia fled, was for a time forced to fall back on its own resources. These icons are markedly provincial yet highly expressive, with their vivid colours and unsubtle, folkloric designs. They are best seen in Novgorod's Museum of Architecture and Ancient Monuments.

One superb example is the mid-15th-century *Battle of the Novgorodians with the Suzdalians*, an unusual work in that it is not based on a biblical event, but commemorates a battle that took place in 1169. The subject matter and its treatment reveal much about its Novgorodian creators; this town of merchants, a member of the international Hanseatic League, was a place of down-to-earth people, interested in concrete facts and simple storytelling set out in a decorative and easily comprehensible manner. Although the painterly language derives from Byzantium, there is nothing particularly spiritual about the bold and rhythmic use of reds and whites in the work. And the Novgorodians were not "helped" by this icon; Moscow defeated Novgorod in 1471, and a century later the city fell completely under the dominance of Moscow.

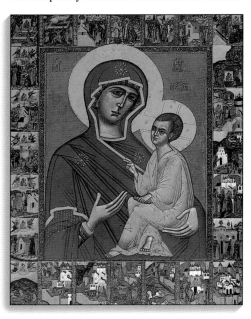

Theofan, Rublyov and Dionisius

In the 15th century, Moscow became the dominant political centre in Eurasia as the Tatar kingdoms began to weaken; obvious in both its imperial aspirations and also in its painting style. Theofan, who moved from Novgorod to Moscow some time before 1400, worked on the iconostasis of the Annunciation Cathedral in the Kremlin together with a young Russian monk, Andrei Rublyov. We know the latter's name from references in contemporary documents, but it was not until 1904, when his famous *Holy Trinity* (now in the Tretyakov Gallery, Moscow) was cleaned for the first time, that scholars were able to get an idea of his style. The panel was painted for the Trinity-St Sergius monastery outside Moscow, in memory of its founder, St Sergius of Radonez (*circa* 1314–92). Rublyov, who had entered the monastery as a monk before leaving to pursue his career as a painter, was asked to return in 1422 in order to decorate the new stone church, and it was during this time that he painted the *Holy Trinity*.

It is difficult to imagine a greater contrast in styles than that between the nervous, expressionistic Theofan and Rublyov. But it was Rublyov who had the greater influence over the next half-century. A late 15th-century *Entombment* (in the Tretyakov Gallery) by an anonymous master uses a combination of mathematics, music and rhythm to achieve a devastating harmony. The theme of the icon is grief, but whereas a European painter would have expressed the grief through facial expressions, the Orthodox painter does not concern himself with private feeling. The grief in this icon is that of the loss of Christ, the son of God, and

AN ICON WITH MIRACULOUS POWERS

The Mother of God of Vladimir is the greatest miracle-working icon of Russia. According to Orthodox tradition, it is one of three likenesses of the Virgin Mary that were painted by St Luke during her lifetime. Legend states that in the 5th century the icon was taken to Constantinople, where it remained until the 12th century (in fact, research suggests it was painted in Constantinople in the early 12th century). It arrived in Kiev in the 1130s and was placed in a convent in Vyshgorod. In 1155 Prince Andrei Bogolyubsky took the icon north on a campaign. As he crossed the River Klyazma, the horses carrying the icon were unable to go forward. Taking this as a sign, the prince built a church

there, in the village of Bogolyubovo (loved by God). The icon was later placed in the prince's new church at Vladimir and it went on to play an important role in Russian history: tsars were crowned in its presence; it accompanied Prince Andrei Bogolyubsky to victory against the Volga Bulgars (it supposedly sent out fiery rays to protect the prince's soldiers); and it is credited with saving Moscow from the Tatars on two occasions, and from the Poles on another. The fame of the icon was such that it was copied all over Russia and all icons of this type are known as *The Mother of God of Vladimir*. It now occupies a slightly forlorn position in the Tretyakov Gallery in Moscow.

even the mountains grieve. Christ's body, bound in white, is laid out, a horizontal, long note, against which a small rhythm of hands and faces is constructed, slowly fading as it moves towards His feet; behind is a rhythm of colour and rhetorical gesture, reaching a high point with the scarlet-robed Mary Magdalene's outstretched arms. Even nature submits itself and inclines towards the dead Christ.

The last major figure in classical icon painting is Dionisius (1450–1508). Again, little can be firmly attributed to him, and the main basis for an evaluation of his style is a cycle of frescoes in the Ferapontov Monastery, 570 km (350 miles) north of Moscow. He deployed a delicate colour scheme, applying pale, translucent washes of paint over fine, precise drawing, to achieve an elegant solemnity. In the Tretyakov Gallery, one can see biographical icons of the sainted metropolitans of Moscow, Peter and Alexei, which exude a dignified mysticism.

When Ivan the Terrible killed his son in 1581, he put an end to the dynasty that had ruled Muscovy since its beginnings. The early 17th century brought military defeat and, for the first time, ideological confrontation with the Catholics to the west. The Poles overran Moscow in 1605 and 1610, and despite the coronation of Mikhail Romanov in 1613, Polish influence and Catholic claims in Russia continued well into the century.

Russia could no longer live behind closed borders, protected from the pervasive culture of the Germano-Latin West. Forced to seek help first from Sweden, and then from England and Holland in order to overcome the military threat posed by Poland, Russia opened herself up to Western trade; it was not long before Dutch engravings, and Piscator's Bible in particular, found their way to Russia, and this inevitably had an effect on icon painting. The best icons were now produced in the tsar's workshops in the Armoury Palace of the Moscow Kremlin.

The 17th century was a period of transition; as so often happens when a culture begins to lose its way, ornament and decoration preoccupied the new generation of painters. Elaborate, jewel-encrusted silver covers that obscured the image, miniature paintings to rival those of

Persia, fine gold decoration; and, to the horror of those who upheld tradition, naturalism. According to Avvakum (*circa* 1620–82), champion of the Old Believers, Christ was portrayed in the new icons "with a plump face, red lips, curly hair, fat arms and muscles… which altogether make him look like a German, big bellied and fat." Theological arguments aside, the golden age of icon painting was dead.

Secular themes

Peter the Great began an enforced Westernisation on an unwilling population. He moved the capital to St Petersburg, a new city without the his-

tory and religious baggage of Moscow, inviting foreign artists and craftsmen to come and work and to teach Russians. St Petersburg was to be the cradle of the new secular art, while Moscow remained a holy city, a city of icons and incense. By the end of the 18th century there were a number of good portrait painters (Levitsky, Rokotov, Borivikovsky) who largely imitated French and German painters, and an embryonic school of history painting. The Romantic Orest Kiprensky (1782–1826) spent most of his unhappy life in Italy, and is remembered for his classic portrait of Pushkin in the Tretyakov Gallery.

Painting recaptured its Russian voice again at the beginning of the 19th century, with Alexei

LEFT: *The Virgin of Tikhvin*, 17th century.
RIGHT: *Harvesting: Summer* by Alexei Venetsianov, an early 19th-century representation of rural Russia.

Venetsianov (1780–1847). While the fashion, in Russia and elsewhere, was for neoclassicism, Venetsianov turned his attention away from Ancient Greece and Rome and focused on Russian peasant life. *Harvest Time: Summer* in the Tretyakov Gallery shows a girl in a traditional, colourful costume, breast-feeding her child while work continues. It is a simplified, rather than an idealised, vision of peasant life, for the idealisation is only in the deliberate beauty of the scene, and the bright, calm colours of the Russian countryside.

The second quarter of the 19th century was dominated by Karl Bryullov (1799–1852) and Alexander Ivanov (1806–58). Each is well known for one monumental work (Bryullov's *Last Day of Pompeii* and Ivanov's *Christ's Appearance before the People*, both in the Russian Museum, St Petersburg), and they were both instrumental in raising the social standing of the artists, who had hitherto served, but not been part of, society. Bryullov, who is alleged to have refused to paint Nicholas I's portrait because the latter turned up late for the first sitting, lived in Italy for many years, and it was there that he painted his masterpiece. Its allegorical allusion to the collapse of antiquity and,

---

by extension, the old regime, has perhaps been overplayed by Soviet critics, but the canvas, for its sheer size and drama, made Bryullov famous all over Europe.

The bourgeoisie

Nicholas I was a severe man, conservative and of bourgeois tastes, and his reign marked a departure from neoclassicism and romanticism, towards genre painting and realism. During the 1840s and early 1850s, Pavel Fedotov (1815–52) painted canvases depicting the bourgeois: the gestures and expressions are often so exaggerated as to be amusing, and social criticism is never far from the surface. During the next decade Vasily Perov (1834–82) produced more serious works; humour was now more bitter, and during the Soviet period, anyone who idealised the pre-Revolutionary past was shown Perov's paintings: drunkenness, poverty, peasant backwardness and the corruption of the Church were among his favourite themes.

By the 1870s, painting and campaigning for social reform had become so intertwined that the Society for Travelling Art Exhibitions, known as the Wanderers, was formed. They took it upon themselves to tour the Empire with their exhibitions, which were intended to educate the population and press for social reform.

The Wanderers are best represented by Russia's greatest realist, Ilya Repin (1844–1930). Repin lived a long, productive life, but his reputation was made with large-scale canvases such as *The Volga Bargehaulers* and *The Zaporozhie Cossacks Writing a Mocking Letter to the Turkish Sultan* (both in the Russian Museum). These monumental paintings have a photographic quality that makes a direct appeal to the viewer. They greatly impressed the people who had never come into contact with painting before. The historical paintings of Vasily Surikov (1848–1916), Vasily Veresh-chagin (1842–1904) and Viktor Vasnetsov (1848–1926), also executed on a huge scale, were similarly didactic. Landscape painting also enjoyed a revival in the second half of the 19th century. Ivan Aivazovsky (1817–1900), an extremely prolific painter of seascapes, achieved enormous fame in Russia and abroad for his dramatic canvases. Among the best is *The Ninth Wave* (Russian Museum). There is a museum devoted to him in Feodosia, his birthplace in the Crimea.

The years between 1885 and 1925, saw the most extraordinary explosion of cultural life in Russia, during which Russian art – not only painting, but also music and literature – was among the most exciting in the world. Instrumental in this was the railway tycoon Savva Mamontov, who gathered young talent about him at his Abramtsevo Estate, near Moscow. Many of the most gifted artists spent time there, and the estate became a hothouse of activity in many media – sculpture, ceramics, architecture and art history – with a particular inclination for the study and revival of Russian folk art.

Mikhail Vrubel (1856–1910), a painter ers to follow his example. One who did so was Valentin Serov (1865–1911). Again, Serov's outstanding characteristic is his sure draughtsmanship; he had the ability to render a face, a figure or an expression in just a few fluid lines. His portrait of the dancer *Ida Rubinstein* (Russian Museum) is outstanding.

Art for art's sake

The year 1898 saw the founding in St Petersburg of the *World of Art* magazine by a group of intellectuals who shared an idealisation of the past and an interest in "art for art's sake". Their worldly outlook now seems both decadent and

whose genius was so extraordinary that he does not fit comfortably in any movement, came to the colony in 1890; he became obsessed with visions of demons, which he painted in great quantity, and died in an asylum. He was perhaps the first to break the mould of the Wanderers' legacy, and to return to painting as an end in itself, rather than as a vehicle for social comment. His genius lay in the twin powers of draughtsmanship and imagination.

Vrubel's break with tradition encouraged oth-

LEFT: *The Last Day of Pompeii* by Karl Bryullov.
ABOVE: *The Zaporozhie Cossacks Writing a Mocking Letter to the Turkish Sultan* by Ilya Repin.

prophetic. This was the pictorial accompaniment to Alexander Blok and the "Silver Age" of Russian poetry. Leon Bakst (1866–1924), one of the founders of the group, became famous in the West as a costume designer for Diaghilev's Ballets Russes in the 1910s, but he is second only to Serov in his abilities as a portraitist. Another member, Nikolay Roerich (1874–1947), explored the theme of ancient Rus in his brightly coloured work. Konstantin Somov (1869–1939), the most "decadent" of all, was fascinated by harlequins, fireworks and ladies in 18th-century costume, which he meticulously rendered on canvas. Boris Kustodiev (1878–1927) joined the group late, in 1911; his work, which sometimes borders on caricature, celebrates the larger-than-life world of the provincial Russian merchant class; enormous ladies at tables straining under the weight of *samovars*, pots of jam, and pies stuffed with sturgeon, buckwheat, boiled eggs and rice. It is a world familiar to readers of Gogol, and one that was shortly to disappear, liquidated in Stalin's camps. Among his best paintings are pictures of fairs, but he was also a fine portraitist, and enjoys the distinction of having

> **OPEN HOUSE**
>
> Two influential, early 20th-century collectors of Impressionist paintings, Sergey Shchukin and Ivan Morozov, opened their doors once a week to allow Muscovites to view these important works.

painted a portrait of the singer *Chaliapin* (Chaliapin Museum, St Petersburg).

The years 1906–11 witnessed the formation of dozens of groups, splinter groups and exhibitions. Two of the most active figures were Mikhail Larionov (1881–1964) and his wife, Natalia Goncharova (1881–1962).

Together with Pavel Kuznetsov (1878–1968), they formed the Blue Rose Group in 1906. Kuznetsov's main preoccupation was with colour, and from Symbolist beginnings, influenced by Puvis de Chavannes, he reached his artistic peak in the 1910s and 1920s, when he painted a series of mystical landscapes of the Caucasian steppes. Goncharova drew her inspiration from Russian folk art and icon painting, and her best work, with its strong linear rhythms and striking colour scheme, reworks Byzantine draughtsmanship.

Larionov delighted in the unexpected and the shocking. Close in spirit to his contemporaries, the Futurist poets, he was the first Russian neoprimitivist, and produced a series of paintings of soldiers in which anatomy is deliberately distorted; in 1913 he turned to semi-abstract painting, having devised a system known as Rayism, by which he painted not objects but the rays emanating from objects, which by their intersection could define space.

Moscow's avant-garde

In 1910, Larionov helped to organise the first exhibition of the Knave of Diamonds group, which included works by foreign artists, and four compositions by Wassily Kandinsky (1866–1944). It was an important event in the history of the avant-garde, for it generated an independent Moscow-based group.

Kandinsky, who spent much of his career in Munich, can be considered the first true abstract painter; his brand of expressionism was concerned primarily with spirituality, and to achieve it he used explosions of colour and line, often including traces of figurative elements. Kazimir Malevich (1878–1935), meanwhile, began his career with Symbolist paintings, moved on to neoprimitivist works inspired by Larionov, but towards 1912 was beginning to develop a style of his own, which he called Suprematism. This was an attempt to break from representation of the visible world, to concentrate on space and through painting to forge a link with absolutes of everything and nothing. The supreme symbol of this period is his painting *Black Square* (*circa* 1914), which is everything its name suggests.

A similarly uncompromising attitude towards art and the public is found in Vladimir Tatlin's work (1885–1953). His legacy is Constructivism; a type of semi-abstraction by which he sought, often with the help of relief, to penetrate the essence of objects, and then of material itself. Among his greatest works, however, is a self-portrait of 1911 in the Russian Museum. Painted in tempera, it recalls icon painting in its use of curved lines and highlights.

The dream like world of Marc Chagall (1887–1985) is represented by early paintings in the Tretyakov and Russian Museums. He was the youngest of the avant-garde painters, spent most of his life abroad, and other than a penchant for neoprimitivism had little in common with his contemporaries.

Kuzma Petrov-Vodkin (1878–1939) also sought to use the language of icon painting: his large canvases are built of areas of strongly contrasting colours, usually including a brilliant, almost luminous red. He deliberately manipulated space to give an impression of flat-

talents to propaganda and public information art. The works of the photographer Alexander Rodchenko (1891–1956) and the poet-artist Vladimir Mayakovsky (1893–1930) were to define international poster and book design effectively until the 1980s. But disillusionment set in, and while some artists chose exile, those who remained and sought to practise their art were finally brought down by an official decree of 1932, which established Socialist Realism as the only acceptable form of art.

Now began a strange period during which many talented artists applied some of the more acceptable discoveries of the avant-garde to

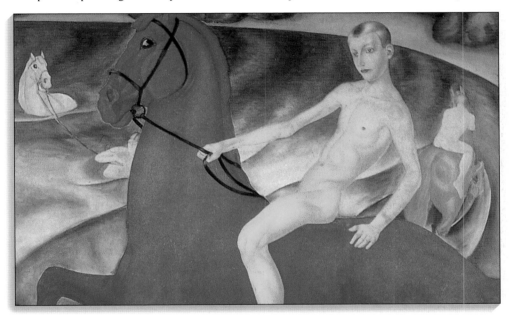

ness, and played with shadow and highlight in such a way that his figures seem, as in icon painting, to be illuminated from within. The Russian Museum contains several outstanding examples of his work, including *The Bathing of the Red Horse* (1912).

This frenzy of artistic activity took place against a background of political intrigue, World War I, the Revolution and finally the Civil War. Many avant-garde artists greeted the new society with open arms, applying their

utopian paintings on Soviet subjects. Some confined themselves to the new heroes of proletarian society – the workers and peasants, sportsmen and women, students at the new literacy colleges – but others went still further, producing vast works showing Lenin and Stalin, Party Congresses and political meetings.

This was a time for huge public commissions, for works of art to fill skyscrapers, for paintings, mosaics, for metro stations, creating palaces for the people. Many of these Stalinist buildings and their interiors survive, a symbol of the utopian euphoria which reigned, and which is often disregarded in Cold War assessments of the Soviet past.

LEFT: *Portrait of Chaliapin* by Boris Kustodiev.
ABOVE: *The Bathing of the Red Horse* painted by Kuzma Petrov-Vodkin in the early 20th century.

But there was no "underground" at this time: the underground was a post-war, post-Stalin phenomenon. Artists such as Pavel Filonov (1883–1941) and Vladimir Sterligov (1904–1973) continued to work throughout the 1930s and 1940s, but were not allowed to exhibit. They designed book covers and scenery, taking one or two students, to whom they passed on the knowledge that they alone possessed.

With the "thaw" of the 1950s

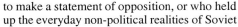

LEFT: *Improvisation* by Wassily Kandinsky, 1911.

OFFICIAL ART

The Soviet era was a time of opportunity for the willing artist. Painters such as Samokhvalov and Deineka represent the best official art of the period, although there were many second-rate artists who came to the fore due to their willingness to compromise with political demands.

and 1960s, a flood of artists who propounded "formalist" – non-Socialist Realist – theories emerged, tolerated but not accepted by the authorities. The true divide between official and unoffical became clear at the end of the 1960s. While "acceptable" painters such as Andrey Mylnikov and Boris Ugarov produced bland, non-controversial pictures of Pushkin, of power stations, of Moscow as the symbol of a contented Soviet Union – but without the inspirational mood of the 1930s – the underground came into its own. Sots Art and Moscow Conceptualism – which produced artists such as Erik Bulatov, Ilya Kabakov and Komar and Melamid, artists who used the Soviet clichés

to make a statement of opposition, or who held up the everyday non-political realities of Soviet society for scrutiny – were just the tip of the iceberg. St Petersburg, meanwhile, retained its emphasis on formal qualities, on line and colour. Artists became more radical, and in 1974 they showed their works publicly – which resulted in the bulldozing of a whole exhibition in Moscow in that year.

Searching for direction

But with the 1980s and *perestroika*, the relaxation of controls, and the massive explosion in exhibitions – public exhibitions, not cramped in small apartments – Russian art found itself facing a crisis. Despite the massive popularity of Russian art abroad, the lesser artists of the underground had made their reputations on opposition, on the expression of dissent. Once the point of opposition was removed, Russian art had to learn to see itself not as a political statement, but as an expression of intellectual and artistic aims.

Moscow and St Petersburg, which still dominate the art scene, have emerged from the crisis, but remain divided as ever. St Petersburg remains a city of painting, sculpture and creativity. Timur Novikov's New Academy of Arts propagandises a return to the values of - pre-Revolutionary art, to beauty, to neoclassicism. Meanwhile Moscow's artists continue to place emphasis on conceptualism and performance, with Alexander Brener spraying a dollar sign on a Malevich, and Oleg Kulik taking on the persona of a dog, biting visitors to the gallery. In early 2005, Moscow held its first ever Biennale of Contemporary Art, bringing over 40 artists from 22 countries to the city for a one-month festival. In the spirit of growing repression and censorship of the Putin regime, works critical of the Russian establishment were quietly vetted. But since Moscow is quick becoming a major world art market, more and more artists only care about what sells or is fashionable, and shy away from things that might cause problems with the authorities ❑

LEFT: *Improvisation* by Wassily Kandinsky, 1911.
RIGHT: *Colour Dynamic Composition* by Aleksandra Alexandrovna Ekster (1884–1949).

LITERATURE

Russia's literary heritage is one of the greatest in the world. At every step it reflects the tragic, comic, glorious history of the country

Russian literature is rooted in an ancient oral tradition which lives on in the national passion for jokes, elaborate toasts, proverbs, fairytales and aphorisms. The literary tradition began with the *byliny*, folk tales told by minstrels in the courts of Kiev over 1,000 years ago, and continued with *The Lay of Igor's Host*, a kind of 12th-century Russian *Beowulf*. The opening words of this long saga are known to every educated Russian, and even in pale translation can send a shiver up the spine: "Is it not fitting, o my brothers, to begin with the old songs, the hard tales of Igor, son of Svyatoslav, and his battles..."

Literary genius

But the man held to be the founder of modern Russian literature is Alexander Pushkin. He was born in 1799, in an age when French was still considered the only language suitable for literary expression, and Russian was held to be the argot of the kitchen and the farmyard.

Pushkin's work took Russian to new and undreamed-of heights. His instinctive feel for the cadences of the Russian tongue, acquired at the knee of his peasant nanny, was transmuted by his genius into deathless lyric poetry, prose, verse novels and plays. It is present, too, in the long poem, *The Bronze Horseman*, and the verse novel *Evgene Onegin*.

Pushkin's place in Russian literature cannot be overstated; he is not just its source, he is the landscape against which its story unfolds. He set the pattern for Russian men of letters in other ways, too: he was harassed by the authorities (Tsar Nicholas I acted as his own personal censor), and he met a tragic end, killed in a foolish duel at the age of 37.

Pushkin's immediate heir was Mikhail Lermontov. He circulated a bitter poem immediately after Pushkin's death blaming the philistine court of Nicholas I for the loss of Russia's great poet. The authorities paid Lermontov the

compliment of exiling him to the Caucasus, and, not for the last time, official punishment boosted a young writer's reputation. In the dramatic mountains of the south, Lermontov wrote poetry which developed the existential idea of the "superfluous man", the view that in Nicholas's Russia, indeed in the world at large, there is no

outlet for the energies of men of talent and feeling, so life consists of frittering away time on meaningless diversions such as love and war, and in taking what solace there is in nature. This philosophy is expressed with deep eloquence in his novel, *A Hero Of Our Time*. Lermontov lived by the idea, breaking hearts and picking fights until he, too, was killed in a duel. He was 26.

A very different light was cast on Russia by Nikolai Gogol, the third great literary talent of Russia's first flowering. Gogol's gift was for the grotesque. His hilarious short stories (*The Two Ivans*, *The Nose*, *The Overcoat*) are populated with pompous provincials, uppity civil servants, and all sorts of shallow, greedy

PRECEDING PAGES: Yevgeny Yevtushenko at work.
LEFT: Leo Tolstoy on his estate at Yasnaya Polyana.
RIGHT: Alexander Pushkin, Russia's literary hero.

gargoyles. But beneath the surface runs a dark seam of fear: perhaps his clownish world is not a burlesque, perhaps humanity really is that ugly. Gogol himself certainly came to believe so. One senses it in his farce, *The Government Inspector*, and in the novel *Dead Souls*, written as he descended into a private hell of religious mysticism and inexplicable guilt.

Great storytellers

The next generation comprises the three giants of Russian letters: Ivan Turgenev, Fyodor Dostoyevsky and Leo Tolstoy. All three dealt with the burning issues of their day – serfdom,

of serfs, and many readers think it is his best.

Turgenev was a Western writer: moderate, restrained and economical. Dostoyevsky was the opposite: his books are full of madly excitable people given to passionate ideas and dizzying swings of emotion, people who are buffeted by sin and repentance, who are, in a word, Russian. Dostoyevsky used this gallery of tortured souls to explore the biggest questions: good and evil, freedom and responsibility, salvation and damnation. His mature novels – *The Brothers Karamazov*, *Crime and Punishment*, *The Devils* – are strong meat, and profoundly absorbing works of art.

While Dostoyevsky's doleful gaze was fixed

Russia's Asiatic and European heritage, the revolutionary movement. But what makes all three of them great is that their works rise above the issues that inspire them. They are all marvellous storytellers. For example, Turgenev's Bazarov, the hero of *Fathers and Sons*, was interpreted by contemporaries to be a vicious caricature of a revolutionary idealist; but modern readers see a well-meaning man whose rational world is thrown into turmoil when he falls in love with a beautiful widow. Turgenev's portrayal of women is one of his strengths; he is also masterful and compassionate when portraying the oppressed: his first book was *Hunter's Sketches*, short stories about the lives

on the dark vortices of the Russian soul, Leo Tolstoy could not tear his eyes from the great, gaudy pageant of Russian society. Tolstoy the Preacher wanted to condemn its frivolity, but Tolstoy the Artist could not resist glorying in it all. This tension is at the heart of both *War and Peace* and *Anna Karenina*, either of which might justifiably be named the greatest novel ever written. *War and Peace*, a vast panorama of the Napoleonic era, is the more ambitious work. Its scope is as deep as it is broad. The focus zooms in and out, alighting at one moment on the daydreams of a teenage girl, at another on great armies in battle. To read the book is like climbing a mountain: it takes stamina and dedication to get there, but the view from the summit is magnificent.

Tolstoy was a nobleman by birth, as had nearly all Russian writers been since Pushkin. At the turn of the 20th century, the voice of the bourgeoisie made itself heard in the stories and plays of Anton Chekhov. The boredom and sense of failure that hangs around his heroes can be seen as a reflection of the political impotence and shallow roots of the middle classes, soon to be uprooted and borne away on a tidal wave of revolution.

WINNING WORDS

Five Russian writers have won the Nobel prize for literature. They are Ivan Bunin, Mikhail Sholokhov, Boris Pasternak (who was forced to refuse it), Alexander Solzhenitsyn and Joseph Brodsky.

Immediately before the Revolution Russian poetry re-asserted itself. Never before had so many gifted and varied poets arisen at one time. There were the Symbolists who elevated poetry to a kind of mystical religion of which they were the high priests; there were the Futurists, bold experimenters who refused "to cling to Pushkin's coat-tails", as Vladimir Mayakovsky put it, and who wanted to remake the language as the Revolution would remake the country; there was the rowdy peasant Sergei

Poets and proletarians

The future belonged to the working masses, whose authentic coarse tones resound in the vibrant, colourful works of Maxim Gorky (his play *The Lower Depths* and his autobiographical sketches *Childhood, Apprenticeship and My Universities*). He was the first truly proletarian writer, and later became a kind of godfather of Soviet letters. To his credit, he used this position of authority to protect young writers from the excesses of the Stalinism regime.

LEFT: Maxim Gorky and his literary circle.
ABOVE: Anton Chekhov.
RIGHT: Fyodor Dostoyevsky.

Yesenin whose life and poetry are a long lament for the doomed Russian countryside; there were the Acmeists, exquisite craftsmen who saw poetry as a refined verbal architecture; and there were poets who either stood apart from these movements or transcended them: Alexander Blok, Boris Pasternak, Anna Akhmatova.

Prose came back into fashion in the 1920s, and dramatic accounts of the revolutionary upheaval vied for attention with joyful comic writing, much of it hailing from Russia's sunny south: Babel's *Odessa Tales* and *Red Cavalry*, Sholokhov's *And Quiet Flows the Don*, the anecdotal short stories of Zoshchenko and Zamyatin, Ilf and Petrov's *Twelve Chairs*.

Promoting the cause

In the 1930s Stalin's grip on the arts tightened. Henceforth literature was to be harnessed for the socialist cause. It was still a high calling because writers are, said Stalin, "engineers of the human soul", and as such a vital element of the production line which turns out right-minded Soviet citizens. This mandate was, of course, a death sentence on real literature. Indeed, it led directly to the death of many writers: Yesenin and Mayakovsky had already committed suicide in despair; Osip Mandelshtam, Nikolai Gumilev and Isaak Babel were swallowed up by the Terror. Of the first rank of writers only Pasternak and

Akhmatova survived. Akhmatova's poetic account of those years, *Requiem*, is a monument of world literature and a testament to her dignity.

The novelist Mikhail Bulgakov once remarked that "manuscripts don't burn", meaning that the impulse to create and consume literature is made stronger when it is attacked. Stalin failed in his attempt to amputate the human spirit, and the Soviet people's hunger for books was made all the sharper. This is why it was common in the USSR to see queues of people waiting to buy some slim volume of civic verse or collection of short stories. Bulgakov was himself one of the writers who satisfied Russians' spiritual hunger. *The Master and Margarita*, his tale of how the devil visits Moscow and wreaks havoc, is one of the most profound (and funny) novels of the century. Russians are always amazed to learn that it is not revered in the West as it is at home.

A brief thaw

The Master and Margarita was published only in 1965, 25 years after Bulgakov's death. This was the time of the Thaw, the heady period under Khrushchev when many banned works saw the light of day. The key event of the Thaw was the publication of *One Day in the Life of Ivan Denisovich*. This short story, a pitilessly truthful snapshot of *gulag* life, was the debut work of Alexander Solzhenitsyn. It made him famous overnight and led to a flood of camp memoirs as "rehabilitated" writers unburdened themselves of their terrible experiences.

Poets also benefited from the Thaw. There appeared in the 1960s a group of young poets – Yevgeny Yevtushenko, Andrei Voznesensky and others – who chose to declaim their verse to an

---

VOICES OF DISSENSION

Russia has had dissidents for almost as long as it has had books. One of the first was Alexander Radishchev, whose account of serfdom under Catherine the Great, earned him long years in Siberia. A more sinister precedent was set when the 19th-century philosopher Peter Chaadayev was declared insane for criticising the tsarist regime. But dissidence is now associated with the Soviet era, especially its last years when the system was oppressive enough to punish free thinkers, but not so despotic as to murder them. The leading anti-Soviet writer of this time was Alexander Solzhenitsyn. His novels *Cancer Ward* and *First Circle*, and his history of the camps, *The Gulag Archipelago*,

were all published abroad. He was exiled in 1970, but returned home to see his work printed in his native land. Solzhenitsyn was the godfather of dissidence, but there was never a unified movement. Indeed, dissidents often objected to each other as much as they did to the state. *Inakomysliye* (thinking otherwise) covered all kinds of writing and opinions: Marxist historian Roy Medvedev, religious poet Irina Ratushinskaya, human rights activist Andrei Sakharov, Nobel laureate Joseph Brodsky, *samizdat* heroes Sinyavsky and Daniil, and comic novelist Vladimir Voinovich. All are worth reading for their own sake, as well as for what they have to say about the repressive regime.

audience. Some of them set their poems to music, and the best – Bulat Okoujava, Vladimir Vysotsky, Alexander Galich – were hugely popular because their subjects were so often taken from humdrum Soviet reality: trolleybuses, communal flats, the lives of geologists, hockey players.

As the Brezhnevian winter set in many free-thinking writers found themselves out of favour with the censors. Popular works passed from hand to hand in typewritten copies, a home-made method of publication which became known as *samizdat* ("self-publishing", a pun on the state publishing organisation, Gosizdat). Works by banned Westerners and Russian

from the intelligentsia was to let them read whatever they wanted. He did just that, and for a couple of years there was a reading frenzy, as eager *intelligenty* devoured the poetry of Marina Tsvetaeva, the satires of Aksyonov and Zinoviev, and (at long last) the novel *Doctor Zhivago*. There was a simultaneous boom in new works, of which the best was *Children of the Arbat*, Anatoly Rybakov's memoir of a Moscow childhood.

The post-Communist era, by contrast, has been marked by a descent into pulp with cheap, low quality detective thrillers becoming more and more popular. However, there are serious writers whose work is both popular and

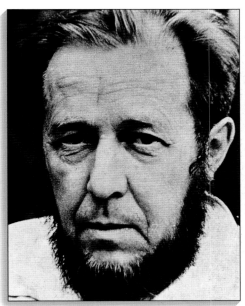

emigrés – George Orwell, Vladimir Nabokov, Aldous Huxley, Joseph Brodsky – were all read in the 1970s, but secretly by torchlight.

In search of a modern Tolstoy

By the time of *glasnost* officially approved literature had grown stagnant, and the best writing of the Soviet period was banned or bowdlerised by the censor. Even politically harmless classics were unavailable. In this absurd situation, all Gorbachev had to do to win sympathy

LEFT: *Anna Akhamatova* by Natan Altmann, 1914.
ABOVE: Vladimir Mayakovsky.
RIGHT: Alexander Solzhenitsyn.

provocative. The most famous of these are Victor Pelevin and Vladimir Sorokin, the latter's *Golobuye Salo (Blue Lard)* book was the object of a court action by a pro-Kremlin youth movement Iduishii Vmeste (Moving Together) due to its descriptions of homosexual acts between Stalin and Khrushchev. Still, most Russians are reading less and less, as many modern forms of entertainment become popular. Print runs are ridiculously small, with 20,000 copies for a piece of contemporary literature considered a huge success. If anything, young people today are more likely to be reading the latest sex tips in *Cosmo or GQ* than having a copy of Tolstoi or Gogol to hand. ❏

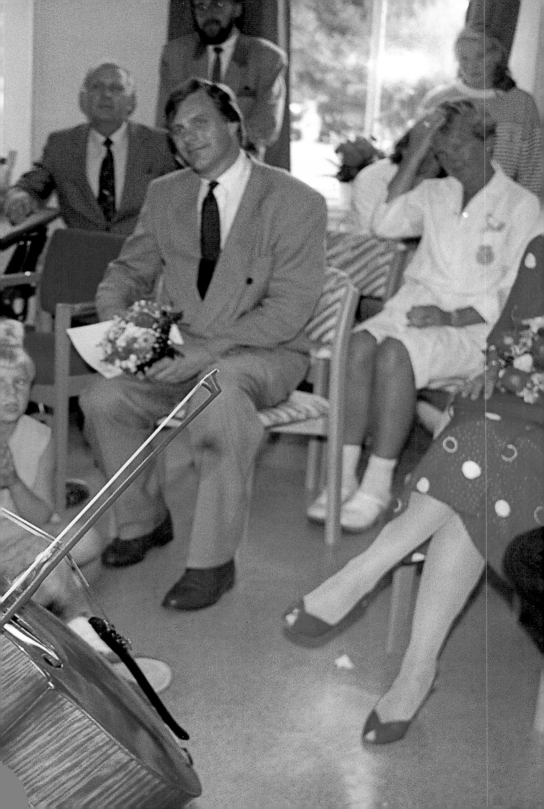

THE MUSIC MAKERS

*Influenced by their early folk and ecclesiastical traditions, the country's musicians
have created, to worldwide acclaim, an authentic Russian sound*

R ussian music is often said by those outside the country to have dated from the
1830s and 1840s, when Mikhail Glinka
became the first Russian composer to obtain
European recognition. In fact, the country has a
rich musical tradition that originated in the folk
songs of the eastern Slavs who settled in the

region about 1,300 years ago. This folk music,
which celebrated all events of life from working in the fields to weddings and festivals,
served as the foundation for the great Russian
classical musical tradition that burst forth in the
mid-19th century.

The first professional musicians (*skomoroki*)
appeared in the 11th and 12th centuries in the
courts of the Russian princes in Kiev and Novgorod. *Skomoroki* were travelling troupes of
actors who played a variety of instruments
unique to Russia, such as the *guslee* (stringed
instrument), *rozhok* (wind instrument) and
volinka (wind instrument akin to the bagpipes).
The Orthodox Church also played a strong role

in the development of Russian music from the
10th century when it became the religion of the
state. Its liturgical monotone and style of
singing had a powerful impact on the Russian
composers of the 19th and 20th centuries.

But the Church had a negative effect, too,
causing Russia to become isolated from the
musical trends in Europe. Orthodox liturgy dictated that only the human voice could be used
in divine worship, and for a long time secular
performers were regarded by the Church as
"messengers of the devil who turn people's
minds from God with songs and trumpets and
games". The only instrument permitted by the
Church were bells, and the Russians developed
bell-ringing to a sophisticated level. Today,
after 70 years of silence under Communism,
the art of bell-ringing is enjoying a revival; the
resonant pealing can be heard on Saturday
evenings and Sundays before services.

Despite the dominance of the Church, Tsar
Ivan III created a secular court choir in the 15th
century. Towards the end of the 16th century, as
contact with the West increased (Elizabeth I,
for example, sent an organ and virginals to Ivan
the Terrible), even church music began to move
with the times. By the 17th century, five-line
notation, polyphony and major and minor keys
were gradually introduced to the liturgy, allowing it to obtain a richer sound and effect.

With the foundation of a court theatre during
the reign of the enlightened Alexis Mikhailovich
(1645–76), a secular musical tradition grew
from the seeds sown by Ivan III, but it was
during the reign of Peter I that the greatest
innovations occurred. By moving the capital
from Moscow to his new city of St Petersburg
in 1703, Peter transformed conservative, pious
Muscovy into the modern state of Russia at a
stroke. Along with all the architects and craftsmen imported to modernise his backward country came foreign musicians to play in the new
military bands and sing in the new state choir.
Music soon became an integral part of everyday
court life. Yet Peter was not very musical himself, so music-making remained entirely foreign

in origin. For the vast majority of the population, hearing music meant either going to church or listening to folk songs.

By the mid-18th century the Russian court had its own orchestra, and a special theatre was built for the performance of opera, which soon became the rage among the aristocracy, thanks largely to the patronage of the imperial family. Indeed, opera became so popular in the 18th century that wealthy landowners such as Count Sheremetev (whose enchanting minia-

NOBLE PASTIME

Music-making in the 18th century was dominated by enthusiastic nobles whose expertise left much to be desired, yet there was a great deal of talent around, particularly in composition.

originally a serf musician) and their successors Alexander Alyabev and Alexei Verstovsky should not be overlooked, even if their Italian training meant that their music did not sound very Russian. They were the first Russian musicians to compete with foreign counterparts on their own level, and they did much to raise musical standards.

Peter the Great's relentless westernising encouraged the nobility to regard Russian culture with contempt, but the upsurge of patriotism which

ture theatre can be visited at Ostankino) were soon setting up their own companies and orchestras on their estates, using serfs as well as foreign artists as performers.

Glinka marks a turning point

It is customary to view Mikhail Glinka (1804–57) as the first genuinely Russian composer. But the achievements of 18th-century composers such as Dmitri Bortnyansky, Maksim Berezovsky and Yevstignei Fomin (who was

---

PRECEDING PAGES: Mstislav Rostropovich, cellist.
LEFT: travelling musicians.
ABOVE: Mikhail Glinka, 19th-century opera composer.

followed Napoleon's defeat in 1812 swelled hearts with national pride. A new generation of artists, musicians and writers appeared on the scene who were anxious to create a genuinely Russian culture.

Among them was Glinka, whose two operas marked a turning point in the history of Russian music. Both *A Life for the Tsar* (1836) and *Ruslan and Lyudmila* (1842) combined Western techniques of composition with music that was clearly inspired by native folk sources. They were unashamedly Russian works.

Glinka's operas are traditionally considered to be the cornerstone of classical Russian music. His musical plays laid the foundation for the Russian symphonic school, and his vocal compositions are the first examples of the Russian romance. Alexander Dargomizhsky (1813–69) continued the search, begun by Glinka, for a national Russian musical style.

Since opera was government-controlled in tsarist Russia, the conservative tastes of the St Petersburg aristocracy for foreign music in particular continued to determine what works were performed. Public concerts, which were held on a regular basis from the end of the 18th century, were

allowed only during the five-week period of Lent, when the Imperial theatres were closed. There was still no professional training available for budding Russian musicians.

A distinctly Russian sound

Anton Rubinstein (1829–94), the virtuoso pianist and composer who did the most to change this situation during the liberal years of Alexander II, was more concerned with raising general standards of musicianship than with promoting specifically Russian music. He founded the Russian Musical Society in 1859 (the first organisation that was allowed to hold concerts throughout the winter season)

POOR RELATION

Under Nicholas I thousands of roubles were spent on the resident Italian opera troupe, while the Russian Opera had to struggle to make ends meet.

and the St Petersburg Conservatoire in 1862. Similar institutions were founded in Moscow by Rubinstein's brother Nikolai. Not all Russian musicians favoured Rubinstein's reforms.

In particular, the group of Slavophile composers which gathered around Mily Balakirev in the 1860s vigorously opposed the professionalism of the Conservatoire training and its classical Western orientation. In an attempt to keep Russian music free from foreign contamination and preserve its independent status, Balakirev (1837–1910) started a rival Free School of Music.

Together with Alexander Borodin (1833–87), who earned a living as a well-respected chemist, Nikolai Rimsky-Korsakov (1844–1908), who forged a successful career in the navy, Modest Musorgsky (1839–81) and César Cui (1835–1918), Balakirev set about promoting a native Russian musical tradition, believing that art belonged to the people and should be realistic in style.

It is to these composers that Russian music owes much of its distinctive sound. Drawing on the melodies of native folk song and Eastern music, they sought inspiration in the legends of Russian history and literature. Borodin based his opera *Prince Igor* (1874) on a 12th-century epic poem, Musorgsky turned to Pushkin for his masterpiece *Boris Godunov* (1874), and Rimsky-Korsakov created magical operas that had their source in Russian fairytales.

A contemporary of the "Five" was Pyotr Tchaikovsky (1840–93), one of the first students at the St Petersburg Conservatoire. Despite his tuition by foreign professors, the Russian element in his music is unmistakable. Besides the six major symphonies, the piano concertos and the ever popular ballets, Tchaikovsky is also best remembered for his operas, which drew on the works of Pushkin and Gogol. *Evgene Onegin* and *The Queen of Spades* are perhaps his greatest works in this genre.

By the end of the 19th century, Russian music was being performed regularly, and the conservatoires of St Petersburg and Moscow were producing composers, conductors and performers of great talent. With the exception of the Imperial theatres, the government had little control over musical life.

The brightest stars at the turn of the century were the singer Fyodor Chaliapin and the composers Sergei Rachmaninov (1873–1943) and Alexander Scriabin (1872–1915), the most famous graduates of the Moscow Conservatoire where they studied with Sergei Tanyeyev (1856–1915), a composer, pianist and musical theorist who had been Tchaikovsky's student.

Rachmaninov, best known for his major contributions to the piano repertoire (but also a composer of some magnificent symphonic works), was himself a highly accomplished pianist, and was able to earn a good living on the concert platform during his long years of

– Sergei Prokofiev (1891–1953) and Dmitri Shostakovich (1906–75).

Composers of the 20th century

Igor Stravinsky (1882–1971) and Sergei Prokofiev became the real innovators in the field of composition. Stravinsky, one of the great musical giants of the 20th century, came to world prominence when Diaghilev staged his ballets, *The Firebird* (1910) and *Petrushka* (1911), in Europe as part of his famous "Ballets Russes" seasons. His *Rite of Spring* (1913) was considered so modern when it was first performed that it caused an uproar all over Europe.

exile after the Revolution. Scriabin, in whose works the influence of Wagner, Liszt and Chopin can be clearly heard, formed close links with the mystical Russian Symbolists who emerged in the early years of the 20th century.

Nikolai Rimsky-Korsakov shaped the musical life of St Petersburg at this time. It was his students, including the music professors Anatoli Lyadov (1855–1914) and Alexander Glazunov (1865–1936), who in turn influenced two of the leading Russian composers of the 20th century

Stravinsky continued to blaze new paths in music for the rest of his long career, his eclectic works transcending narrow national boundaries. Like Rachmaninov, he lived in exile after 1917, visiting his homeland only in 1962.

Prokofiev completed his studies, as Stravinsky had, at the St Petersburg Conservatoire with Rimsky-Korsakov, but he too left the country in the wake of the Revolution, leaving Russia bereft of its greatest talents; he returned in the mid-1930s.

The Soviet muse

While the 1917 Revolution had a cataclysmic effect on musical life in Russia, with theatres closing and concert series abandoned, it also

LEFT: Pyotr Tchaikovsky, composer.
ABOVE: Dmitry Shostakovich working on his Seventh Symphony in besieged Leningrad, 1941.

injected it with energy. The years just after the Revolution were a time of experimentation. Many people attended the opera for the first time and vast musical and dramatic spectacles were organised to commemorate the events of 1917.

Music became an important weapon for propaganda purposes. But until new composers appeared who could write morally uplifting Socialist music, the Bolsheviks were content for the old repertoire to be performed. Innocuous opera titles were often changed for ones that were more politically charged.

The greatest period of artistic tolerance came during the 1920s. Two rival musical organisa-

tions formed in 1923: the avant-garde and modernist Association of Contemporary Music, which favoured experimentation, and the Russian Association of Proletarian Musicians, which was the more militant of the two, dismissing all past music as bourgeois and alien.

The period from the 1920s to the 1940s was the heyday of the composer and music teacher Nikolai Myaskovsky (1881–1950), who wrote 27 symphonies, among other works. Other talented composers to appear during the 1920s were Nikolai Roslavets (1881–1944), later a victim of the purges, whose major contribution to the development of atonal music is now beginning to be recognised, and Alexander

Mossolov (1900–71), whose famous orchestral work full of mechanical sound effects, *The Iron Foundry* (1926), is a testament to the early years of Soviet industrialisation.

By far the most gifted composer to emerge during the early years of Soviet power was Dmitry Shostakovich (1906–75), whose *First Symphony* was first performed in 1926 when he was just 20 years old, and followed by another masterpiece, his opera *The Nose* (1928), based on Gogol's short story.

For a time, Leningrad (as St Petersburg became known) vied with Berlin to be the centre of musical experimentation, but towards the end of the 1920s, as ideology came to play a bigger role in artistic life, the freedoms enjoyed by Soviet artists gradually disappeared.

Music for the masses

In 1932, the Union of Soviet Composers was formed and music was placed under direct government control. Composers were told that they had to write music according to the doctrine of Socialist Realism. In other words, music had to be understandable to the masses and nationalistic in character. It was to depict "reality in its revolutionary development".

It was not until 1936, however, that composers really came under pressure to conform. Shostakovich's great operatic masterpiece *Lady Macbeth of Mtsensk* was first performed in Leningrad to great acclaim in 1934, but things started to go wrong following a Moscow performance in January 1936 attended by Stalin. The next day an editorial entitled "Chaos Instead of Music" appeared in *Pravda*. Shostakovich's opera, and avant-garde music in general, was subjected to a merciless attack. He responded with his *Fifth Symphony*, a darkly ambiguous work subtitled "A Soviet Artist's Reply to Just Criticism". His relationship with the authorities was ever after to be tortuous and complicated. It determined the content of the music he was to write over the next four decades. But while Shostakovich paid lip service to the ideology of the Soviet regime, beginning with his *Fourth Symphony*, he carried out subtle resistance to the established order, as did most composers.

Accusations of decadence

The attack on Shostakovich in 1936 signalled the beginning of a systematic destruction of the

Soviet musical intelligentsia. After the temporary hiatus caused by World War II, the purges intensified. During the first Congress of Composers held in 1948, Shostakovich, together with Prokofiev, Aram Khachaturian, Myaskovsky, and a number of others, was found guilty of "formalism". By refusing to write music filled with bright, optimistic melodies, these composers were accused of following the "cult of atonality, dissonance and disharmony", which reflected the "decay of bourgeois culture".

MUSICAL HERESY

In the 1940s and 1950s Western music was banned from the concert platform and in the classroom was denounced as "decadent" and "reactionary".

thing of a shock for these young Russians to hear the music of Schoenberg and Webern for the first time. It was a brief thaw. Another bleak period of isolation and repression followed Khrushchev's removal from power in 1964. In the musical sphere it was spearheaded by Tikhon Khrennikov, who presided as head of the Union of Composers from 1948 until its collapse in the aftermath of the 1991 coup.

The Soviet conservatoires, however, produced an array of outstanding talents, among

Khrushchev's accession to power heralded the thaw in cultural life, symbolised by the great success of Shostakovich's *Tenth Symphony* in 1953. Restrictions began to be slowly relaxed and contacts with the West were cautiously resumed.

Stravinsky was allowed to return to Russia in 1962 and visits made by Western musicians such as Leonard Bernstein, Glenn Gould and Aaron Copland made a huge impact on the new generation music students. It came as something

them the pianist Svyatoslav Richter, the conductor Gennady Rozhdestvensky and the violinists David and Igor Oistrakh. Young Soviet musicians and conductors took gold medals in international competitions.

The opera and ballet troupes of the Bolshoi Theatre, the symphonic orchestra under Mravinsky and Svetlanov, as well as many other talented musicians successfully made tours to the West to great acclaim. And in Moscow, the International Tchaikovsky Competition has enjoyed great prestige since its inception in 1958.

Despite all these glittering successes, many greatly gifted artists, including the cellist

LEFT: the pianist and conductor Vladimir Ashkenazy's heralded return to Russia in 1989.
ABOVE: Moscow Music Academy.

Mstislav Rostropovich, the violinist Gidon Kremer and the pianist Vladimir Ashkenazy, were forced either to emigrate abroad or defect. Meanwhile, "official" composers continued to churn out leaden operas and orchestral works, and were rewarded for their efforts with trips abroad and privileged lifestyles, while avant-garde composers such as Alfred Schnittke (1934–98), Sofia Gubaidulina, Nikolai Karetnikov (1930–93) and Edison Denisov (1929–96) made a living in the best way they could, knowing that their works could never be performed to the public.

Their music, which represented a defiant and triumphant statement of the values they steadfastly continued to believe in, also faithfully reflected the troubled times in which they lived.

Together with a growing interest in the musical avant-garde, one of the leading figures of this era was Giorgi Sviridova (1915–98) who embodied the national musical traditions. From the 1960s to the 1980s, Sviridov's creative talents were especially prevalent in choir and vocal-symphonic genres.

A new flowering

All this changed when Mikhail Gorbachev came to power in 1985. With *glasnost* came an explosion of Soviet cultural life, as artists and writers were allowed to travel abroad freely, and previously forbidden works were published and performed. Rostropovich and Ashkenazy both made much-publicised return visits to Russia, concert repertoires widened and Russian music started to become popular in the West.

Today, the St Petersburg school of music is best represented by Galina Ustvolskaya, Lucian Prigozhin (1926–94), Sergei Slonimsky, Boris Tishchenko, Yuri Falik, Alexander Knaifel, and their younger colleagues. Notable musicians from the Moscow school include Boris Tchaikovsky (1925–96), Vyacheslav Artemova, Eduard Artemov, Vladimir Martinov, and the husband-and-wife team of Dmitry Smirnov and Elena Firsova.

Amid the general economic crisis in Russia, which has left musicians, orchestras and musical institutions struggling to survive financially, musical life continues to thrive and is even enjoying a period of revival. The number of symphonic and chamber orchestras has been growing in recent years, and music festivals and competitions have become an inherent part of the music scene. Traditional concert venues are being supplemented by churches, whose warm acoustics and rich decor contribute to the ambiance.

Opera and ballet companies such as the Mariinsky (formerly Kirov) Theatre tour abroad and Russian conductors and musicians are much sought after internationally. All this goes to show that Russia has retained its status as a music superpower. ❏

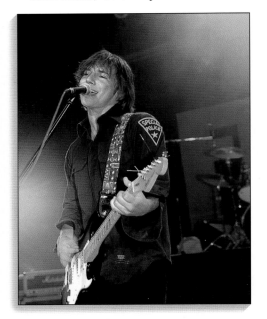

THE POP-ROCK SCENE

Russian pop stars are generally unknown in the West. One recent exception to this is the group Tatu who made headlines outside of Russia. Some other pop stars to look out for are Alsu (a girl singer from Tartarstan), Ivanushki International and Slivki. Russian rock enjoyed its heyday in the period in and around *perestroika*. Groups from this period such as Kino and Akvarium continue to be popular to this day. Among the most recent popular acts are Mummi Troll, from Vladivostock and Zemfira, from Ufa. Live music is still very popular in Russia and new, and not so new, bands can be seen playing live in clubs.

LEFT: Mummi Troll, a ground-breaking rock band from Vladivostok.

The Film Makers

Film, said Lenin, was one of the most important tools in forging a socialist society. Indeed, the Soviet Union built up a powerful film industry that was useful in forming the mentality of the new socialist man, as well as providing entertainment in a drab world. Cinemas were built in every town. Cheap tickets and a limited choice of other forms of entertainment meant that large crowds were always assured.

Since the collapse of the Soviet Union, Russian film has struggled to find its bearings. The economic crisis in the 1990s meant just a handful of films were made each year. The national film industry, facing a dire lack of investment and dwelling on depressing topics, could not compete with Hollywood, and piracy made cinema a losing proposition.Since 2002, all that has changed. As many as 70 films are now produced annually, and the highest-grossing film of all time was a 2004 Russian sci-fi film, *Nightwatch*, which surpassed even *Lord of the Rings* at the Russian box office.

Contemporary directors such as Nikita Mikhalkov, Alexander Sokurov and Alexander Rogozhkin, have adjusted successfully and produced some fine works. Rogozhkin's *Peculiarities of the National Hunt* (1995), a comedy about Russian hunters and the national character, is a rare example of a financial blockbuster. Less commercially successful, but a favourite with critics was Sokurov's *Russian Ark* (2002). Its 96-minute journey through Russia's history was shot in a single take and includes all the rooms of the Hermitage.

Mikhalkov's *Burnt by the Sun*, a chilling film about Stalin's purges, won the 1995 Academy Award for Best Foreign Film. Sergei Bodrov's *Prisoner of the Mountains* and Pavel Chukrai's *The Thief* were also nominated in 1996 and 1998 respectively. The former is about Russia's brutal war in Chechnya, while the latter tells the tale of a boy growing up in Russia, in the care of a thief, amid the destruction wrought by World War II.

Despite the economic problems, gaining the freedom to create has been a significant development. Some directors have broken away from the state-owned, former monopoly film studios to create their own, such as the STV Film Studio in St Petersburg and NTV-Profit in Moscow.

RIGHT: the award-winning Russian film *Burnt by the Sun*, directed by Nikita Mikhailkov.

Since 1896, when the first film in Russia was shown in St Petersburg's Aquarium Theatre (now a Chinese restaurant) Russian film has been a tale of two cities – Moscow and St Petersburg. The state-owned Lenfilm, founded in 1918, is known for intellectual and artistic classics, as well as experimental work, in the vein of Alexander Sokurov's acclaimed film *Mother and Son* (1997). St Petersburg's film industry, however, is in a poor shape compared to its Moscow counterpart. Mosfilm has always produced light-hearted or politicised films, such as the popular comedies of Leonid Gaidai. In 1998 it received a boost when the mayor of Moscow, Yuri Luzhkov, donated US$15 million

towards film making and another US$5 million for new equipment. St Petersburg has so far gone without such a sponsor.

The Moscow-based Gorky Film Studio made a name for itself at the end of the 1990s with its production of low-budget intellectual movies aimed at young people. St Petersburg's private STV studio has done much to help young directors. It produced Alexei Balabanov's 1997 hit, *Brother*, a brutal and realistic film about growing up in Russia's criminal world.

Today, the Russian film industry looks set to take off. The two major film studios are up for privatisation, and there is a surplus of fine young talent, primed by a strong flow of investment from both the state and private sector. ❑

RIDING THE SLOW TRAIN TO VLADIVOSTOK

The Trans-Siberian Railway is one of the epic journeys. It takes over a week to travel its length, and the route lies through Russia's dark heart

A trip across Russia on the Trans-Siberian Railway is more like an ocean voyage than a train ride. The cities of Siberia are strung along the route like islands, and each one is like a new port of call. Half the fun of getting to them lies in the empty stretches between landfall, when you get to know your fellow-travellers.

The Trans-Siberian is also the best way to *feel* the immensity of the Russian hinterland, as for day after day the train ploughs its chugging furrow through dense, dark forest. The journey is perhaps more spectacular in winter, when the snow fields extend to the horizon and the glare from this great unruffled white blanket is blinding. In summer, Siberia is hot and dusty, though the longer days mean there are more hours in which to soak up the view, fewer to spend in your compartment with a pack of cards and a bottle of vodka.

The classic Trans-Siberian route will take you to Vladivostok – "Conqueror of the East" – on Russia's Pacific seaboard. From there it is a short hop in a plane to Japan. But another option is to dip south along the Trans-Mongolian, skirt the shining banks of Lake Baikal, and strike out across the Gobi Desert to China. Either way, at the end of a week you will be a seasoned train-dweller: for days after you will continue to feel the rhythmic hammering of the wheels beneath your feet.

▷ **COACH MAKER**
It is worth making friends with the conductress, who will then keep you supplied with tea and gossip.

▷ **ALL ABOARD**
Stops are a chance to stretch your legs. But do not stray too far from the train: they do not always stick to the timetable, and have been known to leave early.

▽ **MOVABLE FEAST**
The restaurant cars are of unpredictable quality. Be sure to take plenty of dry and canned food with you, to be on the safe side.

MOCKBA

◁ ON TO THE GOBI
This train is branching south through the Gobi Desert to Ulan Baatar. Some trains go through Mongolia and all the way to Beijing.

△ PASSING TRADE
One can often buy food en route. But in hard times shops close when the train arrives, so that travellers do not clean them out.

△ SWING A CAT
Compartments for two are small but cosy. They are neatly designed to convert daily from bedroom to sitting room and back.

▽ END OF THE LINE
Vladivostok is the last stop. Once a closed city, it is now a boom town doing more business with Tokyo than with Moscow.

THE IRON ROAD TO THE EAST

The Trans-Siberian Railway was one of the great engineering projects undertaken during the period of rapid industrialisation under the last two tsars. It was begun in 1890, and its primary purpose was to link European Russia with the new city of Vladivostok, which had been founded only 30 years before, but had grown rapidly into a major port. Like the great railroads of the American West, the Trans-Siberian also had the effect of opening up the land for urban adventurers. All the old towns on its route – Yaroslavl, Yekaterinburg, Krasnoyarsk, Irkutsk, Khabarovsk – grew bigger when they became staging posts along the iron road. The railway was finished in 1905, just in time to serve as a supply line in the Russo-Japanese war. In 1918 it carried the tsar and his family on their last journey to Yekaterinburg. The railway played a military role once again in 1941, when thousands of factories in European Russia were rapidly dismantled and shipped wholesale down the line to Siberia, where they churned out tanks and guns beyond the reach of the advancing Germans.

PLACES

A detailed guide to the entire country, with principal sites clearly cross-referenced by number to the maps

Travel to Russia becomes more exciting each year because of the greater freedom to explore. Even now that so many of the former republics such as the Baltics (Estonia, Lithuania and Latvia) and Asian states have gained their independence, Russia remains a vast, enigmatic and diverse territory.

The European North, which stretches into the Arctic Circle, is one of Russia's wildest and most beautiful regions. One of the main attractions of St Petersburg and the palaces which surround it is the splendour, principally reflected in the architecture, of the imperial past. A tour to St Petersburg often takes in the country's capital, Moscow, as well. The question as to which city is superior has been hotly debated for more than two centuries and continues to this day among both Russians and foreigners.

Even though two-thirds of Moscow was burnt by Napoleon in 1812, the city gives us a feel for the age and history of the country and, with its myriad onion-domed churches, for holy Russia, too. Equally, with some of its many monuments to Communism intact, we are made aware of the more recent Soviet past. The city's Russianness attracts some people as much as St Petersburg's European-ness attracts others.

The theme of holy Russia continues as one explores the Golden Ring of churches, kremlins and medieval towns which surrounds Moscow, and a boat trip on the Volga takes in rural Russia as well as such towns and cities as Astrakhan along its banks. The mountainous southern region of the Caucasus, with its spa towns and hot springs, attracts walkers and climbers alike.

The Ural Mountains mark the boundary between Europe and Asia, with the forests, lakes and rivers of Siberia extending to the shores of the Pacific and Arctic oceans. Cutting through Russia, from Moscow in the west to Vladivostok in the east, is the famous Trans-Siberian railway.

Belarus and Ukraine are included in this book, because both geographically and culturally they are closely linked with Russia and they share a common history – Kiev, capital of Ukraine, is where the traveller will discover the origins of "Rus". Crimea, with its hot climate and beaches, is still one of the most popular holiday areas for many Russians, though it is now part of Ukraine.

The dramatic differences between the lands that make up Russia, Belarus and Ukraine add to their great appeal. You can tailor a visit to suit your own interests and at last wander freely without an accompanying guide. ❏

PRECEDING PAGES: the Trans-Siberian railway; an effective way to travel in the northeast; driving across Lake Baikal in winter.
LEFT: Catherine Palace, Pushkin, a present from Peter the Great to his wife.

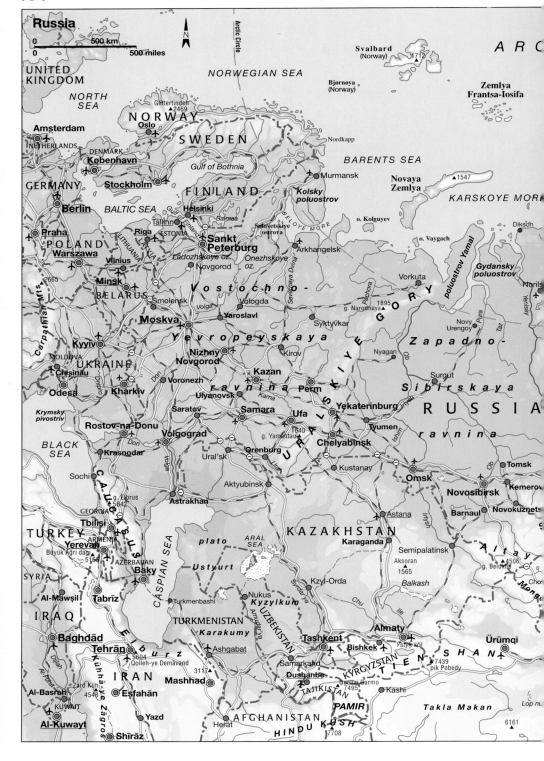

Russia

0   500 km
0   500 miles

ARC

UNITED
KINGDOM

NORWEGIAN SEA

Svalbard
(Norway)   ▲1712

Bjørnøya
(Norway)

Zemlya
Frantsa-Iosifa

NORTH
SEA

NORWAY

Ghtertinden
▲2469

Oslo

SWEDEN

Nordkapp

BARENTS SEA

Novaya
Zemlya   ▲1547

KARSKOYE MOR

Amsterdam

NETHERLANDS

DENMARK

København

GERMANY

Stockholm

FINLAND

Gulf of Bothnia

Helsinki

BALTIC SEA

Tallinn

Saimaa

Murmansk

Kolsky
poluostrov

BELOYE MORE

o. Kolguyev

Dikson

o. Vaygach

Berlin

Praha

POLAND

Warszawa

Rīga

ESTONIA

Sankt
Peterburg

Solovetskiye
ostrova

Arkhangelsk

poluostrov Yamal

Gydansky
poluostrov

Norils

LITHUANIA

Vilnius

Ladozhskoye oz.

Novgorod

Onezhskoye
oz.

Vorkuta

GORY

Yenisey

Minsk

BELARUS

Smolensk

Vostochno-

Vologda

Severnaya Dvina

Pechora

1895

g. Narodnaya

Zapadno-

Novy
Urengoy

Pura

Taz

2665

Carpathian Mts.

Moskva

Volga

Yaroslavl

Syktyvkar

KIYE

Nyagan

Ob

Kyyiv

Yevropeyskaya

Nizhny
Novgorod

Kirov

Surgut

Sibirskaya

MOLDOVA

Chişinău

UKRAINE

Don

Voronezh

Kazan

r a v n i n a

Perm

URAL'SKIYE

Yekaterinburg

Irtysh

RUSSIA

Odesa

Kharkiv

Ulyanovsk

Kama

Ufa

1640

Tyumen

r a v n i n a

Krymsky
pivostriv

Saratov

Samara

g. Yamantau

Chelyabinsk

Ishim

BLACK
SEA

Rostov-na-Donu

Don

Volgograd

Orenburg

Kustanay

Omsk

Tomsk

Krasnodar

Ural'sk

Ural

Kemerov

Sochi

CAUCASUS

g. Elbrus
▲5642

Astrakhan

Aktyubinsk

Ob

Novosibirsk

GEORGIA

Astana

Barnaul

Novokuznets

Tbilisi

ARMENIA

TURKEY

Büyük Ağrı dağı
5165

AZERBAIJAN

Baky

CASPIAN SEA

plato

Ustyurt

ARAL
SEA

KAZAKHSTAN

Karaganda

Semipalatinsk

Aksoran
1565

Altay

g. Belukha
▲4506

Cho

Mong

SYRIA

Al-Mawşil

Tabrīz

Turkmenbashi

Nukus

Kyzylkum

Syrdar'ya

Kzyl-Orda

Chu

Balkash

Ile

IRAQ

Baghdād

Dijlah

Tehrān

Elburz

5604

Qolleh-ye Demāvand

Ashgabat

3117

TURKMENISTAN

Karakumy

Amudar'ya

UZBEKISTAN

Samarkand

Tashkent

Bishkek

Dushanbe

Almaty

Ysyk-köl

KYRGYZSTAN

TIEN SHAN

7439
pik Pobedy

Ürümqi

Kashi

Al-Başrah

KUWAIT

IRAN

Eşfahān

Mashhad

Kuh-e Garmo
7495

TAJIKISTAN

PAMIR

Lop n

Takla Makan

6161
▲

Al-Kuwayt

Yazd

Herat

AFGHANISTAN

HINDU

KUSH

7708

Shīrāz

Zard Kūh
4548

Zagros

Kūhhā-ye

IC OCEAN

CHUKCHI SEA

USA

mys Dezhneva

Bering Strait

St Lawrence

o. Vrangelya

Chukotsky poluostrov

BERING SEA

VOSTOCHNO- SIBIRSKOYE MORE

Pevek

Anadyrsky zaliv

Anadyr

1785 ▲

Severnaya Zemlya

Novosibirskiye ostrova

Koryakskoye nagore

2562 ▲

MORE LAPTEVYKH

mys Chelyuskin

o. Karaginsky

Komandorskiye ostrova

poluostrov Taymyr

Taymyr

1146 ▲

Tiksi

Verkhoyansky

Yana

Indigirka

Kolyma

khrebet Cherskogo

g. Pobeda ▲3003

zaliv Shelikhova

Srediny khrebet

4688 ▲ vlk. Klyuchevskaya Sopka

Verkhoyansk

2389 ▲

Lena

khrebet

Aldan

Magadan

poluostrov Kamchatka

Petropavlovsk- Kamchatsky

g. Kamen ▲1664

Sredne –

Vilyuy

Yakutsk

Amga

o. Iony

m. Lopatka

SEA OF OKHOTSK

Kurilskiye ostrova

sibirskoye

Mirny

Aldan

Shantarskiye ostrova

oloskogore

adkamennaya Tunguska

Lena

Vitim

Stanovoy khrebet

2255 ▲

o. Sakhalin

1609 ▲

Angara

3072 ▲

Stanovoye

Tynda

Zeya

Amur

Tatarsky proliv

nagore

Komsomolsk- na-Amure

Yuzhno- Sakhalinsk

Krasnoyarsk

Bratst

oz. Baykal

Chita

Shilka

Da Hinggan ling

Argun

Khabarovsk

2090 ▲

Blagoveshchensk

Irkutsk

Ulan-Ude

Yichun

Ussuri

Sikhote – Alin

2290 ▲

Hokkaidō

3491 ▲

g. Munku-Sardyk ▲

nisey

Selenga

Kerulen

Hailar

Qiqihar

Songhua jiang

oz. Khanka

Sapporo

Changajn Nuruu

2800 ▲

Ulaan Baatar

Harbin

Nakhodka

Vladivostok

SEA OF JAPAN

Sendai

tajn Nuruu

Changchun

Honshū

MONGOLIA

GOBI

Shenyang

2034 ▲

2750 ▲ Paektu-san

NORTH KOREA

JAPAN

Fuji-san ▲3776

Tōkyō

Baotou

Beijing

Lüda

P'yŏngyang

Sŏul

Nagoya

Osaka

Tianjin

SOUTH KOREA

CHINA

Shijiazhuang

Pusan

Shikoku

Kitakyūshū

Yinchuan

Huang he

Jinan

Qingdao

YELLOW SEA

Kyūshū

6305 ▲

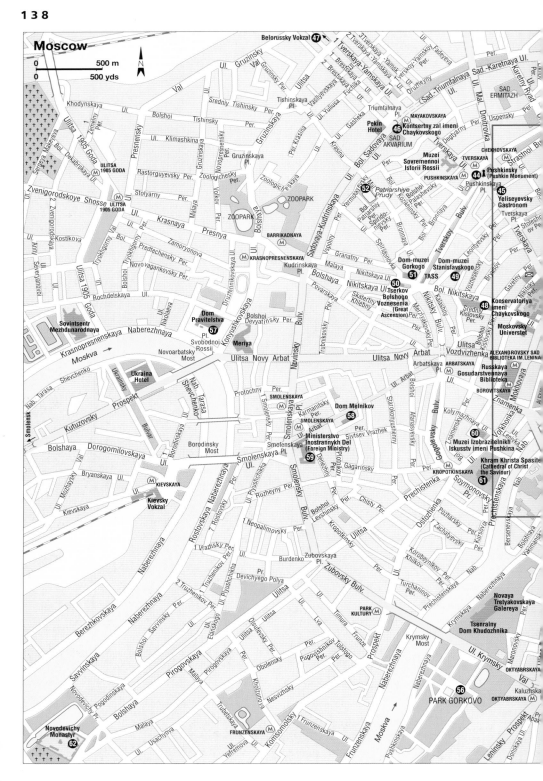

Moscow

MOSCOW

Russia's capital beckons exploration. Here domed cathedrals, baroque palaces and soaring Soviet edifices compete for attention amid the bustle of modern European city life

Map on page 142

Moscow's first mention in historic chronicles is a brief note in an annal written in 1147 indicating that there was a small settlement surrounded by small hills on the banks of the Moskva River. Such limited mention is not surprising: Moscow lay on the extreme borders of the Suzdal Knyazhestvo (principality), the centre of which was far to the southwest in Kiev. When Prince Yuri Dolgoruky arrived in 1156, Moscow must have been no more than a cluster of wooden huts. However, he saw its potential as an outpost against the Tatar Golden Horde and ordered a kremlin (fortification) to be built.

Historians believe the name Moskva derives from an old Slavonic word meaning "wet", probably an allusion to the marshy countryside that surrounded the site. The broad Moskva River winds through the city and used to be swelled by a number of smaller streams and rivers, so the site was ideal for a fortress. However, the Tatars still torched it at regular intervals, even after Grand Prince Ivan Kalita ("Moneybags") built stone walls around the settlement in the early 14th century. The walls were made of limestone and earned Moscow the name "belokamennaya" (literally white-stone).

As Ivan Kalita's power and prestige grew, so did Moscow. But his real coup was managing to persuade the Russian Metropolitan to move the Holy See from Vladimir to Moscow. As chief centre of both religious and secular power, Moscow was on the map. The city blossomed during the reign of Ivan III, in the late-15th century. Ivan dealt with the Tatars effectively and was the first prince to take the title "tsar", the Russianised form of Caesar. To match his new status, he imported Italian architects to create a new kremlin. Many of the cathedrals and the walls they built still stand.

PRECEDING PAGES: a scarecrow burns in Moscow's Masienitsa Festival. **LEFT:** St Basil's Cathedral. **BELOW:** monument to the worker and the woman collective farmer.

The Kremlin

When the Italian architects Fioravanti, Ruffo and Solari had finished their job in 1495, praise was effusive and another "eighth wonder of the world" was added to that already lengthy list. But the accolade was not entirely undeserved. The imposing red-brick walls running around the **Kremlin ❶** are 2,230 metres (7,316 ft) long, 20 metres (65 ft) high and 6 metres (20 ft) wide in some places. It has four gates and 19 towers. Inside, the Italians created three stone cathedrals to replace the humble wooden structures that had existed. These came to symbolise tsarist power: the Uspensky was used for coronations, the Blagoveshchensky for baptisms and weddings, and the Arkhangelsky for funerals.

The main entrance for visitors (open Fri–Wed 10am–6pm, last entry 4.45pm) is the **Troitskaya**

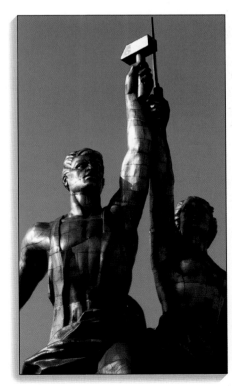

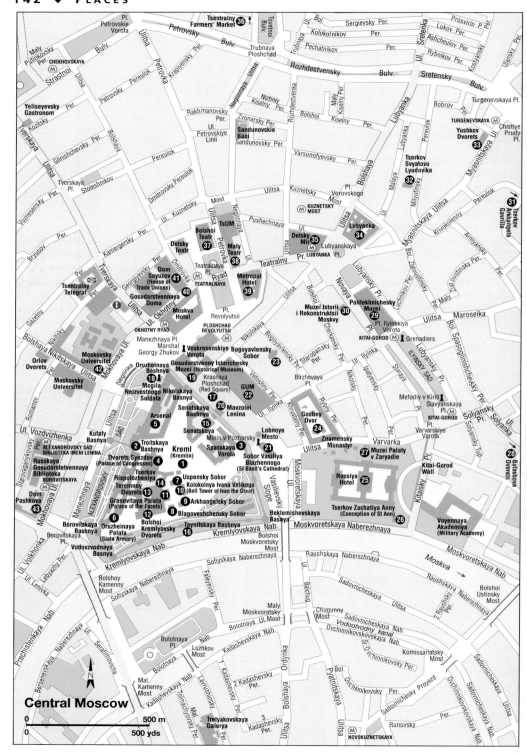

Central Moscow

N

0   500 m
0   500 yds

Bashnya ② (Trinity Tower) that crosses Alexandrovsky Gardens and the Neglinka River (which was channelled into a large stone underground pipe on the orders of Catherine the Great in the 18th century). In pre-Revolutionary times this gate was used for regal entrances. Napoleon, in 1812, obviously didn't know this – although his army entered the Kremlin this way, he used the **Spasskaya Vorota ❸** (Spassky Gate). He is supposed to have lost his famous tricorn hat in the process, making it unlucky, according to popular lore, to pass through the Spassky Tower wearing a hat.

At one time the Kremlin was considered almost impregnable. Its southeastern side is protected by the Moskva, and a deep moat, which once linked the Moskva and Neglinka rivers, takes care of the remaining walls. The **Arsenalnaya Bashnya** (Arsenal Tower) had its own well which fed a secret reservoir and an underground passage to the Neglinka River. During long sieges, the garrison could thus come and go as they pleased.

Although the Russian tricolour now flutters above the Kremlin, the symbols of Soviet power are still apparent in the red stars topping five of the towers. These have been there so long (since 1937) that most Muscovites don't feel strongly about their removal. But there is one Soviet eyesore that still makes Muscovite blood boil – the steel and glass **Dvorets Syezdov ❹** (Palace of Congresses) that was planted in the middle of the Kremlin in 1961. (The architect, Mikhail Posokhin, is also responsible for the soulless Novy Arbat, formerly Kalininsky prospekt.)

Several ancient monasteries inside the Kremlin walls were demolished in Soviet times, but the complex retains its ancient beauty. The former **Arsenal ❺** buildings were constructed by Peter the Great between 1701 and 1736 and its

Trams, buses and trolleybuses operate from 6am to 11.30pm. You'll need a talon (ticket), obtainable in strips from street kiosks, the conductor or the driver.

ĂBELOW: the Kremlin Cathedral.

The Cap of Kazan, made for Ivan the Terrible in the 16th century to mark his victory over the Tatars in Kazan, features in the Armoury Museum collection.

BELOW: Kremlin's Gate Tower.

facades are hung with Napoleonic military trophies. The **Oruzheinaya Palata** ❻ (State Armoury) at the foot of the **Borovitsky Bashnya** (tower) houses the oldest Kremlin museum. It has armour, but pride of place goes to the valuables accumulated by the Russian aristocracy, in particular diamonds and jewellery.

The three original cathedrals still dominate the heart of the Kremlin, with the grandiose **Uspensky Sobor** ❼ (Cathedral of the Assumption), built by Fioravanti, as centrepiece. This is a prime example of European Renaissance building combined with Byzantine traditions. Inside is a remarkable collection of frescoes devoted mainly to the Virgin Mary, in addition to the famous 14th-century Trinity icon. It is here that the city's bishops and patriarchs were interred.

To the south is the contemporary **Blagoveshchensky Sobor** ❽ (Cathedral of the Annunciation), which was built as a private church for Moscow's Grand Princes. The cathedral started life as a three-domed, galleried building in the Pskov style (Ivan III had opted for Russian rather than foreign stonemasons for this particular project). As this was essentially a private church, the builders set it on a very high foundation so that its entrance would be accessible from the second floor of the royal palace. Ivan the Terrible thought the cathedral should be more imposing, so he ordered the addition of four small chapels surmounted by a cross and cupola. The result matched Ivan's nickname, so two more domes were added to restore the building's balance.

The Annunciation is generally regarded as superior to the other early cathedrals. Built on the site of a wooden structure of the same name, it inherited the original church's iconostasis, painted by two of the greatest names in Russian iconography: Feofan the Greek and Andrei Rublyov. Its floor is tiled with agate and jasper, a gift from the Shah of Persia. Portraits of the Grand Princes hang alongside biblical fathers and Greek and Roman luminaries such as Aristotle, Plutarch and Virgil: doubtless an attempt by the princes to portray themselves as enlightened rulers.

Next to the Annunciation is the **Arkhangelsky Sobor** ❾ (Archangel Cathedral), built in the early years of 16th century by Venetian architect Alevisio, nicknamed Novy (the new), because an Italian of the same name had worked in Moscow before him. It was here that the princes and tsars were coronated, married and buried until Peter the Great built his new capital in 1712. Seventeenth-century murals of dead aristocrats watch over the bronze sarcophagi containing their remains.

The Kremlin's focal point is the **Kolokolnya Ivana Velikogo** ❿ (Bell Tower of Ivan the Great). Started by Ivan, it was augmented by Boris Godunov. Some said he undertook the building work as a penance for murdering Prince Dmitry, the legitimate heir to the throne. Although Boris had been elected tsar, many people saw him as an upstart: they must have been delighted to see the bell tower grow shakier the taller it rose – like the tsar's hold on power. But it survived and is still the tallest structure in the Kremlin. It carries the inscription: "By the grace of the Holy Trinity and by order of the Tsar and Grand Prince Boris Fyodorovich, Autocrat of all Russia, this temple was finished and gilded in the second year of their reign."

Ivan III was a prolific builder. The **Granovitaya Palata** (Palace of the Facets) is perhaps the most fabulous of the secular buildings he initiated. Unlike any other structure in Moscow, the palace is a pure example of Italian Renaissance architecture, designed by Ruffo and Solari. It was here that the tsars received foreign ambassadors and other dignitaries and the whole place was decorated as a showpiece. The frescoes are painted on backgrounds of gold, and you'll even find a portrait of Ivan the Terrible in the guise of the "Just Knight" in the Hall of Facets.

These are the oldest buildings in the Kremlin, but over the centuries myriad others have been erected between them. Until the modern Palace of Congresses was built, the most recent was the **Bolshoi Kremlyovsky Dvorets** (Great Kremlin Palace) built by Konstantin Thon, architect of the Cathedral of Christ the Saviour. Just in front is the spectacular **Teremnoy Dvorets** (Terem or Belvedere Palace), now only accessible through the Great Kremlin Palace. Built along the lines of traditional wooden houses, it was first occupied by Mikhail Romanov's family. The first of his line, Mikhail (1613–45), and later his son Alexis, used this palace to conduct state affairs. It was meant to convey the power and unity of the Russian state so the interiors are lavish to say the least. Before becoming tsars of Russia, the Romanovs were just one of many noble families. Young Mikhail was elected tsar by a council of all Russia following a long period of popular unrest and occupation by the Poles. The Poles were finally driven out in 1612 by a patriotic army that rallied to Russia's banner at the religious settlement founded by St Sergius just outside Moscow. Led by Prince Pozharsky and organised by a patriotic merchant called Minin from Nizhny Novgorod, the national army advanced on the capital and forced the Poles and the pretender they had put on the throne to flee. Pozharsky and Minin were immortalised in bronze in 1818; their statue stands outside the entrance to St Basil's Cathedral on Red Square.

Tucked between the Uspensky and Palace of the Facets is the tiny **Tserkov Rizopolozheniya** (Church of the Deposition of the Robe), commissioned by Patriarch Geronty in 1480 to commemorate an argument with Ivan III about whether a church procession should follow the course of the sun or vice versa. The religious leader threatened to resign if Ivan didn't admit he was wrong. The Grand Prince finally gave in and the church was built by masons from Pskov (Geronty wasn't having any of the new-fangled Italian-style architecture in vogue in Moscow at that time). Initially, the church served as a private chapel for the Russian patriarchs, but it was requisitioned by the Romanovs for their own use in 1653.

The eastern side of the Kremlin is reserved for government buildings. The main structure is late 18th-century and was designed by Matvei Kazakov for the Moscow Department of the Senate, which was then located in St Petersburg. After the Revolution, Moscow became the capital and the top floor of the **Senat** was used by Lenin as an apartment building from 1918 to 1923.

Although the buildings inside the Kremlin are the main attractions, some of the 20 towers that line the

Map on page 142

TIP

The best time to visit Moscow is during the summer months of May to August when the temperature is around 18°C (62°F) and can rise to 30°C (86°F). In the snowy winter the temperature can fall as low as –30°C (–22°F).

BELOW: Tsar Bell on display outside the Bell Tower of Ivan the Great.

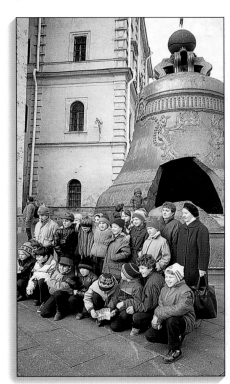

An eternal flame burns on the Tomb of the Unknown Soldier in the Alexandrovsky Gardens along the west wall of the Kremlin.

BELOW: two of the city's war heroes.

walls are worth mentioning. The oldest, **Taynitskaya Bashnya** (Tower of Secrets) in the southern wall, has fascinated scholars for centuries. It has an underground passage to the river, but it is also thought to have been the site of Ivan the Terrible's famous library. The collection was started by his grandmother, Sofia Paleologue, who brought a wealth of manuscripts to Moscow as part of her dowry. Some believe the library is still hidden beneath the Kremlin walls, probably under the Arsenal Tower overlooking the Alexandrovsky Gardens. A Russian scholar thought he had found it in 1934 but Stalin ordered him to stop searching.

Another of the towers that shouldn't be missed is the **Spasskaya Bashnya** (Spassky Tower) located by the Spasskaya Vorota. Built in 1625, its Gothic and Renaissance splendour served as a fitting background for the state entrances of the tsars. In the 20th century, the guard of honour for Lenin's mausoleum passed through here on the choreographed march to the revolutionary's tomb.

Red Square

Touching the wall as you leave the Kremlin is supposed to bring you luck and ensure your return. **Krasnaya ploshchad** (Red Square) adjoins the eastern side of the Kremlin, but to get there you have to leave the Kremlin through Trinity Gate and walk round as only top brass are allowed to use the Saviour's Gate on the square itself. Walk through **Alexandrovsky Gardens**, with its lime trees and remarkable 19th-century grotto in the Kremlin's wall, past the **Mogila Neizvestnogo Soldata** (Tomb of the Unknown Soldier) – a popular spot for wedding pictures – and turn right. The ketchup-coloured building on your left is the city's **Gosudarstvenny Istorichesky Muzei** (Historical Museum; open Mon–Sat 10am–6pm, Sun 11am–8pm; closed first Mon of the month; last entry

one hour before closing time), which houses a rare collection of artefacts tracing Russian history up to the present day. Red Square started life as the eastern moat protecting the Kremlin, but this was eventually filled in and the resulting square was cobbled in the 15th century. For much of its history the square was crammed to bursting point with wooden market stalls where merchants from all over the world set up shop. The whole place formed a major fire hazard and the Great Fire of Moscow that destroyed much of the old city in 1737 started here.

The **Mavzolei Lenina** ❷⓿ (Lenin Mausoleum; open Tues–Thurs, Sat & Sun 10am–1pm), which partially obscures the red Kremlin wall, still houses the great man's embalmed body, but people no longer queue for hours to see the waxen features. The building itself was designed by Shchusev in 1930.

The area of the Kremlin wall between the Nikolskaya and Senatskaya towers is the burial place of top Soviet statesmen, public figures and military leaders. Here lie such names as Maxim Gorky, Lenin's wife, Nadezhda Krupskaya, spaceman Yuri Gagarin, nuclear physicist Igor Kurchatov, and John Reed, the American journalist whose book on the birth and early years of the Russian Revolution, *Ten Days That Shook the World*, was a revelation to subsequent generations of Marxists throughout the Western world. It describes Western governments' attempts to undermine and destroy the Revolution, and until the 1960s seemed to explain and even justify the burgeoning paranoia and suspicion of the young Soviet state.

Sobor Vasiliya Blazhennogo ❷❶ (St Basil's Cathedral) is to Moscow what the Eiffel Tower is to Paris, or Big Ben is to London. It is essentially Muscovite. There is a story that Ivan the Terrible had the architects blinded so they could not build anything like it again. Ivan shaped Red Square and much of old

Map
on page
142

BELOW: Historical Museum from Maneznaya Square.

The 40-ton bronze Tsar Cannon was cast in a Moscow foundry in 1586. The biggest cannon in the world, it was once positioned in Red Square to repel enemy attacks, but never fired a shot.

Moscow. He built St Basil's, more properly known as the Pokrovsky Sobor (Cathedral of the Veil), to commemorate major victories over the Tatars. Every victory (nine in all) added a new chapel to the structure, each one dedicated to the saint on whose day the victory was won. The whole golden-domed complex became known as St Basil's when one of the chapels was dedicated to Basil the Blessed, a holy man who predicted that Ivan would murder his first-born.

In the 17th century Red Square became a centre of political debate and was the venue for many popular uprisings. The **Lobnoye Mesto** (a raised circular platform in front of the cathedral) was used for religious services and for reading tsarist decrees. The square served also as a place of execution (it is said that as a child Ivan the Terrible had a small wooden tower built on top of the Spasskaya Tower so he could watch beheadings in private). Later the leader of the 1671 peasant revolt, Stenka Razin, was executed here and in 1648 the Streltsy mutineers and supporters of Tsarina Sofia, Peter the Great's half-sister, also met their deaths on Red Square.

It's hard to judge just how the wooden city of Moscow looked because Muscovites put it to the torch in order to frustrate the imminent arrival of Napoleon and his troops in 1812. By the time Napoleon arrived he found the buildings in flames and anybody who was anybody, and a lot who weren't, gone.

In retrospect, you could say Moscow should be grateful to Napoleon. The reconstruction transformed the city from a medieval warren of small alleys and streets into an elegant capital whose main streets and quarters were dominated by stylish mansions. In charge of the massive project was an architect called Osip Bovet. He restored the Kremlin wall and rebuilt the shopping galleries that lined the eastern side of Red Square. These were later replaced by the still magnificent

BELOW:
Moskva River
and the Kremlin.

GUM ㉒ building, with its pastel interiors and ornate fountain. GUM opened in 1893, was nationalised in 1921 and celebrated its centenary by returning to the private sector following an auction of the retail units that make up what was once the most up-market shopping mall in Russia. In the late 19th century another red-brick building was added to the northern end of Red Square, just opposite the Historical Museum. It housed the city's Duma or council until the Revolution. After Lenin's death it became a museum devoted to the father of the country and housed the city legislature, both of which have now moved to other locations, although the Lenin Museum recently hosted a contemporary arts exhibition.

On Manezhnaya Sqaure, just off to the right of Red Square, is the newly restored **Voskresenskiye Vorota** (Resurrection Gate) with a tiny chapel. The gate was pulled down by Stalin to make way for tanks that used to roll across Red Square on revolutionary holidays. Next to the gate is the **statue of Marshal Georgy Zhukov**, who led the Soviet Army to victory over Germany in 1945.

A street by any other name

The Kremlin and Red Square may have been the heart of the original city, but its arteries were the old quarters that clustered around them. The city was built in rings, with main roads to important towns, such as Smolensk, Tver and Kaluga, radiating in a wagon-wheel pattern that still exists today. Not surprisingly, these roads became major thoroughfares and until the Revolution were simply named after the places they led to. Since 1917 they have had different names – Kalininsky prospekt (now Novy Arbat), ulitsa Gorkogo (now Tverskaya) and Leninsky prospekt respectively. In day-to-day speech and on street signs most of them have reverted back to their original names. Other street

Map on page 142

The name "Red" Square was a happy coincidence when the Bolsheviks came to power in 1917. In old Russian the word "red" also means beautiful and this is the source of the square's name.

BELOW: GUM, Moscow's famous shopping mall.

names are clues to the trades and businesses once conducted there, e.g. Meshchanskaya (Petty Bourgeois Street), Zhivoderka (Abattoir Road) or are derived from a monastery or church.

The Kremlin formed the central ring, followed by the former **Kitai-Gorod wall** which bordered the Kremlin to the northeast. The wall was 2.5 km (4 miles) long and had 12 towers and several gates. Built in the mid-16th century around the original market-place, its name derives from the Mongolian word for "middle", i.e. middle fortress. It is thought that Ivan the Terrible's mother, Elena Glinskaya, first coined the name – she came from a place called Kitai-Gorod in Poland. These walls have not survived, but remains can be seen on Teatralnaya ploshchad, close to the Metropol Hotel, and on Kitaisky prospekt in Zaryadye.

The third ring accounts for Moscow's reputation as the "white city". These walls ran 9 km (5 miles) along what is now the **Bulvarnoye Koltso** (Boulevard Ring), had 10 gates and 17 blind towers, and were built of white stone. They were constructed in the early 16th century and served as a sturdy defence for the outskirts of Moscow until they were demolished in the late 18th century.

The final ring, **Zemlyanoi Val** (Earthern Wall), was constructed at the end of the 16th century and was really a rampart. Two hundred years later it was replaced by gardens which gave their name to a whole area: the **Sadovoye Koltso** (Garden Ring) follows the course of the original ramparts.

Merchants of Moscow

BELOW: fashionable dressing.

Many of the old streets of Kitai-Gorod lost a lot of their original charm at the same time. This was one of Moscow's liveliest quarters and runs due east from the north end of Red Square. **Nikolskaya** (formerly October 25 Street) was

SUBTERRANEAN MOSCOW

Moscow has a secret which the Kremlin says nothing about: an underground city with one section beneath the suburb of Ramenki about 6 km (4 miles) southwest of Red Square. It was designed to accommodate 30,000 party élite and their families for as long as 30 years in the event of a nuclear war. Ivan the Terrible laid the foundations of subterranean Moscow to give his *oprichniki* militia secret access from his palace to various parts of the city. The KGB, successor to the *oprichniki*, built a tunnel to ferry prisoners from prison to their headquarters. But these efforts were nothing compared to the refinements of Leonid Brezhnev in the 1960s and 1970s. The Ramenki complex was built on several levels over 202 hectares (500 acres) with streets wide enough to take cars. It has its own metro linking it to central Moscow and Vnukovo airport. There are cinemas and swimming pools, and warehouses filled with food.

As for the old jest about Moscow's "wedding-cake" ministry buildings being perilously close to the breaking strain of the earth's crust, it seems that they are almost as deep underground as they are tall, and each has its own stop on the private "Metro 2" and other concealed links with the underground warren.

known as the "street of enlightenment" as the city's first higher education facility, the Slavonic-Greek-Latin Academy, was located at Nos 7–9. Further up the street on the same side is a magnificent Russian Gothic building with a sundial adorning its facade. Built in 1814 as the Orthodox Synod's printing house, it printed the first books in Russian. Today, it is the History and Archives Institute.

Turning right into **Bogoyavlensky Pereulok** you'll see the magnificent **Bogoyavlensky Sobor ㉓** (the Church of the Manifestation) on your right, parts of which are 13th-century, but whose main facade is a typical example of 17th-century Moscow baroque. It was founded in 1290 by Prince Daniel Nevsky, the same man who built a string of fortified monasteries, including the Danilov, around the city. Ilyinka used to be the Moscow equivalent of Wall Street, but during the Soviet era the bank buildings and the Mercantile Exchange (at No. 6) were confiscated and turned into public offices – the Exchange became the Soviet Chamber of Commerce and Industry. Contemporary photographs show a lively commercial street cluttered with bright advertisements. Today it's all rather grey.

If you go right into **Ilyinka** (formerly Kuibyshevskiy) **ulitsa** and left into **Khrustalny Pereulok** (Crystal Alley) at the exchange corner you'll see the **Gostiny Dvor ㉔** (Old Merchant Arcade), another of the city's famous shopping arcades. When it was completed in 1805 by the Italian architect Quarenghi it was considered a major accomplishment. Its elegant, white Corinthian pillars still retain their original magic. The building, which was warehouse space for decades, has now been restored to its original glamour.

At the south end of Khrustalny turn into **Varvarka** (formerly Razin Street). Ironically, the revolutionary name given to this once exclusive street of nobles

Map on page 142

Moscow has several colourful food markets (rynky). *Tsentralny Rynok (Central Market) is on Tsvetnoy Bulvar.*

BELOW: the White House, Russia's government building.

The Mayakovsky Museum, Myasnit-skaya ulitsa 3–6, is devoted to the life of the poet Vladimir Mayakovsky, who worked here before his suicide in 1930 (open Fri–Tues 10am–5pm, Thurs 1–8pm; closed Wed).

BELOW: checking out the pet market.

and wealthy merchants' homes was that of the Cossack rebel Stenka Razin. Little remains of the old street. Around 20 tiny churches and a number of houses were demolished to make way for the staggering **Rossiya Hotel** ㉕ complex, reputed to be the biggest in the world with more than 5,000 rooms. There is, however, contant speculation about the Rossiya's future. There are rumours, as yet unconfirmed, that it is soon to be demolished. For the moment though it continues to accept guests. But a stretch of the old Kitai-Gorod wall is still extant, along with the small **Tserkov Zachatiya Anny** ㉖ (Church of the Conception of St Anne), which was built at the time of Columbus's voyage to America.

To the right you'll see the Vasilievsky Slope running down to the **Bolshoy Moskvoretsky Most** (Bridge), which German teenager Matthias Rust used as a landing strip on his extraordinary flight to Moscow in the mid-1980s. The world held its breath when it was revealed that a teenager in a light plane had managed to dodge Soviet radar. As detente was well established and the Cold War beginning to thaw, most people thought Rust would be sent home with a slapped wrist. In the event, the Soviets imprisoned him for a short period before quietly letting him go home – on a scheduled flight, of course.

The humble-looking white-stone, wooden-roofed building (No. 8) was once the English Embassy. It was presented to English merchants by Ivan the Terrible in the mid-16th century when the tsar was considering marriage to Queen Elizabeth I of England. The building was restored in the 1970s. Next door is the **Znamensky Monastyr** (Monastery of the Sign), with its five domes. Started in 1684, the belfry was added in 1789 and today the second floor is used as a venue for classical and religious music concerts. The building beside it (No. 10) was the home of Mikhail Romanov, the first tsar of the dynasty which ruled

Russia for more than three centuries. The house had fallen into disrepair, but in the late 19th century it was restored; only the ground floor is original. Now a museum, the **Muzei Palaty v Zaryadie** ㉗ (open Wed–Mon 10am–5pm), it shows how the Russian nobility lived. The interiors are stunning.

Slavyanskaya ploshchad runs northwest and if you cross it at its southern end you turn right onto **ulitsa Solyanka** (Salt Street). For centuries, this eastern quarter was the centre of the artisans' guilds and it became notorious in the 19th century for prostitutes, brothels and criminals. The central marketplace at the top of **Podkolokolny Pereulok** was known as the Khitrovo and the pickpockets who thrived there were said to be so clever that they once stole a bronze cannon from the grounds of the Kremlin. To escape public disgrace, the Governor-General of Moscow ordered his men to find the cannon at all costs. As usual, the local police set up a meeting with the criminal bosses and the cannon was back in its place next day. But there's a twist to the tale. It was discovered that the returned cannon had itself been stolen from the opposite side of the Kremlin wall; the first cannon was never recovered.

You can easily spend a couple of hours in this picturesque quarter which is bordered by the Yauza River whose embankment makes a pleasant walk up to the **Yauza Boulevard**, the starting point of the Boulevard Ring. Solyanka and the main thoroughfares in the vicinity were popular residential streets for the nobility. Most of their mansion homes have either disappeared or have been turned into institutes or academies. The former home of the Naryshkin family at 14a is now the Obstetrics Institute. Peter the Great's mother was a Naryshkin and the family liked to remind everyone of its royal connections, so the palace they built (all gone now) had more than its share of pomp and circumstance. The

Map on page 142

BELOW: painting eggs for Easter.

Court of Wards erected in the 1820s and the 18th-century Foundling Hospital at Nos 14 and 16 are now the buildings of the Academy of Medical Science. Solyanka runs into Yauzskaya and ends up in **Taganskaya** (formerly Internatsionalnaya ulitsa). Worth seeing is the former **Batashova Dvorets**  (Palace) at No. 1, another aristocratic legacy. Now the 23rd City Hospital, the palatial building set back off the street in its own landscaped gardens is a real jewel.

On Slavyanskaya ploshchad, you could opt to walk up Lubyansky Proyezd and turn right onto **ulitsa Maroseika** (formerly Bogdan Khmelnitsky Street). To your left in the central garden you'll see the **monument to the Grenadiers** killed at the battle of Plevna during the Russo-Turkish War in 1887. At the top of the square is the **Politekhnichesky Muzei** (Polytechnic Museum), which was built between 1874 and 1907. It houses more than 40,000 exhibits tracing the development of Russian technology and science (open 10am–6.30pm; closed Mon and last Thurs in month).

On **Novaya ploshchad** to the left of the museum is a former Baptist church (No. 12) which is now the **Muzei Istorii Moskvy** (Museum of the History of Moscow; open Tues, Thurs, Sat & Sun 10am–6pm; Wed & Fri 11am–7pm; closed last day of month). The museum charts the changes in the city since 1812.

The old embassy quarter

A walk along ulitsa Maroseika, which runs into Pokrovka (formerly Chernishevsky), takes you into the old embassy quarter. A lot of embassies can still be found here and in the area around **Chistiye Prudy** (Clean Ponds). Like most old cities, certain quarters of Moscow came to be associated with particular nationalities. In Ivan the Terrible's day, much of the land behind the Clean Ponds was owned by German merchants. To the northwest, the French set up shops in the streets around Markhlevskogo and Malaya Lubyanka; the English and Poles gravitated to Myasnitskaya (Kirov) Street between Markhlevskogo and Chistiye Prudy. By the end of the 17th century, Moscow's wealthy boyars had bought up much of the land and built superb palaces.

A cluster of noble dynasties dominated the area – the Dolgoruky family lived on Kolpachny Pereulok 1, the Lopukhins at Starosadsky 5, and the Botkins at Petroverigsky Pereulok 4 – all to the southwest of Chistiye Prudy. Their grand palaces are overshadowed by the splendid **Tserkov Arkhangela Gavriila** (Church of the Archangel Gabriel) on Telegrafny Lane. Grand Prince Menshikov had the church built in the early 18th century and the tower still bears his name. Menshikov's aim was to top the Kremlin Bell Tower. It was the tallest building in Moscow and an old tsarist decree prevented the erection of anything higher. The Grand Prince was something of a favourite with Peter the Great, but when the tower was struck by lightning in 1722 no one lifted a finger to put out the ensuing fire which consumed the giant bronze statue of Gabriel mounted on top. The disaster was seen as a sign of God's displeasure with the tsar's favourite. Muscovites had good reason to be angry with the tsar – he had moved the capital to St

BELOW: a quiet moment at the church of the Archangel Gabriel.

Petersburg some years earlier, relegating Moscow to provincial status. Another church worth seeing is **Tserkov Svyatovo Lyudovika** ❷ (St Ludovic's; Lubyanka Malaya 12). It's a working Catholic church founded by the French in the early 19th century.

Map on page 142

Myasnitskaya to Lubyanka

The corner of Myasnitskaya (formerly Kirov) ulitsa and Chistiye Prudy (formerly Kirov) ploshchad is dominated by what remains of the grand **Yushkov Dvorets** ❸ (Palace), built in the late 18th century by architect Vasily Bazhenov, when most of the aristocracy became interested in philanthropy and art collections. The Yushkov family were famous for their balls. It is said that one Yushkov scion held a soirée that lasted three days – it ended only when the whole district had become disrupted by the crowds that had come to gape at the fireworks, music and the gorgeously dressed guests. From 1844 until recently the Yushkov Palace housed the Academy of Art and Sculpture.

Next door is an amazing looking building that was constructed in the late 19th century for the tea-merchant Perlov. He was hoping to entertain the Chinese emperor's ambassador during Nicholas II's coronation celebrations so the classical three-storey house-cum-tea-shop was topped by a Chinese pagoda. The envoy never turned up, but the pagoda still graces the roof. Today, the shop sells tea from Georgia among a variety of brands.

A statue of Felix Dzerzhinsky, Lenin's closest associate and founder of the KGB, once cast a stony stare over Moscow's citizens in Lubyanskaya ploshchad. It was one of the first to go following the unsuccessful coup against Mikhail Gorbachev and his reformers in 1991. The busy square now has its old name

The imposing Polytechnic Museum is devoted to technological advances in such fields as mining, electronics and space travel.

BELOW: Moscow's majestic Metro.

back, although it also has some creepy connotations. **Lubyanka Prison** ❸❹ in the headquarters of the Federal Security Service, formerly the KGB, on the north-east side of the square can still send shivers up spines. It seems an odd location for the city's biggest children's store, but **Detsky Mir** ❸❺ is almost next door. It was built on the site of the Moscow foundry which in the 1580s produced the bronze Tsar Cannon now on display in the Kremlin.

The city's shopping centre

If you walk westwards down ulitsa Okhotny Ryad (formerly Marx prospekt) you'll come to **Neglinnaya ulitsa**, in the city's main shopping centre. Neglinnaya takes its name from the river which used to flow down to the Moskva on this site but has long since been channelled deep underground. The area became a mecca for shoppers in the last century when it was noted for its French fashion stores. Russia's first department store (now **TsUM**) was built in the late 19th century on **ulitsa Petrovka** behind the Maly Teatr.

Nearby, on 1st Neglinny Pereulok, are the **Sandunovskie Bani**, the oldest public baths in the city. Built for a wealthy boyar's courtesans, they are elaborate. Taking a bath in Russia is a social event (although they don't go in for mixed bathing) and traditionally you would drink *kvas*, a home-brewed non-alcoholic drink resembling root beer, while steaming yourself clean.

At Trubnaya ploshchad (Pipe Square), Neglinnaya crosses the Boulevard Ring and runs into **Tsvetnoi** (Flower) **Boulevard**, now famous for its excellent, though expensive, **Tsentralny Farmers' Market** ❸❻. In the old days, its park was best known as a shelter for the homeless. At Trubnaya, you may opt to turn right and walk a block to the busy ulitsa Sretenka, running northeast.

BELOW: a bouquet from the flower-seller.
RIGHT: the Bolshoi Theatre.

Sretenka terminates at **Sukharevskaya ploshchad** which was named after the tower that stood here until the 1930s. Sukharev was the only officer who remained loyal to Peter the Great during the Streltsy rebellion and the grateful tsar erected the tower in Sukharev's honour. Later on the square's associations were less lofty: it hosted an officially recognised weekly market for stolen goods. Permission for the market was granted by Governor Rostopchin following the great fire of 1812. When the wealthy Muscovites returned home, they found their homes stripped bare and scoured the market in the hope of retrieving their valuables.

This is also the location of the **Doctor Sklifasovsky Hospital** which was founded by the noble Sheremetyev family. Sheremetyevo, Moscow's international airport, is built on what was once one of their country estates. Turn left at Trubnaya, and walk along Petrovsky and Strastnoi Boulevards to **Tverskaya** (formerly Gorky) ulitsa, the city's main drag. Tverskaya leads to the Kremlin, with Teatralnaya ploshchad on the left.

Teatralnaya ploshchad

Two main thoroughfares come together on Teatralnaya – Neglinnaya and Petrovka (named after the Vysoko-Petrovsky monastery built by Prince Ivan Kalita). The world-famous **Bolshoi Teatr** ❸ (Bolshoi, meaning "big", Theatre) dominates the northern side of the square. Formerly known as the Grand Imperial Theatre, it was built in 1825 and restored and remodelled following a fire some years later. Although internationally acclaimed as perhaps the world's greatest ballet company, nowadays the Bolshoi is feeling the pinch. Founded by the tsars, it became a Soviet flagship and as such enjoyed hefty state subsidies. Decades of neglect of the building's structure and rifts between performers and management have left the Bolshoi in a shaky state.

However, efforts have been made to rekindle the theatre's glory, and the government has released funds to revamp the Bolshoi as a part of an ensemble incorporating several buildings surrounding the square.

The Bolshoi's near neighbours are the **Maly Teatr** ❸ (Maly, "little", Theatre), the oldest drama hall in the city, and to its left, the **Detsky Teatr** (Central Children's Theatre). The Detsky opened in 1921 and was Moscow's first professional theatre for children.

Famous hotels and mansions

The eastern side of Teatralnaya ploshchad is home to the glamorous fin-de-siècle **Metropol Hotel** ❸, designed by a Scottish-Russian team, William Walcott and Leo Kekushev. Restored to its original glory, it is once again the best and most exclusive hotel in town. It's worth having a coffee in one of the ornate lounges if the room prices are beyond your reach. Opposite is the site of the **Moskva Hotel**, which in a true Russian manner is being pulled down and replaced with an exact replica containing all modern conveniences and 600 fewer rooms – undoubtedly priced much higher. Another new advancement is that guestrooms will be allowed to overlook the Kremlin. The KGB had forbidden this luxury in the original

Map on page 142

TIP

When in the vicinity of TsUM, check out Petrovka 38, an imposing classical building that has housed the Moscow police department since the Revolution.

BELOW: a new look for Maneznaya Square.

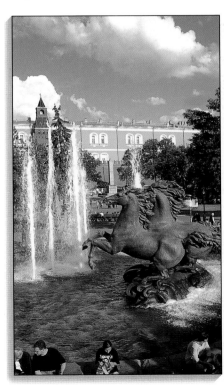

Gorky Park is a favourite place of relaxation for Muscovites, with its amusement park and Disney-style rides. It lies southwest across the Moskva River from the Kremlin.

BELOW: Moscow's State University.

design. Eccentricities aside, this recreation will prevent the designers at Stolichnaya vodka from rethinking their label which has featured this famous facade for decades; though they may consider adding some scaffolding for a few years.

Okhotny Ryad ⓵ was once a big covered market place where hunters would trade game, rabbits and such. Small stalls selling meat, fish, fruit and vegetables made it one of the dirtiest places in Moscow. The booths were dismantled after the Revolution, but following the 1991 coup people remembered the tradition and set up their own stalls. The city authorities had to designate special areas in the suburbs as flea markets so people could practise "market economy".

On the corner of Okhotny Ryad and ulitsa Bolshaya Dmitrovka is a green-painted, white-colonnaded former mansion. Once the Nobles' Club, it is currently the **Dom Soyuzov** ⓵ (House of Trade Unions). The mansion originally belonged to Prince Vasily Dolgorukov, the city's military commander in the early 1780s. In 1783 it was sold to the newly established Assembly of the Nobles, who started a very exclusive club in the building. Said to be the most beautiful house in Moscow, the interior is stunning, but the building is only open to the public when the white and gold **Kolonny Zal** (Hall of the Columns) is used as a concert venue. Keep your eyes open for these concerts, because in the old days the hall saw the likes of Pushkin, Lermontov and even Leo Tolstoy tripping the light fantastic under the crystal chandeliers.

Moscow had a number of clubs for different social classes. The Tradesmen's Club was located in what is now the Stanislavsky Theatre on the street of the same name. The English Club has become the **Muzei Sovremennoi Istorii Rossii** (Museum of the Modern History of Russia; Tverskaya ulitsa 21; open Tues–Sat 10am–6pm, Sun 10am–5pm; closed last Fri of the month), while the Central House of Artists now occupies the former German or Schuster Club.

Walk west down Okhotny Ryad to the river and if you follow its route, you'll pass **Moscow University's** ⓵ oldest building. Set slightly back from the street and fronted by a small garden, the classical yellow mansion was constructed between 1776 and 1793 by Matvei Kazakov and restored after the 1812 fire by Domenico Gilardi.

Just opposite on your left across the four-lane highway is the site of the former Manege, whose construction commemorated Russia's victory over Napoleon in the 1812 Patriotic War. It was used for exhibitions until 2004, when it burnt down in mysterious circumstances.

If you follow Okhotny Ryad down to the river, past the white marble **Russkaya Gosudarstvennaya Biblioteka** (Russian State Library, formerly the Lenin Library) on your right, you'll see an astounding palace, **Dom Pashkova** ⓵.

Built in the time of Peter the Great by the son of one of his administrators, Peter Pashkov, it was designed to vie with the Kremlin in magnificence and style. The money to build this gloriously baroque mansion had come from Pashkov's father Igor, who had made a fortune by investigating the bookkeeping of the governor of Siberia, Prince Matvei Gagarin. Pashkov claimed the prince was lining his own pockets on the proceeds of lucrative diamond and grain deals. Although well liked by the Siberians, Matvei was hanged and a great deal of his wealth and estates along with a few thousand serfs passed to the punctilious Pashkov and his family.

The last of the Pashkovs presented the palace to Moscow University which, in its turn, gave it to Count Rumyantsev to house his collection of art and manuscripts. After the Revolution, the art works were removed to the Pushkin, but the books remained and the mansion is now part of the state library.

Tverskaya ulitsa

Moscow's best-known street is **Tverskaya ulitsa**, the main thoroughfare since the early 19th century when wealthy nobles began building new palaces and imposing mansions in Moscow. Tverskaya was the main road to St Petersburg, so members of the tsar's entourage were constantly shuttling between the two cities along this thoroughfare. It had two triumphal arches in Pushkinskaya (formerly Tver Gate) ploshchad and at Belorussky Station. When Pushkinskaya Square was extended in the 1930s, the arch was dismantled brick by brick and relocated in Kutuzovsky prospekt across the river. The most incredible things were done to Tverskaya in the 1930s as part of Stalin's master plan to create a Communist capital of awe-inspiring proportions. It was straightened and widened. Several major buildings were moved deeper into the existing blocks of houses, including the former Governor General's residence which housed the Moscow Council of Deputies after the Revolution and is now the Mayor's Office; it also gained two storeys in the process.

The **Pushkin Monument** ⓴, about a third of the way up the street, was moved from one side of the boulevard to the other, into the small square in

Map on page 142

The Russian State Library (Lenin Library) holds 30 million books in 247 languages.

BELOW: peddling icons in the park.

The famous Filippov Bakery on Tverskaya is renowned for its raisin pie, said to have originated from before the Revolution when a police chief found a cockroach in a bun he was sold. Filippov ate the cockroach, saying, "But this is a raisin!" Then he bought a pound of raisins and created his raisin pie.

front of the grubby-looking Rossiya Cinema; the majestic Strastnoi Monastery was knocked down to accommodate the movie theatre. The building at No. 14 Tverskaya housed one of Moscow's biggest food stores. It was bought in 1898 by an entrepreneur called Yeliseyev who owned a chain of grocers. The "supermarket", **Yeliseyevsky Gastronom** ⑮, on the ground floor amazed even sophisticated Muscovites. The shop, which lay three-quarters empty in the hungry late 1980s and early 1990s, is now filled with imported Western groceries and luxury items.

About half-way up Tverskaya, is **Triumfalnaya ploshchad** (formerly Mayakovskogo). The **Kontsertny zal imeni Chaykovskogo** ⑯ (Tchaikovsky Concert Hall) was built in 1940 to mark the centenary of the composer's birth. It has a giant 20-tonne pipe organ with 7,800 pipes and is a venue for the International Tchaikovsky Competition (tel: 299 3681). Across the square is the old **Pekin Hotel**. It has been done up and serves Chinese food. At the end of Tverskaya is **Belorussky Vokzal** ⑰ (station), the terminus for trains from Western Europe and the start of the road to Sheremetyevo International Airport.

Nikitskaya

Parallel to Tverskaya is **Bolshaya Nikitskaya ulitsa** (formerly Gertsena). In the 16th century, this was the old road to Tver (known as Kalinin in the Soviet period). Ivan the Terrible stationed a garrison on this stretch of the road and it was later a coveted site for boyar mansions. The **Orlov Dvorets** (Palace), at No. 5, is typical of 18th-century classical architecture. At No. 11, the former home of the Kolychev boyars is now the voice department of the Moscow Conservatory and was recently returned to the splendour of its original elegance.

BELOW: statue of Tchaikovsky.

Maps on pages 138 & 142

The **Ekaterina Romanovna Vorontsovoi Dvorets** (Palace) is at No. 12. Ekaterina (1744–1810) was one of the first patrons of the arts in Russia. A great friend of Catherine the Great, Voltaire and Diderot, she developed into a true philanthropist and spent her fortune on sponsoring students, lectures and literary publications. She was head of the Russian Academy of Sciences from 1783 until 1796. After her death, the palace was bought for the Moscow Conservatory of Music, **Konservatoriya imeni Chaykovskogo** ❹❽. Tchaikovsky, Glier and Neuhaus taught Rachmaninov and Scriabin here and the Great Hall is a venue for the International Tchaikovsky Competition held every four years. The Lesser Hall presents chamber music and recitals.

Not all the best palaces are on the left of the street. The **Menshikov Dvorets** (palace), for example, is a classic piece of Moscow Empire style, incorporating six Corinthian columns in its facade. Unfortunately it is partly obscured by a hospital, so you have to reach it from Gazetny Pereulok (formerly Ogaryova).

Theatre buffs should head for the **Dom-muzei Stanislavskogo** ❹❾ (Stanislavsky Museum; open 11am–6pm; Wed, Fri, 2–9pm; closed Mon, Tues), just up the street and round the corner to the right at No.7. Stanislavsky transformed theatrical practice, and in particular the business of rehearsal. He made his actors literally live their part: they stayed in costume and in character day and night in order to achieve an understanding of the role. The desired result was a theatre which was convincing because it was realistic, rather than moving because it was mannered and rhetorical. The Stanislavsky approach has had a lasting influence on Hollywood, where his ideas were developed by Lee Strasberg of the Actors' Guild, and practised by followers of his such as James Dean, Marlon Brando and Robert De Niro.

BELOW: winter games on Patriarchs' Ponds.

Moscow has seven railway stations and five airports. It has 132 metro stations on its 213-km (132-mile) underground network. Its two river ports are accessible from the sea by the Volga River and the Moscow Canal.

BELOW: an artist on the Arbat.

At the same corner, Nikitskaya is crossed by Nikitsky (formerly Suvorovsky) Boulevard – the building on your right belongs to the **ITAR-TASS** news agency. If you cross Nikitsky here, Nikitskaya continues on the opposite side of the boulevard but twists off to the left, turning into Malaya Nikitskaya. The church on your left is the **Tserkov Bolshogo Voznesenia** ❺⓪ (Great Ascension). Besides having the best choir in the city, it is also a centre of monarchist activity.

Turn right onto Spiridonovka (formerly ulitsa Alekseya Tolstogo) to find the side entrance to the fabulous Art Nouveau **Dom-muzei Gorkogo** ❺❶ (Gorky Museum; open Thurs, Sat & Sun 10am–5pm; Wed & Fri noon–7pm; closed last Thurs in the month), which fronts Malaya Nikitskaya.

The house was commissioned at the turn of the 20th century by the merchant Stenka Ryabushinsky. Its architect, Fyodor Shekhtel, was the most exciting of the day and he finished the lyrically imposing building in 1902. It is one of the finest examples of an Art Nouveau interior in Russia – or indeed anywhere in Europe. Be sure to go inside, and don't miss the ceilings. When Gorky returned to the young Soviet Union in the early 1930s, he was presented with the house although he liked neither it or its architect.

Follow Spiridonovka to the next corner on the right and turn down Spiridonievsky Pereulok. This will bring you to Malaya Bronnaya. Turn left and the street leads to **Patriarshiye Prudy** ❺❷ (Patriarchs' Ponds), where Mikhail Bulgakov set the opening scene of his famous novel *Master and Margarita*. On the corner is Margarita, a restaurant. In the 19th century, this was Moscow's student quarter.

In 2002 there was an attempt to erect monuments to Bulgakov near the pond, as well as to carry out extensive reconstruction of the area. Both of these plans

TRETYAKOV GALLERY

On the south bank of the Moskva, opposite the Kremlin, is one of the greatest collections of Russian art in the country. The newly renovated **Tretyakovskaya Galereya** (Tretyakov Gallery; open: 10am–7.30pm; closed Mon), Lavrushinsky Pereulok 10, spans 1,000 years of Russian art, from early icons to 20th-century works. The building itself is in the Russian style – an urban interpretation of a boyar's mansion built in 1900 to house the collection accumulated by the brothers Pavel and Sergei Tretyakov in the late 19th century. The two men, who had made their fortunes in textiles, later donated their collection and palace to the state. On the gallery's ground floor, the remarkable icon collection includes the Byzantine *Mother of God of Vladimir* and Andrei Rublyov's 15th-century *The Trinity*. You'll find 17th- and 18th-century portraits upstairs. The work of the 19th-century Wanderers such as Ilya Repin, and 20th-century paintings by Kandinsky, among others, feature alongside sculptures and engravings. A short walk to the west brings you to the **Novaya Tretyakovskaya Galereya** (New Tretyakov Gallery; open 10am–7.30pm; closed Mon), Krymsky Val 10, housing Soviet and post-Soviet art. Communist statues pulled down after the 1991 coup have found refuge in its garden.

were met with strong resistance from local residents: many people felt that the pond itself served as a good enough monument to *"The Master and Margarita"* and that any redevelopment of the area was unnecessary. In the end the residents were victorious and the pond, albeit after being drained and refilled, remained as it was.

South across the river

The area opposite the Kremlin on the south side of the Moskva River, between the bridges of Kamenny and Moskvoretsky around the **Tretyakovskaya Galereya** ⓢ (Tretyakov Gallery; *see box on page 162*), comes as something of a surprise after the appalling 20th-century urban planning generally apparent in the old heart of the city. **Zamoskvorechye** (literally "beyond the Moskva River") was the artisan centre in the 17th century, hence street names such as Kadashevskaya (barrel-maker) and Novokuznetskaya (blacksmith). The nobility moved in during the 19th century and built palaces and mansions. Today, it is embassy country and the classical 19th-century buildings, with their chantilly stucco, give an idea of what Moscow must have been like before the Revolution.

Donskoy Monastery is named after the miracle-working "Mother God of the Don" icon.

The **Muzei V Tropinina** ⓢ (Tropinin Museum; open Mon, Thur & Fri noon–6pm; Sat & Sun 10am–4.30pm; Shchetininsky Lane 10), of 18th- and 19th-century portraiture is near the Tretyakov and shouldn't be missed.

When Prince Daniel Nevsky built his string of fortified monasteries in the 13th century, he dedicated the best and most beautiful to his patron saint. The **Svyato-Danilovsky Monastyr** ⓢ (Danilov Monastery) still stands today, enclosed by its white walls, due south from Moskvoretsky Most (Bridge) at the end of ulitsa Bolshaya Ordynka. Recently, it was restored to its former gold-domed splendour and returned to the Orthodox Church. The patriarch now has his residence here.

BELOW: the new Cathedral of Christ the Saviour.

While south of the river, don't miss **Park Gorkovo** ⓢ (Gorky Park). It surrounds the land-scaped Neskuchny Garden (literally "not dull") created by the millionaire industrialist Demidov on the south bank of the Moskva in the mid-18th century, the name of which derives from the fantastic collection of plants that lined the pathways. Today, Demidov's mansion is home to the Academy of Sciences. Leninsky prospekt, along the south side of the park, is known as the Avenue of Soviet Science because more than 30 research centres are located here.

West to Old Arbat

Walking westwards up ulitsa Vozdvizhenka from the Manege on Okhotny Ryad, you can't miss the broad eyesore of ulitsa **Novy Arbat** (formerly Kalininsky prospekt) starting at Arbatskaya ploshchad and ending at the **Dom Pravitelstva** ⓢ (Russian Government building) overlooking the Moskva River. In the 18th century, the Romanov, Naryshkin and Sheremetyev families all had houses on this part of the street.

Novy Arbat is dissected by Nikitsky Boulevard at Arbatskaya ploshchad and to your left is the beginning of the **Old Arbat**. The name derives from the Arabic word for suburb, *rabat*. More than five centuries old, Arbat was the starting point of the road to Smolensk.

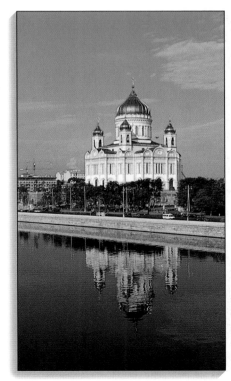

Map on pages 138–9

In the 18th century the Arbat was popular with the aristocracy, who held soirées and literary salons in their homes. The Russian writer and revolutionary Alexander Herzen called it Moscow's St Germain, and true to its reputation the Arbat again became a mecca for artists when *glasnost* began. Satirical and political cartoonists, painters and sculptors, who couldn't get access to official art galleries, began exhibiting their work on the pedestrianised street. It has subsequently become a tourist trap, but in spite of that, the cafés, buskers and souvenir sellers make it lively and fun.

One building you shouldn't miss is the **Dom Melnikov** ⑱ (Melnikov House), tucked down a side-street off the Arbat in Krivoarbatsky Pereulok, about half-way along the pedestrian street on the left-hand side. It doesn't look particularly promising, which is why people rarely find the constructivist jewel built by one of the most innovative and creative Russian architects.

Konstantin Melnikov was a founder member of the avant-garde arts movement that flourished in the first decade after the Revolution. Along with artists such as Kandinsky and El Lissitsky, he formulated a new and iconoclastic approach to the arts. But the movement which influenced the Bauhaus and De Stijl schools was short-lived in Russia. Only a few of the buildings remain. Melnikov's house is one of them. Stalin decided that the proletariat should have neoclassical facades on their apartment blocks, but Melnikov built himself a family home, a white cylindrical structure with lozenge-shaped windows.

The Arbat ends on Smolenskaya ploshchad (Square), an enormous intersection which is dwarfed by the **Ministerstvo Inostrannykh Del** ㉙ (Foreign Ministry). There are seven of these Stalinist "wedding cakes" in the city: all

BELOW: an ice house in Gorky Park.

were built in the late 1940s and 1950s. You either love them or hate them, but they are part of Moscow's heritage and have added their own specific contribution to the city's skyline.

Map on pages 138–9

On the arts trail

Following Peter the Great's lead, the nobles of the 18th century began taking the kind of Grand Tour that created the fabulous aristocratic art collections of other parts of Europe. The great Russian collectors, the Rumyantsevs, Golenishchevs, Shchukins and Morozovs, were both catholic and discerning in their tastes. Their collections were nationalised by Lenin in the early 1920s and brought together in the **Muzei Izobrazitelnikh Iskusstv imeni Pushkina** ⑥ (Pushkin Fine Arts Museum; ulitsa Volkhonka 12, two blocks southwest of the Kremlin).

The museum was founded at the end of the 19th century as a school of art and incorporated copies of all major sculptural works from around the world (the notion being that Russian artists could study the greats without leaving home). The reproductions are still there, but the Pushkin also has a wealth of original works, from ancient Egyptian art to a collection of Impressionists and Post-Impressionists, including Cézanne, Gauguin, Matisse and Van Gogh. It is housed in a purpose-built turn-of-the-20th-century neoclassical style building (open Tues–Sun 10am–6pm).

Opposite the museum is the newly rebuilt **Khram Khrista Spasitelya** ⑥ (Cathedral of Christ the Saviour). The new church is a constructed copy of the original, which was built between the 1830s and 1880s. It soon became the outstanding symbol of the city. It was not just a church, it was also a monument

BELOW: Zurab Tsereteli's giant sculpture of Peter the Great.

SCULPTURE IN THE CITY

Walking around Moscow, you cannot escape the sight of a curious structure in the middle of the Moskva River between the new Cathedral of Christ the Saviour on the north bank and the New Tretyakov Gallery on the south. The giant sculpture of a figure on a sailing boat is Peter the Great. It is one of the many creations of Zurab Tsereteli, Moscow's most controversial sculptor. Tsar Peter I, founder of St Petersburg, is known to have detested Moscow, and it is a bizarre twist of fate that this sculpture has found a home here. According to Tsereteli's critics, it was originally intended to represent Christopher Columbus and had been commissioned by the United States for the 500th anniversary celebrations of the discovery of North America. The US is said to have rejected it on first sight. The 60-metre (200-ft) bronze body had to be disposed of somehow and Tsereteli subsequently won a commission from Moscow's mayor, Yuri Luzhkov. The reincarnated statue raised an outcry in Moscow, but has so far survived a massive public campaign for its removal as well as a demolition attempt. You can sample other works by Tsereteli studded around Moscow, including interiors of the Cathedral of Christ the Saviour and his animalistic forms in the Okhotny Ryad shopping mall.

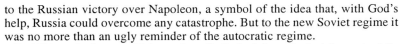

Map on pages 138–9

The Novodevichy Monastyr (Convent) is Moscow's second most important religious centre.

BELOW: window of Novodevichy Convent.
RIGHT: the International Friendship Fountain.

to the Russian victory over Napoleon, a symbol of the idea that, with God's help, Russia could overcome any catastrophe. But to the new Soviet regime it was no more than an ugly reminder of the autocratic regime.

In 1931, to the horror of Muscovites, Stalin had the cathedral dynamited. In its place he planned to erect a gigantic skyscraper which, in turn, would also be the largest in the world. It was called the Palace of Soviets, and it was in effect a temple of communism. It was to be crowned with a statue of Lenin so colossal that its upper half would have been permanently lost in the clouds. But the plan was never realised. The skyscraper could not be made to stand up, and the gaping hole of the foundations was turned into the Moscow open-air swimming pool.

The demolished cathedral became a forbidden topic in the USSR, a non-building. It was as if the Cathedral of Christ the Saviour had never existed. But when communism collapsed, the resurrection of the church became a *cause célèbre*. The energetic mayor of Moscow, Yuri Luzhkov, took up the baton. It was built in the astonishingly short space of three years in order to be ready for Moscow's 850th anniversary celebrations, and stands as much a monument to Luzhkov's tenure of office as a place of divine worship.

New Maiden Convent

The tsars had a love-hate relationship with the Orthodox Church. Some tsars used the Church for their own purposes, installing relatives as patriarchs, but others were suspicious of its power over the people. During the Soviet era, most of the Church's wealth and real estate were confiscated by the new authorities. But the Church and its members struggled on and when liberalisation took place it made a comeback.

In the meantime, Muscovites who wanted to be baptised sneaked off to Sergyev Posad (formerly Zagorsk), one of the few surviving Orthodox enclaves, 65 km (40 miles) north of Moscow. You only have to look around Moscow to see just how powerful the Church was, and is becoming again. Some of the city's major landmarks are religious, in spite of Stalin's efforts to redefine the skyline.

Perhaps one of the most beautiful religious complexes is the **Novodevichy Monastyr ⓸** (New Convent of the Maiden; open Wed–Mon 10am–5.30pm). To the southwest of the Kremlin, strategically placed on a bend in the river, the convent was founded by Vasily III in 1524.

From a distance the white walls topped by red roofs and 16 golden domes look picturesque, but the convent's history is chequered. The strong walls and fortified towers were used as a prison for trouble-making female nobles. A string of well-born women from influential families ended up imprisoned here, including Peter the Great's half-sister Sofia and his first wife Evdokia.

While you are at the convent take the time to visit the cemeteries: Chekhov, Gogol and Bulgakov lie buried in the old one, while Khrushchev and other Soviet big-wigs can be found in the new cemetery (open Wed–Sat 11am–4pm). ❑

PALACES BENEATH THE STREETS

Muscovites are extremely proud of their metro system, and they have every right to be. It is clean fast, efficient, cheap – and spectacular to look at

In most cities the metro is a dull way to get around: there is not much for a visitor to look at 20 metres (65 ft) under the ground. In Moscow, on the other hand, the metro is a primary tourist attraction. The stations are justly famed for their sumptuous and unique decoration. Where else in the world is the rumbling approach of the train heralded by a delicate tinkle of chandeliers?

The metro is a good way to travel for practical reasons, too. In a Russian winter, it makes sense to do one's waiting in the damp warmth of the underground rather than at a freezing bus stop. Throughout the cold months armies of *babushkas* (grandmothers) are employed to mop up the slush which passengers carry into the station vestibules on their winter boots.

The metro has its own very definite etiquette. When it comes to boarding a train it is every man or woman for themselves, and in rush hour it is a scrum between the people getting on and those getting off. But once on the train, invalids and pensioners have an indisputable right to seats.

This right is in the *Rules For The Use of the Metro*, a Soviet-era document which is displayed in every train. The first rule of the metro states, in true bureaucratic fashion, that passengers must obey the rules.

△ **POLISHED VAULTS**
Mayakovskaya, with its elegant arches, is true Art Deco chic. This shiny interior would not look out of place inside New York's Chrysler building.

▽ **UNDERGROUND ART**
Now that socialist realist statuary is out of fashion, Ploshchad Revolutsii (Revolution Square) is one of the few places you can see monumental Soviet art.

◁ **NEW SOVIET MAN**
The figures at Revolution Square portray the strata of an idealised Soviet society: workers, peasants and (left) serious-minded members of the new intelligentsia.

DIGGING TUNNELS FOR SOCIALISM

△ **LIGHT FANTASTIC**
Komsomolskaya is one of the busiest stations because it serves three railway terminals. It is also one of the most ornate, with its giant chandeliers and a terrace round the platforms.

The building of the metro was the centrepiece of the first Five-Year Plan. Like many of the industrial undertakings of the 1930s it was a symbolic project, intended to show that socialism could achieve anything capitalism could. The first line to be built was the red one, which runs to the southwest of Moscow. The stretch from Palace of Soviets station (now Kropotkinskaya) to Frunzenskaya was opened with much pomp in 1935. Kropotkinskaya itself is one of the most beautiful and restrained stations. It is lined with marble taken from the façade of the demolished Cathedral of Christ (now reconstructed nearby). It was only later, in the 1940s and 1950s, that it became fashionable to build in a style that one might call Soviet baroque. Newer stations are mostly utilitarian. In the suburbs, metro stations are lined with blank, easy-to-clean tiles. To enjoy the gaudy architecture of the metro, stay inside the Circle Line.

▷ **GOOD NEIGHBOURS**
The grand mosaics at Kievskaya tell the happy story of Russian-Ukrainian relations: two peoples working to the same communist goal.

△ **NEXT STOP...**
The names of stations are not always obvious, so visitors should listen for the recorded announcements: "Doors closing, next stop..."

▷ **GOING DOWN**
Many metro stations were built in the war years and used as shelters. Park Pobedy, opened in 2003, is the deepest station in the world.

THE GOLDEN RING

Map on page 174

The princely towns of the Golden Ring reached their zenith before Moscow was even conceived. Here, beneath gilded onion domes, is the historic centre of ancient Muscovy

The Golden Ring (Zolotoe Koltso) comprises a dozen medieval towns northeast of Moscow that once formed Russia's political, spiritual and cultural heartland. Despite heavy Soviet destruction, these towns have managed to retain many of their architectural features and, together with Moscow and St Petersburg, top the list of Russia's most popular tourist destinations. While Suzdal and Sergiyev Posad are the most visited towns – due to their proximity to the capital – other smaller, more remote towns are no less attractive for their peaceful rural charm.

Sergiyev Posad

Situated 70 km (44 miles) north of Moscow on the Yaroslavl road, **Sergiyev Posad ❶**, makes for a perfect day-trip from Moscow. It is built around the **Trinity Monastery of St Sergius**, founded in the mid-14th century by St Sergius of Radonezh – a holy man revered for his role in uniting Russia against the Tatars. Today, the remains of St Sergius are kept in the white stone **Trinity Cathedral** (Troitsky Sobor), also noted for its splendid icons painted by Russia's celebrated master Andrei Rublev and his school of icon painters. Behind Trinity Cathedral, the **Vestry** (Riznitsa) displays the lavish gifts amassed by the monastery over the centuries (monastery grounds open 8am–9pm; tel: 254-45356; vestry open 10am–4pm, closed Mon; tel: 254-45342).

The **Cathedral of the Assumption** (Uspensky Sobor), resplendent with its blue domes speckled with gilded stars, was completed on the orders of Ivan the Terrible in 1585. A modest tomb outside the west door contains the remains of tsar Boris Godunov. The pretty **Chapel-at-the-Well** (Nadkladezhnaya Chasovnya) nearby was built over a spring where pilgrims now queue to collect holy water. The five-tier bell tower once had as many as 42 bells. Along the southern wall, the bulky 17th-century **Refectory Church of St Sergius** (Trapeznaya Tserkov Sv Sergeya), once a dining hall for pilgrims, now holds morning services in winter when the Assumption Cathedral is closed.

Pereyaslavl-Zalessky

This small town on the main road between Moscow and Yaroslavl, 50 km (30 miles) northeast of Sergiyev Posad, was founded in 1152 by Prince Yuri Dolgoruky and is famous for being the birthplace of Alexander Nevsky. The highlight of **Pereslavl-Zalessky ❷**, or Pereslavl Beyond-the-Woods, is the Kremlin with its solid **Cathedral of the Transfiguration of the Saviour** (Spaso-Preobrazhensky Sobor), one of the oldest edifices in Russia, built in the mid-12th century. A bust of Alexander Nevsky stands across the

PRECEDING PAGES: Trinity Monastery of St Sergei. **LEFT:** frescoes decorate an Orthodox cathedral. **BELOW:** domes of the Trinity Monastery of St Sergei.

St Sergei of Radonezh, founder of the Trinity Monastery at Sergiyev Posad.

BELOW: a farmer fetches water.

square together with three other churches, including the once-beautiful, but now badly run-down **Church of Peter the Metropolitan** (Tserkov Petra Mitropolita), built in 1585. On the banks of Lake Pleshcheevo, a young Peter the Great built a mock flotilla and thus laid the foundation of the Russian Navy. The history of this fleet is told in the **Botik Museum** on the southern bank of the lake. The museum's treasure is the *Fortuna*, one of a pair of Peter the Great's ships which have survived to this day (open Mon–Fri 9am–5pm, Sat & Sun 10am–5pm; tel: 08535-31910). Southwest of the Kremlin, the pretty **Goritsky Monastery** was founded in the early 14th century, although today its oldest standing buildings date from the 17th century. It is worth a visit and has a small **museum** (open Wed–Sun 10am–5pm; tel: 08535-38100).

Rostov-Veliky

Rostov-Veliky ❸, or Rostov the Great, is one of the Golden Ring's finest towns with its rustic Kremlin and monasteries that dot the landscape. Situated 220 km (137 miles) northeast of Moscow on the shores of Lake Nero, Rostov-Veliky is also the Golden Ring's oldest town. It was first mentioned in chronicles dated 862. By the end of the first millennium AD it was one of the biggest spiritual and trading centres in all of Russia. Entering the town from the south offers a fairy-tale panorama of the Kremlin and the **Monastery of St Jacob** across Lake Nero. The town has retained much of its pre-Soviet charm and consists mainly of *isbas* (huts) surrounded by wild open spaces. Founded in the 12th century on the shore of the lake, the breathtaking Kremlin is framed by a 1-km- (½-mile-) long wall and has a large central square which is full of flowers during the summer.

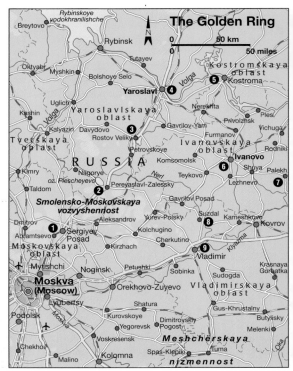

Map on page 174

The 16th-century **Cathedral of the Assumption** (Uspensky Sobor), behind the Kremlin's northern wall, is magnificent despite its dilapidated state. Its five domes symbolise Christ and the four apostles. Next to it towers the great 17th-century belfry and 15 bells, each with its own name, the biggest weighing 32 tons. Bells are the symbol of Rostov-Veliky and locals say that the Kremlin's bells can be heard for 18 km (11 miles). The two imposing **gate-churches** (Tserkov Voskreseniya and Tserkov Ionna Bogoslova) and the **Church of the Saviour-over-the-Galleries** (Tserkov Spasa-na-Senyakh) have bright 17th-century frescos but are open only from May to October to protect them from the cold. The former **law court** flanking the north gate has an interesting museum of *finift*, Rostov's traditional hand-painted enamelware, while the **Red Chamber** (Krasnaya Palata) and the **White Chamber** (Belaya Palata) in the south section house a museum of church antiques and a picture gallery (Kremlin grounds and museums open daily 10am–5pm; tel: 08536-61717).

Yaroslavl

Yaroslavl , 250 km (155 miles) northeast of Moscow, is by far the largest town on the Golden Ring with over 620,000 inhabitants. In 1010, the Kyivan prince Yaroslav the Wise founded a fort in a small locality on the banks of the Volga called **Medvezhy Ugol** (Bear Corner) and is said to have gained the locals' allegiance by killing a bear with an axe. The bear became the town's emblem and figures to this day on Yaroslavl's coat of arms.

As Yaroslavl grew into a major trading centre, rich merchants eager to compete with Moscow donated huge sums for the construction of churches all over the city. One of Yaroslavl's finest churches is the redbrick **Church of the Epiphany**

TIP

A number of agencies in Moscow offer English-language tours of the Golden Ring. Patriarshy Dom Tours, Vspolny Pereulok 6, tel: 753 0003. Intourist, Stoleshnikov Pereulok 11, tel: 923 8575. Mosco Gostiny Dvor, Ulitsa Ilinka 4, tel: 956 5445.

BELOW: winter sunset at Suzdal.

A simple axe and chisel were the only tools used to construct some of the traditional buildings preserved in Suzdal's Museum of Wooden Architecture and Peasant Life (open Wed–Mon 9.30am–3.30pm).

BELOW: typical wooden house at Abramtsevo.

(Tserkov Bogoyavlenia), built in the 17th century just off Bogoyavlenskaya ploshchad. Opened recently after being used as a storage facility for decades, this elegant church is decorated with the city's traditional hand-painted ceramic tiles and has rich frescoes and a carved iconostasis.

The 12th-century **Monastery of the Transfiguration of the Saviour** (Spaso-Preobrazhensky monastyr) encloses the imposing **Cathedral of Transfiguration** (Preobrazhensky sobor) dating from 1516. The north section of the cathedral once housed the monastery library where Russia's literary treasure, *Slovo o Polku Igoreve*, a kind of Russian *Beowulf* written in the 12th century, was discovered in the late 18th century. The spiky golden globes on the bell tower, which you can climb for a sprawling view of the city, were added in the 19th century.

All the monastery's churches are closed between October and May to preserve their frescoes. Every year for two weeks starting on 19 August, the local brewer organises a high-profile classical music festival in the monastery grounds (monastery grounds open 9am–5.30pm, until 7pm in summer; museums open 10am–5pm; tel: 0852-304072).

Another of Yaroslavl's highlights is the graceful **Church of Elijah the Prophet** (Tserkov Ilyi Proroka) with its tall, candle-shaped bell tower, built in the mid-17th century by wealthy brothers who dealt in fur and jewellery. Located on Sovietskaya ploshchad, it contains splendid frescos painted in just three months (open May–Oct Thurs–Tues 10am–1pm & 2–6pm). A walk along the picturesque Volga embankment will take you to the **Museum of Music and Time**, packed with the fascinating collection of old clocks, musical instruments, bells and samovars gathered by the eccentric actor and magician John

ABRAMTSEVO ARTISTS' COLONY

The Abramtsevo country estate, 60 km (37 miles) northeast of Moscow near Sergiyev Posad, occupies a special place in Russian culture. Early in the 19th century it was owned by the novelist Sergei Aksakov and frequented by writers such as Nikolai Gogol and Ivan Turgenev. In the 1870s it was purchased by the railroad and industrial tycoon Savva Mamontov, who put it at the disposal of some of the country's leading artists for the specific purpose of preserving its national heritage. It became the cradle of the neo-Russian style – the Russian variation of the Romantic and nationalist movements that swept Europe in the 19th century, and strove to preserve Russian folkloric traditions and skills. Abramtsevo was frequented by a wide range of prominent painters such as Ilya Repin, Mikhail Vrubel, Isaak Levitan, Valentin Serov, Viktor Krasnetsov and Vassily Polenov. Russia's legendary opera singer Fyodor Chaplyapin made his debut at the estate's theatre.

The heyday of Abramtsevo came to an abrupt end when Mamontov's business empire collapsed in 1899. Today the estate's wooden buildings house a Museum of Literature and Art (open Wed–Sun 10am–5pm; tel: 254-32470).

Mostoslavsky. Call in advance to book a tour in English, preferably with Mostoslavsky himself (open daily 10am–7pm; Volzhskaya naberezhnaya 33A; tel: 0852-328637/727212).

Map on page 174

Kostroma

Located 70 km (44 miles) east of Yaroslavl, **Kostroma ❺** was once a key cultural and trading centre on the Golden Ring, but a devastating fire in 1773 and economical difficulties have made it an impoverished town with a struggling tourist industry. Still, this somewhat run-down city does not lack charm and is well worth a visit if only for its wonderful **Monastery of St Ipaty** (Ipatevsky Monastyr) on the broad Kostroma River – a tributary of the Volga. According to legend, a Tatar ancestor of the Godunov dynasty founded the monastery in the 14th century after recovering from a severe illness. The monastery was handed over to the Romanovs in the 17th century. The splendid **Trinity Cathedral** built by the Godunovs in 1590 has some of the Golden Ring's most vibrant and best-preserved 17th century frescoes as well as a magnificent baroque carved iconostasis; it also houses a museum of icons. The large building across the courtyard with the wallpaper paint job is the Romanov Chambers, which house a **Museum of Romanov Relics** (monastery grounds and museums open daily 9am–5pm; tel: 0942-312589).

TIP

Suzdal is one of the better places to stay. It is well served by hotels, including the traditionally furnished wooden *izby* (peasant cottages) around Pokrovsky Monastery.

Suzdal

Some 100 km (65 miles) south of Kostroma, **Suzdal ❻** was first chronicled in 1024 and became the capital of Yuri Dolgoruky's Rostov-Suzdal principality in the early 12th century *(see page 30)*. Established on fertile soil on the banks of

BELOW: cottages in old Suzdal.

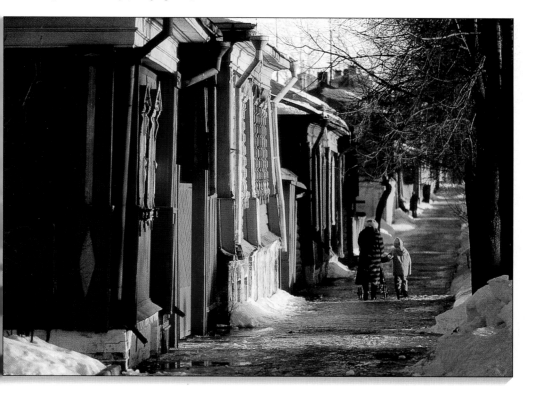

Map on page 174

Suzdal has a good choice of restaurants serving traditional dishes such as mushroom soup, meat as the merchants cooked it, and medovuka, *a Russian drink made from honey.*

BELOW: Church of the Intercession, Vladimir.
RIGHT: *Mother of God* icon from Yaroslavl.

the Kamenka River, it was always a wealthy town with a thriving trade. This made it a prime target for invaders, but generous donations by tsars and rich merchants helped it rise from the ashes of any assault on its wealth.

In the 19th century, the railway constructed between Moscow and Nizhny-Novgorod bypassed Suzdal, sparing it from industrialisation. Today the town has over 100 architectural landmarks dating from the 13th to the 19th century over an area of just 9 sq. km (3 sq. miles).

The **Intercession Convent** (Pokrovsky Monastyr) was founded in 1364 and was long used by tsars as a place to exile their unwanted wives. The convent's history is retraced in a museum on the left of the main entrance. The three-domed **Cathedral of the Intercession** (Pokrovsky Sobor) was built in the early 16th century (monastery grounds open 24 hours, museum open Fri–Tues 10am–6pm; tel: 09231-20609).

Further north, the **Saviour Monastery of St Euthymius** (Spaso-Yevfimevsky monastyr) is Suzdal's biggest monastery. Built in the 14th century to protect the northern flank of the town, its fortress-like redbrick walls contain several churches and museums.

In the city centre, the 11th-century Kremlin includes a few streets and several churches, its highlight being the **Nativity of the Virgin Cathedral** with its blue and gold cupolas, magnificent 13th- and 17th-century frescoes, and two rare 13th-century Damascene doors (gilded copper). The cathedral was reopened in summer 2005 after 12 years of restoration works.

South from the Kremlin across the river is the open-air **Museum of Wooden Architecture and Peasant Life** (Muzei Derevyanovo Zodchestva) exhibiting traditional peasant log houses and wooden churches built without using a single nail (buildings open May–Oct Thurs–Tues 9am–6pm).

Vladimir

Vladimir ❼, 35 km (22 miles) south of Suzdal and 190 km (113 miles) northeast of Moscow, was founded by Prince Vladimir Monomakh in 1108 on the banks of the Klyazma River but is thought to be much older. As Kiev's authority began to fade in the 12th century, Vladimir became the capital of medieval Russia, a status that was brought to an end in the 13th century by the Mongol invasion and the rise of Moscow.

Little remains of Vladimir's ancient roots, but the city nevertheless makes for a pleasant stopover on the way to other, more picturesque Golden Ring towns.

The interior of the imposing yet graceful **Assumption Cathedral** (Uspensky Sobor) are adorned with precious frescoes of the Last Judgement painted by Andrei Rublev and Daniil Chorny in 1408.

Nearby, the white-stone facades of the exquisite **Cathedral of St Dmitry** (Dmitrievsky Sobor), built between 1193 and 1197, are carved with a multitude of animals, plants, and hunting scenes.

Vladimir's 12th-century **Golden Gates** (Zolotye Vrata) were built as replicas of Kiev's Golden Gates and are a mix of triumphal arch and fortress. The gates now house a **Museum of Military History** (open Fri–Wed 10am–6pm; tel: 0922-322559). ❑

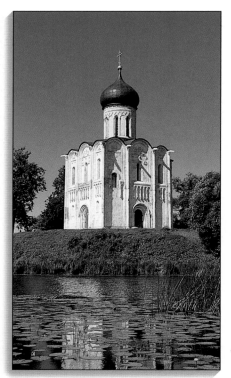

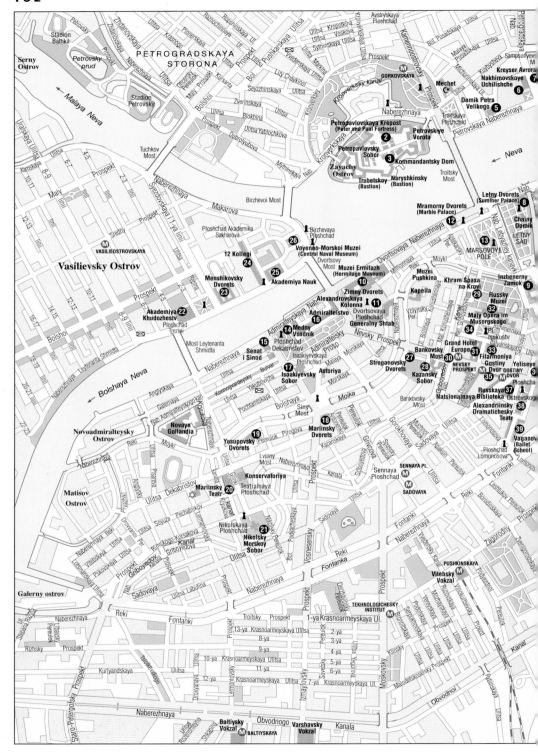

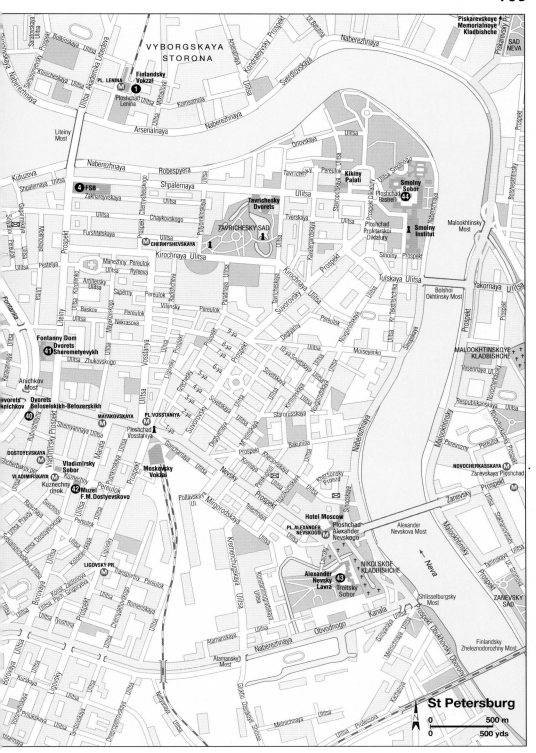

VYBORGSKAYA
STORONA

St Petersburg

0 ——— 500 m
0 ——— 500 yds

ST PETERSBURG

St Petersburg is Russia's cultural capital, a stately city of islands, bridges and classical 18th-century palaces on the northern shores of the Baltic

Map on page 182–3

Sankt Pitersburkh, Sankt Peterburg, Petrograd, Leningrad, Saint Petersburg – just as the city's name has changed over the centuries, so has its fortune. The history of St Petersburg has been one of continued struggle, destruction, and rebirth. Perhaps it is this constant tumult that has made it a living inspiration to some of the world's greatest cultural figures.

St Petersburg rose out of a swampy backwater on the Neva River delta at the beginning of the 18th century when Peter the Great realised his dream to build a new capital, a "Window on the West", that would open the way to European enlightenment and raise Russia out of its medieval past. Peter named his new capital using the Dutch pronunciation, Sankt Pitersburkh: he was enthralled with all things Dutch as he considered its civilisation to be the most advanced. Bringing "civilisation" to Russia, however, came at a medieval price. Historians estimate that at least 100,000 people died of exposure and disease while building the new capital. But by the end of the 19th century, when the city was called "Piter" by its inhabitants, it had indeed become great as the tsar-founder had envisaged and was a leading European cultural and scientific centre.

PRECEDING PAGES: Peter and Paul Fortress. **LEFT:** Alexander Column. **BELOW:** window in the Bolshevik headquarters, 1917.

A change of name

When World War I began in 1914, anti-German sentiment convinced Tsar Nicholas II, a cousin of the German Kaiser Wilhelm, to change the capital's name to the more Russian sounding Petrograd. Then in March 1918, the Bolsheviks, who had seized power in a *coup d'état* in October 1917, moved the capital back to Moscow while the German armies advanced on the "cradle of the Revolution".

As the Communist order established itself, it, too, wished to honour its heroes. In 1924, Petrograd's name was changed to commemorate the recently deceased founding father of the new Russian state. The city of Peter became the city of Lenin, Leningrad.

By 1924, a decade of world war, civil war, famine, class strife, and finally the forces of nature – the city was hit by a devastating flood in that year – had left the former imperial capital in ruins. The magnificent buildings remained, but gone was the soul of a great civilisation as the cream of its society was either dead or had left the country in exile. With the onset of World War II the city experienced yet more suffering and destruction.

Undaunted, the people of Leningrad worked once again to rebuild their city into an important cultural, industrial and scientific centre. With the collapse of the Soviet Union in 1991, many of these accomplishments were swept away by the winds of change. Nevertheless, the new freedom allowed the city to

The winter climate in St Petersburg is harsh, with strong winds and snow between November and late March. In summer, from the end of May to early July, there is an air of festivity due to the extraordinary White Nights, when the sun sets for no more than two hours.

win back its historical name and memory. St Petersburg celebrated its 300th anniversary in May 2003 and many long-awaited repairs were made.

A beautiful misfit

From the beginning, St Petersburg has been something of an anomaly, a beautiful misfit, and a showpiece city. Peter the Great's vision of building a capital to rival the great cities of Europe seemed foolhardy to many, but in the end the great and stern tsar had the last laugh.

Peter gave his European designers – mostly second-rate, unemployed Italian, German and French architects – a huge amount of space to play with. Hence the city's layout of massive perspectives and boldly symmetrical lines. The streets and buildings, although low, dwarf pedestrians. To appreciate the exterior of a building fully you have to view it from a distance, preferably from another island. This is particularly true when looking at the Hermitage.

As your eyes move along the city's embankment, the perfectly rectangular buildings disappear from sight into the vast flat Russian expanse and one architectural defect becomes obvious: with the exception of St Isaac's Cathedral, the Admiralty and the Saviour on the Blood Cathedral, the buildings lack towers and turrets to accentuate their presence.

Tsarist tastes

Of course, Peter the Great is not directly responsible for the St Petersburg that we see today, and few examples of the buildings of his era remain. His taste was simple and sparse. The preferences of his daughter, the Empress Elizabeth (1741–61) were much more fanciful. Her favourite architect, Bartolomeo

BELOW: aerial view of St Petersburg.

Rastrelli, liked colours and tended to decorate buildings as one would a cake for a great occasion, with piping and swirls. Catherine the Great (1762–96) was less frivolous in her tastes, but buildings were nevertheless grand in scope, and became even more so in the reign of Alexander I (1801–25) when they were designed to reflect the glory of Russia's victory over Napoleon and increasing foreign expansion.

Map on pages 182–3

Commerce and industrialisation before the Revolution brought the first railways, which linked Moscow and St Petersburg in 1851. Fine examples of Art Nouveau sprung up at the turn of the 20th century. Following the Revolution, the architecture of Stalin in the 1930s and 1950s was kept to the outskirts. One outstanding feature of Stalin's time was the construction of the Leningrad metro, which started running in 1955. Besides the metro decorations (particularly impressive on the Kirov-Vyborg line) there is little art of the Soviet period in the centre of the city. However, 101 statues and busts to Lenin still stand. Some are in public places, but most are at factories and institutes. You will find a huge statue of Lenin outside **Finlandsky Vokzal** ❶ (Finland Station).

St Petersburg trams and buses run from 5.30am until midnight.

Despite extensive damage to older buildings during World War II, most of them have been rebuilt and faithfully restored to their original state. Since Putin came to power, the city has benefited from large amounts of investment, and many buildings are being renovated.

Literary connections

Architecture tells us much about a city, but equally revealing, particularly in St Petersburg, are the impressions of its famous writers whose works have immortalised many of its sights. Alexander Pushkin (1799–1837), Russia's equivalent

BELOW: chess players in a city square.

Peter the Great is usually represented as a young man (as here), but in the grounds of Peter and Paul Fortress there is a sculpture by Michael Chemyakin portraying him in later life.

BELOW: Peter the Great as the Bronze Horseman.

of Shakespeare, depicted St Petersburg's forbidding aspect in his poem *The Bronze Horseman*. The statue of Peter the Great, located on the river side in front of Isaakiyevsky Sobor (St Isaac's Cathedral), is known as the Bronze Horseman. In Pushkin's poem it comes to life and bears down on an enfeebled and terrified clerk called Evgeny. Pushkin also describes St Petersburg high life in his poem *Evgeny Onegin*. The hero, one of literature's great dandies, becomes bored and disillusioned by an endless round of balls, restaurants and women.

Tolstoy takes up the same theme in his novels *War and Peace* and *Anna Karenina*, contrasting the spontaneity and simplicity of Moscow life with that of St Petersburg, which he saw as false, artificial and corrupt. Dostoyevsky, in marked contrast, wrote of low life and the poor.

In the poem *The Twelve*, Alexander Blok found in the 1917 Revolution a vision of the city's rebirth and the Second Coming of Christ. But he quickly became disenchanted with the barbarity of the Bolshevik regime, and died an untimely death in 1921.

Evgeny Zamyatin, in his short story *The Cavemen*, compared post-Revolutionary St Petersburg to a society of cave-dwellers, whose civilised values are subverted when the protagonist is forced to beg and then steal firewood in order to exist for just one more day.

A city under siege

Records of the city's suffering also exist in living memory. The older generation remembers the Siege of Leningrad (in Russian "Blokada") during World War II when the city was completely cut off from the outside world for almost 900 days. The Germans invaded Russia in July 1941 and reached Leningrad in

August of that year. The town was encircled and cut off from September, when mass bombing began. Soviet troops finally broke through the blockade in January 1943 and provisions reached the city through Finland Station, but the siege did not end until January 1944 when the Germans were beaten back. Victory left nearly one million dead, most from starvation. Some 470,000 victims of the blockade are buried at the **Piskarovskoye Memorial Cemetery** on the northern outskirts of the city. The sheer size of this cemetery, with the dead buried in mass graves, gives a more chilling impression of the loss of life than any statistic.

Sts Peter and Paul Fortress

The most appropriate place to begin a tour of St Petersburg is **Petropavlovskaya Krepost ❷** (Peter and Paul Fortress; fortress grounds open Thurs–Tues 9am–10pm; museums open Thurs–Tues 10.30am–6pm; closed last Tues of month), built during the time of the Great Northern War, 1700–21. The first stone was laid on 16 May 1703 Old Style (unlike Europe and the USA who by this date had switched to the new Gregorian Calendar, Russia still used the calendar of Julius Caesar, which was 13 days behind the Gregorian).

The fortress, built on **Zayachy Ostrov** (Hare Island) according to plans drawn by Peter himself, was designed to stave off the enemy, occupying as it did a strategic position at the dividing point of the Neva into the Malaya (Small) and Bolshaya (Big) Neva. It became a notorious prison – the Bastille of tsarist Russia. In 1917 the **Kommandantsky Dom ❸** (Commandant's House) was one of the Bolshevik command posts for the storming of the Winter Palace. But today such an infamous place has become a favourite area for relaxation, and many city-dwellers flock to the beach in front of the fortress on pleasant days. Though

Map on pages 182–3

BELOW: soaring spire of Peter and Paul Fortress.

CITY OF ISLANDS

St Petersburg is Russia's largest seaport and second-largest city with an official population of just under 5 million. It lies 60°N, on the same latitude as Alaska, Hudson Bay, the southern tip of Greenland and Oslo. While the city originally straddled 101 islands at the mouth of the River Neva, which sweeps majestically through its centre, many have since disappeared as the rivers, streams and canals have been filled in. Today, the "Venice of the North" is situated on 42 islands linked by 432 pedestrian, car and rail bridges. Twenty of these are drawbridges, some of which rise each night between 2am and 5am, from April to the end of November, to allow the passage of sea-going ships. The Neva flows westerly from Lake Ladoga, 74 km (46 miles) to the east, into the Gulf of Finland. Here, where it branches into three arms, separating the Petrograd Side and Vasilievsky Island from the mainland, the main channel is 400 metres (437 yards) wide.

Today, granite embankments contain the 68 rivers, canals, channels and streams which separate the islands. These waterways, Lake Ladoga and the sea freeze over in winter and icebreakers have to be used to keep the port open throughout the year.

During the White Nights of June, crowds gather at 2am on both sides of the River Neva, near the Hermitage, to watch the raising of the drawbridges to allow sea-going vessels to pass.

it is forbidden to swim there, many do, even in winter. There are various buildings to see within the fortress, as well as temporary exhibitions. The major features are **Petrovskiye Vorota** (Peter's Gates), built by Domenico Trezzini, who also designed the cathedral. The gate, originally built in wood and later in stone (1717–18), has hardly changed since it was built. The bas-relief above the tsarist emblem of the double-headed eagle depicts the Apostle Peter overthrowing Simon the Magus, an allegory of Russia's victory over the Swedes.

Petropavlovsky Sobor (Sts Peter and Paul Cathedral) is rectangular in layout and quite unlike a traditional Russian place of worship. It bears a tall spire standing at 122 metres (400 ft), which was the tallest building in the city until the Television Tower (316 metres/1,036 ft) was built. On the top is an angel carrying a cross. In 1830, Pyotr Telushkin, a roofer, climbed to the very top, with the aid of just a rope, to repair the cross which had been struck by lightning.

Inside the church are the white marble tombs of most of the Romanov emperors and empresses, as well as grand dukes. Peter the Great's tomb lies in the far right-hand corner. The remains of the last Russian tsar, Nicholas II, his wife, three of their children, and four servants were buried here in 1998 having been transported from Yekaterinburg in the Urals where they were murdered in 1918. Their grave is in **Yekaterinsky Pridel** (St Catherine Chapel), which is to the right as you enter through the main cathedral entrance. The last ruling Romanovs have been consigned to this private chapel for two reasons: Nicholas II renounced the throne; and commoners are buried with the royal family. The tombs of Alexander II, the tsar liberator who freed the serfs but was none the less blown up by leftist terrorists, and his wife are in great contrast to the others. Theirs are the only ones not made of marble, but made instead from Altai jasper and Urals rhodonite.

BELOW: the cruiser *Aurora* outside the Nakhimov Naval Academy.

In 1717 the fortress became a prison for political prisoners and the cells are now open as a museum in the **Trubetskoy Bastion**. One of its first prisoners, who was later beaten to death, was Peter the Great's son Alexei, who was falsely accused of plotting against his father. Other distinguished inmates were Fyodor Dostoyevsky; Alexander Radishchev, author of *A Journey from St Petersburg to Moscow*, in which he criticised autocracy and serfdom; Nikolai Chernyshevsky, a Revolutionary democrat and author of *What is to be Done?*; Lenin's elder brother, Alexander Ulyanov, who was executed for taking part in the plot to murder Alexander III, and the socially orientated writer Maxim Gorky, who wrote a Revolutionary proclamation calling for the overthrow of the monarchy.

In the Soviet period, political prisoners were taken to KGB **headquarters** ➍ (now FSB) on Liteiny prospekt in a building nicknamed the "Big House", and not without reason: it is the tallest, biggest building in the city centre.

Peter and Paul Fortress has six bastions, one named Gosudarev (Ruler's) in honour of Peter the Great, and the rest named after his closest companions who supervised the construction of the fortress. A cannon shot is fired every day at noon from the **Naryshkinsky Bastion**.

On the banks of the Neva

On the river banks on the other side of Troitsky Most stands **Domik Petra Velikogo** ➎ (Peter the Great's Wooden Cabin), which is now a museum (open Wed–Sun 10am–4pm). Although protected by stone on the outside, inside there is a perfectly preserved, two-roomed hut. It was made out of rough pine over a period of three days in 1703. Peter lived here for six years while overseeing the building of the city.

BELOW: view from the Grand Palace at Peterhof, southwest of St Petersburg.

The Metchet (Mosque), built on Kronversky prospekt, in 1912 is the only mosque in the city.

Moored in front of the blue **Nakhimovskoye Uchilishche** (Nakhimov Naval Academy) on Petrogradskaya Embankment – designed in the style of Petrine baroque and completed in 1912 – is the cruiser *Kreyser Avrora* (*Aurora*; open for tours Tues–Thurs, Sat & Sun 10.30am–4.30pm), famous for its part in the 1917 Revolution. At 9.45pm on 25 October 1917, the *Aurora* fired a blank round, the signal for the Bolshevik forces to storm the Winter Palace, the seat of the provisional government. Prior to this, between 1904 and 1905, it served the tsarist government at the Battle of Tsu-Shima against Japan. Today, the cruiser once again flies the tsarist-era naval flag of St Andrew whose blue diagonal cross on a white background is common in St Petersburg, home of the Russian fleet.

On the opposite side of the river is the tsar's modest **Letny Dvorets** (Summer Palace; open May–March Wed–Mon 11am–6pm) built by Domenico Trezzini in 1710. It has retained most of its original features, occupying two floors of identical layout, one for the tsar and one for the tsarina. Its simple exterior was later decorated with terracotta panels depicting scenes from mythology – including allegorical portrayals of the Northern War.

Letny Sad (the Summer Garden) in which the palace stands is the oldest garden in the city. Much of the work was done by the architect Jean Baptiste LeBlond. It was originally a formal garden with many rare plants and trees, an aviary and a grotto, but its appearance has changed over the years as Venetian statues were commissioned and buildings such as the **Chainy Domik** (Tea House) and a statue of Ivan Krylov (1768–1844), the author of children's fables, have been added, but it is still one of the city's most peaceful and shady places.

The path through the centre of the gardens leads as far as the Fontanka Canal

BELOW: Hermitage Museum.

and the red **Inzhenerny Zamok** ❾ (Engineer's Castle, also known as St Michael Castle). The castle was built by Catherine the Great's son, Tsar Paul I, with strong walls and a moat to prevent any attempt at assassination, the fate of which had befallen his father, Tsar Peter III, at Catherine's hands. But such efforts proved in vain: military officers bribed the guards and murdered Paul just 40 days after he had taken up residence; Paul's son, Alexander I, was complicit to the murder which put him on the throne. So much for 18th-century Russian family cohesion. The castle acquired its current name when it became a school for engineers in 1819. Its most famous student was Dostoyevsky.

The Hermitage Museum

The **Muzei Ermitazh** ❿ (Hermitage Museum; open Tues–Sat 10.30am–6pm, Sun 10.30am–5pm; last ticket one hour before closing) consists of five buildings, **Zimny Dvorets** (the Winter Palace), the Small Hermitage, the New Hermitage, the Old Hermitage and the General Staff building. Architect Bartolomeo Rastrelli started work on the Winter Palace in 1754, during Empress Elizabeth's reign. He built it, to use his own words, "solely for the glory of all Russia". It was home to the imperial family, with the exception of Paul I, until 1917, when it became seat of the provisional government.

The **Hermitage Collection** was originally the private collection of Catherine the Great. She collected in earnest, instructing her ambassadors in Europe to buy not just individual pictures, but entire collections. She housed them in her retreat ("Hermitage") and only a select few were permitted to see them. The museum was not open to the public until 1852. During the siege in the 1940s, most of the artworks were successfully evacuated. Although renowned for its collections of Western European art, including early 13th-century Italian works, French Impressionists and modern art, the Hermitage has other important departments, notably those of prehistoric cultures, Oriental and classical antiquities, as well as an exhibition of gold treasures that are among the finest in the world.

Of equal interest is the architecture of the interior: the Jordan Staircase, Great Hall, Large Throne Room and Gallery of the 1812 War, to name a few *(see Insight On the Hermitage, page 206)*.

Palace Square

Behind the Hermitage is the impressive **Dvortsovaya ploshchad** ⓫ (Palace Square), with its towering **Alexandrovskaya Kolonna** (Alexander Column) designed by August de Montferrand to commemorate the victory of Russian armies in the Napoleonic War during the reign of Alexander I. It is made from a granite monolith transported from the northern shore of the Gulf of Finland. This 47.5-metre (156-ft) column is held together entirely by its own weight. On the south side of the square is the curved, sprawling, neoclassical **Glavny Shtab** (General Staff building), designed by Carlo Rossi (1775–1849). Its arch is decorated with a chariot of victory and statues of warriors.

Rossi designed many buildings in St Petersburg, most of which are painted pale yellow as opposed to the pale greens and blues preferred by Rastrelli.

Map on pages 182–3

St Petersburg is a federal city, with the official status of a "subject of the Federation". It is one of Russia's 89 regions, and the head of the city is called "governor" not "mayor".

BELOW: the ornate Jordan staircase at the Hermitage Museum.

Dvortsovaya ploshchad (Palace Square) is a popular venue for rock concerts during June's White Nights Festival.

BELOW: Alexander Column in Palace Square with the General Staff Building behind.

Before the Revolution many of the government buildings – with the exception of the Admiralty – were painted dark red (for example, the General Staff building, the Winter Palace and the Senate and Synod).

At the corner of Palace Square is Millionnaya ulitsa (Million Street), which runs behind the Hermitage to the Field of Mars. At the beginning of Millionnaya ulitsa the porch of the New Hermitage building is supported by figures of Atlas designed by a German architect, Leo von Klenze (1784–1864). At the end of the street is the **Mramorny Dvorets ⑫** (Marble Palace). It is faced with marble, which is a rarity in this city of plaster facades. The palace was commissioned by Catherine the Great for one of her favourites, Grigory Orlov, and the task of designing it went to the Italian architect Antonio Rinaldi (1709–94). Before the Revolution the palace was the home of various grand dukes, but in 1937 it became the city's Lenin Museum. Now it belongs to the Russian Museum and houses the Ludwig Museum collection of contemporary art which was a gift to the Russian Museum from Germany's Ludwig Foundation (open Wed–Mon 10am–6pm).

The tsar used to review his troops in **Marsovoye Pole ⑬** (Field of Mars). It was redesigned after the 1917 Revolution by Lev Vladimirorich Rudnyev, who later built the skyscraper of Moscow University. Some Communists who fought and died in the Revolution and Civil War are buried here, where an eternal flame burns. But since the fall of communism few Russians pay their respects, and many wish that those who died had not even bothered to make that ultimate sacrifice.

Decembrists Square

Along the embankment from the Hermitage is the city's most famous statue: **Medny Vsadnik ⑭** (The Bronze Horseman), depicting Peter the Great on a

Map on pages 182–3

rearing horse. It was cast by the French sculptor Etienne Falconet and completed in 1782. The head of Peter the Great was designed by Falconet's pupil, Marie Collot, who never earned the recognition she deserved for this particular work.

The square in which the statue stands, **Dekabristov ploshchad** (Decembrists Square) is where, on 14 December 1825, tsarist troops fired on 3,000 revolting soldiers and spectators, many of whom were innocently driven into action by revolutionary-minded young officers who wanted to turn Russia into a republic. The yellow buildings of **Senat i Sinod** ⓯ (the Senate and the Synod) were designed by Carlo Rossi between 1829 and 1832.

Nearby stands the golden spire of the **Admiralteistvo** ⓰ (Admiralty). This was one of the first buildings of the city, built in 1705, then replaced between 1806 and 1823 by the present neoclassical structure designed by Andrei Zakharov. It was used as a naval headquarters and shipyard. At the top of the spire is a weather-vane in the form of a ship, the emblem of the city. From the Admiralty the main streets of Nevsky, Gorokhovaya and Vosnesensky stretch out like a fan. The fountains in front of the Admiralty are surrounded by statues of Russia's cultural heroes, including the writers Nikolai Gogol and Mikhail Lermontov, the composer Mikhail Glinka and the poet Vasily Zhukovsky.

St Isaac's Square

Isaakiyevsky Sobor ⓱ (St Isaac's Cathedral) stands in the square behind. It was built over a period of 40 years in the first half of the 19th century by the French architect Auguste de Montferrand. The dome is covered with 100 kg (220 lb) of pure gold. Forty-three types of stone and marble were used to decorate the lavish interior, including the lapis lazuli and malachite columns of the iconos-

BELOW: winter in the Field of Mars.

St Petersburg is the home of the Russian Navy, which celebrated its 300th anniversary in 1996. Its headquarters are in the Admiralty.

tasis. Among the general surfeit of visual splendour is a statue of the architect carrying a model of the cathedral in his hand. Montferrand very much wanted to be buried here, but his wish was denied by the tsar because of the Frenchman's Catholicism. In the middle of St Isaac's Square stands a statue of Nicholas I on a prancing horse, by Pyotr Klodt. According to a Russian saying commenting on the obvious parallel with The Bronze Horseman: "The fool [Nicholas I] chases the wise man [Peter I] but St Isaac's stands in between."

Mariinsky Dvorets (Mariinsky Palace), on the south side of the square, is now home to the city's Legislative Assembly. It was built between 1839 and 1844 by Andrei Stakenschneider. The palace was a present from Nicholas I to his daughter Maria. The bridge in front crossing the River Moika is **Siny Most** (Blue Bridge) and is the widest in the city. Further along the Moika in the direction of **Novaya Gollandia** (New Holland) is **Yusupovsky Dvorets** (Yusupov Palace; open for tours 11am–5pm) at No. 94, home of Rasputin's chief assassin. Rasputin was murdered here in 1916. The rooms have been restored to evoke the eerie atmosphere of the night of the murder; there is even a creepy wax figure of Rasputin. Behind the red brickwork of Novaya Gollandia, Peter the Great stored his ship-building timber.

Theatre Square

BELOW: the golden spire of the Admiralty building.

The Moika turns a bend along the Kryukova Kanal, bordering **Teatralnaya ploshchad** (Theatre Square), home of the Mariinsky (formerly Kirov) Theatre and, opposite, the **Rimsky-Korsakov Conservatory**. The **Mariinsky Teatr** , founded in 1783 (but renamed in 1884), is where many of Russia's operas and ballets were first performed, including Mussorgsky's *Boris Godunov* (1874) and Tchaikovsky's *Sleeping Beauty* (1890). Dancers such as Kschessinska, Pavlova and Nijinsky made their debut here. The ballet company has recently outperformed Moscow's Bolshoi. In 2003 a fire swept through a storage annexe several blocks from the theatre destroying the costumes and many of the sets. A French post-modernist design for the new Mariinsky stage, planned next to the imperial building, has evoked great controversy. Though it has been officially approved, opponents in the government are fighting to have it altered into something that does not clash so drastically with the historical neighbourhood. Maria, from whom the theatre took its name, was the wife of Alexander II. Kirov – Secretary of the Leningrad Communist Party from 1926 until 1934 – was murdered at Smolny, then Communist Party headquarters. This triggered Stalin's purges of the 1930s. Beside Kryukova Kanal in **Nikolskaya ploshchad** (St Nicholas Square) is the blue and gold **Nikolsky Morskoy Sobor** (Cathedral of St Nicholas), also known as the "Sailor's Church". This cathedral is often compared with Rastrelli's Smolny Cathedral, and is considered one of the finest examples of Russian baroque.

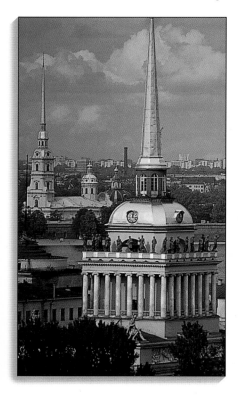

Vasilievsky Island

On the other side of the river, facing the Bronze Horseman, is one of the oldest parts of the city, **Vasilievsky Ostrov** (Vasily's Island). One of its more "modern" buildings overlooking the river is the **Akademiya Khudozhestv** (Academy of Arts), built by Catherine the Great in 1757 as a training ground for professional painters, architects, sculptors and engravers. In front of it, on a granite pier, stand two **sphinxes** which date from the 13th century BC. They were brought to St Petersburg from Egypt in 1832. The **obelisk** standing on the eastern side of the Academy commemorates Russia's victory over the Turks under Field-Marshal Rumyantsev in the 18th century. The next building is the **Menshikovsky Dvorets** ❷ (Menshikov Palace), now a branch of the Hermitage Museum (open Tues–Sun 10.30am–4.30pm). Alexander Menshikov was a friend and close associate of Peter the Great. As Menshikov's palace was finished before Peter's, it was used for large-scale entertainment. Peter staged an extraordinary event for his niece here: a wedding feast attended by dwarfs.

Walking east along the embankment, the terracotta-coloured building is called **12 Kollegi** ❷ (Twelve Colleges). Peter housed his *kollegia* (ministeries) here; it is now part of St Petersburg University. The building's construction, in which a number of architects, including Rastrelli, participated, was set as a competition – Russia's first. Construction took 19 years and was completed in1741. To its east, the **Akademiya Nauk** ❷ (Academy of Sciences) was built to house the expanding collection of the **Kunstkamera** (Chamber of Curiosities; open Tues–Sun 11am–5.45pm; closed last Wed of month), a museum of anthropology and ethnography next door. Inside, beneath the dome, is a collection of genetic freaks, embryos and human organs, all of which held a particular fascination for Peter the Great.

Vasilievsky Island's easterly "spit" offers one of the best views of the city. Many newlyweds come here to be photographed. The magnificent building

Map on page 182–3

TIP

Mariinsky Theatre tickets can be more expensive for foreigners. In 1998 the Supreme Court ruled that price discrimination on the basis of nationality is illegal, yet the theatre and some museums circumvent the law by giving "discounts" to Russian citizens, and making foreigners pay the full price.

BELOW: interior, St Isaac's Cathedral.

Siberian mammoth, one of the exhibits at the Zoological Museum of the Academy of Sciences (open Sat–Thurs 11am–5pm).

which dominates the spit is the **Voyenno-Morskoi Muzei** (Central Naval Museum; open Wed–Sun 11am–6pm; closed last Thurs of month). Before the Revolution it was the Stock Exchange. Until the 1880s this point of Vasilievsky Island was the city's port. The red columns were the lighthouses; they are decorated with the prows of boats representing four Russian rivers: the Volga, Dnieper, Neva and Volkhov.

Nevsky prospekt

The 4.5-km (3-mile) **Nevsky prospekt**, which runs southeast from the Admiralty to Alexander Nevsky Most (bridge), is the most famous street in the city. Apart from the splendid architecture of Nevsky prospekt, there is plenty of activity at street level. People might not walk gracefully or pose as in days gone by, and the street is not as clean as in Nikolai Gogol's time ("how spotlessly clean are its pavements swept and, good gracious, how many feet leave their marks on them!"), but Nevsky prospekt remains a good place to take the city's pulse.

Starting from **Admiralteisky prospekt**, the first important street which crosses the Nevsky is **Malaya Morskaya**. Gogol lived at No. 17. Here he wrote the first chapters of *Dead Souls*. Pyotr Tchaikovsky died at No. 8. The next street is the once-fashionable **Bolshaya Morskaya**, home of the famous Fabergé shop (No. 24), still a jewellers, but having lost its former glory. The Nevsky crosses the River Moika where, on the right-hand side stands the red and white **Stroganovsky Dvorets** (Stroganov Palace), home of one of Russia's leading families. It was designed by Rastrelli, architect of the Winter Palace. The next street on the left, **ulitsa Bolshaya Konushennaya**, leads to the former stables. The residents of No. 13 Bolshaya Konushennaya included the Russian

BELOW: Stroganov Palace.

writer Ivan Turgenev and, later, the ballet dancer Nijinsky. The musician Rimsky-Korsakov lived at No. 11. A short distance along Nevsky prospekt, on the right, stands the majestic **Kazansky Sobor** ❷ (Kazan Cathedral) with its 90 metre- (295 ft-) high dome and 96 columns, designed by the architect Andrei Voronikhin in the first decade of the 19th century. In the square in front are statues of the heroes of the 1812 war, M.I. Kutuzov (who is also buried here) and M.B. Barclay de Tolly. From the 1930s, the cathedral was a Museum of the History of Religion and Atheism. Religious services have been restored and its cross has been replaced. Opposite, at No. 28 Nevsky prospekt, is the Art Nouveau pre-1917 Russia head office of the Singer Sewing Machine Company. You can't miss the huge globe on the roof.

As you cross the **Griboyedov Kanal**, the multi-coloured domes of **Khram Spasa na Krovi** ❷ (Church of the Resurrection; open Thurs–Tues 11am–7pm), also known as the Saviour on the Blood, are visible. Built on the site of Alexander II's assassination, this church has been extensively restored.

Two interesting bridges by the same architect, W. Traitteur (1825–26), cross the Griboyedov as it flows away from Nevsky prospekt to the right. The first is **Bankovsky Most** ❸ (Bankers' Bridge) on which stand guard two golden-winged griffins. The bridge is so named because the large building in front, housing the Institute of Finance and Economics, used to be the Russian Central Bank in tsarist times. Most of the country's gold supply was stored here; in ancient mythology, griffins stood guard over gold. Further down is **Lvinny Most** (Lion Bridge) where two lions hold the suspension cables of the bridge in their mouths.

Continuing eastwards along the Nevsky, on the left-hand side in ulitsa Mikhailovskovo is the luxurious **Grand Hotel Europe** ❸. The street on which it stands leads into **ploshchad Iskusstv** (Arts Square), home of the Russian Museum.

The yellow classical building of the **Gosudarstveny Russky Muzei** ❸ (State Russian Museum; open Wed–Mon 10am–5pm) was built by Rossi between 1819 and 1825 for Grand Duke Mikhail, Alexander I and Nicholas I's younger brother. Unlike the Hermitage it houses only Russian art and is a smaller, more manageable museum. The exhibits span almost 1,000 years of the history of Russian art, from a magnificent icon collection through works by avantgarde artists such as Malevich and Kandinsky to contemporary work. Also in ploshchad Iskusstv stands the **Sankt Peterburzhskaya Filarmoniya** ❸ (St Petersburg Philharmonia) and the **Maly Teatr operi i Baleta imeni Mussorgskogo** ❸ (the Small Musorgsky Theatre of Opera and Ballet). In the middle of the square is a statue of Pushkin by one of the city's leading sculptors, Mikhail Anikushin.

Back on the Nevsky prospekt, with ploshchad Iskusstv behind you, notice the long yellow and white facade of **Gostiny Dvor** ❸ on the right-hand side. This is one of St Petersburg's largest department stores. Two blocks along the Nevsky on the left-hand side, at No. 58, is Yeliseyevsky, a food shop with an extravagant Art Nouveau interior, built by the rich merchant **Yeliseyev** ❸ and once the grandest delicatessen in St Petersburg.

Map on page 182–3

Plaza, on Birzhevaya ploschad, is one of the city's most elite venues, frequented by politicians and businessmen. Luxury cars draw up at the entrance under the watchful eyes of burly guards.

BELOW: shopping in a city arcade.

BELOW: Beloselsky
Palace.

Sadovaya Ulitsa runs beside Gostiny Dvor to **Sennaya ploshchad** (Hay Square), a traditionally seedy area. Raskolnikov, in Dostoyevsky's *Crime and Punishment*, wandered here, where "types so various were to be seen that no figure, however queer, would have caused surprise".

To the right just after the junction of Sadovaya ulitsa and Nevsky is **ploshchad Ostrovskogo**, a huge square with a statue of Catherine the Great surrounded by her most prominent court officials, some of whom were her lovers. This square is named after the playwright Alexander Ostrovsky. Its buildings include the **Rossiskaya Natsionalnaya Biblioteka** ❸ (Russian National Library; not open to the public) and the **Alexandriinsky Dramatichesky Teatr** ❸ (Alexander Theatre of Drama), with its white Corinthian columns.

Behind the theatre, leading away from the right-hand corner of the square, is **ulitsa Zodchego Rossi** (Architect Rossi Street). This street has perfect proportions with the width of the street equalling the height of the buildings. Among its buildings is the **Vaganova Ballet School** ❸, the training ground for some of the greatest names in ballet, including Pavlova, Nijinsky, Nureyev, Makarova and Baryshnikov.

Back on Nevsky prospekt, the next canal is the **Fontanka** with its impressive **Anichkov Most** (Anichkov Bridge). The horses which decorate the bridge are the work of sculptor Pyotr Klodt; during World War II they were buried underground in the nearby gardens of the **Dvorets Yunikh Pionerov** (Palace of Young Pioneers), as were many of the city's other famous statues.

Behind Anichkov Bridge stands the dark-red **Dvorets Beloselskikh-Belozerskikh** ❹ (Beloselsky-Belozersky Palace), built by Stakenschneider in 1847–48 for Prince Beloselsky-Belozersky.

Map on pages 182–3

To the left, on the banks of the Fontanka, is the yellow **Dvorets Sheremetyevykh** ❹ (Sheremetyev Palace), built by Chevakinsky between 1750 and 1755. One of its outbuildings, the **Fontanny Dom**, houses the **Muzei Anni Akhmatovoi**, the literary museum of Anna Akhmatova, one of Russia's greatest poets (open Tues–Sun 10.30am–5.30pm; closed last Wed in month).

At the next junction, Liteiny prospekt, is the famous second-hand bookstore, **Bukinist** (No. 59). To the right, **Vladimirsky prospekt** leads to a side street, Kuznechny Pereulok, where the **Muzei F.M. Dostyevskovo** ❷ (Dostoyevsky Museum) is located. Here, the writer lived and died (open Tues–Sun 11am–5.30pm; closed last Wed in month). Nearby is the 18th-century, five-domed **Vladimirsky Sobor** (St Vladimir Church).

At the very end of Nevsky prospekt is **ploshchad Alexander Nevskogo**, where the **Hotel Moscow** stands. Here is the **Alexander Nevsky Lavra** ❸, the oldest and most beautiful monastery complex in the city. Alexander Nevsky crushed two separate invading Swedish and German armies in the mid-13th century and was later canonised. His remains are buried inside the Lavra.

There are several cemeteries inside the Alexander Nevsky Lavra, where some of Russia's most famous citizens are buried. In the **Lazarus Cemetery**, where Peter the Great's sister, Natalya Alexeyevna, lies, you will find the graves of famous architects, including Carlo Rossi and Andrei Voronikhin. The composers Mikhail Glinka, Pyotr Tchaikovsky, Modest Musorgsky and Nikolai Rimsky-Korsakov are buried in the **Tikvin Cemetery** opposite, together with Fyodor Dostoyevsky. Today, most famous people from the arts world are buried in the **Volkhov Cemetery**, a short drive away from the Lavra complex.

The twice-weekly St Petersburg Times is the city's only English language newspaper. Covering politics, business and culture, it is one of the few independent voices – more than half of its readers are Russian.

BELOW: the study in which Dostoyevsky wrote *The Brothers Karamazov*.

Crowds stood and cheered on Anichkovsky Most (Anichkov Bridge) when the horses were returned after World War II.

BELOW: Monplaisir at Petrodvorets.

Smolny Cathedral and Institute

Another religious building not to be missed is **Smolny Sobor ㊹** (Smolny Cathedral), situated northeast of Nevsky prospekt. Designed by Rastrelli, this pale blue and white building in the shape of a Greek cross seems to float rather than stand on the horizon. Smolny means "tar" and the site of the cathedral was used as a tar yard until 1723. Although construction began in the mid-18th century, the cathedral was not finished until the end of the 19th century.

In 1764 Catherine the Great created an institute next to the cathedral "for the education of well-born young ladies", the first of its kind in Russia. The **Smolny Institut** was housed in the yellow, neoclassical building designed by Giacomo Quarenghi between 1806 and 1808. In August 1917 this building became the headquarters of the Bolshevik Central Committee, and it was from here that Lenin led the uprising in October of that year.

Opposite the cathedral, two blocks along **Shpalernaya ulitsa**, are the **Kikiny Palati** (Kikin Palace) and **Tavrichesky Dvorets** (Tauride Palace). Kikin was an associate of Peter the Great and although the palace has been rebuilt the basic structure dates from 1714. The Tauride Palace was built between 1783 and 1789 for Grigory Potemkin. Potemkin was one of Catherine the Great's favourites, arguably no less than co-regent in view of his influence over her. He is remembered for annexing the Crimea in 1783.

Out-of-town palaces

A visit to St Petersburg is not complete without a trip to one or more of the five palaces now open to the public. Petrodvorets, the Catherine Palace at Pushkin (Tsarskoye Selo), and Pavlovsk attract the most visitors. They have been almost fully restored following the devastation of German occupation in World War II. The palaces at Oranienbaum and Gatchina are undergoing major restoration work.

Petrodvorets (Peterhof grounds open Tues–Sun 9am–10pm; Grand Palace open Tues–Sun 10.30am–5pm; closed last Tues of month; Hermitage, Monplaisir currently closed; Marly closed Tues and last Wed), Peter's summer palace, is situated on the Gulf of Finland, 29 km (18 miles) west of the city. One of its most striking features is its fountains (which are turned off in the winter). The original palace was built by Peter the Great in 1720 to the design of Jean-Baptiste LeBlond. It was much simpler than the version that now stands, which was embellished and enlarged by Empress Elizabeth. But traces of Peter the Great and LeBlond show through the baroque glitz. They chose the magnificent site on a natural slope – a Versailles by the sea – and were responsible for the intricate fountains, a major feat on land consisting of marshy clay.

Looking at pictures of Petrodvorets after the ravages of World War II, one wonders it was ever rebuilt. Some, but by no means all of its treasures were smuggled out in time to escape bomb damage. The Grand Cascade is the focal point of the water gardens in front of the **Grand Palace**, with the famous statue of Samson rending apart the jaws of a lion.

The gardens contain three pavilions. The first, the **Hermitage**, was where Peter entertained, helped by a "dumb waiter" device – a section of the round table was lowered below ground to be cleared and replenished. The **Marly** is built in a simple Dutch style and **Monplaisir**, at the water's edge, became Peter's favourite retreat; he could see the sea from his bed.

Inside, his taste is reflected in the beautiful oak staircase, oak study and the elaborate throne room, where his original throne sits. Catherine the Great later introduced such rooms as the Portrait Gallery, with its portraits of 368 women in different costumes.

About 12 km (7 miles) along the coast is **Oranienbaum** (open Wed–Mon 11am–5pm; Chinese Palace open June–Sept), built by Alexander Menshikov. It was the construction of Oranienbaum that inspired Peter the Great to build Petrodvorets. In the summer the **Chinese Palace**, built by Catherine, is open to the public, along with the **Coasting Pavilion**, though its rollercoaster with wooden toboggans no longer stands.

A Russian version of Versailles

Pushkin (formerly Tsarskoye Selo, the Tsar's Village) can be reached by train from St Petersburg's Vitebsk Station. This station is well worth seeing for its splendid Russian Art Nouveau interior. It was the first Russian station and the line between here and Tsarskoe Selo was the first Russian railway (1837).

Peter the Great's wife, Catherine I, chose the site for a stone country house, intended as a surprise for her husband while he was away in Poland. It seems to be the fate of each royal palace to be altered by successive monarchs and Peter's daughter, the Empress Elizabeth, decided to build a new and more

Frequent pilgrimages are made to the grave of St Ksenya Blazhennaya (the Blessed), in Smolenskoye Cemetery. The 18th-century saint was endowed with gifts of healing and prophecy, and to this day many claim miracles from her.

BELOW: Catherine Palace, Pushkin.

THE AMBER ROOM MYSTERY

Of all the works of art that disappeared from St Petersburg's palaces during World War II, few have captured the imagination of historians and treasure hunters as much as the Amber Room. This priceless 18th-century masterpiece was made by German craftsmen in the early 1700s for the Prussian King Friedrich I's palace in Charlottenburg, Berlin. His son gave it to Peter the Great in 1716. In 1754 the Amber Room was mounted in the Catherine Palace at Pushkin. It comprised six large oak wall panels, covering 100 sq. metres/yards, inlaid with six tons of amber, wall mirrors, and Italian mosaics containing precious stones. The room prompted one 18th-century British ambassador to call it the Eighth Wonder of the World. In 1941 the Nazis were said to have removed it to the German city of Königsberg (now Russian Kaliningrad) where it was last seen in 1945. Recent reports suggest that it was Red Army troops, occupying a Königsberg castle during the war, who lost it in a fire: Russia had destroyed one of its greatest treasures, and officials have been concealing the fact ever since. Over the past 20 years Russian craftsmen worked to recreate the room at the Catherine Palace. German natural gas giant, Ruhrgaz, gave about US$3 million to the restoration project, which was completed in 2003.

Map on pages 182–3

The summer resort of Pushkin (Tsarskoye Selo) is said to have had the first electric street lighting in Europe. It was renamed on account of the poet having studied at the Lycée.

BELOW: flute-player at Catherine Palace. **RIGHT:** the gilded domes of the Church of the Resurrection of Christ.

opulent palace here in 1741. She asked Rastrelli to model it on Versailles. It was enlarged by subsequent rulers, particularly by Catherine the Great, whose architect, the Scotsman Charles Cameron, gave the palace a more stately feel, but above all it is Elizabeth's own creation. The extravagant, baroque design is symbolic of the mood which dominated during her reign. In 1941 Tsarskoye Selo was occupied by the German Army, which left the town and palace in ruins.

The interior of the restored **Bolshoi Yekaterinsky Dvorets** (Catherine Palace; open Wed–Mon 10am–5pm; closed last Mon in month), like its exterior, is a mixture of styles by different architects: for example, the baroque of Rastrelli and the classicism of Cameron. The Great Hall, with its massive mirrors, wood carvings and glistening gold is perhaps the most sumptuous of all.

There is a great deal to see in the park, including the Upper and Lower Baths, the Hermitage, the great pond, the fountain of the milkmaid with the broken pitcher, inspired by one of La Fontaine's fables, and the Caprice. When visiting a palace that has been so highly restored, it is important to see the ruins, so a visit to the **Chinese Palace** is also recommended. In the grounds stand the **Alexander Park and Palace**. This smaller, more classical palace, only part of which is open to the public, was presented to Alexander I by his grandmother, Catherine the Great, on the occasion of his marriage.

A gift for Paul and Maria

The next stop on the Electric Railway, some 4 km (2 miles) further, is **Pavlovsk**. The palace at Pavlovsk (open Sat–Thurs 10am–5pm; closed first Mon of month), much smaller than the others, was built by Catherine the Great for her son Paul and his wife Maria Fyodorovna. The architect, who was also commissioned to redesign the palace gardens in accordance with the then fashionable English style, was again Charles Cameron. Later, an Italian architect, Vincenzo Brenna, was brought in. The land was originally chosen for the royal hunt, on account of the abundant elk and wild fowl. The rooms inside the palace reflect the personalities of Paul and his wife. Paul's militaristic interests can be seen in the Hall of War, Throne Room and Hall of the Maltese Knights of St John. His wife's Hall of Peace forms a pleasant and intended contrast.

The tapestries in the Carpet Room represent motifs from Cervantes' *Don Quixote*. There is a lot of French furniture on display, embroidered French curtains in the Greek Hall, and in the Hall of Peace a tripod-vase of crystal and red-gold produced in the St Petersburg glass factory in 1811. In Maria Fyodorovna's boudoir stands a piano imported from London. There is also a large collection of Sèvres porcelain pieces and a clock in Paul's study presented to him by Pope Pius VI.

The most important features of the large gardens are the Temple of Friendship (the friendship between Maria and her mother-in-law), the Centaur Bridge, the Cold Baths, the Apollo Colonnade and the Pavilion of the Three Graces. In time Paul transferred his affections to the palace at **Gatchina**, 45 km (28 miles) south of St Petersburg (open Tues–Sun 10am–5pm). This stone-built palace changes colour according to the time of day. ❏

THE HERMITAGE: ART AS POWER

The Hermitage collection of Old Masters, sculptures, antiquities and archaeology remains a powerful symbol for St Petersburg and Russia

Art has always been political in Russia. Catherine II bought her first collection of 225 paintings in 1764 to get one up on Frederick of Prussia, who could not afford them. She went on to purchase vast national collections one after another – the Campana collection in Italy, the Crozat collection in France and the Walpole collection in England – until she had more than 4,000 paintings and 10,000 drawings. The sale of these works of art to Russia aroused storms of disapproval and political censure but, in each case, it also proved Catherine's wealth, power and cunning in the international arena.

The 19th century added rich archaeological collections – archaeology being a patriotic and political science important in proving the glory of the Russian land – and more paintings and applied art. All this came to the Hermitage, heir to the imperial collections, along with thousands of confiscated works including, after 1917, those of the Impressionists. During the Soviet era the Hermitage collection was a symbol of Soviet learning and magnificence, and today, with its 3 million pieces, it remains a great source of pride to Russians everywhere.

▷ **RICH COLLECTION**
The Benois Madonna by Leonardo da Vinci (above) and this 19th-century Russian silverware indicate the breadth of the Hermitage collections.

△ **THE WINTER PALACE**
Rastrelli's baroque palace (1754–62) dominates the central body of the Neva and the immense Palace Square. It is most beautiful at night, when richly lit.

▽ *LADIES OF ARLES*
The stunning display of Impressionist and Post-Impressionist canvasses includes this painting by Van Gogh, as well as work by Monet, Sisley and Pissaro.

AN IMPERIAL RETREAT

Catherine the Great inherited Rastrelli's new Winter Palace when she came to the throne in 1762. She wanted a more intimate space, however, and added a small pavilion to be a "Hermitage", with room for her art and tables for private dinners. She then added a second pavilion and galleries, forming the Small Hermitage (1764–67), and a Large Hermitage along the waterfront (1771–87). Here she hung her fast-growing collection, played billiards, and, after the addition of the theatre (1783–87), allowed guests to wander around after performances. In the 1830s Nicholas I decided to open the museum to the public. The New Hermitage opened in 1852. The Winter Palace was added to the museum after 1917, although for some years it was a Palace of Culture, showing films and lectures to the masses.

◁ THE JORDAN STAIRCASE
Once ambassadors ascended this staircase to be received at court. Today visitors can admire the stunning white marble and gold interior.

▷ SASKIA AS FLORA
Masterpieces by Rembrandt such as *The Sacrifice of Isaac*, *Return of the Prodigal Son*, *The Holy Family* and *Descent from the Cross* fill almost a whole room.

◁ THE RED ROOM
Space is flattened and tilted in Matisse's seminal picture of 1908. The fabric shown remained in the artist's studio to his death; he used it in many works.

▷ SCYTHIAN STAG
Visit the magnificent collection of gold, from 7th-century BC Scythian and Ancient Greek items to Oriental daggers and jewellery.

THE EUROPEAN NORTH

The North of Russia is a land of great beauty, of harsh winters and summer "white nights", where the life, traditions and architecture of old Russia can still be experienced

Map on page 212

Russians often say that the medieval city of Vologda, 500 km (310 miles) east of St Petersburg, is the gateway to the north, an area stretching from Finland in the west to the Urals in the east, and north to the Beloye More (White Sea) and Barents Sea.

The importance of the north dates from medieval times. When Kiev came under the Mongol yoke, many Russians fled north, taking their skills with them. Monks settled the region and founded monasteries which grew into important cultural centres. By the end of the 15th century, with the formation of a single Russian state under Muscovite rule, the northern border needed defending. A series of fortresses was constructed, often in the form of monasteries and with the active help of the monks such as at Solovetsky.

A rich heritage

In 1553 Richard Chancellor, an Englishman, opened up the northern waterways and foreign merchants sailed along the rivers Sukhona and Severnaya Dvina (Northern Dvina) en route to Moscow. Arkhangelsk (Archangel) was founded as a trading port and flourished, along with other towns such as Veliky Ustyug. Huge fairs attracted goods and traders from both East and West, from England, Holland, Greece, Armenia, China and Persia. There was a large community of English merchants in Arkhangelsk and an English wharf in the port. Local crafts – nielloed metalwork from Ustyug, carved ivory from Kholmogory – were valued all over Russia.

The north is rich in wooden churches, reflecting the wealth of the area between the 16th and 18th centuries, when the church was the centre of social and administrative life in a community. Indeed, the social significance of churches was so great that the *galilee* (covered "porch") was often larger than the church itself – in the case of the church of St Nicholas in the monastery of Muyezero, four times its size.

Peter the Great was in part responsible for the decline of the area when he ruled that the Gulf of Finland would be Russia's "Window on the West" and not Arkhangelsk as was previously. With the foundation of St Petersburg in 1703, the glorious days of the Russian north were suddenly over. Peter westernised his country by looking west rather than north. For 150 years the region was isolated from the mainstream of Russian life and the fairs and markets died for lack of goods. Towns and villages dependent on trade declined to provincial status.

What may have seemed to be a tragedy was, in ethnographical terms, the area's salvation. When the north was rediscovered in the late 19th century by ethnographers, then by artists, they found a society

PRECEDING PAGES: an admiring crew. **LEFT:** cubs at play. **BELOW:** an elderly inhabitant.

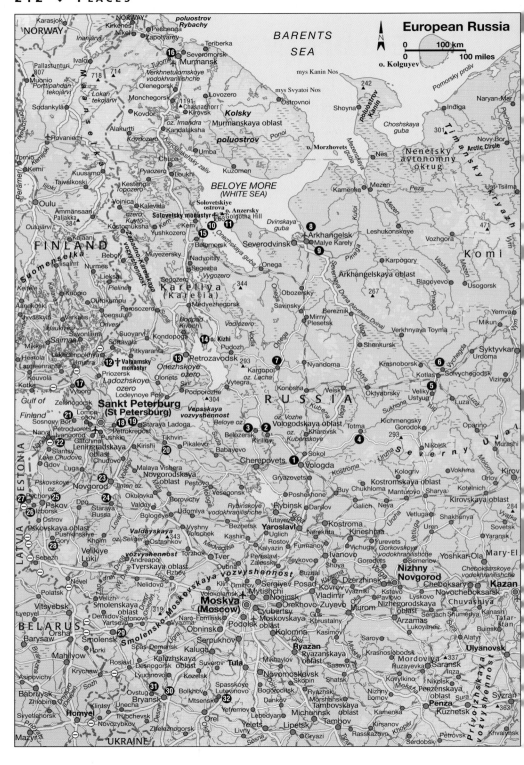

Map on page 212

which was living in the past. Not only were there hundreds of stone churches and monasteries set in magnificent landscapes, but there was a wealth of wooden buildings, religious and secular. What's more, the population had maintained age-old traditions, preserving fairytales, folk songs and customs which had already disappeared from much of Russia.

Artists flocked to the region. Nationalist composers such as Balakirev and Rimsky-Korsakov collected folk songs, incorporating the melodies in numerous compositions. Their art and music opened up the north to the world. For today's traveller who wants to get close to traditional Russian life and architecture, to understand how people lived in the past, this is the only place to go.

Gateway to the north

Ivan the Terrible fortified **Vologda** ❶, building a **Kremlin** (fortress) to strengthen control over the north which became an important trade route with Europe during his reign. He received Chancellor here on his memorable voyage, and from here a Russian envoy was sent to England. The chronicles record how Ivan personally oversaw the building of **Sofiysky Sobor** (Cathedral of St Sophia), 1568–70, though, according to legend, when a red tile fell on his head as he walked round his new church the irate tsar set off for Moscow leaving the cathedral unconsecrated for 17 years.

The cathedral stands on the high bank of the River Vologda, in the centre of what was once the Kremlin. Its late 17th-century frescoes combine medieval monumentality and the contemporary decorative manner. The archbishop's residence, an attractive huddle of buildings by the cathedral, includes the baroque **Palati Iosifa Zolotovo** (Palace of Joseph the Golden), 1764–69.

Vologda itself is a charming city best seen from the river with its 18th-century churches and secular buildings running along the embankment. Of particular note are the **Tserkov Svyatikh Konstantin i Yelena** (Church of Sts Constantine and Helen), 1690, with its typical tent-shaped, free-standing belfry and, among the secular buildings, the **Dom Admirala Barsha** (Admiral Barsh Mansion), the neoclassical **Skuliabinskaya Bogadelnaya** (Skuliabin Almshouse) and the wooden **Dom Levashova** (Levashov House), as well as the enchanting wooden **Dom Zasetskikh** (Zasetsky House), 1790–95.

Monasteries of the north

On the northern edge of Vologda, on the road to **Beloye Ozero**, is the **Spaso-Prilutsky Monastyr** (Monastery of the Saviour on the Bend). To get the best view climb the steep wooden staircase under the roof of the Water Tower. From here you can see the oldest and most typical northern building in the complex: the stone **Spassky Sobor** (Cathedral of the Saviour), 1542, the jumble of buildings around it and, over the walls, the Sofiysky Sobor. During Napoleon's invasion of Russia, treasures from the Kremlin and many Moscow monasteries were stored here.

Rather than go by road, take a boat from Vologda to the **Kirillov-Belozersky Monastyr** (St Kirill-Belozersky Monastery), which stands on the edge of

BELOW: the Vologda Tower and Moscow Gate of the Kirillov-Belozersky, Monastyr, Vologda.

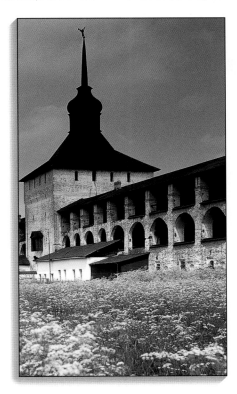

The Monastery of Ferapontov contains remarkable 16th-century frescoes by the artist Dionisius.

BELOW: looking out to the Gulf of Finland.

Siverskoye Ozero (Lake Siverskoye), 120 km (72 miles) to the north. The boat winds past wooden windmills and churches before arriving at **Kirillov** ❷, where the monastery emerges from behind the trees, its white stone buildings and domes reflected in the water. The monastery was founded in 1397 and by the 17th century was one of the richest foundations in Russia, largely due to the sale of salt. Vasily III, tsar of Russia in the early 1500s, came here to pray for a child by his apparently barren wife, Elena, and the following year they were blessed with a son, who became Ivan the Terrible.

There are a number of 15th- and 16th-century churches, but the star is the **Uspenskaya Sobor** (Cathedral of the Assumption) with its superb frescoes and 17th-century iconostasis. Twenty kilometres (12 miles) northeast from the St Kirill-Belozersky Monastery is the **Ferapontovsky Monastyr** (Monastery of St Therapont) on the banks of **Borodavskoye Ozero** (Lake Borodava). Its main claim to fame lies in the frescoes in the **Rozhdestvensky Sobor** (Cathedral of the Nativity of the Virgin), painted in the first few years of the 16th century by Dionisius and his sons. The superb cycle, devoted to the life of the Virgin, is regarded as Dionisius's swan song. A romantic local legend attributes his appearance this far north to the death of his beloved wife and his subsequent desire to find peace in the monastery.

The town of **Belozersk** ❸, 40 km (25 miles) north of Kirillov, retains much of its wooden 19th-century appearance, plus the symbols of its wealthy past: the massive **Uspensky Sobor** (Cathedral of the Assumption), 1553, devoid of ornament; the heavy **Preobrazhensky Sobor** (Cathedral of the Transfiguration), 1670s, and the jolly **Vsemilostivogo Spasa** (Church of the Most Merciful Saviour), 1723. Most impressive of all are the remains of the ancient fortress, the high earthen ramparts which run around the old town.

Totma ❹, 200 km (124 miles) east of Vologda, is an attractive small town with superb 18th-century churches displaying fine monumental brickwork. Lunacharsky, the first Soviet Commissar for Enlightenment and friend of numerous avant-garde artists, was exiled here by the tsar between 1902 and 1904.

Veliky Ustyug ❺, 250 km (155 miles) north of Totma, is now a sleepy provincial centre. Once it was one of the great market towns of the north – hence "Veliky" (Great) – and its tiered churches, monasteries and mansions are strung out along the river. The 17th-century **Uspensky Sobor** (Cathedral of the Assumption) is the eighth building on the site. Of particular note are the **Tserkov Zhawn-Mironosets** (Church of the Holy Women), 1714–22, the baroque **Tserkov Simeona Stolpnika** (Church of Simeon the Stylite), 1725–65, and the **Mikhailo-Arkhangelsky Monastyr** (Monastery of the Archangel Michael), not to mention the wealth of 18th- and 19th-century mansions such as the **Dom Shilova** (Shilov House) on the embankment. It is an easy walk across the old town.

The Stroganov Masters

One of the richest periods in the history of Russian art is linked with the so-called Stroganov Masters, artists employed by the wealthy Stroganov family, who made their fortune from the salt mines along the

Severnaya Dvina River. The Stroganovs settled in **Solvychegodsk** , 80 km (48 miles) north of Veliky Ustyug, and founded many fine churches, such as the fortress-like **Blagoveshchensky Sobor** (Annunciation Cathedral), 1560–79, which was the Stroganovs' own church, treasury and citadel, standing adjacent to their grounds. The cathedral is still rich in icons and frescoes.

They also founded the **Yavleniya Bogorodtsi Monastyr** (Monastery of the Presentation of the Virgin), 1689–93, its carved white stone details set off against the red brick and coloured tiles. The local museum contains many more icons and pieces of applied art linked with the Stroganovs and the town still has plenty of picturesque wooden buildings. Solvychegodsk is a well-known health resort, with salt and mud baths, particularly good for the relief of rheumatism.

Arkhangelsk region

In the region bordering the White Sea is the small town of **Kargopol** ❼, 427 km (257 miles) south of Arkhangelsk, yet another point on the important trading waterways of the north. Its key position on the River Onega led to a boom between the 16th and 17th centuries, manifested in the highly decorative white stone **Blagoveshchensky Tserkov** (Church of the Annunciation). The opening up of the northern trade route created the need for a port near the mouth of the Severnaya Dvina on the White Sea. In 1584 the town of Novye Kholmogory was founded; it later became known as **Arkhangelsk** ❽ (Archangel). By the beginning of the 18th century this was the centre of Russian shipbuilding. Now it is a big timber-logging and fishing area, known to the West through centuries of foreign trading links and the area's occupation by anti-Soviet Allied European and US troops immediately after the Revolution (1918–19). The great Russian scientist and poet

Arkhangelsk's nearby satellite town of Severodvinsk was one of the most top-secret cities in the Soviet era. It was, and still is, the centre of nuclear submarine production for the Russian Navy.

BELOW: Vologda with the Cathedral of St Sophia.

Petrozavodsk ("Peter's factory"), capital of Kareliya, was founded by Peter the Great as an iron foundry and cannon factory, and to this day it is famous for its iron-casting work.

Mikhail Lomonosov was born close to the town. Thirty km (18 miles) outside Arkhangelsk is the open-air **Muzei-zapovednik Derevyanova Zodchestva** (Wooden Architecture Museum Reserve; open summer 10am–5pm, winter 10am–3pm; closed Tues) at **Malye Karely ❾**. The forests make an effective backdrop for wooden churches, *izby* (cottages) and outhouses, many of them superbly decorated with carved window surrounds, eaves and crests running along the roof. The museum also holds concerts and provides a home to craftsmen.

Solovetsky islands

Arkhangelsk is a departure point for the **Solovetskiye Ostrova** (Solovetsky islands) in the White Sea, familiarly known as Solvki. This name has a particular ring to those whose relatives were imprisoned or died in the Solovetsky Special Purpose Camp, one of the camps the writer Solzhenitsyn called the "gulag archipelago". **Solovetsky Monastyr ❿** (Solovetsky Monastery) was a medieval fortress and major border post, and this can be seen in its grim, grey aspect, defensive walls and towers rising above the White Sea. The high windows recall embrasures, and the two 16th-century cathedrals were once linked by secret underground passages containing huge vaults for food and a hidden water supply in case of siege. Political and religious opponents were despatched here from the Middle Ages onwards. They were held in cells in the walls and towers and beneath the cathedrals.

The area is of outstanding natural beauty and this particular part of the White Sea has a comparatively moderate climate. You can take a tour on a small boat around the islands. The church on **Golgotha Hill ⓫** on **Ostrov Anzersky** (Anzersky Island) is a good place from which to look over the whole archipelago.

BELOW: transport around the Cathedral of the Transfiguration (c.1744) on Kizhi Island, Kareliya.

Exploring Kareliya

The western side of the region, northeast from St Petersburg, is the Republic of **Kareliya**, with its richly forested, flat landscape dotted with lakes. To see what the area has to offer, take a five-day trip on a river boat. The tours start from St Petersburg (longer cruises from Moscow) and take in the Valaam islands on Ladozhskoye Ozero (Lake Ladoga), Petrozavodsk (capital of Kareliya) and Ostrov Kizhi (Kizhi Island). On the boat tour, the **Valaam islands** come into view early on the second morning. Energetic passengers are advised to skip the organised tour and lecture and walk the 5 km (3 miles) through the woods to **Valaamsky Monastyr** ⑫ (Valaam Monastery). Returned to the Orthodox Church's possession in 1990, the monastery is an active religious community, with a farm and workshops, and tourism is now big business. The buildings, outlying cells and chapels, are being restored: major damage to the frescoes in the **Preobrazhensky Sobor** (Cathedral of the Transfiguration) was caused by over-officious guardians covering them with Perspex, thus trapping moisture and causing the paint and plaster to flake off.

The capital of Kareliya, **Petrozavodsk** ⑬, on the banks of Onezhskoye Ozero (Lake Onega) was founded in 1703 to serve a cannon foundry nearby. Despite the destruction wrought during World War II, Petrozavodsk is an attractive town, built on a series of plateaux rising from the water. The neoclassical **Kruglaya ploshchad** (Round Square) survived the Nazis.

About 70 km (43 miles) north of the town of Petrozavodsk is **Vodopad Kivach** (Kivach waterfall), the best of many on the River Suna, set in the midst of a vast nature reserve.

Petrozavodsk is a good springboard for exploring the northern reaches of

Map on page 212

TIP

Kareliya is home to some of the oldest volcanic rock and soil in the world – almost 3.3 billion years old. Petrozavodsk's Geological Research Institute in the Kareliyan Science Centre organises tours.

BELOW: Valaam Island, Lake Lagoda.

DISAPPEARING FORESTS

The Republic of Kareliya (pop. 800,000), which borders Finland, is three-quarters covered with forest. Naturally, logging and paper industries account for most of its economy. But Kareliya is only now learning that it needs to respect its environment to ensure a healthy and prosperous future. During Soviet times, these forests were only partly exploited as the area bordering Finland was left untouched to minimise the country's contact with the decadent West. Since the collapse of the USSR, however, the Russian economy has become a free-for-all and Russian *biznessmeni* along with their Western partners are taking advantage of the country's weak legal system to exploit the forests for all they're worth.

Approximately nine percent of Kareliya's forests are virgin old-growth areas, considered the oldest and most biologically diverse in Europe. They are protected by Russian and international law. In the first half of the 1990s, parts of these forests were not merely destroyed, but almost no effort was made to re-plant. In 1996, foreign timber companies agreed to a Greenpeace-sponsored moratorium on the purchase of old-growth timber from Kareliya. Still, illegal logging flourishes as corrupt officials turn a blind eye.

Modern Murmansk's role in World War II is highlighted in the Muzei Militarny Severnogo Morskogo Flota (Museum of the North Sea Fleet), ulitsa Tortseva 15 (open Thurs–Mon 9am–5pm).

Lake Onega and the island of **Kizhi** , a unique museum of wooden architecture. The 22 domes of the **Preobrazhenskaya Tserkov** (Church of the Transfiguration), 1714, are made entirely of wood and without the use of nails. The iconostasis inside the church is also of interest, not least because it is curved rather than straight. The interiors of some houses look much as they did when they were still home to local peasants.

Murmansk and the far north

Heading north, you come to **Belomorsk** ⑮, from where it is possible to take a trip to the Solovetsky islands. If you are intending to go to **Murmansk** ⑯, the journey north takes in some stunning scenery at any time of the year. And if one should be brave enough to go during the cold, dark winter months, you might be lucky enough to see the Northern Lights. To members of the older generation, Murmansk is equated with the Allied Forces who defended the town and port during World War II. It was through here that supplies from the West reached the rest of Russia. The port was founded in 1916 with British assistance (even the first houses were brought over from the UK) on the Barents Sea, which does not freeze thanks to the North Cape Stream. It rests between two low hills by the mouth of the River Kola and it is here, 68.5° north, that you really appreciate the meaning of a long winter night: the sun does not rise for two weeks.

The Leningrad region

BELOW: cooling off at Petrozavodsk.

The area around St Petersburg, still known as the **Leningrad region**, is well worth exploring if you get the chance. Northwest of the city, between (Lake Ladoga) and the Gulf of Finland, the landscape is dominated by country houses

Map
on page
212

(dachas) belonging to residents of St Petersburg. Part of the region belonged to Finland until 1940, and some of the best houses here were Finnish built. Now the area is dotted with sanatoria and wooden houses, often huddled round picturesque lakes. It is ideal for cross-country skiing in winter.

The last town on the Russian side of the border is the Swedish-Finnish medieval city of **Vyborg ⓱**. This area changed hands many times between the 13th and 20th centuries. It may not seem very Russian, for many of its buildings are left over from Finnish rule. **Vyborgsky Zamok** (Vyborg Castle) dates largely from the 16th century, and there are defensive towers from the 14th, but buildings from all periods survive, and the early 20th-century Art Nouveau buildings are especially striking. If you like follies, then the early 19th-century castle burial vault will be of interest. The peace and quiet of Vyborg has been disrupted since the late 1980s, as this has become the main crossing point for Finnish and Russian tourists and business people, and a busy freight route.

Petrokrepost ⓲, famous to those familiar with Russian history as Schlusselberg, lies 30 km (18 miles) east from St Petersburg, towards Lake Ladoga. The town's main claim to fame is the **krepost** (fortress) which was used as a prison in pre-Revolutionary times. Peter the Great's sister was imprisoned here, and in 1887 Lenin's brother, Alexander Ulyanov, was executed in the yard for his role in an attempt on Alexander III's life. **Staraya Ladoga ⓳**, 100 km (60 miles) along the south side of the lake, is noted for its 12th-century **Tserkov Giorgaya Pobedonostsa** (Church of St George) filled with marvellous frescoes, and other 17th-century buildings. Sixty km (37 miles) to the southeast is **Tikhvin ⓴**, worth a visit for its 16th- and 17th-century monuments and the **Dom Muzei Rimskovo-Korsakova** (Rimsky-Korsakov House Museum).

BELOW: river fish drying in the wind.

Going west along the south bank of the Gulf past Petrodvorets and the imperial summer palaces, you come to the closed city of **Sosnovy Bor** ㉑, best known for its nuclear power station. On reaching the border with Estonia at **Narva** ㉒, jump out on the Russian side, which is called **Ivangorod**, and take a look around the fortress there. Also, notice the strong difference in lifestyle between the Russian and Estonian sides of the border.

South of St Petersburg

In times of war, Novgorod withheld supplies of salt from its enemies, and used it as a powerful bargaining tool.

Novgorod and Pskov ruled the roost when the Tatars took over the rest of ancient Rus, building up trading links with the Hanseatic League and protecting themselves against attacks by the Poles and Livonians with heavy fortifications. Rich merchants built themselves churches galore.

When Russia was united under the rule of the Moscow princes at the end of the 15th century, Ivan III invited Pskov and Italian architects and craftsmen to help in the building of the churches in the Moscow Kremlin. The local monasteries were centres of learning, and Novgorod's historical chronicles and texts, scratched on pieces of dried birch bark, are known to historians all over the world.

The area suffered appallingly from the Nazi occupation. Whole villages were burned, complete with all their inhabitants. Buildings of interest that have survived or have been restored are concentrated in the two main towns.

Novgorod ㉓ has a rich past. At its height, the principality ruled from here spread all the way up to the White Sea and west to present-day Poland. Its power did not always work to the city's good, however. In 1570, for example, Ivan the Terrible butchered some 60,000 of Novgorod's citizens when they rebelled against his rule. Despite all the wars, the city has numerous monu-

BELOW: Cathedral of St Sophia in Novgorod.

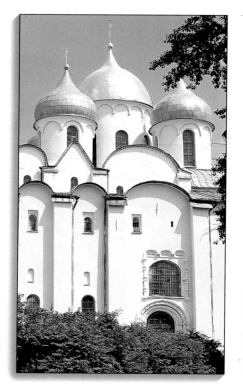

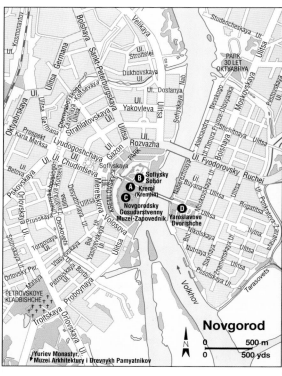

ments. The **Kremlin**  built on the bank of the River Volkhov is at the heart of the old city. It is dominated by the magnificent 11th-century **Sofiysky Sobor B** (Cathedral of St Sophia). Inside are 12th-century frescoes, including a portrait of Constantine and Helen, and the remains of 11th-century mosaics. One of the most surprising things to be found here is the east portal, with 12th-century bronze doors made at Magdeburg, taken – according to legend – from the fortress of Sigtunain in 1187. They are a superb example of Western European Romanesque metalwork tucked away in the heart of Russia. **Novgorodsky Gosudarstvenny Muzei-Zapovednik C** (Novgorod State Museum; open Wed–Mon 10am–6pm) is also housed here. It has a wealth of icons and church utensils. The monument outside the building, erected to commemorate the millennium of Russia in 1862, is by the sculptor Mikhail Mikeshin.

On the opposite bank of the river is **Yaroslavovo Dvorishche D** (Yaroslav's Courtyard), a pretty ensemble of 12th- to 16th-century churches. It was thought to have been the residence of the princes of Yaroslav until the end of the 14th century. There are plenty of other churches in town, some in the most unexpected places. If you count fewer than 30 as you wander round you have missed a fair number. Outside the town, only a short bus trip away, are two more sights. The **Yuriev Monastyr** (St Yuri Monastery) is still being restored, but work is coming along nicely (open Wed–Mon 10am–6pm), and there is the excellent **Muzei Derevyannovo Harodnovo Zogchestvo Vitoslavits** (Vitoslavlitsy Museum of Wooden Architecture) just across the road.

South of Novgorod, on the other side of Ilmen Ozero (Lake Ilmen) at the confluence of two rivers, is **Staraya Russa 24**. More intimate than Novgorod, the town is also rich in churches, for this was the centre of salt production.

Maps:
Area 212
City 220

The countryside south of Pskov forms the backdrop for much of Pushkin's writing. His family estate is near Pushkinskiye Gory.

BELOW: residents of Novgorod, 1880.

Map on page 212

Fyodor Dostoyevsky and his family spent their summers in Staraya Russa from 1872, and part of *The Brothers Karamazov* is set here. His house is now a museum: the **Dostoyevskovo Muzei** (Dostoevsky Museum; open Tues–Sun 10am–5.30pm; closed last Thurs of month).

For many people outside Russia, all they know about **Pskov** ㉕ is that it was here, in the royal train, that Nicholas II signed his abdication. Lake Chudovo, where the hero of Eisenstein's film *Alexander Nevsky* defeated the Teutonic Knights in the famous battle on the ice in 1242, is not far from the city.

Like Novgorod the town is dominated by its fortress and churches. They played a bigger defensive role than those in Novgorod, because of the ever-present danger from across the nearby border. Pskov's **Kremlin** is more fairy tale in appearance than that of Novgorod. Instead of square red-brick towers, here we have heavy, round, squat towers with wooden roofs.

The **Troitsky Sobor** (Trinity Cathedral), built in 1669, still dominates any view of the town. This white structure was not only a church, but also the place where the state council sat in session and where important state documents were kept. The **Kutekrom Bashnya** (tower) in the corner of the Kremlin walls was where the poet Pushkin liked to look down over the river.

Outside the old town are yet more religious buildings. The magnificent **Spaso-Preobrazhensky Sobor** (Cathedral of the Transfiguration) in the Mirozhsky Monastyr, decorated in the 12th century by Greek masters and their Russian apprentices, is a world in itself. The frescoes definitely merit a visit.

About 30 km (18 miles) along the main road to the west of Pskov, you find **Izborsk** ㉖. The village is built around the remains of a medieval fortress. Another 20 km (12 miles) further on, nestling in a deep ravine, is the 16th-century **Pskovo-Pcherskaya Lavra** (Pskov Monastery of the Caves) at **Pechory** ㉗, its picturesque beauty matched only by the strangeness of its underground caves, used as burial vaults for monks. Of particular note is the **Uspensky Sobor** (Cathedral of the Assumption), erected on the site of an ancient cave church. The monastery is still a religious institution, and it is possible to come here for a retreat.

Pushkin's estate

Even Russians indifferent to the medieval history of the Pskov area do not remain unaffected by its connection with the poet Alexander Pushkin (1799–1837). The **Mikhailovskoye** estate at **Pushkinskiye Gory** ㉘ (Pushkin Hills), 130 km (80 miles) south of Pskov, belongs to an ensemble of three estates and the nearby **Svyatogorsky Monastyr**. The estates were restored after the war and the parks returned to their former glory. Amble slowly round the grounds and drop into Pushkin's study, where he worked during his exile, then take a peek into the small cottage where his old nanny lived (open Tues–Sun 9am–4.30pm; closed last day of month).

The other estates here, **Petrovskoye** and **Trigorskoye**, are all reflected in Pushkin's poetry and prose. Mikhailovskoye and Trigorskoye form the background to *Evgene Onegin*, and the monastery features in *Boris Godunov*. ❑

BELOW: country life. **RIGHT:** dressed in national costume for the midsummer festival of Ust-vym.

Map on page 212

THE SOUTHWEST

The cathedrals, fortresses and war memorials of the southwestern steppes bear witness to the region's many rulers. It was here that Ivan Turgenev found inspiration

St Petersburg
Moscow

PRECEDING PAGES: whooper swans. **BELOW:** Smolensk's Bogoyavlensky Cathedral.

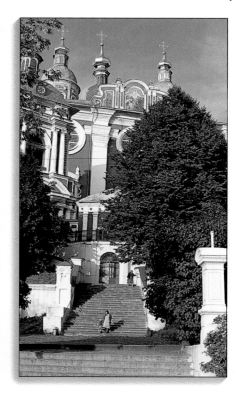

The perennial question of whether southwestern Russia is Asian, Western or forms a separate culture is as relevant today as ever it was. Never more so than in a region that has struggled through 1,100 years of being sniped at, ravaged and plundered, from all sides. Yet despite countless changes of ruler, southwestern Russia remains fundamentally *russkiy*. It was here that the Russian Empire was forged.

Kievan Rus, which covered western Russia and parts of present-day Ukraine and Belarus, emerged after the 860s when the Varangians (Vikings) arrived to lord over and protect the Slavic tribes. It was as Rus that the area gained its Slavic identity and from this word we get *russkiy*, which refers to the Russian people and all matters personal, homely and non-imperial.

From 1054, Kievan Rus was divided into principalities. These lasted into the 12th century from which point the history of **Smolensk** ㉙ offers a typical catalogue of the tumultuous battles and power struggles which have marked Russian history, causing Rus to expand into imperial Rossiya in an attempt to survive.

From the 12th century to the 20th, Smolensk and its region have passed from Kievan to Tatar, Lithuanian, Muscovite, Polish, Russian, French, German, Soviet and now finally back to Russian rule. Situated on the upper River Dneiper (Dnepr), "the gate of Russia" was first mentioned in 863. It soon became an important centre along the trade route between Moscow, 390 km (242 miles) to the northeast, and the West. Indeed, the town gets its name from the Russian word for tar, *smola*, because it was here that the river traders tarred their boats.

At the centre of the old town is Cathedral Hill on which the vivid green and white **Uspensky Sobor** (Assumption Cathedral) stands, on ground hallowed since 1101. This 18th-century church has a gilded interior and a wooden iconostasis carved by the Ukrainian, Sila Trusitsky. The town's three 12th-century churches – Sts Peter and Paul, St John the Divine and the Archangel Michael – are also worth a visit.

The main attraction of Smolensk is the **city wall**. Built by 300,000 people between 1596 and 1602, the 15-km (9-mile) long, 15-metre (49-ft) high wall was known as "the precious necklace of Russia". Precious indeed, considering that regent Boris Godunov forbade anyone in Russia to build themselves a stone edifice during its six years of construction.

For art lovers, the **Kartinnaya Galereya** (Art Gallery; open Tues–Sun 10am–6pm; ulitsa Krupskaya), has a valuable collection of icons, and the **Muzei Skulptury S.T. Konenkova** (Konenkova Museum; open 10am–6pm; ulitsa Mayakovskaya 7; tel: 0812-32029) has some fun exhibits, including *matryoshka* dolls.

City in the forest

Founded in 985 on the River Desna by Prince Vladimir, **Bryansk** ㉚, 325 km (200 miles) southwest of Moscow, lies in the heart of a 12,000-sq. km (4,630-sq. mile) forest and has a rich and brutal history. The forest has ensured the survival of the inhabitants of Bryansk on many occasions, most notably during World War II when 60,000 people fled from the invading Germans and lived in huts in the woods, forming a formidable partisan movement. The Bryansk fighters are remembered at **Partizanskaya Polyana** (Partisan Field) on the Orel road, just outside Bryansk where there is a museum (open daily 10am–4.30pm; tel: 0832-951717), preserved huts, and a wall on which are recorded the names of the 8,000 partisans who died. You may also spot some of the wild boar, brown bears and elks which roam the forest.

South of the city, the working **Svensky Monastyr** (Sven Monastery) is a reminder of the days when Bryansk was also a significant trading town. Furs and jewellery were sold here at the Sven Fair, which reached its zenith in the 17th century. The huge **Uspensky Sobor** (Assumption Cathedral), commissioned by Ivan the Terrible, has not withstood the test of time, but the two gate churches are relatively intact (entry on request). The view from here is splendid.

The region has been home to many artistic heroes. In **Ovstug** ㉛, 48 km (30 miles) northwest of Bryansk, the picturesque estate of nature poet Fyodor Tyutchev makes an interesting day trip (open Wed–Mon). The village of **Spasskoye Lutovinovo** ㉜, 70 km (43 miles) north of Orel and 340 km (211 miles) south of Moscow, is where Ivan Turgenev wrote *Fathers and Sons* and *A Nest of Gentlefolk* in the 1850s on his family estate. It is well worth a visit (museum open Wed–Mon 10am–5pm; tel: 08646-57247/23948). ❑

A memorial to the World War II Battle of Kursk – Belgorod road, 115 km (71 miles) south of Kursk – features a museum (open Tues–Sun 10am–5pm), T-43 tank, TaK fighter plane, trenches and a wall, out of which are sculpted the faces of tank crews.

BELOW: the city wall, Smolensk.

ALONG THE VOLGA

*The mighty Volga, Europe's longest river, has played a
major role in the development of Russia, as
the ancient towns and villages along its banks testify*

Map
on page
230

For many centuries the Volga has been like a mother feeding the Russian nation. It has witnessed numerous battles and wars, and has always stirred strong feelings in Russian hearts. It begins just north of Moscow in Valdayskaya Vozvyshennost (the Valdai Hills), not far from the picturesque Lake Seliger, and flows 3,530 km (2,195 miles) south to the Caspian Sea.

From time immemorial, people have gravitated to the river. One of the best preserved of the early settlements is **Veliky Bulgar** (Great Bulgar), the former capital city of the Volga Bulgars, near **Posileniye Bulgar** (Bulgar Village) in Tatarstan. Other great sites include the remnants of Itil and Sarai, former capital cities of the Golden Horde, not far from Volgograd and Astrakhan.

The **Povolzhye** (Volga Region) comprises the middle and lower parts of the river from Kazan to Astrakhan. **Kazan ❶** (pop. 1.1 million) is the capital city of Tatarstan, a sovereign republic in the Russian Federation. It was founded in the second half of the 13th century, and in the mid-15th century became the capital of the Kazan khanate. In the second half of the 15th and in the early 16th centuries Moscow princes besieged the city repeatedly. In 1552 it became part of the Russian state and in the 18th century developed into a major administrative, trade, industrial and cultural centre.

The **Kazan Kremlin** is a marvellous ensemble of 16th-century architecture. Particularly handsome are the towers. They include the **Spasskaya Bashnya**, a 45-metre (147-ft) high clock-bearing tower begun in 1555, the seven-tier 55-metre (180-ft) high **Suyumbiki** with its stone dome and gate leading to the Sovereign's yard, and the **Tainitskaya** towers.

Kazan is famous for its **university**, which is one of the oldest and most respected in Russia. Its students have included illustrious scholars, writers and politicians, notably Lenin, Lobachevsky and Leo Tolstoy. Kazan is also the native town of Tatar poet Musa Jalil and Russian singer Fyodor Chaliapin.

Around 74 km (46 miles) downstream, travelling southwest from Kazan, the Volga joins the Kama, its largest tributary. Just south of here is the town of **Ulyanovsk ❷** (formerly Simbirsk), pop. 650,000, occupying both banks. It was founded in 1648 to protect the southeastern outskirts of the Russian state from incursions. It is perhaps most famous for being Lenin's birthplace, hence its name: Lenin's original surname was Ulyanov – "Lenin" was one of the many revolutionary *noms de guerre*.

Another 125 km (78 miles) downstream from Ulyanovsk, a truncated cone of the Karaulny mound and the Kabatskaya hill rise on its right bank. This is where the **Zhiguli Hills** begin, the most beautiful part

LEFT: fisherman grapples with a sturgeon.
BELOW: flooded willows.

Along the Volga

of the Volga. On the left bank of the river, opposite the village of **Usolye**, stands **Tolyatti** ❸ at the bottom of the Zhiguli Hills. A modern city, it is well known for its **Volzhsky Avtozavod** (Volga Car Factory), which produces Zhigulis, Ladas, Sputniks and Samaras.

Further downstream, approximately half-way down the Volga's entire length, stands the town of **Samara** ❹ (known as Kuibyshev between 1935 and 1991), extending for dozens of kilometres along the bank. A broad staircase leads from the bank to the city centre, and a cast-iron grille adorns a riverside park. Named after the Samara River which flows into the Volga at this point, the town was built in 1586 as a fortress on the Volga's left bank. The easternmost town on the protected trade routes along the Samara bend. The town was an important crossing point, and used for monitoring the nomads' movements around the Trans-Volga's steppes. By the early 19th century Samara had grown considerably, and only its centre was confined by the disintegrating fortress. Though known as an industrial town throughout its history, Samara is especially proud of its theatre, which is one of the best local theatres in Russia. Samara's Drama Theatre, **Teatr imeni Gorkogo**, named after Maxim Gorky, can be found on Ploshchad Chapayeva.

After Samara the Volga turns sharply to the west. The landscape here is stunningly beautiful. The right bank with its steep and high cliffs is mountainous while the left bank is a lowland of emerald-green meadows.

Trading centre

After Samara comes **Saratov** ❺ (pop. 1 million), a modern industrial town, founded on the left bank of the Volga in 1590. In 1674 the town was moved to the right bank, to a sloping hollow surrounded by the **Lysaya, Altynnaya** and **Uvekskaya Mountains**. In the first 100 years of its existence it was little more than a small fortress designed to protect river trade routes from raids by nomads. During the reign of Peter the Great, the city's central square was called Gostinaya, on account of the **Gostiny Dvor** (rows of shops) built for merchants. The **Sobor Svyatoi Troitsi** (Trinity Cathedral) was built in Gostinaya Square in 1695. In the 18th century Saratov emerged as a major trading centre. The production of salt on **Elton Ozero** (Lake Elton) boosted the city's development. The first industrial enterprises date from that time. In the late 18th century grain became a key commodity, along with salt and fish.

In 1798 Saratov was made the centre of a *guberniya* (a pre-Revolution term equivalent to "province", which has now been reintroduced) and awarded a coat of arms. Like many other Russian towns, Saratov was a wooden town and as a result, it often suffered from fires. There was a particularly devastating fire in 1810, which prompted new city planning. In 1865 a new theatre was built of stone; this has survived as the **Teatr Operi i Balleta** (Opera and Ballet Theatre) on Teatralnaya ploshchad 1 (Theatre Square).

Also here is the **Muzei Iskusstv imeni Radishcheva** (Radischev Art Museum; ulitsa Pervomayskaya 75; tel: 8452-243627), which opened in 1885 (open Tues–Sun 10am–6pm; closed last day of month). It contains rich collections of paintings, sculptures, porcelain and furniture. The city's main street, Moskovskaya ulitsa, leads to Muzeinaya ploshchad (Museum Square), a remnant of old Saratov. Its major feature is the **Stary Sobor** (Old Cathedral) and, nearby, the former theological seminary, with arcades and columns. The **Muzei Kraiyevedeniya** (Museum of Local Lore; ulitsa Lemontova 34; tel: 8452-282496) is worth a visit (open Tues–Wed 10am–4pm, Thurs–Sun 10am–5pm).

Some 394 km (244 miles) downstream from Saratov stands the town of **Volgograd ❻** (pop. 1 million). During the 13th century the area was occupied

Map on page 230

Vologgrad's eternal flame burns in memory of those who lost their lives here during World War II.

BELOW: Volga embankment, Volgograd.

NIZHNY NOVGOROD

Perhaps the most successful city after Moscow in terms of economic development in post-Communist Russia, is Nizhny Novgorod (known as Gorky in the Soviet era, after the writer Maxim Gorky who was born here). Situated 250 km (155 miles) upstream from Kazan, Nizhny (pop. 1.6 million) is historically closer to the towns of the Zolotoye Koltso (Golden Ring), but is nevertheless seen as a major city of the Volga Region and indeed Russia. Two giants of Soviet engineering have their roots here: MiG, the soviet aircraft manufacturer, and GAZ, the Gorky Avto Zavod (Gorky Car Plant), producer of the Volga saloon car. In the mid-1990s, GAZ alone had 350,000 employees. The city became infamous for being the place of exile for the dissident, physicist and Nobel prize winner, Andrey Sakharov in the 1980s. His flat is now a museum, **Muzei A. D. Sakharova**, Prospekt Gagarina 214 (open Sat–Thurs, 10am–5pm; tel: 8312-668623). Nizhny Novgorod was founded in the early 13th century. Its **Kremlin** houses the **Arkhangelskoye Sobor** (Cathedral of the Archangel Michael), built in 1631 and the 19th-century governor's house, now the **Khudozhestvenny Muzei** (Art Museum; open Wed–Mon 10am–5pm; tel: 8312-390855). Many of the city's churches are undergoing restoration.

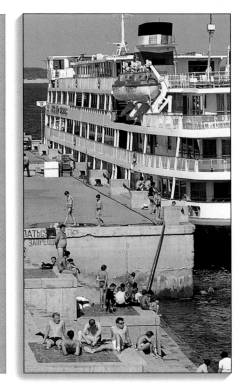

The Mother Russia memorial of Mamaev Kurgan in Volograd was built to commemorate the Battle of Stalingrad, 1942.

by the Golden Horde. When the Kazan and Astrakhan khanates eventually collapsed in the second half of the 16th century, a new town called Tsaritsyn was built on the island where the Tsaritsyn River flows into the Volga. It was designed to protect the country's southeastern borders.

The town suffered numerous raids by nomads, and the Don Cossacks, who rose in rebellion against the ruling regime, entered the town more than once. Peter the Great attached great importance to the town and built a barrage more than 60 km (38 miles) long and a rampart about 12 metres (40 ft) high. In 1765, Catherine the Great issued a decree allowing foreigners to settle in Russia. Among Tsaritysyn's newcomers from Western Europe was a sizeable colony of Germans, whose neighbourhood became known as Sarepta.

By the 19th century the town had lost its function as a fortress and become a trading and industrial centre. With the introduction of railways, industry developed rapidly, and soon saw-mills and cast-iron foundries were operating.

In the winter of 1942–43 the town (then called Stalingrad) was the focus of the key battle which marked the turning point in World War II. Fierce fighting lasted for 200 days and nights; some 300,000 of Hitler's crack troops lost their lives and the whole town lay in ruins.

After the war, the town was built anew. It extended along the Volga for nearly 100 km (60 miles). New factories, houses and parks were built. The memorial on **Mamaev Kurgan** (Mamaev Mound) by the sculptor Vuchetich and architect Belopolsky was built to commemorate the battle. It depicts a group of grieving citizens carrying wreaths to put on the heroes' graves. Behind the sculpture is a ramp paved with granite slabs and on both sides of the ramp are granite blocks resembling anti-tank teeth; they are engraved with the dates of all the major

battles that took place near the town. The ramp ends with an 11-metre (36-ft) high sculpture of a warrior with a submachine-gun and a grenade in his hand. Behind him, near the terrace with red flowers, rises a wide staircase with high walls on both sides showing the town's ruins. The staircase leads to a gigantic sculpture of a female figure symbolising the **Mother Russia**, a sword high in her hand.

There are extensive views of the city and the river from the bottom of the main monument and from the top of the mound. Try and visit the **Muzei - Izobrazitelnykh Iskusstv** (Fine Arts Museum; ulitsa Port-Saida), to see its collection of Russian paintings and Palekh boxes (open Tues–Sun 10am–5pm). The **Planetary** (Planetarium; ulitsa Gagarina 14), was presented to Volgograd by Germany. It is one of the few of its kind in the country (shows every hour, 10am–4pm).

Cultural crossroads

Downstream from Volgograd, the river turns to the southeast, flowing along the sandy-clay steppe of the lower Volga area. The right bank of the river near **Astrakhan ❼** (the last town on the Volga) is 12 metres (40 ft) high. Astrakhan lies in the Volga's delta, straddling 11 islands separated by channels and rivulets and has a population of approximately half a million. In the 18th century Astrakhan was on the Caspian Sea; today the sea falls short by some 200 metres/yards).

In the 8th century, 10–12 km (6–7 miles) upstream on the Volga's right bank stood **Itil**, the capital city of the Khazar (Turkic-speaking nomadic tribes). The name "Astrakhan" was first used in the 13th century. In 1558 Ivan IV's troops captured Astrakhan without a fight and annexed it to Moscovy. Another turning point in the town's history was 1558, when New Astrakhan was founded on

Map on page 235

BELOW: Astrakhan, in the Volga delta.

the opposite, left bank. The first wooden fortifications were built here. Between 1582 and 1589 they were replaced by a stone fortress: the **Astrakhan Kreml A** (Kremlin). This has seven towers, three of them with gates. **Krasnie** (Red) and **Nikolskie** (St Nicholas) gates, located in the Kremlin's northwestern part, led to the Volga. The third **Prechistenskaya Bashnya** (Prichisten Tower), with a bell tower incorporated in the eastern wall, led to the suburb **Bely Gorod** (White Town). Close to the Prechistensky Gate is the **Uspensky Sobor B** (Cathedral of the Assumption). The cathedral is a marvellous monument built by the serf-architect, Dorofei Myakishev, in 1698. From all sides, it is surrounded by a two-tier gallery decorated with filigree carved stone, creating an impression of light and air. The upper church with five graceful domes rises from this unusual, seemingly weightless pedestal. The Cathedral of the Assumption together with the place of execution and a high bell tower, built in the 19th century, make up a majestic architectural ensemble. The pseudo-Russian details overload the facades of the structure, but its tiers, evenly diminishing as they rise, make the bell tower look austere.

The **Troitsky Sobor C** (Trinity Cathedral), built between the late 16th and 18th century on the opposite side of the Kremlin territory, looks modest compared with the Cathedral of the Assumption. But in terms of craftsmanship, it is a large and intricate complex.

Many of the Kremlin's architectural structures date from the 19th century. Of particular interest are the Guard House (1807) and the **Kirillovskaya Chasovnya** (St Kiril Chapel). In the early 19th century, the chapel's original 17th-century structure was enclosed in a classical shell. The main portal (17th-century) is hidden behind the short massive Doric columns. Another architectural structure that has survived on the territory of the former Bely Gorod is the Tower of the **Preobrazhensky Monastyr D** (Transfiguration Monastery). Its snow-white octahedron, adorned with multi-coloured belts and insets and crowned with a dome, is magnificent.

Not far from the Preobrazhensky Monastery there is the **Demidov Homestead E**, at ulitsa Sverdlova 55, another architectural legacy of the 17th and 18th centuries. It was the largest and the most important home in the town. The Demidovs were an ancient merchant family in Russia. The size of the building was immense and even today it occupies half the block.

Among the churches that have survived outside the Kremlin's boundaries is the **Ioann Zlatoust F** (St John Chrysostom; ulitsa Volzhskaya 14). It was built in 1763, and its octahedron-on-tetrahedron composition was common in Central Russia. The church was reconstructed more than once, the final version in the form of a cross, incorporating the decor associated with classicism. The entrance to the church is adorned with a figure of Christ. The bent figures of angels on the western façade of the belfry express grief.

Buildings in classical style became a regular feature in towns after 1769. The early 19th century gave rise to such imposing and outstanding buildings as the **City Technical School G** and the **Department for the Supervision of the Kalmyk People H** at

BELOW: boatman on the Volga River.

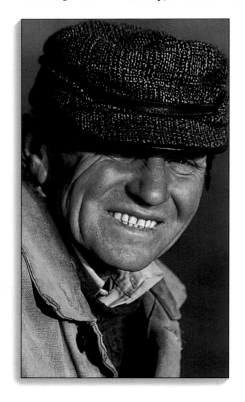

See map below

ulitsa Volodarskoga 22. Stone structures were built not only in the centre of Astrakhan but in the outskirts, too. A striking example is the surviving building of the hospital on Parobichev Hill. Eastern merchants, who enjoyed extensive privileges, settled in Astrakhan. They built their trade rows and lived in tight-knit communities in the centre of Bely Gorod. The surviving structures of the Indian and Persian homesteads were built in the 19th century.

Foreign merchants also built their own religious institutes, hence the **Belaya Mechet** ❶ (White Mosque; ulitsa Zoi Kosmodemyanskoi 41), and the **Chernaya Mechet** ❷ (Black Mosque; ulitsa Musy Dzhaliya 26), erected by Strakhan Tatars in the mid-19th century. In the eastern part of town, at the confluence of the Kutum River and the canal stands a Roman Catholic church, **Katolicheskaya Tserkov,** dating from the 18th century. Such architectural imports form a magnificent contrast to Astrakhan's other buildings.

Equally impressive are the commercial buildings that served the merchants. The merchants' estates on the Kutum's northern bank also illustrate the luxury of the times. One of the most interesting features of Astrakhan's architecture of the 19th century is the elaborate metalwork. A strong Oriental influence is evident in the fancy grilles, balconies, arches and gates.

The **Kartinnaya Galereya B.M. Kustodieva** ⓚ (Kustodiev Art Gallery; open Tues–Sun 10am–5pm; ulitsa Sverdlova 81; tel: 8512-226409) is named after Astrakhan's most famous native resident, Boris Kustodiev, a graphic artist and colourist. It contains works by artists from the 18th and 19th centuries and modern masters.

The city is still expanding. New buildings are constantly appearing, both in the centre and on the outskirts. The best of these complement the old town. ❑

TIP

Boat tours of the Volga delta reserve can be arranged through Intourist in Astrakhan (Sovietskaya Ulitsa). Don't miss the red lotuses which bloom in August.

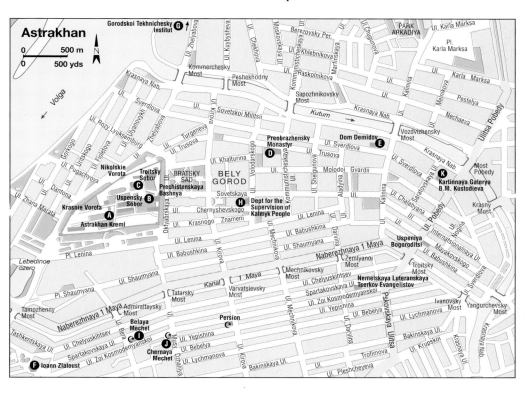

THE URALS

Marking the border between Europe and Asia, the Ural Mountain region is the industrial heartland of Russia, where modern cities rise out of a landscape of forests and lakes

Map on page 240

To picture the Urals, imagine smokestacks, factories and heavy industry. That is how leaders of the old USSR envisaged this mountain chain, and they proceeded to transform it into a succession of massive state-owned industrial enterprises. The region has never attracted many tourists, partly because Soviet leaders declared most of the Urals off-limits to foreigners – bans that were lifted only in the *perestroika* years. Today, foreigners in the area are generally businessmen sifting through the tattered remains of Soviet industry in search of investment opportunities.

There are still some areas of outstanding natural beauty where lakes and hiking paths dot the landscape, but the lack of tourist facilities make them inaccessible for everyone except the experienced traveller in Russia. The 2,000-km (1,250-mile) long Ural Mountain range – stretching between the Kara Sea in the north and Kazakhstan in the south – is not the insuperable geographical barrier one imagines: it is less than 2,000 metres (6,500 ft) at its highest point and has never been a serious obstacle to invasion from either direction. But in the absence of any other geographical feature it has long been taken to mark the divide between European Russia and Siberia, and by extension, between Europe and Asia.

The Ural Mountains date back 250 million years. Until the 15th century they were sparsely inhabited by a variety of local tribes. By contrast, today's Urals accommodate more than 20 million inhabitants, covering five regions: Sverdlovsk, Perm, Chelyabinsk, Orenburg, Kurgan, and two republics, Udmurtiya and Bashkortostan. The Urals' rich reserves of iron ore, coal, precious minerals and ferrous and non-ferrous metals eventually attracted large-scale European migration in the 18th century. Between 1752 and 1762 alone, 55 factories were built in the region, and industrial centres sprouted up in Yekaterinburg, Perm and Orenburg.

Industry moves in

Russia's devastation during World War II brought a boom to the Urals. After the German army roared across much of the European part of the USSR, Stalin moved 1,300 factories and hundreds of thousands of people to beyond the Urals for protection – not only from ground troops, but also from the Luftwaffe. The new Ural industrial base tripled capacity and was able to supply 40 percent of the Soviet Union's military needs for the war. The German armies never came close to the Urals, and historians cite Stalin's relocation of Soviet industry as a decisive factor in the outcome of World War II. Today, of course, distance is no barrier, as Gary Powers showed in 1960 in his U2 spy plane. He was however, shot down over Yekaterinburg.

PRECEDING PAGES: the Ilych Reserve at Pechora. **LEFT:** Yekaterinburg. **BELOW:** selling *tvorog* (curd cheese) at the Central Market in Yekaterinburg.

Yekaterinburg was named after Catherine the Great. During Soviet times it was known as Sverdlovsk after the Bolshevik leader Yakov Sverdlov who is said to have arranged the execution of Tsar Nicholas II.

Today's American-produced jets are less likely to be shot down as they fly into the city's increasingly busy international airport.

Following the war, Soviet authorities continued to expand heavy industry and the manufacturing of weapons. Traditional rural life in the region changed permanently as people flocked to the cities to work. Between 1940 and 1979, the Urals' urban population more than doubled. Even though the Urals still has one of the lowest population densities in Russia, it claims one of the highest outputs in heavy industry and defence sectors.

By the final years of Soviet power, the Urals accounted for a third of the country's steel production and a quarter of its cast iron. "The economic region of the Urals plays an important role in building the material and technical base of Communism," the country's main encyclopaedia enthused. The intense industrialisation has also made the Urals one of the most polluted regions in the world, resulting in staggering health problems for local inhabitants.

Capital of the Urals

Yekaterinburg ❶ (pop. 1.5 million), omitted from many tourist maps until 1990, is the Urals' most important urban centre and is Russia's third city (a popular claim of many large Russian cities). It is the first major Russian city in Asia; 40 km (25 miles) to the west along the highway, a 4-metre (13-ft) high memorial marks the Asian-European border. The city spreads out around the Iset River and is surrounded by taiga (forests).

The winter here lasts for about five months, from November to April, and the temperature may fall to -40°C (-40°F). The summer, which normally lasts no more than two months, maintains an average temperature of 20°C (68°F).

BELOW: at work on the production line.

Like most major cities in the Urals, Yekaterinburg's history has been closely associated with industry. The city was founded in 1723, and within five years the area had set up an ironworks, the first of many industrial enterprises attracted by the abundant raw materials of the region. It remained modestly populated for many decades with just 10,000 people at the start of the 19th century, but the population exploded under socialism, climbing from 100,000 in 1917 to four times that number at the end of World War II. The war triggered an industrial boom in the city, and the area became one of the Soviet Union's most important manufacturing centres for years afterwards. With its solid industrial base, Yekaterinburg is one of the few towns outside European Russia to make real progress in market reform.

Map on page 240

Yeltsin's home town

Modern Yekaterinburg is best known for its political sons, the first president of the Russian Federation, Boris Yeltsin, and Nikolai Ryzhkov, prime minister during Gorbachev's presidency. Yeltsin was born into a poor family some 150 km (93 miles) from Yekaterinburg, in **Butka**. He spent most of his life in Yekaterinburg, first studying at the Urals Polytechnic (now the Urals State Technical University), then building a career in the construction industry while rising through the ranks of the Communist Party.

Many remember Yeltsin as a tough but popular leader, and locals still recall the day that party officials came to visit in 1985. Yeltsin was later summoned to the capital to become chief of the Moscow party, effectively taking up the post of mayor of the city. With Gorbachev's blessing he used this post as a power-base for reform at the heart of the Soviet Empire. He did not know that he would be staying on in Moscow as president of a new Russian state.

A remarkable sight in modern Yekaterinburg are the old wooden houses, complete with carved window frames and other details. Many of these are still used as homes and offices.

BELOW: a cross marks the site of Tsar Nicholas II's execution at Yekaterinburg.

DEATH OF A TSAR

Yekaterinburg is most famous in the history books not for its industry, but for its role in the execution of Tsar Nicholas II following the Bolshevik Revolution. After seizing power in 1917, the Communists imprisoned Nicholas and his family, moving them to several locations before bringing them to Yekaterinburg in April, 1918. The family was confined to a brick home formerly belonging to a local businessman, Ipatyev. Accounts of the royal family's end were wrapped in secrecy throughout the Soviet period, but historians believe that guards treated the family cruelly during their final days. In July the Bolsheviks decided to dispose of the tsar once and for all, to avoid him being recaptured by the anti-Bolshevik forces that were then threatening the town. The tsar was moved into the basement of the house and informed that he was about to die. The historian William Henry Chamberlain wrote: "The tsar did not understand, and began to say 'What?' whereupon Yurovsky shot him down with his revolver. This was the signal for the general massacre. The other executioners emptied their revolvers into the bodies of the victims." The bodies were taken into the surrounding woods and left in a shallow grave. In 1998 their remains were removed to St Petersburg for reburial.

A folk display in Yekaterinburg's History Museum.

Exploring Yekaterinburg

Town planners have thankfully kept most of the industry outside the town centre, creating instead pleasant wide avenues lined with trees and modern apartment blocks and offices.

Start your sightseeing by walking south, away from prospekt Lenina (Lenin Avenue), the city's main street, along ulitsa Karl Liebknecht. The first major sight – a few minutes' walk, to the right – is the **Oblastroy Kraevedchesky Muzei Ⓐ** (Regional History Museum; ulitsa Malisheva 46; open Wed–Sun 11am–5pm). Here you'll find an interesting historical collection starting with late tsarist rule and continuing through to the present. Highlights include pre-Revolutionary photographs and objects from Yekaterinburg, a photographic record of the men who killed Tsar Nicholas II and his family, and objects connected with the original inhabitants of the Ural region, including tents, hunting implements, and fur garments.

The **Muzei Molodyozhi Ⓑ** (Youth Museum; ulitsa Karl Liebknecht 32; open Mon–Fri 9am–7pm, Sat 1–7pm during summer), once belonged to the Komsomol Communist youth organisation. The museum now takes an imaginative look at Soviet history and has opened a radical exhibition on Soviet life. Displays include a maze of mirrors, said to illustrate the futility of Soviet bureaucracy, and a man walking through a glass wall, showing how Russians are looking forwards and backwards at the same time. In another room there is an artist's rendition of what the world would look like after nuclear war.

A five-minute walk north up ulitsa Karl Liebknecht is the **Khram-Pamyatnik na Krovi Vsekh Svyatikh** (Church-Monument on the Blood of the All Holy), the golden-domed church which was consecrated in July 2003 on the 85th

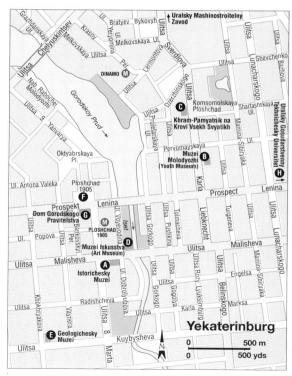

Yekaterinburg

anniversary of the execution of Russia's last tsar and his family. The church is built on the site where the tsar, Nicholas II, his wife Alexandra and his five children were shot dead.

The executions took place in the basement of a house belonging to an engineer named Ipatyev and this house came to represent a link with earlier times in the decades following the revolution. However, in 1977, the Kremlin, increasingly worried that the **Dom Ipatyeva ❻** (Ipateyev's House) could become a place of worship, ordered the local party boss, Boris Yeltsin, to remove it. A few days later the bulldozers were driven up to the house in the middle of the night. By the next morning, nothing was left of the building.

There are several museums a few blocks west of Prospekt Lenina. In an area that is the site of the city's original settlement is the **Muzei Iskusstva ❹** (Art Museum; ulitsa Voyevodina 5; open Tues–Sun 11am–6pm), home to mostly Russian paintings. The large building's centrepiece is a 4.5-metre (15-ft) high iron pavilion crafted in an intricate Oriental style for display in Paris in 1900. Other highlights include local metal sculptures, a popular and traditional art form of the area.

The **Geologichesky Muzei ❺** (Geological Museum; ulitsa Kuybysheva 39; open Tues–Sat 10am–5pm) houses an interesting collection of some 600 minerals found in the Urals, including malachite, topaz, a 748-kg (1,650-lb) crystal and meteorites.

If you return to prospekt Lenina and walk one block to the east, you'll come to **ploshchad 1905** (1905 Square) ❻, Yekaterinburg's main square and the home to the **Dom Gorodskogo Pravitelstva ❻** (City Hall; prospekt Lenina 24), which was built between 1947 to 1954 by German prisoners captured during World War II. Here you will find a large statue of Lenin erected in 1957.

On the east side of town, where Prospekt Lenina starts, is the **Uralsky Gosudarstvenny Tekhnichesky Universitet** (Urals State Technical University) ❼, the largest university in the Asian part of Russia, which once had 20,000 students, 7,000 teachers and employees and occupied several blocks of town with its own hospital, hostels and hotels. Known for its strong science and engineering departments in particular, the school has produced a series of prominent Soviet and Russian officials, including Boris Yeltsin and his wife, Naina, who met as students here. At one time 12 graduates of the school were on the Central Committee of the Communist Party. More recently the university has experienced harder times, since local industry has cut back its need for university-level engineers.

Although hardly worth a tourist visit, **Uralsky Mashinostroitelny Zavod** (Urals Factory of Heavy Machine Construction), ploshchad 1 Pyatiletki, on the north part of town is famous throughout Russia and once ranked as one of the largest factories in the world. A machine tool and heavy plant factory, "Uralmash" once employed a staggering 50,000 people in the area. As a Soviet publication of 1991 stated: "For many decades, this name was the symbol of the newest, most powerful, most progressive technology in the country." The introduction of market

Map on page 242

BELOW: Urals State Technical University.

TIP

A useful precedent was set recently when a western journalist took a local hotel to court, and won, over the inflated "tourist" price list. Now no hotel in the area will dare to charge a visitor more than a local.

BELOW: Central Market in Yekaterinburg.

economics to Russia gave this factory, and many others, a harsh slap in the face. Output fell dramatically, and Uralmash management reduced the number of workers to 18,000.

Steel city

A name virtually synonymous with Soviet industrialisation, **Magnitogorsk** ❷ (pop. 450,000) is also one of the world's most polluted cities. Ironically, this most Soviet of places, 113 km (70 miles) into Asia from the European divide, was designed by a US firm. When the Soviet Government decided to increase exploitation of the Urals' rich iron ore deposits, which had already been mined for hundreds of years, they turned to the McKee corporation of Cleveland, Ohio (at the time selected US businesses were free to co-operate with the new but underdeveloped Soviet state). McKee was called upon to help in the design of Magnitogorsk, and it drew its inspiration from the US steel plant in Gary, Indiana, which was at the time the largest iron and steel plant in the world. The American firm was paid US$2.5 million in gold for its services. The construction of Magnitogorsk began in 1929; pig iron was already in production by 1932, and steel was being manufactured by the following year.

The initial name of the plant launched during the USSR's first Five-Year Plan was the Stalin Magnitogorsk Metallurgy Kombinat. Workers in this model industrial project settled in an area called Sotsgorod, a Russian-language abbreviation for "The Socialist City". The city's population rapidly expanded to 146,000 by 1939, and it soon became one of the country's major industrial centres. The area still stamps out huge quantities of steel: in 1990 Magnitogorsk produced 25 percent of all Soviet goods containing metal.

Accidents and experiments

Founded in 1736 as a defensive fortress, **Chelyabinsk** ❸ (pop. 1.2 million) is the administrative centre of the southern Urals. It grew rapidly in the 19th century as a trading centre along the railway. Located 200 km (125 miles) southeast of Yekaterinburg, the city was an important industrial centre for the manufacture of T-34 tanks and Katyusha rocket launchers during World War II. Nowadays, the city produces nearly one-fifth of big-bore pipes produced in the country, one-third of smelted ferroalloys and ball-bearing steel, over 60 percent of stainless steel, and about 40 percent of road-building machines.

The Chelyabinsk area is also the site of two of the worst nuclear accidents in the post-war period. In September 1957, a mechanism designed to cool nuclear waste failed in nearby **Kyshtym** and contaminated the area with radioactive material. For years the incident was shrouded in secrecy. From 1951 to 1961, the Mayak (Lighthouse) nuclear bomb plant 100 km (80 miles) northwest of Chelyabinsk dumped huge quantities of radioactive waste into a local lake. The lake has since evaporated, but the radioactive dust remains a lethal threat. Travel agencies arrange tours, including visits to a biophysics centre specialising in treatment of the victims of radiation, and meetings with local scientists specialising in nuclear and energy problems.

The main sights are the **Geologichesky Muzei** (Geology Museum; open Tues–Sun 10am–5pm; ulitsa Truda 98, tel: 3512-630186), highlighting Ural minerals; the **Kartinnaya Galereya** (Picture Gallery; open 10am–6pm; ulitsa Truda 92), containing work by Russian and foreign artists from the 15th to the 20th century; and the **Muzei Prikladnykh Iskusstv** (Applied Art Museum; open Tues–Sun 11am–6pm; ulitsa Revolutsii 1), showing off the best of local masters.

Orenburg ❹ (pop. 500,000), an industrial centre founded in 1735, is located near the site of one of the most grotesque experiments of the Cold War. According to recent press accounts, in 1954 the Red Army exploded an atomic bomb near the city during military exercises. Subsequently, local villagers suffered a 50 percent increase in cancer, and of the 44,000 soldiers who participated all but 1,000 died prematurely. Orenburg is home to the Military Aviation Academy where Yury Gagarin, the first human in space, studied. A jet which he used is located at the entrance to the academy.

In and around Perm

On the European side of the Urals, **Perm** ❺ is another large industrial centre (pop. 1 million). It was founded in 1723 as a village around a factory. From 1940 to 1957, Perm was renamed Molotov, in honour of the Soviet foreign minister who signed the non-aggression pact with Nazi Germany in 1939. Perm's highlight is the **Gosudarstvennaya Kartinnaya Galereya** (State Picture Gallery; open Tues–Sun 10am–6pm; Komsomolsky prospekt 4; tel: 3422-129524), with its fine display of 16th–19th-century icons, sculptures and Russian and foreign paintings. The **Etnografichsky Muzei** (Ethnographic Architecture Museum; open daily 10am–6pm; tel: 3422-997182) at **Khokhlovka**, 45 km (28 miles) north of Perm, preserves examples of pre-20th-century rural life. ❑

Map on page 240

BELOW: waiting for public transport.

THE EUROPEAN SOUTH

*This is Russia with a southern flavour. Here, you can soak up the
sun in the Black Sea resort of Sochi or sample
the curative mineral waters of the Caucasian Mountains*

Map
on page
250

The European south, or northern Caucasus as it is also called, stretches across the south of the Russian Federation, bounded by the Black and Sea of Azov to the west and the Caspian Sea to the east. The scenery is diverse: from the fertile black-earth steppe of the Don to the north, to the snow-capped Caucasian mountains to the south; from the subtropical Black Sea coast to the semi-desert areas by the Caspian. The vegetation is equally varied: coniferous forests at the foot of the mountains, subtropical vegetation along the shores, high meadows carpeted with mountain flowers and rush-filled river valleys.

Both the subtropical climate and the mineral-rich soil in the northern Caucasus make it an extremely fertile area and a wide variety of fruits and vegetables grow in abundance. Just north of Sochi at **Dagomys** ❶ are the most northerly tea plantations in the world, producing Krasnodarsky tea, a large percentage of which goes for export. Tobacco, including rare oily kinds, is another important resource. Despite the harsh legislation during Mikhail Gorbachev's anti-alcohol campaign when nearly one-sixth of the Soviet Union's vineyards were destroyed, the northern part of the Caucasus is still renowned for its vineyards. In the small town of **Abrau-Dyurso**, west of the Black Sea port of Novorossiysk, vintners have been producing one of Russia's best champagnes for more than 150 years.

The Caucasus has been home to dozens of different peoples over time, resulting in the ethnic diversity which characterises the region to the day. It covers more than six autonomous republics and is home to Ukrainians, Russians, Circassians, Adygeis, Kabardians, Balkars, Ossets, Ingushi, Chechens, Greeks, Abkhazians, Georgians, Armenians and Estonians. The Kuban Cossacks (named after the river which runs through Krasnodar) and their descendants live on the plains to the north of the Caucasus. Their capital is **Krasnodar** ❷ (pop. 630,000). Before the Revolution, Krasnodar was called Yekaterinodar – from *Yekaterina* (Catherine) and *dar* (gift). Catherine the Great gave this city to the Kuban Cossacks in return for conquering southern lands for the Russian crown. Today it is the capital of the **Krasnodarsky Kray** region, an area rich in minerals, especially oil, and famous for its wheat.

PRECEDING PAGES:
the Caucasian
Mountains.
LEFT: a wild iris.
BELOW: raising
lambs in the hills.

The Black Sea coast

The Black Sea is an internal and virtually isolated body of water, which is contaminated below 200 metres (656 ft) with hydrogen sulphide. Although marine life is sustainable only in the top 200 metres/ yards, the Black Sea supports a variety of different fish, three species of dolphin and more than 13 types

Triumphal Arch at
Novocherkassk, the
19th-century capital
of the Don Cossacks
near Rostov-on-Don.

of jellyfish. It is fed by a large number of rivers, which dilute the salt content and keep the sea clean. **Novorossiysk** ❸ is southern Russia's principal port. It has become especially important since Ukraine gained independence and Russia's naval base in the Crimean port of Sevastopol moved in part to Novorossiysk. Another vital Black Sea port is **Tuapse** ❹, south of Novorossiysk, where most of the Russian oil tankers berth.

Sochi

Russia's most popular beaches stretch along the east coast of the Black Sea from Tuapse to Georgia. The best known resort is **Sochi** ❺. Like the rest of the coast, Sochi is protected from cold northerly winds by the Caucasus and enjoys a subtropical climate. The area around Sochi has evidence of habitation dating back to prehistoric man. The first official Russian settlement on the River Sochi was the coastal fortress of Aleksandria, founded in 1838 to prevent Ottoman expansion in the area. The fortress came under constant attack, not by the Turks but by the local Caucasian peoples and 15 years later it was evacuated by the Russian garrison as the Crimean campaign began. Russian troops returned in 1864 and by 1866 the local inhabitants had been subdued. Alexander II ordered that the region be "settled" by Russians and Ukrainians.

Sochi began developing as a tourist destination in the late 19th century. In the Soviet period it became a popular holiday destination among Russians and their leaders. You can still see the *dachas* (country houses) of some the politicians – Stalin, Khrushchev, Brezhnev – who spent holidays here. Indeed, Khrushchev was on holiday at his Black Sea *dacha* just along the coast in Pitsunda (now in the Republic of Abkhazia) when he was removed from power in 1964.

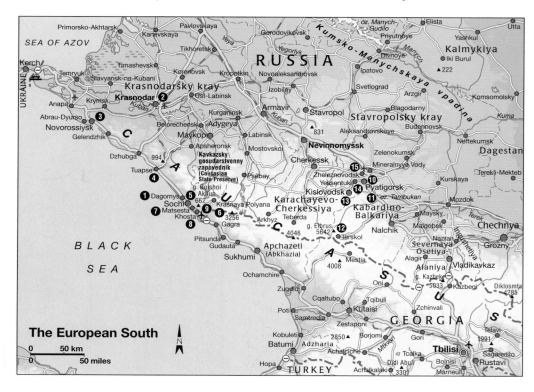

Sochi's popularity is further boosted by its numerous *sanatorii* (therapeutic hotels) and *doma otdykha* (rest-houses), which offer cures and treatments for various illnesses using local spa therapies. Many Soviet trade unions had therapeutic hotels in Sochi to which their members could come on holiday with their families. A number of these *sanatorii* still exist and you can generally arrange to stay at one by turning up at the door. Sochi remains a favourite destination for conferences, and hosts an annual international film festival in June.

Like all the Russian Black Sea beaches, those in Sochi are pebble rather than sand. They drop away steeply into the sea making them excellent for swimming. You can walk most of the coast along the romantic seafront promenades and through the parks lush with magnolia palm and cypress. Most popular of Sochi's parks is the botanical garden, **Park Dendrariy** Ⓐ, with more than 1,600 different types of trees. Next to Dendrariy Park you will find the **Derevo Druzhby** (Tree of Friendship). Although it looks similar to an orchard, it is in fact one tree to which, in honour of visiting foreign representatives, 40 different citrus fruits have been grafted – Japanese tangerines, Italian lemons, American oranges and Indian grapefruits, to name a few.

Kurortny prospekt Ⓑ is the main street in Sochi, where most of the major hotels are situated. The prospekt begins in the north at Platanovaya alleya (Platan Alley, named for the plane trees which line it) at **Park Rivyera** Ⓒ and traverses the length of Sochi crossing several small rivers. In the evening, life shifts from the seafront cafés to restaurants and cafés along Kurortny.

Sochi has a number of museums including a good art gallery, **Muzei Izobrazitelnykh Iskusstv** Ⓓ (Sochi Art Gallery) at Kurortny prospekt 51, which features a collection of paintings, drawings and sculpture from the

Maps:
Area 250
City 252

TIP

The best time to visit Sochi is in autumn when there are long hours of sunshine and the humidity is low. Spring comes early to the coast and flowers bloom in late March.

BELOW: *borshch* (beetroot soup), a popular dish in the Caucasus.

A TASTE OF THE CAUCASUS

The cuisine of the northern Caucasus and the Black Sea coast is influenced both by the bordering country of Georgia and by the local inhabitants. Here you will find Ukrainian *borshch* (beetroot soup) alongside Georgian *kharcho* (a spicy meat and tomato broth). You can try Russian *pelmeni* (a type of ravioli served with sour cream or vinegar) and Georgian *khinkali* (a larger spicier version of *pelmeni*). As well as traditional Russian breads there are Armenian *lavash* (a soft pancake-thin unleavened bread) and Georgian *khachapuri* (a delicious hot cheese-filled bread). On the beach vendors often come by selling hot corn on the cob, roasted hazelnuts and *semochki* (sunflower seeds). Another unusual seaside snack is *churchikhela*, a Georgian sweet made of hazelnuts or walnuts strung on a piece of string and coated with hot grape juice, which solidifies as it cools. An integral part of summer picnics is *shashlyk*, a type of marinated kebab cooked on long skewers over charcoal embers. The Armenian version is wrapped in *lavash* and cheese. In the seafront cafés try locally caught trout in delicious Georgian *bazha* (walnut and coriander sauce), and finish your meal with an excellent Turkish or Greek-style coffee and a *paklava* (pastry) made with fresh mountain honey.

A pleasant half-day excursion can be made from Sochi to Dagomys Tea Farm to sample the local brew in attractive surroundings.

17th to the 20th century (open Tues–Sun 10am–5.30pm). **Muzei Istorii Goroda-kurorta Sochi** (Sochi History Museum; ulitsa Ordzhonikidze 29; open Tues–Sun 9am–6pm), contains exhibits from the earliest evidence of pre-historic habitation through to the modern day.

The **Muzei Pisatelya Nikolaya Ostrovskogo** (Ostrovsky Literary Museum; open Thurs–Tues 10am–6pm) is dedicated to Nikolai Ostrovsky, a revolution-ary writer who fought in the Civil War following the October Revolution. Unable to hold a pen as a result of his injuries, he dictated his novels to his wife. The museum has three sections: a house-museum dedicated to Ostrovsky and a literary collection at ulitsa Pavla Korchagina 4; and at Krasnaya Polyana, 50 km (34 miles) into the mountains, a house-museum (open Thurs–Tues 10am–5pm) dedicated to the Estonians who settled in the Caucasus in the 19th century, in particular the writer Tommsaare.

The foothills of the Caucasus

Most compelling of all is the countryside around Sochi. This area is very pop-ular with the Russian political elite and President Putin often skis here. If you don't have a car, there are plenty of tour operators located on Kurortny who arrange moderately priced bus trips into the mountains surrounding Sochi. One of the most spectacular routes is the journey to the mountain village of **Krasnaya Polyana** (Beautiful Glade), 50 km (30 miles) from Sochi and 600 metres (1,970 ft) above sea level. The road up to Krasnaya Polyana snakes along ledges cut into steep mountain gorges providing breathtaking views. Along the way, look out for two crowbars sticking out of the rock, a memorial to the workers who died while building this treacherous road between 1897 and 1899. A fork

BELOW: Black Sea port of Sochi.

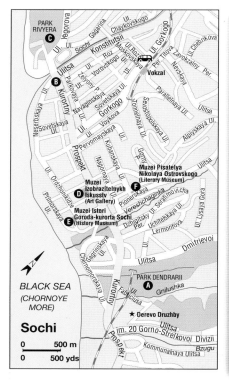

in the road takes you to a place called **Medvezhy Ugol** (Bears' Corner), an allusion to the brown bears that roam these parts, along with wild boar and deer. There is also a Narzan mineral water spring. Archaeological finds suggest that the area was inhabited first in the Stone Age. At the turn of the 20th century it was a hunting preserve for the tsar and his family. Today, as the **Caucasian State Preserve**, it is famous for its herd of bison.

Krasnaya Polyana, which is a favourite place of relaxation for President Putin, is surrounded by snowy mountain peaks, at the foot of which are dense forests. Footpaths lead to an arboretum and the remains of the tsar's hunting lodge, and to river valleys, waterfalls and alpine meadows. There are several places to stay that make a good base for hiking trips in the summer months and skiing in the winter. **Matsesta** ❼, 12 km (7 miles) southeast of Sochi, is the region's main spa town. In local Circassian, *matsesta* means "fire water". The sulphur waters turn bathers' skins bright red; they also help to treat systemic disorders, ulcers, and skin diseases. The marble *banya* (baths) date from tsarist times.

About 25 km (15 miles) from Sochi is **Khosta** ❽, another spa with hot mineral springs. It can be reached by train, bus, or boat. The pleasant beaches here are less populous than those in the centre of Sochi. Three kilometres (2 miles) inland is a forest preserve containing trees as old as 800 years. Here, too, are all that remains of an 11th-century fortress believed to have been built by Genoans. Nearby is a collection of cork oaks brought from Portugal, France, Spain and Algeria.

Mt Bolshoi Akhun ❾ with a 662-metre (2,171-ft) observation tower, is 20 km (12 miles) inland from Sochi. From the top of the tower there is an excellent view of the snow-topped peaks of the high Caucasus, the coastline beyond

BELOW: carrying water from the well.

LITERARY HERO

Mikhail Yurevich Lermontov (1814–41) is one of Russia's leading romantic writers whose life and works are integral to the Caucasus. He is best known for his novel, *Hero of our Time*, a large part of which is based in Pyatigorsk. As a child, Lermontov visited the region on several occasions and his earliest poems refer to the local landscape and culture. Lermontov was exiled to the Caucasus in 1837 for writing a poem alleging that the tsarist regime was to blame for Pushkin's death. A year later he returned to St Petersburg, where his reputation as a writer grew. His work was characterised by his cynical views on contemporary society and his criticism of the tsarist regime. In 1840 he was exiled to the Caucasus again, this time to a military post. The following year, strangely reminiscent of the plot of *Hero of Our Time*, Lermontov quarrelled with another officer and was killed in a duel just outside Pyatigorsk. You can still visit the Academic Gallery, Bulvar Gagarina, where the character "Pechorin" first sees "Princess Mary", and the Spa Research Institute, prospekt Kirova, site of the fashionable balls in the novel. The author's cottage can be seen at the Lermontov Museum Reserve, ulitsa Lermontova (open Wed–Mon 10am–5pm; closed last Thurs in month).

Map on page 250

The Caucasians are famous for their curative mineral water springs, reputed to improve the heart and vascular systems, nervous system, stomach ailments, gynaecological problems and skin diseases.

BELOW: abundant tomato harvest.
OPPOSITE: southern gentlemen.

Sochi, and even the Abkhazian resort of Pitsunda. A little way from the tower are the **Agurskiye vodopady** (Agur waterfalls). There are good restaurants at the foot of the tower and by the waterfalls serving Caucasian food and wine.

Spa towns of the northern Caucasus

Mineralnyye Vody (Mineral Waters) is a resort region made up of four main towns: Kislovodsk, Pyatigorsk, Zheleznovodsk, and Yessentuki, all of which are connected by trolleybuses. The area is located on the northern spur of the central Caucasus. Summers are warm, 20° to 25°C (68°–77°F) and long, winters are mild and the sun shines nearly 300 days a year. The marvellous climate, curative waters, lush vegetation and mountain scenery have lured the health-conscious for nearly two centuries. The region is also known for its abundance of fruits and vegetables, dry and sweet wines, cognacs and, of course, drinking waters. Today there are a few Intourist hotels as well as the numerous *sanatorii*.

Pyatigorsk ❿ (Five Peaks), the region's oldest spa, was founded 200 years ago on the southern slopes of **Mt Mashuk** (993 metres/3,257 ft). It has 43 mineral springs and its own research institute for the development of new cures. You cannot visit Pyatigorsk without coming across reference to the Russian poet and author Mikhail Lermontov (1814–41) who died here fighting in a duel *(see box on page 253)*. The **Lermontovskaya Galereya** (Lermontov Gallery) is situated in the town's central park among the mineral springs and grottoes. **Ozero Tambukan** ⓫ (Lake Tambukanskoye), 11 km (6 miles) from Pyatigorsk, is renowned for its mud, which is said to improve muscle tone and blood vessels.

Gora Elbrus ⓬ (Mt Elbrus), Europe's highest peak, is a 168-km (104-mile) drive south. The region is noted for its horse farms. Races are held at the local hippodrome from May to September).

Kislovodsk ⓭ (Sour Waters), 40 km (25 miles) southwest of Pyatigorsk, claims to have the best climate in the region. Founded in 1803, Kislovodsk is renowned for its Narzan mineral water. In the local language, *narzan* means "drink of the gods"; it is used in medicinal baths. The town is surrounded by beautiful landscapes, including a 12-hectare (30-acre) artificial lake. Nearby is a strange rock formation known as the **Zamok Kovarstva i Lyubvi** "Castle of Perfidy and Love" from which, the story goes, a young shepherd boy and wealthy local girl who were in love but forbidden to marry made a pact to throw themselves to their deaths. The shepherd jumped, but the girl did not. Here you'll find the Caucasian restaurant **Zamok** (Castle). Order the delicious fresh trout.

Halfway between Pyatigorsk and Kislovodsk is **Yessentuki** ⓮, named after a local mineral water that is prescribed for stomach, intestinal, and urological disorders. Built in the early 19th century, the spa is known for its Gothic and Greek-style architecture and for its mud baths. **Zheleznovodsk** ⓯ (Iron Waters), the smallest of the four spa towns, is 630 metres (2,066 ft) above sea level. It was built at the recommendation of the General Aleksei Yermolov who fought in the Caucasian war. Local sites include the Mauritanian-style **Ostrovsky Baths** (1893), the **Emir of Bukhara's palace**, and the **permafrost caves**. ❏

SIBERIA AND THE FAR EAST

Siberia may seem awesome in size, but the delights of Irkutsk's wooden houses, the rugged mountains of Altay and the wonders of Lake Baikal are easily accessible by plane or train

Map
on page
260

In 1982, Russian geologists exploring a remote region of the Siberian taiga near Gornaya Khasiya, found a family of *raskolniki* (Russian Orthodox Old Believers) who had been living in hiding since tsarist times and knew nothing of the fall of the tsar and the rise of Soviet rule. Such is the vastness of the great Siberian plain.

Exploring Siberia measures up to a lifetime's ambition, not a holiday. But for a determined and hardy traveller, much of the flavour of this remote part of the world can still be savoured in the Russian and Soviet-era outpost towns that dot the vast Siberian taiga from the Urals to the Pacific, the Arctic Ocean to Mongolia. Travel in Siberia tends to take two forms: stop-offs along the Trans-Siberian Railway and city-jumping on Aeroflot internal flights. With the easing of travel restrictions during the 1990s, even more exotic excursions are also possible: deep tundra snow-mobiling, boat cruises up the Yenisey and Lena rivers with a helicopter shuttle in between, and hunting and fishing expeditions.

Adventurous travelling requires careful planning, with the help of private Russian travel agencies. In Siberia, the best of the agencies are in Irkutsk, but be warned: where amenities are concerned, Siberia makes Moscow seem like Paris. Many towns have no restaurants or hotel rooms. A hefty dose of patience is as important to a traveller as bottled water.

The region's geography

Covering 12.5 million sq. km (4.8 million sq. miles), Siberia is a geo-political invention rather than a physical, geographical identity. The name Siberia comes from the Mongolian *sibi*, which means "sleeping land". It encompasses a wide range of terrain, related by little more than the remoteness of European Russia to the west and China and Mongolia to the south. The Buryats in Ulan-Ude consider themselves residents of Siberia just as much as the Yakuts living near the Bering Strait.

A journey from west to east Siberia starts at the rolling Urals and passes immediately on to the great primeval forests of the taiga. The taiga is almost equal in size to the whole of Western Europe. It stands pretty much as it has for millions of years, since logging is economically impractical in the remote forests.

Further east is the River Ob, running north from the Altai Mountains through Gorno-Altaysk to Barnaul, Novosibirsk, just missing Tomsk and then meandering north towards the Arctic Circle where it enters the Obskaya Guba. This is Russia's longest river, 5,410 km (3,362 miles), and the first of a network of rivers flowing north to the Arctic Ocean. The others include, from west to east, the Yenisey, Angara and Lena. To the south of the taiga is the world's biggest

PRECEDING PAGES: Siberian reindeer. **LEFT:** Nentsy mother and child. **BELOW:** Siberian tiger on the prowl.

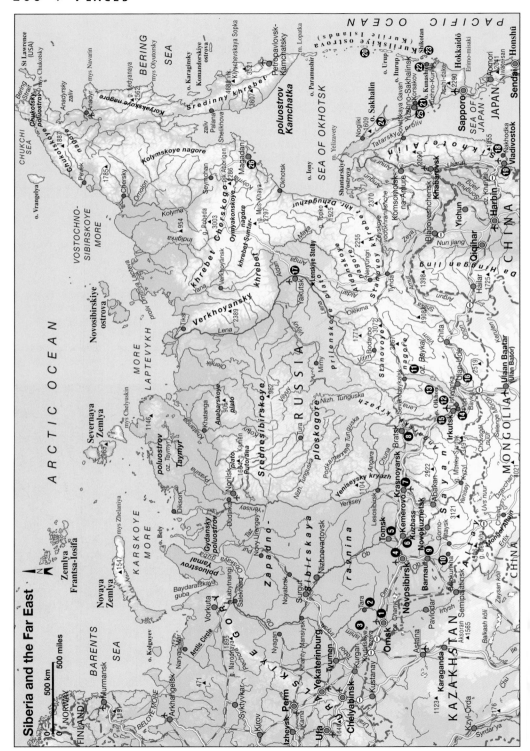

Siberia and the Far East

bog, the Urmany. The region has some of the richest oil reserves in the world, which, together with oil rigs in the Severnoye More (North Sea), once accounted for 95 percent of the Soviet Union's hard currency earnings. Foreign oil workers are beginning to explore the region, but roads cannot be built over the soft ground. Further east is Ozero Baykal (Lake Baikal), "the Pearl of Siberia", and the boundary between Siberia and the Russian Far East. To the north, Siberia hugs the Arctic Circle, passing over the diamond-rich region of Yakutiya and on to the Bering Strait. Siberia peters out on the island of Big Diomede, within sight of the US island of Little Diomede, seven time zones away from where it starts.

Map
on page
260

A little history

Though sporadic fur-trading was underway by the 11th century, the process of "opening" Siberia to Russia did not really begin until 1552 – the year Ivan the Terrible liberated Kazan from the Tatars and created a gateway for expansion.

Siberia has endured two great waves of exploration and settlement. The first occurred during the expansion of tsarist Russia, when Russian explorers reached the coast of California. Expansion was characterised by brutal suppression of native peoples followed by waves of exiles and serfs seeking freedom. The explorer credited with doing most to open up Siberia is the Cossack Yermak, an outlaw who travelled with a band of mercenaries in the hope of winning the tsar's favour and pardon. Yermak was killed in 1564, but not before founding the fortress of Tomolosk on the River Ob. Successive explorers and settlers continued to arrive right up to the time of the Bolshevik Revolution in 1917.

The greatest wave of Siberian settlement came with Stalin's first Five-Year Plan in 1929, which called for the rapid transformation of Russia from an agrarian to an industrial society. This daring, ultimately brutal programme led to the founding of thousands of small and medium-sized industrial towns across Siberia.

BELOW: Siberian portrait.

Industrial expansion led to ecological disasters for many regions, as improper care was taken to guard the delicate environment. Today, Siberia is littered with leaky oil pipelines, ill-conceived reservoirs, nuclear waste disposal sites, and blighted by short-sighted logging and thousands of smoke-spewing factories. The only thing that has protected Siberia from environmental ruin is its vastness.

During this period of settlement, enthusiastic *komsomoltsy* (young Communists) were encouraged to go to Siberia to work on one of the hundreds of large industrial projects designed to transform Russia into a modern, industrial power. It was a heroic undertaking, embarked upon in the most idealistic years of Soviet rule. Many elderly Russians who took part speak fondly of those hard and heady achievements of their youth.

The Trans-Siberian Railway

The world's longest continuous train journey, the Trans-Siberian Railway, crosses seven times zones along its 9,299-km (5,778-miles) route from Moscow to Vladivostok, passing from a stretch across the north Gobi Desert to a 4,000-metre (13,125-ft) high mountain pass in the remote Amur Mountains. It actually

TIP

Since travel restrictions to Siberia have been lifted, it is more likely that a visitor will be invited into a local home than hassled about his or her camera. But both events occur and it is important to have all your documents in order, including a visa valid for all destinations.

BELOW: gate to an Old Believers' enclave.

comprises three routes: the Trans-Siberian, the Trans-Mongolian and the Trans-Manchurian railways, the last two making the connection to Beijing. The railway was built to counter Western Europe's commercial shipping fleets and to break their monopoly on trade with the Orient. Tsar Alexander III dreamed of creating a faster route to the Orient. Due to political upheavals this aim was never achieved, but the Trans-Siberian railway did support Russia's expansion into Central Asia and allowed it to keep a grip on its Far East holdings as far south as Vladivostok.

The ability of Russia to transport troops and weapons quickly to these remote areas allowed the country to become the world's largest empire. Construction began in 1890. At the time, it was the world's most ambitious engineering project. The entire stretch from St Petersburg to Vladivostok was finished in 1905 *(see Insight On The Trans-Siberian Railway, page 124).*

Western Siberia

Siberia's second-largest city, **Omsk ❶**, approximately equidistant at 800 km (498 miles) from Yekaterinburg in the northwest and Novosibirsk in the southeast, is also one of its oldest. It was founded in 1716 as a fort city and later became a place of exile. Among those banished here was Dostoyevsky, who spent four years in Omsk until 1854. Before the 18th century, Omsk traders supplied Asian markets with slaves, who were kept on **Katonsky Ostrov** (Katon Island) until they could be sold. Two forts can still be visited: **Staraya Krepost** (Old Fort), built in 1716, and **Novaya Krepost** (New Fort), built by the Russians at the end of the 18th century. Today, Omsk is the administrative centre of western Siberia with a population of 1.2 million. It is regarded as having one of the best museums

of fine art in Siberia, **Istoriko-Kraevedchesky Muzei** (Art Museum; ulitsa Lenina 23A; tel: 3812-314747; open Tues–Sun 10am–6pm), featuring a collection of 7,000 artworks, as well as exhibits on peasant life of different peoples.

From Omsk there are day tours to **Tara ❷**, a Siberian fort town 300 km (186 miles) north, founded in 1594. It is also possible to visit **Krutinskiye Ozera ❸** (Steep Lakes), comprising three beautiful natural lakes (Ik, Saltaima and Tenisa), 200 km (125 miles) to the northeast of Omsk. During the warm summer months, these lakes and the surrounding area are popular among local families as a weekend getaway for hiking and swimming.

Novosibirsk ❹, Siberia's largest city, 700 km (435 miles) east of Omsk, is the quintessential, dull Soviet city covered with pre-fab housing. It was built predominantly as an industrial centre. Indeed, the city is a virtual monument to Stalin's single-minded drive to industrialise Russia. Its airport is Siberia's hub, and nearly all flights between Moscow and the Far East refuel here. Attached to the city is the research centre of **Akademgorodok** (Academic Town), a prestigious Soviet-scale think-tank that was badly affected by the brain-drain of the early 1990s. Novosibirsk has the usual array of theatres and worthy museums, but one museum does stand out: the **Istorichesky Muzei** (Local History Museum; Krasny prospekt 23; tel: 3832-271543 and Vokzalnaya Magistral 11; open Wed–Sun 10am–6pm), which does an excellent job of documenting the history, geography and ethnic make-up of Siberia. It even includes the requisite woolly mammoth display.

The town of **Tomsk ❺**, 400 km (248 miles) northeast of Novosibirsk, is perhaps best known for its academic prowess: it has more professors per head than any Russian city, the oldest university in Siberia and its **Botanical Gardens**, 36 Prospekt Lenina is thought to be one of the finest in the country.

Map on page 260

Negotiate the price of your journey with the taxi driver before setting off. Official taxis don't always use their meters.

BELOW: travelling on the Trans-Siberian railway.

TIP

The countryside around Tomsk is beautiful, but harsh: beware of ticks in the summer (June–July) as tick-borne encephalitis can be a real danger.

Rich pickings

At the centre of the **Kuzbass** coal-mining region, **Kemerovo** ❻ is politically and economically critical to Russia. It is the prime supplier of the country's coal. Founded in 1918, the modern Soviet-era city is now ringed by seven large coal mines, which employ nearly every inhabitant in the town. The only reason for tourists to come to Kemerovo is to see a genuine Russian coal mine (the mines are working mines, not tourist attractions, but a day trip can be arranged privately), although the city **Kemerovsky Istoriko-Arkhitekturny Muzei Krasnaya Gorka** (Regional Museum of Nature, History, Architecture and Ethnology; ulitsa Krasnaya Gorka 17; tel: 3842-642726; open Tues–Sun 10am–4pm) has some interesting exhibits. It is possible to arrange a train trip from here across the taiga to the **zapovednik** (nature preserve) 50 km (31 miles) to the south of Tomsk.

Krasnoyarsk ❼, 1,000 km (620 miles) from Novosibirsk and 600 km (373 miles) east of Kemerovo, is one of the latest Russian cities to open up to foreign tourists, though it's hard to imagine there will be much of a rush to visit it. Founded in 1628 along the River Yenisey, Krasnoyarsk became a place of political exile. Today it is choking in industry: iron, aluminium, heavy machinery and agricultural equipment are all manufactured here. The pride of the town is the 18th-century **Pokrovskaya Tserkov** (Church of the Protection of the Virgin; ulitsa Mira). However, the city does have several museums, including the **Krasnoyarsky Kulturnno-istorichesky Tsentr i Muzeiny Kompleks** (Krasnoyarsk Cultural and Historical Centre and Museum Complex; ploshchad Mira 1; open Tues–Sun 10am–6pm). The *Saint Nikolai*, the ship on which Lenin supposedly sailed into exile in Sekhushenskoye in 1897, is on ulitsa Dubrovin-

BELOW: the shores of Lake Baikal.

skoyo. Vasily Surikov, the 19th-century artist, was born and lived in Krasnoyarsk and his house, **Muzei-usadba V. I. Surikova,** can be visited (ulitsa Lenina 98; tel: 3912-231587; open Tues–Sat 10am–6pm; closed last day of month).

Wood and water

Founded in the late 1600s by Cossacks, **Bratsk ❽**, 600 km (373 miles) east of Krasnoyarsk, has been overtaken by progress – literally. The old city is now under the reservoir of the **Bratsk Hydroelectric Station**, once the largest in the world. New Bratsk, founded in 1955 as the logging and wood processing centre of central Siberia, is an ecological nightmare where production targets take precedence over all other concerns, although attempts to clean up the region have begun. The extent of the ecological disaster is clearly evident on a drive out to the taiga. Winds whip over vast, denuded expanses of land where no replanting has taken place. Bratsk, however, is not without attractions. Before the basin that held Old Bratsk was flooded, workers transported all the historic buildings to a nearby hillside. The result is a wonderful **Otkryty Muzei Etnografii** (open-air museum; open Tues–Sun 10am–5pm) devoted to the wood-working skills of Bratsk's first residents. Several *logizby* (peasant cottages), barns, and *bani* (bathhouses) have been constructed here. The highlight is a wooden church, built without a single nail.

Altay Mountains

The territory of Altaisky Kray, in the south of Western Siberia, bordering Kazakhstan and the Respublika Altay (Republic of Altay), is an ideal place for the adventure tourist to experience the Russian outback. What with its natural

Map on page 260

The tourist office in Krasnoyarsk offers trips along the Yenisey River; outings to the striking rock formation of Krasnoyarskiye Stolby (Krasnoyarsk Pillars), as well as hunting packages.

BELOW: winter weather.

Theatres, opera houses and concert halls provide popular entertainment throughout Siberia and the Far East.

beauty – one-third of the territory is covered by woods – mountains, low rainfall and pleasant summer temperatures of around 20°C (68°F), it makes an ideal centre for hiking, rafting and climbing.

The starting point for exploring the region is **Barnaul 9**, the administrative centre of the territory, founded in 1730. It lies 230 km (143 miles) southeast of Novosibirsk on the River Ob and is accessible by plane, train and bus from Novosibirsk. There are two museums worth seeing in town: **Altaisky Kraevedcheskii Muzei Hstorii** (Altay Museum of Regional Studies and History; ulitsa Polzunova 46; tel: 3852-234551; open Wed–Sun 10am–5.30pm), was founded in 1823 and claims to be the oldest in Siberia. It pays homage to Barnaul's most famous citizen, the inventor Ivan Polzunov. **Gosudarstvenny Khudozhestvenny Muzei Altaiskogo Kraya** (Altay State Art Museum; prospekt Lenina 88; tel: 3852-611888; open Wed–Sun 10am–6pm) is the region's main art gallery containing Russian works from the 16th to 20th centuries.

In the resort of **Belokurikha ⑩**, 200 km (124 miles) to the south, the combination of the local spring waters and pure mountain air creates an ideal atmosphere for the Russian sanitorium and indeed it is home to several specialised *doma otdykha* (rest homes, similar to Western health farms). Here, you can ski, trek, make use of the medical facilities or simply enjoy the scenery.

Lake Baikal

BELOW: the central market in the Ulan Ude region near Lake Baikal.

A trip to Siberia is not complete without seeing the "Pearl of Siberia," **Ozero Baykal** (Lake Baikal) ⑪, the 636-km (395-mile) long stretch of water which lies 66 km (41 miles) east of Irkutsk. One of the world's great lakes, Baikal is more than simply Siberia's top tourist attraction, it is a force of nature. For

once, Russian statistics are not gratuitous. The lake holds 20 percent of the world's fresh water and its maximum depth plunges to 1,637 metres (5,370 ft) *(see Insight On Lake Baikal, page 272)*. Lake Baikal offers so many endemic species (1,500) and so much geological diversity that the study of the lake has created a new scientific discipline: Baikology.

Its most famous indigenous species is the *nerpa*, the world's only freshwater seal. Sturgeon and *omul* (similar to salmon and trout) feature among the marine life. The lakeside village of **Listvenichnoe**  makes an interesting day-trip from Irkutsk, where the extraordinary ecology of the area is best explained in a small museum at the **Muzei Baikolovedeniya Limnologicheskogo Instituta** (Baikal Limnological Institute).

Whatever the season, weather on Baikal is unpredictable. The lake is ruled by a micro-climate in which storms may rise and fall without passing over the shoreline. Weather often bears little relation to that in Ulan-Ude or Irkutsk. Even on the lake, it may change drastically in minutes. The first snow appears in early October, and the lake is frozen from January to May. The best beaches can be found near the entrance to **Ostrov Olkhon** (Olkhon Island) on the lake's west shore, about one and a half hours northeast by car from Irkutsk.

Port Baykal is a charming village 65 km (40 miles) southeast of Irkutsk, a former crossroads on a now dead-end line of the Trans-Siberian Railway. Timber, coal and sand from around the lake is ferried to the port where it is loaded onto rail cars which leave once a day. There are no tourist facilities to speak of, but a stroll through the town gives a delightful sense of what life on Baikal is like for the locals.

Well worth a visit is Muzei Zodchestva i Etnografii (the Museum of Wooden Architecture and Ethnography) in Taltsy, 47 km (30 miles) south of Irkutsk on the road to Baikal (open 10am–5pm).

BELOW: carved lintel decorates a Siberian home.

Irkutsk

Irkutsk (pop. 600,000) is arguably the most appealing Siberian city and the one best developed to accommodate tourists, mainly as a result of being the launching point for excursions to Lake Baikal. It is located along the Angara River, about 30 minutes by car north of the southernmost tip of the lake.

It was founded in 1662 by Russian Cossacks, as a place of exile on the crossroads to Mongolia and China. Its most famous residents were the Decembrists, who were exiled there following an unsuccessful coup against the tsar in December 1825. A museum dedicated to the Decembrists is located in **Dom Volkonskikh** (the house of Count Sergey Volkonsky; Pereulok Volkonskogo 10; tel: 3952-277532; open Tues–Sun 10am–5.30pm).

For many years a centre of the defence industry, the city is undergoing enormous change as it retools itself in the post-Cold War period. The growing tourism industry is seen as a possible saviour for the depressed region. The fur trade, the timeless Siberian standby, is also growing in importance. Irkutsk's largest factories are a tannery, a shoe and a fur factory. Other manufacturing industries include heavy machinery, timber and building materials. The population is a comfortable mixture of Russians and assorted peoples, including about 20 percent Buryats, the Mongolian Buddhist descendants who settled

Lake Baikal's southern shore. The city has expanded to cover both banks of the Angara River, but the historical and commercial centres are located on the west bank. Though the central districts are characterised by the usual Soviet-era concrete blocks and monuments to the Great Patriotic War (World War II), the older outer districts still feature wood-frame homes, even Russian log *izby*.

A beautiful **riverside park** has been constructed along ulitsa Gagarina, across from the Intourist Hotel, and this is the best starting point for a tour of the city. Begin at ulitsa Karla Marksa and proceed to the bridge at the city's promenade. Looping back, take ulitsa Lenina, making sure you stop by at the city's **central market**. This four-storey indoor bazaar of clothing, electronics and other soft goods draws enthusiastic Siberians from hundreds of miles.

Most of the shops in Irkutsk can be found between the central market and ulitsa Karl Marx. From ulitsa Karl Marx, proceed back to the river, passing the delightful **Krayevedchesky Muzei** (Local History Museum), across from the large concrete obelisk. The museum has several departments across town – the central building at ulitsa Karl Marx 2 houses the departments of History and Natural History (open Tues–Sun 10am–6pm; tel: 3952-333449). There is also an exhibition hall in the **Spasskaya Tserkov** (Church of our Saviour; ulitsa Sukhe-Batora; open Wed–Mon 10am–6pm).

Other places to see when in Irkutsk include: the **Muzei Izkusstv imeni Sukhacheva** (Art Museum; ulitsa Lenina 5), named after Sukachev – it also has exhibition halls at ulitsa Karl Marx 23 (open Wed–Mon 10am–6pm). For plays and concerts check out the **Irkutsk Dramatichesky Teatr** (Irkutsk Drama Theatre; ulitsa Karl Marx 14; tel: 3952-333361); and the **Irkutsk Filarmoniya** (Philharmonic; ulitsa Dzerzhinskogo 2; tel: 3952-241100).

Izba, the peasants' wooden cottage, is traditionally made from five walls and a roof. The fifth wall divides the building in two for either the expanding family or livestock, whichever the more pertinent.

BELOW: a Buryat Lamaist monk.

SEAT OF BUDDHISM

The greatest attraction of Ulan-Ude is the Ivolginsk Datsan, the seat of Buddhism in Russia, 30 km (19 miles) west of the town. The temple was opened in the 1960s ostensibly to show the world that religious tolerance existed in the Soviet Union. In reality, it was all a charade. The KGB had secretly sent a dozen agents to Ulan Bator, Mongolia, to become sufficiently familiar with the rituals of Buddhism to open the datsan. The KGB agents enjoyed large *dachas* in the mountains and were driven to the temple each day in *Zil* limousines. In the late 1980s the pretence became reality as more and more curious Buryats attended the temple. The temple, modest by the standards of Tibet or other Buddhist centres, is in a splendid setting with snow-capped peaks towering over the plain and a small mountain stream running nearby. Its colourful interior contains numerous images of the Buddha, Buryat paintings and a museum. Today, it may be visited without official supervision. Follow the path along the datsan's inside walls: the prayer wheel (spin it gently as you pass) is said to write a prayer 1,000 times for each spin. You may visit a service at the main temple – generally held in the morning – but keep to the rear of the building as the main part is reserved for the lamas.

Republic of Buryatia

On the east side of Baikal, the capital of the Republic of Buryatiya, **Ulan-Ude** ⓰, is beginning to discover its identity having been closed to foreigners until 1988. Perhaps no city in Russia today shows the diversity of the country better than Ulan-Ude. Buryat culture and language, which bear a close resemblance to those of Mongolia, were nearly extinguished under Soviet rule. Today, though 50 percent of the population are Buryats, few people can speak Buryat. However, young people are beginning to show an interest in Buddhism and the Dalai Lama has visited Ulan-Ude to encourage the re-education of the Buryat people.

Ulan-Ude lies on the badly polluted Selenga River, which winds its way through Mongolia to Lake Baikal. To the south, a desert stretches to the Mongolian border. To the north a range of mountains frames the southern shore of Lake Baikal. It is laid out like the archetypal Soviet city. The central square, an enormous stretch of empty asphalt, is overlooked by what is surely the biggest head of Lenin in the world. On the outskirts, wooden homes are common, reminders of the city's status as a Cossack frontier town.

Diamond-studded Yakutia

In theory you could reach Yakutsk from Baikal by water; in practice it would, at best, be very difficult. The mighty Lena river meanders north from Baikal around the Udokan Mountains towards the Verkhoyansky Mountains where it widens and continues north to the Arctic Ocean. Where the Lena widens, the town of **Yakutsk** ⓱, which dates from the first wave of Russian exploration in 1632, can be found. It is best reached by air on regular flights from Moscow, Irkutsk and Vladivostok.

Map on page 260

Cakes on sale in a Siberian market.

BELOW: at work in all weather on a natural gas plant.

Today, visitors to Vladivostok can stroll along the docks and freely shoot pictures of the naval fleet – a stark contrast to the days when a careless photo could trigger an international incident – but the locals may still scold you for doing so.

BELOW: prisoner in Sakhalin, 1894.

Like most outposts of its kind, Yakutsk was founded by Cossacks, working to please the tsar, who permitted them freedom in an empire of serfs. Later it became one of the cruellest places of exile, notorious for its brutal cold.

The city might have remained a simple outpost had it not been for the discovery of enormous mineral riches in the region, including diamonds, gold, oil and gas. Today Yakutsk is the capital of the Yakutiya Republic, a swathe of far northern Siberia covering more than 2.6 million sq. km (1 million sq. miles).

Yakutsk itself is a dull Soviet city, but it offers an excellent base for exploring the native Yakut and Evenki villages on the tundra. The town has 15 museums: there is a fine **Muzei Istorii i Kultury Narodov Severa imeri Yaroslavskovo** (Museum of North Peoples; prospekt Lenina 5/2; tel: 41122-422689; open Wed–Sun 10am–5pm), providing a glimpse of how Yakutiya's native peoples lived before the Soviet era. **The Permafrost Institute** (Merzlotnaya ulitsa 1; tel: 41122-334423) operates tours only upon request, taking visitors into its underground research chamber, beneath the earth's frozen crust.

You can take a hydrofoil to **Lenskiye Stolby** (Lena Pillars), giant rock formations about an hour upstream from Yakutsk. Cruises on the Lena and a trip to **Derevnya Yakutsk**, the old village of Yakutsk, are also offered.

Far Eastern ports

Nakhodka  was a Soviet-era solution to the problem of closing Vladivostok to foreign shipping in the 1950s. It was the commercial port and the end of the Trans-Siberian Railway line, while Vladivostok was the naval port.

Taking a plane or train further east will bring you to **Vladivostok** at the base of the Sikhote-Alin Mountains, bordered by China to the west and the Sea of Japan to the east. Vladivostok is sometimes called the "San Francisco of Russia", a reference to its Pacific location and its steep streets. But that's as far as the comparison goes with this Soviet naval city, which was completely closed to foreign shipping between 1958 and 1991. It was first taken from the Chinese in 1860 and has since become the country's main port in the Far East.

The twists and turns over the steep streets offer visitors many beautiful views of the city and the ocean. The climate is pleasant with summer temperatures reaching 20°C (68°F) and winter lows rarely dipping below -15°C (5°F).

Volcanic isles

The **Kurilskiye Ostrova** (Kurile Islands), a chain of volcanic islands extending from Kamchatka to the northern Japanese island of Hokkaido, would probably be unheard of outside Sakhalin if they were not the subject of a territorial dispute between Russia and Japan over the South Kuriles, which Japan claims, but which Russia took in World War II.

The islands are stunningly beautiful all year round, with towering volcanoes sloping into violent seas. The Russians have done very little to develop them, except for creating a number of small fishing villages and a naval base situated on Shikotan. The journey by sea takes one and a half days from the closest port,

Korsakov ㉑, on the island of Ostrov Sakhalin. Ships also leave daily from Vladivostok, weather permitting, and take three days.

With a population of 6,000, **Yuzhno-Kurilsk** ㉒, a fishing village on the island of **Ostrov Kunashir**, is the capital of the Kurile chain, and the most accessible destination in the group. At its southern tip, the island is within 12 km (7 miles) of Japan, whose hills are clearly visible from most points on the island. The village itself is little more than a maze of rickety huts and a fishing plant.

The island has a small **Muzei Yestestvoznaniya** (Museum of Natural History) in the town square. At the entrance a Japanese face is carved into a stone, a compelling reminder of the island's former landlords. From Yuzhno-Kurilsk it is possible to arrange boat trips to nearby **Ostrov Shikotan** ㉓, the most beautiful island in the chain, with a sunny micro-climate.

Russia's Alaska

The island of **Ostrov Sakhalin** ㉔ has long held an exotic allure for Russians as a remote land of possibilities. Rich in natural resources such as oil, gas and non-ferrous metals, it is Russia's Alaska. Passed between Japan and Russia during the 19th and 20th centuries, Russia finally occupied Sakhalin in the last days of World War II. The capital of **Yuzhno-Sakhalinsk** ㉕ was founded in 1881 at the base of Mount Bolshevik. Surrounding the city are virgin forests blanketing mountainous terrain, which provide a spectacular backdrop.

It is difficult to imagine what would draw a foreign tourist to **Magadan** ㉖, a remote gulag centre in northeast Siberia where winter temperatures can plummet to −65°C (−85°F). It was first named on maps in 1939 and it relies on building materials manufacture and a small fishing industry. ❑

Map on page 260

TIP

The best time to visit Yakutsk is between June and August. On 25 June the city hosts the Ysykh festival, a colourful celebration of native Yakut culture.

BELOW: a young resident in remote Yakutsk.

LAKE BAIKAL – THE PEARL OF SIBERIA

The most beautiful jewel in Siberia's crown is Baikal Ozero, the world's deepest lake, which attracts scientists and tourists alike to its shores

Lake Baikal's crystal clear waters cut a north-south swathe through the mountains and taiga of Siberia, creating a rich habitat for a flora and fauna unique to this region.

Baikal is roughly the size of Belgium. It covers 32,000 sq km (12,352 sq. miles), holds one-fifth of the world's fresh water and is more than a mile deep (1,637 metres/5,370 ft).

SPECIES OF THE LAKE

The lake's most renowned resident, the *nerpa* (Baikal seal), is believed to have been trapped here when the last Ice Age retreated. The seal then slowly adapted to the freshwater environment of its new home. Today, the grey-coloured *nerpa* is a protected species, but the Russian authorities still allow 6,000 to be slaughtered each year for their fur and blubber. About 60,000 *nerpas* inhabit Baikal.

More than 50 species of fish can be found in the waters. Among the more interesting fish is the *golomyanka*, which lives up to 1.5 km (1 mile) below the surface and gives birth to living young. The highly prized Baikal sturgeon can produce up to 9 kg (20 lb) of caviar on reaching maturity, and the *omul*, a member of the salmon family, often appears on the menu as a local speciality.

◁ **HOME FROM HOME**
Wooden homes are typical of the lakeside villages. The Museum of Wooden Architecture near Irkutsk contains fine examples of Siberian buildings.

△ **FINE BALANCE**
The construction of the Irkutsk hydroelectric station in the 1950s led to a rise of 1 metre (3 ft) in the depth of water and caused serious ecological problems.

◁ WHAT'S IN A NAME?
The word Baikal is derived from the Turkish word Bai-Kul, meaning "a rich lake". The lake has been designated a UNESCO World Heritage Site.

△ OBSERVATION POSTS
For the past 50 years Irkutsk State University has been making observations of the Baikal biota at Bolshyie Koty and on the Angara biostation.

OUT AND ABOUT ON THE LAKE

Helicopter trips, horse-riding, hiking and fishing are just some of the summer excursions on offer around Baikal, while in winter, troika rides, skiing and skating top the list – but don't expect anything sophisticated. Irkutsk is the best launching point for trips. Hydrofoils and ferries make regular journeys to lakeside settlements in summer, and travel agencies such as Irkutsk-Baikal Intourist can tailor packages to suit. The southwestern side of the lake is the most accessible. One of the best places to view what is said to be the oldest lake in the world (20 million years) is from the hill behind the Limnological Institute at Listvyanka, 66 km (41 miles) east of Irkutsk. For the more adventurous, a trip to the Khamar-Daban mountains south of Baikal offers the chance to explore taiga, alpine tundra and glacial lakes. Heading northwest is Olkhon Island, a favourite holiday spot for Russians where the *nerpa* seals can be glimpsed off its north coast.

▽ MAKING A LIVING
Fishing, forestry and fur farming are the main occupations. The climate around the lake is ideal for mink and sable; fox and beaver trapping is common.

▷ ICY WATERS
Lake Baikal is fed by more than 300 rivers, and drained by just one, the Angara. For five months of the year it is frozen to a depth of 10 metres (30 ft).

▽ LAKE RESIDENT
The sturgeon *Acipenser baeri* inhabits the shallows of Lake Baikal. It takes between 18 and 20 years to reach maturity.

BELARUS AND UKRAINE

These two independent states share their roots with Russia in the once grand principality of Kievan Rus

Belarus and Ukraine have always been considered close cousins to Russia. Their languages are close enough to be almost mutually comprehensible. Their political fates have been interwoven for centuries. Kiev, the "Mother of Russian cities", was at the heart of the first Eastern Slavic state of Kievan Rus. With the rise of Muscovy, much of Belarus and Ukraine was brought under Tsarist control and ruled from St Petersburg. Next to Belarus (White Russia), Ukraine became known as "Malorossiya" (Little Russia), an epithet that illustrated its provincial and dependent status. More recently, the three countries formed the core of the Soviet Union, making up half of its population and a much greater proportion of its leaders.

Yet to see Belarus and Ukraine only as adjuncts to the powerful Russian state is to see only a part of the story. This historic border-land has two faces; one looks towards Moscow and the east, but the other – smaller but still recognisable – is turned to the west and towards Europe. Much of the history of Ukraine and Belarus, and the origins of many current difficulties, can be found in the unfinished dialogue between the two sides of their national characters.

With independence in 1991, Ukrainians and Belarusians had the opportunity to take charge of their own affairs, maybe even to move out from under Russia's shadow. It was not a comfortable experience. By the mid 1990s, Belarus had re-created its own brand of Soviet-style authoritarianism; by the beginning of the 21st century, after the fall of Milosevic, Belarus was left alone as Europe's least demo-cratic state. Ukraine, on the other hand, was keen to avoid being left on the margins of the continent, but remained unsure of its vocation and hesitant in its actions. While Ukraine's neighbours in Central Europe were following a fairly direct path from state planning to a market economy, Ukraine's own road took in more than a few twists, turns and dead ends. It is still not clear where this journey will lead: the economic situation remains critical, and wealth and political power have been concentrated in few hands. And with Viktor Yushenko's victory in the 2004 presidential election, the Ukraine's future, and its relationship with Russia, remains as unclear as it has ever been.

Meanwhile, the visitor will find much of interest: Orthodox cathe-drals, Tatar palaces, Polish castles and elegant Hapsburg frontier towns sit side by side with grandiose Soviet developments and mon-uments to the fallen of two World Wars. Kiev is a thriving modern city and cultural centre; hiking, fishing and *dacha* life are features of the countryside; and in season the Black Sea resorts buzz with hol-iday atmosphere and the legendary hospitality of the people. ❑

PRECEDING PAGES: the trident is the symbol of Ukrainian independence; Yalta's waterfront, Crimea. **LEFT:** the dramatic Lastochkino Gnezdo (Swallow's Nest), near Yalta, was built in 1912 for a German oil magnate.

BELARUS AND UKRAINE: A SHORT HISTORY

The history of these two countries is both longer and initially grander
than that of Russia, which subsequently overwhelmed them

Belarus and Ukraine owe their origins to strategic geography. The Varangians (Vikings) who opened up trade links between the Baltic Sea and the Black Sea in the 9th century rowed rather than walked, and therefore the most convenient route was along rivers from the Baltic. The Dvina was the most heavily travelled river, because it put traders within porterage distance of the Dnipro (Dneiper) for the journey to Byzantium.

The Varangians acted as catalysts for the development of the early Slav settlements along these rivers. Those settlements on the first leg of the outward journey, the most notable being the principality of Polatsk, were the nucleus of the future Belarus.

The Dnipro leg was dominated by Kiev, and it was on the territory of present-day Ukraine, with a fusion of Scandinavian and Slav influences, that the first great regional political entity was formed in the 9th century – Kievan Rus.

Kievian Rus

In its heyday before the Mongol invasion in the 13th century, Kievan Rus had a place in the first rank of European states. Remarkably soon after Prince Volodymyr's (Vladimir's) conversion to Christianity in 988, Kiev boasted a cathedral modelled on the Hagia Sophia in Constantinople and had more than 400 churches.

From this ancient city sprang the roots of the Russian state. Only in 1050 did the northern Rus principalities, such as Novgorod began to break from Kiev. The region then fell under the "Tatar Yoke", the wave of Mongol invaders that swept across the steppes in the 13th century. A declining Kiev was also sacked by the Mongols in 1240, and only St Sophia's and a couple of hundred houses were left standing.

PRECEDING PAGES: *The Battle of Balaklava, 25 October 1854*, lithograph by E. Walker and O. Norrie. **LEFT:** Ukrainian musicians. **RIGHT:** Tatar couple.

Maintaining traditions

The traditions of Kievan Rus were absorbed by the principalities of Galicia and Volhynia, whose location further to the west allowed them to escape such close Tatar attention. In the mid-

14th century, Galicia and Volhynia ceased to exist: Poland conquered Galicia and Lithuania took Volhynia, including Kiev. These regions, now in western Ukraine, were crucial through the centuries in maintaining Ukrainian cultural and political traditions against the influences of the might of the Russian Empire.

The decline of Kievan Rus in the 13th and 14th centuries coincided with the rise of neighbouring Lithuania and Poland to the north and west, and Muscovy (Russia) to the east. From that time up until the present, and apart from brief periods of self-assertion, the fate of Ukraine (the "borderland") and Belarus was in the hands of these and other foreign powers.

The Cossacks

Incorporation within the Lithuanian state and then the Polish-dominated commonwealth did much to expose Ukraine and Belarus to Western European influences. Poland, ardent champion of the Roman Church, did its utmost to bring Ukraine and Belarus within the Catholic fold.

A compromise between Catholicism and Orthodoxy eventually emerged in the shape of the "Uniate" (Greek Catholic) Church, which retained the Orthodox ritual while acknowledging the temporal power of the Pope, but this development did nothing to ease the religious tensions with Eastern Orthodoxy. Many

Ukrainians and Belarusians remained to take up the new faith and to work under the Polish landlords; others escaped to the periphery of the commonwealth, to the plains of the Dnipro basin and the home of the Ukrainian Cossacks.

The Ukrainian Cossacks were originally a collection of outlaws and fugitives, surviving by hunting, fishing and by grazing cattle along the dangerous border territories between the Polish Commonwealth, Russian Muscovy and the Ottoman Tatars to the south. With time they took on forms of political organisation, including the self-governing entity formed beyond the *porozhy* (rapids) of the Dnipro, which became known as the Zaporizhean Sich. Social

and religious resentment at Polish rule provided the catalyst, and it was from Zaporizhe in 1648 that the Cossack leader, Bogdan Khmelnitsky, launched the great Ukrainian offensive that succeeded in driving the Poles from Ukraine.

Khmelnitsky's dream of a Ukrainian state – the Cossack Hetmanate – was threatened from the west by a Poland eager to reverse its stunning defeat, and was also vulnerable to Tatar incursions from the south. So it was in 1654, by an agreement concluded at Pereyaslav, that Khmelnitsky proceeded to carve a somewhat ambiguous niche for himself in Ukrainian folklore by turning to Muscovy for assistance.

The rise of the Russian Empire

The assurances of autonomy included in the Pereyaslav agreement were undermined as Moscow extended its control. At first Ukraine was split along the line of the Dnipro, with the left (east) bank under Russian control, and the right (west) bank, along with most of Belarus, remaining under the Polish Commonwealth.

However, Poland was subject to partition three times at the end of the 18th century, and Catherine the Great delighted in "recovering" Belarus and most of Ukraine. The exception was Galicia which became part of the Austro-Hungarian Empire, a fact that explains the very different architectural styles in such western Ukrainian cities as Lviv and Chernivtsi.

Catherine's attention was also drawn to the strategic goal of securing access to the Black Sea. With the help of Alexander Suvorov, Russia's most successful general, Ottoman forces were pushed out of southern Ukraine and Crimea became part of the Russian Empire.

Under the Russian Empire, the Ukrainian and Belarusian lands lost much of their former national distinctiveness. The territories were reorganised into provinces governed from St Petersburg, conversion to Russian Orthodoxy was encouraged, and any signs of nationalism were dealt with harshly by the tsarist authorities.

At the westernmost edge of the empire, Belarus, in particular, was in the front-line of any conflicts with other European powers. In the 19th century the territory had to withstand the invading armies of Napoleon; 140 years later it bore the brunt of Hitler's "Operation Barbarossa" against the Soviet Union. Therein lies the explanation for the singular lack of historical buildings in Belarus.

The Crimean War

During the mid-19th century Ukraine's Crimea became the focus of a long and bitter war between the Russian Empire on one side and Britain, France, Ottoman Turkey, Piedmont and Austria on the other. The Crimean War marked the end of 40 years of comparative European tranquillity following the defeat of Napoleon, and reflected the Western Powers distrust of Russian expansionism and in particular Tsar Nicholas's designs on a declining Ottoman Empire.

THE LIGHT BRIGADE

Theirs not to reason why,
Theirs but to do and die:
Into the valley of Death
Rode the six hundred.

— ALFRED, LORD TENNYSON

Personal animosities and misunderstandings among senior officers sent the Light Brigade on a suicidal mission into a valley lined on three sides by Russian artillery. Almost half were killed on the spot. The appalling conditions endured by troops were brought to public attention by the first generation of war reporters. They were alleviated in turn by the heroic efforts of nurses, most famously by Florence Nightingale, and then by the long-overdue reappraisal of provisions for humanitarian treatment of soldiers.

The Allies headed for war expecting a swift victory over the Russian forces, but in the event the war was long, bloody and hard won. One of its most famous episodes was the misguided Charge of the Light Brigade during the Battle of Balaklava, immortalised by Alfred Tennyson's haunting refrain about the futility of the charge (*see above*). The 600 in question were some of the most venerated troops in the British Army, the 11th Hussars, whose misfortune was to be subject to the particular failings of a command system based on patronage rather than merit.

LEFT: a 17th-century engraving of a Cossack.
ABOVE: nursing the wounded in the Crimean War.

The 20th century

As the Russian Empire collapsed during World War I, national movements in Ukraine and Belarus fought against strong opposition for independence. Ukrainians received their first taste of modern self-government with the proclamation of the Ukrainian National Republic in 1918, governed from Kiev, and a Western Ukrainian National Republic based on the territories that had been part of the Austro-Hungarian Empire. The republics even agreed to unify in 1919, but by then the tide of events was already turning against independence.

As the Bolsheviks consolidated their hold within Russia, so Poland was reasserting its historical claim to western Ukraine and Belarus. Fighting between these two ancient adversaries was concluded only with the Treaty of Riga in 1921. The western Ukrainian and Belarusian regions became part of Poland. The Ukrainian Soviet Socialist Republic (SSR), with its capital in Kharkiv in the east, and the Belarusian SSR became in 1922 founding members of the Union of Soviet Socialist Republics (USSR).

Starvation and deportation

Between the wars the reinstalled masters of Ukraine and Belarus did everything in their power to suppress any independent national

instincts. In particular, Stalin's genocidal instincts wreaked havoc in Soviet Ukraine. After a period of calm in the 1920s when Ukrainian language use grew, Stalin's assumption of power coincided with a vicious offensive against the two social bases of Ukrainian nationalism – the peasants and the educated classes.

The cost of the remarkable pace of Soviet industrialisation under the first five-year plans was borne by the peasantry. While iron and steel furnaces and hydroelectric plants were being built, the forced collectivisation of agriculture destroyed traditional country life. Impossible production quotas were enforced at gunpoint. Forced to give up all their food to the state, 7 million Ukrainians died in the famine of 1932 and 1933. Purges aimed at eliminating "nationalist deviation" resulted in the repression or execution of four-fifths of Ukraine's cultural elite.

Stalin's brutality encouraged many Ukrainians and Belarusians to regard Hitler as a liberator. But, far from helping them achieve self-rule, the Nazis regarded them as fit only for servitude, and millions were transported to the Reich as slave labour to support the German war effort. Those who remained were caught in the direct clash between Nazi and Soviet forces. More than 8 million Ukrainians and Belarusians died – and hostilities didn't end with the Nazi defeat in 1945. Hundreds of thousands of real and alleged Nazi collaborators, former German prisoners of war and repatriated slave workers, Ukrainian "bourgeois nationalists", and others suspected of disloyalty were sent to Siberian concentration camps. The Ukrainian Insurgent Army, continued its

A QUESTION OF IDENTITY

Questions of Ukrainian and Belarusian identity lead straight back to their complex national histories. For much of the last 1000 years they would not have called themselves Ukrainians or Belarusians at all, but *Rusyny* (Ruthenians). This identified them with the lands and religion of Kievan Rus, the original East Slavic state. However, as Muscovy grew in power it came to claim also the historical rights to the legacy of Kiev, and the image of Rus became intertwined with the growth of the Russian state.

This was a crucial transformation, since it was on this basis that Moscow took up the imperial mission to reunite all the "Russian" lands. The *Rusyny* were deemed to be

Russian – whether Little Russians (Ukrainians), or White Russians (Belarusians) – and any cultural differences ascribed to the period of "forced" separation and the influence of the hostile Catholic Poles. This interpretation underpinned tsarist and Soviet policies of russification, and today some Russians still deny that Ukraine and Belarus are "real" nations.

Many Ukrainians and Belarusians take a different view, taking their lead from a process of national identification that began in the 19th century. Even those who would not call themselves nationalists still readily volunteer an opinion on how they differ from the Russians.

guerrilla activity against the Soviet authorities until the 1950s.

Independence and beyond

During Soviet times, the Ukraine was known as the "bread basket" of Europe, and two leaders of the USSR, Nikita Khrushchev and Leonid Brezhnev, were born within its borders. Belarus was portrayed as a shining example of Soviet values, its new industries and factories held up as paragons of socialist planning, its people as model Soviet citizens.

After Stalin's death in 1953, a Ukrainian, Khrushchev, became the leader of the Soviet Union, and in 1954 he made a "gift" of the Crimea to his motherland.

Throughout the 1960s and '70s, Ukraine and Belarus, while existing as separate republics within the USSR, and despite the rumblings of discontent from intellectuals in Kiev and western Ukraine, were fully assimilated into the Soviet Union, and life there differed very little from that of life in Russia itself.

The first real moment of outright disapproval of the Soviet system came with the Chernobyl disaster in 1986. The power plant was just 97 km (60 miles) from Kiev and the Ukrainian capital was only saved from a lethal dose of radiation by prevailing winds. The authorities had concealed the danger from the population, and a parade even went ahead in the city. Belarus was less lucky, and its population bore the brunt of the ill wind; cancer rates soared and vast tracts of land become unsuitable for agriculture.

These events, combined with the ascendancy of Mikhail Gorbachev to power, led to the rebirth of nationalist movements, and after the failure of the 1991 coup by communist hardliners, independence was soon declared by both countries.

With the collapse of the USSR, both the Ukraine and Belarus were faced with the unexpected problems of independence. Crime rates rocketed, and there then came the harsh economic lessons that led to shortages and the once unthinkable sight of beggars in the streets.

In Belarus, Alexandr Lukashenko, a former Soviet collective farm manger, ran an election campaign in 1994 that played upon the peoples' nostalgia for the USSR, and was duly elected to the presidency. His tenure has been authoritarian, to say the least, and a referendum held in 2004 to determine if he would be able to stand for a third term was widely condemned by international observers and has turned Belarus into a virtual pariah state.

The Ukraine met independence with enthusiasm, but Ukrainians quickly realised that this was not enough to feed the population, ironic for a country renowned for its extremely fertile black earth. Mismanagement and outright corruption typified the presidency of Leonid Kuchma, and when his unofficial successor,

Viktor Yanukovitch, was voted into power in 2004, peaceful protesters took to the streets in their tens of thousands, claiming that the elections had been rigged, in what became known as the Orange Revolution. Under pressure from all sides, the authorities eventually relented, and in an election re-run, Viktor Yushchenko, a Western-leaning liberal, was voted into office.

The future is uncertain for both Lukashenko's Belarus, and the promised European state that Yushchenko has promised to build in the Ukraine, but the whims and ambiguities of history are things with which the people of both countries are all too familiar. ❏

LEFT: vast numbers of Ukrainians were deported to Siberian labour camps following World War II.
RIGHT: a reminder of Soviet rule in Belarus.

LIFE TODAY IN BELARUS AND UKRAINE

The transition from Soviet rule has not been easy: Belarus has played safe with a Soviet-style economy while Ukraine struggles with the free market

For many Russians, the state of affairs in which Belarus and Ukraine exist as separate states is considered to be a ludicrous, temporary phenomenon. Indeed, their very names, the Ukraine means, roughly, "On the edge (of Russia)", and Belarus "White Rus", indicate the extent to which these two countries are bound up with Russia.

However, Belarus and Ukraine, despite their common Soviet backgrounds and eastern Slavic heritage, have both begun moving away from Moscow's sphere of influence, albeit in very different directions. Belarus, under the autocratic rule of Alexandr Lukashenko, a former Soviet collective farm manager, is now considered to be Europe's only remaining dictatorship; the referendum in which he won the right to a third term in power, and the elections themselves in 2004, were widely dismissed by the international community as staged and undemocratic.

Ukrainians rejected the results of the 2004 election that would have brought the Russophile Viktor Yanukovitch, the choice of Leonid Kuchma, the outgoing president, to power. In protests lasting nearly a month, demonstrators in Kiev and the Ukrainian-speaking parts of the country, took to the streets claiming that the election had been fixed. Meanwhile, with shades of a spy novel, dioxin poisoning was found to be the cause of a face-disfiguring illness of Yushchenko, who accused Ukrainian authorities of trying to poison him in the run-up to the vote. Yushchenko's blood and tissue was found to have concentrations of dioxin 1,000 times above normal levels. Encouraged by the West, the protesters drove Yanukovitch from office and in a second round of elections, Yushchenko, the leader of the so-called "Orange Revolution" was elected. The Ukraine had turned its face firmly towards the West.

PRECEDING PAGES: facade of Shevchenko University, Kiev. **LEFT:** children at play, Platz Jakub Kolas, Minsk. **RIGHT:** young woman from Odessa.

Soviet legacy

The sudden and largely unpredicted break-up of the USSR in 1991 left Ukraine and Belarus facing an independence that they were largely unprepared for. The Ukrainians at least wel-

comed it, overwhelmingly approving the split from the Soviet Union in a referendum, yet soon after their departure from the USSR, their economies all but collapsed as neither country was equipped to cope with the sudden pressure created by free-market forces. The country suffered from hyper inflation and savings were wiped out overnight. Belarus on the other hand was never a passionate believer in independence, and Lukashenko, aware of the people's desire for order, played upon nostalgia for the USSR to with the presidential election of 1994.

The legacy of the Soviet Union, even now, 15 years after the break-up of the USSR, is still very much evident in both countries. In the negative sense this is reflected in the culture of corruption and bribery inherited from Soviet times. As in Russia, many laws from the Soviet era still remain on the statute books, tying both countries up in red tape and hindering economic progress. In Ukraine, Yushchenko has promised to make a break from these reminders, legal and otherwise, of the Soviet past, and his prime minister, Yulia Tymoshenko, has vowed to tackle these problems in the first few months of the new government's rule. It remains to be seen if they will stick to their words, or if this is merely more of the empty posturing intended to curry favour with the West and its investors.

of office expired, Viktor Yanukovitch became the status quo's candidate for the presidency. Yanukovitch had been imprisoned twice; in 1968 and 1970, for robbery and bodily injury respectively. His opponent was Viktor Yushchenko, a Western-leaning politician with an American wife.

The election campaign that followed was one of the most vicious to ever take place on post-Soviet territory, culminating in the bizarre transformation of Yushchenko from a youthful, handsome and charismatic candidate into something resembling an extra from a zombie film – Yushchenko maintained that poison led to his

Another legacy of Soviet times are the strong family ties which people enjoy. Not that there is much choice. With failing health systems and poverty threatening many people, the family is the only support structure which can be relied upon for assistance.

Election problems

The eventual election of Yushchenko in Ukraine in 2004 was seen as a bloodless revolution. Leonid Kuchma's presidency had become vastly unpopular, and there was even evidence to suggest that he had been involved, or at least aware of, the murder/disappearance of a journalist. When his second and final term

facial disfigurement; the president's supporters maintained that he was merely suffering from a rare skin condition.

When the results came in, and it emerged that Yanukovitch had won the presidency, Yushchenko and his supporters refused to accept the result, claiming mass falsification of the poll, pointing to reports of 100 percent turn out in some pro-Yanukovitch areas as evidence. There then began an occupation of Maidan Nezalezhnosti (Independence Square) by protesters who vowed to stay until the election results were annulled. Eventually the Supreme Court declared the elections invalid, and ordered that they be rerun. This time, Yushchenko gained a majority of the vote, severely embarrassing President Putin who had backed Yanukovitch and had already twice congratulated him on the presidency.

In Belarus, in 2004, a referendum to decide whether or not the serving president, Alexandr Lukashenko, should be allowed to stand for a third term was the subject of criticism by electoral monitoring groups. Lukashenko won 77 percent of the vote, and in no uncertain terms told the West to stop interfering in Belarus' internal affairs. Immediately after the referendum there were protest rallies, but these were quickly clamped down on, and never looked like posing a serious threat to the established order.

HARD FACTS

In the decade after independence the Ukrainian economy grew 10 percent every year, compared to an annual reduction of 1.5 percent for Belarus.

"Europe's last dictatorship"

Lukashenko's rule, although perhaps not quite deserving the title of "Europe's Last Dictatorship", which has been bestowed upon it by the United States, is, at the very least, one of the most authoritarian regimes in Europe. Disappearances of journalists are common place, there are allegations of state-run death squads, opposition politicians are imprisoned and, as a visit to the country will show you, Lukashenko is a figure who dominates the country in a way that is extremely unusual for a 21st-century European country.

The news is dominated by the president, his every utterance and proclamation on a variety of subjects repeated in portentous tones on prime-time TV by obsequious newsreaders. The overall impression is that one has stepped back in time, and that the Soviet Union never ceased to exist.

And, like all dictators, Lukashenko is more than adept at inventing new rules that reflect his own personal concerns. When a student group held a demonstration in Minsk, wearing Lukashenko masks to avoid identification by the state security service, he responded by making it an offence to wear masks bearing the president's image. Just a small thing, perhaps, a minor footnote, nothing compared to the disappearances, but it is the daily catalogue

of events like this which gives the country a less than free and open atmosphere.

Although Lukashenko, or "Batka" – "Father" – as he is known among his supporters, once enjoyed genuine popularity in Belarus, especially in rural areas, even his traditional sources of support are now slipping away. In the cities, in Minsk in particular, the opposition, having taken its cue from the "Orange Revolution" in the Ukraine, is becoming bolder, sensing, perhaps, that it is only a matter of time before things

come to a head. Lukashenko, however, as he has already shown, is not afraid of using force to protect his power, and if change is to come, it is unlikely to be in the form of a simple repeat of the bloodless Ukrainian uprising.

Relations with Russia

For obvious political, economic and cultural reasons, ties with Russia, their vast neighbour to the east, are important for both Belarus and Ukraine. Events in Ukraine in 2004 were watched with both interest and concern in Russia. After all, many Russians have relatives in Ukraine, and there are hundreds of thousands of migrant workers in Russia at any given

---

LEFT: workers in Belarus spread hay before winter.
RIGHT: newly-weds pose for a photograph in front of the war memorial in Platz de Sieges, Minsk.

moment, not to mention the large permanent ethnic Ukrainian group within the country.

The election dispute in Russia was viewed as a struggle between the Russian- and Ukrainian-speaking areas of the country, aligned with Russia and the West respectively. The majority of Russians were suspicious of Yushchenko, seeing him as a pawn of the US and NATO. As would be expected, the reporting in Russia of the protests on Independence Square in Kiev was very different from elsewhere.

It is a little-known fact that in the former USSR it is quite common to pay students, pensioners and the unemployed to attend demonstrations, a tactic used by various groups within Russia itself. With this in mind, the images of candle-waving crowds facing down baton-wielding riot squads lacked much of the resonance and drama that they had in the West.

Politically, the whole event was an embarrassment for President Putin who, having backed Yanukovitch, was forced to stand by impotently as Russia's closest ally fell into the hands of the opposition. And when Yushchenko, despite his claims that he wished to maintain good relations with Russia, appointed Yulia Tymoshenko, a fervent Ukrainian nationalist with an outstanding

CHERNOBYL CATASTROPHE

Since April 1986, Ukraine and Belarus have been indelibly associated with a nuclear power station near their common border. Nearly 9 tonnes of radioactive material were released when an experiment with a reactor at Chernobyl in Ukraine went catastrophically wrong. The Soviet authorities evacuated 135,000 people; thousands more were exposed to radiation as the prevailing wind blew north across Belarus. While 32 people at or near the plant died within days, the longer term effects are still being felt in radiation-related illnesses and cancers. The reactor itself was covered with concrete and the plant surrounded by a 30-km (19-mile) exclusion zone.

court order for her arrest in Russia, as Prime Minister, it seemed that relations between the two countries would deteriorate sooner rather than later.

Ideology, so far, seems to have been tempered by pragmatism, and the first few months of Yushchenko's rule have shown a willingness on both sides to compromise, especially where business matters are concerned. The real test of relations may be yet to come. If the Ukraine shows signs of wanting to join NATO, then President Putin may feel that this is one step too far in the wrong direction, and the possibility of US troops being stationed in Kiev is something that Russia simply cannot allow.

As regards Belarus, its oft-mooted union with Russia seems doomed to remain just that. There are signs that Lukashenko may be becoming an embarrassment to Putin, and that the Kremlin is considering backing an opposition candidate in the 2006 presidential elections, perhaps figuring that it would be preferable to have "their man" in power in Belarus than letting events slide towards a repeat of the scenario in Ukraine – a result that would see them lose control over the country completely.

A TRADITION UPHELD

The name of the Belarussian state security service is still the KGB. Unlike Russia and the Ukraine, Belarus never made it a priority to dispense with the infamous name.

tradition, reflected in craft works and in the specialities of their traditional food. In Ukraine, *salo* is particularly popular. Best described as lard or pig fat, it is considered a delicacy. Normally, small slices of the white fat are eaten with black bread, raw garlic, herbs and vodka. It is an acquired taste, to say the least. *Samagon*, home-made vodka, is popular everywhere, the best examples are far better than anything the shops can offer, while the worst are foul-smelling concoctions that will leave you with a splitting headache.

Living off the land

In both Ukraine and Belarus, once you travel outside of the cities, the countryside is spotted with *dachas* (cabins) and allotments, and it is this ability to grow their own food which has enabled many people to maintain some degree of independence from the state by feeding themselves and selling what is left over at farmers' markets.

The Ukraine is blessed with rich "black earth", and both countries enjoy a rich rural

To test *samagon*, put a match to it and see how well it burns. If there is a clear blue flame it is good quality; a yellow flame or oily smoke is not a good sign. DIY *samagon* instruction books are on sale everywhere.

Ice fishing is also popular in both countries during their harsh winters. This consists of walking out onto a frozen river or lake, drilling a hole, and hoping for a bite. Every year, when the thaws come, countless fishermen float off on ice floes, the overstretched rescue services not always reaching all of them in time.

In the summer, the cities empty at weekends and public holidays as people rush to their *dachas*, escaping from the problems of city life.

FAR LEFT: the ruins of the Chernobyl nuclear plant.
LEFT: Ukrainians are tested for radiation.
ABOVE: relaxing in the Black Sea resort of Odessa.

The language issue

Both the Ukrainian and Belarusian languages are closely related to Russian: all three languages are lineal descendents of the Slavic language used in Kievan Rus. Both Ukrainian and Belarusian, to a Russian speaker, have a "rustic" feel, a result of their popularity in the villages and countryside. In western Ukraine the dominant language is Ukrainian, while in the east the main language is Russian. However, attempts to paint the 2004 election dispute as a struggle for power between the two halves of the country are simplistic at best, a result of lazy journalism and Russian propaganda. The

fact was that while Yushchenko had support in the west of the country, and more tellingly, in Kiev (where Ukrainian is used interchangeably with Russian), Yanukovitch enjoyed no real fervent support in the east, with the exception of, perhaps, the mining region of Donetsk.

Russian is spoken and understood everywhere in Ukraine, whereas in the east many people only have a rudimentary knowledge of Ukrainian. It is Ukrainian though, not Russian, that you will find signposted at train stations, post offices, etc.

Russian is the language of music and film in both countries. Even the 2003 film *Okkupatsiya, Misterii* by Andrei Kudinenko, heralded as

a breakthrough for the Belarusian film industry, and promptly banned by Lukashenko, consisted of half Russian and half Belarusian dialogue, with subtitles for Russian speakers.

There has never really been any serious attempt to promote the local languages over Russian, and it is hard to see what could realistically be done without resorting to draconian measures that would only stir up resentment and discord. It is a little known fact that in many places in the Ukraine and Belarus, especially out of the main cities, people speak a mutant mixture of Russian and either Ukrainian or Belarusian, and it is perhaps this which sums up the position that both countries find themselves in today – linguistically and otherwise.

The new generation

A decade and a half has passed since the collapse of the Soviet Union, and a new generation has grown up remembering little of the former superpower. Indeed, a recent survey, carried out throughout Russia, Belarus and the Ukraine, found that children under 10 had little or no knowledge whatsoever of Lenin.

The new generation of Ukrainians and Belarusians resemble their counterparts in the West more than at any time in modern history. They have the same access to information, mostly via the Internet, and are as clued up with contemporary fashions as any group of twentysomethings anywhere in the world, though youth groups impact on the regions' politics in a manner young Western demonstrators could only dream of. The youth organisation PORA in the Ukraine was instrumental in the protests that led to Yushchenko coming to power, although, with an admirable unwillingness to compromise, they immediately went into opposition once the election results were in.

In Belarus, the ZUBR youth organisation has begun resistance to Lukashenko's rule, organising rallies and other events, yet Belarus is not the Ukraine, and the authorities are more than willing to use force to maintain order. The real test of ZUBR's mettle, and indeed the authorities, will surely come in 2006, during the protests that are sure to accompany the next presidential elections.

ABOVE: primary schoolchildren in Odessa, Ukraine.
RIGHT: Lenin's statue stands guard over a boulevard in Yalta on the southern shores of Crimea.

The road ahead

The immediate future for Belarus is uncertain. Revolution remains a distinct possibility, as Lukashenko's regime continues to lose its popularity. Russia may soon see fit to involve itself, if only by supporting an opposition candidate to remove the increasingly erratic Lukashenko.

For the Ukraine, the future rests on Yushchenko's ability to stabilise a country which has just experienced a bitter and divisive election struggle. A subtle touch may be what is needed, but Yushchenko appears bullish in his desire for justice. His government has begun attempts to bring the ex-president, Leonid Kuchma to justice for his alleged part in the murder of Georgiy Gongadze, the journalist whose headless corpse was discovered in woods near Kiev in 2001. This investigation looks set to shed light on a lot of murky deals.

The recent suicide of Yuri Kravchenko, the former interior minister, to whom Kuchma reportedly gave orders to "get rid of" the troublesome Gongadze, is surely only the first development in what promises to be a long and controversial process. It remains to be seen if this is the first step in an attempt to clean up the problems inherited from the Kuchma period, or just political infighting that will make little difference to the lives of the vast majority of Ukrainians.

The Ukraine has indicated its desire to become more closely integrated with Europe, an aspiration that is more than understandable. It is, after all, the largest country entirely situated within the continent. Integration into Europe, it is hoped, will improve the country's economic situation.

However, taking into account the geographical position that the country occupies, its relations with Russia, and, as ever in this part of the world, the past, this may not be as simple as some would like to believe. It is unthinkable to many in Russia that the Ukraine could move so far away politically from Moscow as to, like many former Warsaw Pact countries, require Russians to obtain visas in order to visit the country, and any move towards NATO will surely be met with more than the harsh words received by the Baltic states when they entered the Western defence alliance. ❑

CRIMEA: OUTPOST OF THE EMPIRE

The area where you might see the fewest signs of Ukrainian cultural life is Crimea, which was an autonomous region in the USSR before World War II, and then spent nine years as part of Russia before being transferred to Ukraine in 1954 – ostensibly to mark the 300th anniversary of Ukrainian "union" with Russia from the times of Bogdan Khmelnitsky.

Following the collapse of the USSR, Crimea became a touchstone for Russian sensitivity at the loss of empire. Although rumblings from the Crimean ethnic Russian community, which forms a majority on the peninsula, died down after 1995 this is still a potentially divisive issue.

In all the discussions over Crimea, it is easy to forget that its largest population before 1944 was that of the Crimea Tatars. Identified by Stalin as guilty of collaboration with the Nazis, the entire Tatar population was deported, mostly to Central Asia. This act of calculated barbarism was acknowledged as "groundless" even by the Soviets themselves in 1967, but it was to be another 20 years before the Tatars were allowed to begin returning home. The early returnees managed to rebuild homes while their Soviet roubles still had some value; more recent arrivals have had to settle in makeshift houses around Crimea's capital, Simferopol.

BELARUS

At the crossroads between Poland and Russia, ravaged by
warring armies, Belarus has survived as a nation in its own right
with much of historical interest to offer the visitor

Map
on page
302

M ost visitors arriving in Belarus from the West arrive through the border town of **Brest ❶**, a town that used to be one of the busiest thoroughfares in Eastern Europe. Its name in the 20th century was irrevocably linked with the conduct of war. It was in Brest-Litovsk at the end of World War I in March 1918 that revolutionary Russia agreed a separate peace with the German High Command, surrendering control over Ukraine, the Baltic States, Finland and Poland in exchange for an end to hostilities. This treaty was annulled with the final defeat of the Central Powers in November of the same year.

A more celebrated episode in Brest's modern history was its valiant resistance to Hitler's invading army of 1941. This is immediately apparent to those arriving by railway who see the commemorative plaque within the station building, all the more so to those who venture out of the city centre to the site of the old Brest fortress. Here the garrison of Soviet soldiers held on for six weeks after the Nazi invasion, persuading the German army commanders that the main body of their forces would have to bypass Brest in order to press on towards Minsk. The fortress, **Brestskaya Krepast**, was badly damaged in 1941, and was reduced to rubble as the retreating Nazis fought against the Red Army in 1944. Now partially rebuilt, it houses a museum honouring its Soviet defenders (open Wed–Sun 9.30am–6pm).

PRECEDING PAGES:
square in Minsk.
LEFT: World War II
memorial, Brest.
BELOW: central
Minsk.

Beyond Brest

On leaving Brest, the road to the east passes through the **Belovezhskaya Pushcha Nature Reserve ❷**, 85,000 hectares (210,000 acres) of unspoiled deep forest of the sort that once covered much of Europe. It is now the main sanctuary of the European bison, which was almost extinct by the mid-20th century but is now numbered by the thousand in this area alone. The quantity and variety of wildlife made this forest the favourite hunting ground of the Polish and then the Russian royal families; one remarkable Russian 12-day shoot produced a tally of 36 elks, 53 stags, 325 roebuck, 42 of the famed bison, and 138 wild boar.

Further to the north, nestling near the borders with Poland and Lithuania, is the town of **Hrodno ❸**. Although sacked by Tatars and Teutonic knights in the 13th and 14th centuries, Hrodno managed to avoid the contemporary fate of towns like Brest, being taken with relative ease by the advancing Nazis in 1941. This means that while Hrodno may not have "hero-city" status, it does offer some rare clues as to what pre-war Belarus must have looked like. Of the many historic buildings left standing, the modest 12th-century **Barysahlyebskaya Tserkva** (Church of Sts Barys and Hlyeb) is one of the oldest Belarusian structures left

TIP

Brest has the
unexpected distinction
of hosting one of
the finest Indian
restaurants in the
former Soviet Union.
The Restoran Indija is
at the junction of Karl
Marx and Hoholja
streets.

from the times of Kievan Rus. The castle overlooking the Neman River was
originally built by the Lithuanians in the 14th century, and the baroque **Farny
Sabor** (Farny Cathedral) in the town centre is a reminder of later Polish rule.

One of the most powerful influences in the Hrodno region were the
Radziwills, a family of Lithuanian magnates that rose to prominence when
Barbara Radziwill secretly married the Polish King Sigismund II in 1547.
Although Barbara died four years later, allegedly poisoned by Sigismund's
mother, the Radziwills continued to play a leading role in Polish politics until
the 20th century. The family owned large tracts of land in western Belarus, and
built the imposing castle at **Mir ❹** and the palace and fortress at **Njasvich ❺**.

Another more infamous product of the local Polish nobility was Felix
Dzerzhinsky, the fanatical Bolshevik revolutionary who went on to set up the
first Soviet secret police organisation, the Cheka, in 1917. Dzerzhinsky autho-
rised and supervised the arbitrary terror meted out against real and imagined enemies of the young Soviet state, thereby installing the machinery that was later

to become the KGB. The town of **Dzerzhinsk ❻**, near his birthplace to the west of Minsk, was named in his honour. Ironically, the previous name for this town, Koydanovo, referred to a Mongol commander who had also brought fear into the hearts of the local populace six centuries earlier.

Maps:
Area 302
City 304

The capital city of Minsk

The Belarusian capital, **Minsk ❼**, was a massive casualty of World War II, and anything that looks older than 1945 has been heavily restored or rebuilt. Minsk has grown dramatically since the war and its population has tripled since 1970, but even with its parks and pleasant open spaces it is still difficult to discern many traces of the old town. The 17th-century **Bernardzinskaya Tsarkva ❹** (Orthodox Cathedral of the Bernadine Monastery) and some renovated houses along **Troitskaya Naberezhna** (Trinity Embankment) by the Svislach River hint at a more distant past, but these now look strangely out of place among the monumental Soviet boulevards and apartment buildings.

Among the lost features of Minsk, as indeed of Belarus, are the Jews who became subjects of the Russian Empire as it expanded its borders in the 18th century. Tsarist restrictions on their rights meant that they were confined to the "Pale of Settlement", land along the western edge of the empire and the Black Sea coast. The Russian census of 1897 showed that 5 million Jews were living in the "pale". A hundred years of conflict and persecution, and the possibility of emigration to Israel, has meant that Jews now make up only 1 percent of Belarus's 10.4 million inhabitants.

It is difficult to underestimate the effect that World War II has had both on the landscape and on the Belarusian psyche. The **Muzey Istorii Byalikay -**

Instead of the usual array of national heroes, notes of the national currency feature government buildings and wild animals, including the hare (zaichik) that has become the currency's nickname.

BELOW: Brest Fortress has been partially rebuilt since its ruination in World War II.

Aychynnay Vayny (Museum of the Great Patriotic War; open Tues–Sun 11am–5pm), along the central Skaryna prospekt at No. 25, is a grim reminder of the horrors visited upon the country during the war, but in a country full of memorials the most impressive is still the complex at **Khatyn** ⑧, 60 km (37 miles) north of Minsk. It was built on the site of a village which was destroyed by the Nazis in 1943 as a reprisal for the murder of German soldiers. Only one person survived when the villagers of Khatyn were locked in a single burning building, and the statue of this survivor, Yuzif Kaminsky, dominates the centre of the complex. Accompanied by solemn funereal music, Khatyn also commemorates the hundreds of other Belarusian villages ruined by war and the quarter of the population that lost their lives between 1941 and 1945.

The tragic impression left by Khatyn is both compounded and compromised by the memory of another similar-sounding episode in Soviet history, the murder of thousands of Polish officers by the NKVD (forerunner of the KGB) in Katyn Forest near Smolensk in Russia in 1940. For many years the Soviet Government falsely claimed that the killings were perpetrated by the Nazis, and it was only in 1992 that the Russian Government released documents which proved the complicity of the Soviet authorities in the massacre and cover-up. A few years earlier, in 1988, Belarusians became aware of the atrocities committed by their own government, with the discovery of mass graves in Kurapaty Forest near Minsk containing at least half a million victims of Stalin's terror.

Ancient Belarus

Such wholesale destruction inflicted by modern conflicts means that very little remains of the country's earliest origins, when most of Belarus formed

---

TIP

A sensible precaution to take against the small risk of food contamination is to avoid wild mushrooms and berries, which retain radiation longer than other vegetation, and to steer clear of locally produced milk.

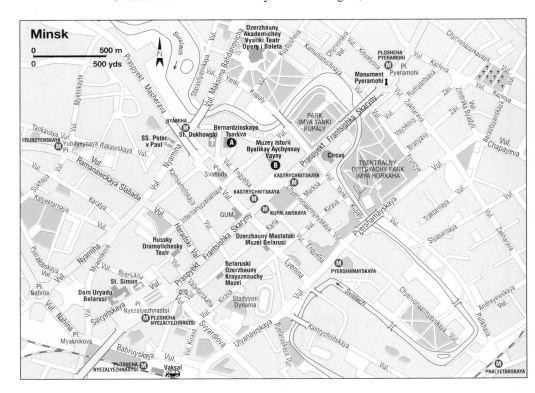

part of the kingdom of Kievan Rus, trading goods along the river grid that linked Byzantium with the Baltics.

The main exception is the quiet northern town of **Polatsk ❾**, whose location along the Dvina River made it the dominant regional centre from the 10th until the 12th century. The **Saphiyskyy Sabor** (Cathedral of St Sophia), originally modelled on the great cathedral in Kiev, was built during this period, although it was substantially rebuilt in baroque style under Polish rule. Polatsk remained influential into the Middle Ages, its ruling élite making enough money from agriculture to send their sons to study at the great European universities.

The influx of Renaissance and humanist influences into Belarus is apparent in the work of Frantsysk Skaryna of Polatsk. He held degrees from the universities of Krakow and Padua, and editions of his translation of the Bible into Belarusian in the 16th century were the first printed books not only in Belarus, but in the whole of Eastern Europe. His and other achievements are celebrated in Polatsk's **Muzey Belarushka Knihadrukavanni** (Museum of Historical Books and Printing; open Tues–Sat 10am–5pm).

Belarus was rarely promoted in Soviet times as a holiday destination and the resulting lack of attention given to tourism make it an occasionally challenging place to explore. Visitors have been put off by worries over the Chernobyl catastrophe whose effects were felt most strongly in southern Belarus, although Western organisations maintain that the risks associated with short stays in the country are insignificant. The national authorities have yet to put much effort into promoting an attractive external image. Yet in return for some patience and perseverance Belarus provides a fascinating portrait of a country that has seen the worst that the 20th century could offer, and survived. ❑

Maps:
Area 302
City 304

Minsk, along with such cities as Kiev and Odessa, was renowned as a major centre of Jewish influence and culture during the 18th and 19th centuries.

BELOW: market place, Minsk.

A COMMONWEALTH IS BORN

In December 1991 the once-mighty Soviet Union was laid to rest in the Belovezhskaya Pushcha Nature Reserve near Brest. In a lodge in the forest, the elected leaders of Russia, Ukraine and Belarus – Yeltsin, Kravchuk and Shushkevich – agreed to replace the USSR with a looser association, the Commonwealth of Independent States (CIS). They proposed Minsk as the administrative centre of the CIS, giving the Belarusian capital a chance to become the Brussels of eastern Europe. As it turned out, the commonwealth has been almost entirely ineffective. Twelve of the 15 former Soviet republics regularly attend CIS meetings, but they have yet to agree on exactly what the organisation should be doing in their name. Russia has been arguing for a closer confederation that could help to restore Moscow's global authority. Other countries, including Ukraine, have been more wary. On the rare occasions when everyone reaches agreement, such as in 1994 on the introduction of free trade, little is implemented. Those who mourn the passing of the Soviet Union have denounced the creation of the CIS as an act of criminal irresponsibility, but even those glad to see the Union behind them still have few kind words to say about the unloved organisation that was born in Belovezh.

UKRAINE

Evidence of Ukraine's chequered history abounds.
The Tatars, Genoese, Poles, Hapsburgs and
Russians have all left their mark on ancient Kievan Rus

Maps:
Area 310
City 312

Generations of Poles and Russians can attest to the difficulty in holding and keeping the borderlands of Ukraine. The lands are flat and famously fertile, broken only by the Carpathian mountains to the west, and by the Crimean peninsula in the south. The region has been a crossroads of migration paths, trade routes and imperial ambitions for centuries, and the evidence left behind goes far beyond the Russian hegemony of the last 300 years. Ukraine includes the frontier towns of the Hapsburg Empire, as well as Polish castles, Tatar palaces, and the remains of old Greek and Genoese trading posts along the Black Sea coast.

Ukraine is also rediscovering its own history, and one of the best examples is **Kiev ❶** itself. From the glorious period at the heart of Kievan Rus when only Constantinople could compete in importance, Kiev was almost completely destroyed by Batu Khan and the Tatars in 1240. It was to take six centuries before Kiev's population reached the same level again, during which time the city was fought over by Lithuanians, Poles and then Russians. It barely survived the chaos and destruction of two world wars in the 20th century, but history is now turning full circle and Kiev is beginning to reassert itself as one of the great European capitals.

PRECEDING PAGES:
Opera and Ballet
Theatre, Kiev.
LEFT: St Sophia's
Cathedral.
BELOW: the
monastery of
Kievo-Pecherskaya.

The upper town of Kiev

The story of early Kiev revolves around the achievements of two men, Volodymyr (Vladimir) the Great and his son Yaroslav the Wise, and a walking tour of the upper town begins at the junction of two streets bearing their names, vulitsya Volodymyrska and Yaroslaviv Val. This is the site of the **Zoloti Vorota Ⓐ** (Golden Gate), the ancient entrance to the city that is now a block away from the Kiev Opera and Ballet Theatre. The gate was built by Yaroslav in the 11th century as part of the fortifications of the upper town and was given its name by the golden dome of the Church of the Annunciation which stood on top. Both the gate and the church were ruined by the Tatars in 1240; what you see today is a 1982 restoration supposedly true to the original design. You can visit the museum inside to find out more about ancient Kiev and for some fine views across the modern city (open Mar–Nov Fri–Wed 10am–5.30pm).

From the Golden Gate, **Misto Yaroslava Ⓑ** (Yaroslav's Town) is reached by walking north up vulitsya Volodymyrska, passing the austere SBU **building** – the Ukrainian successor to the KGB – on your right at No. 33. This gives way a little further on to the open square in front of **Sofiysky Sobor Ⓒ** (St Sophia's Cathedral), and to the left the gold and green domes of the cathedral itself. This is Yaroslav's most enduring memorial, completed in 1031 in honour of his victory in battle against

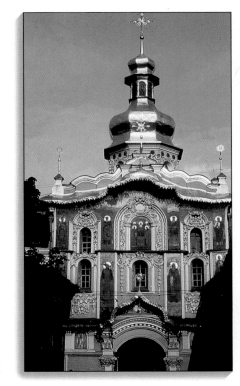

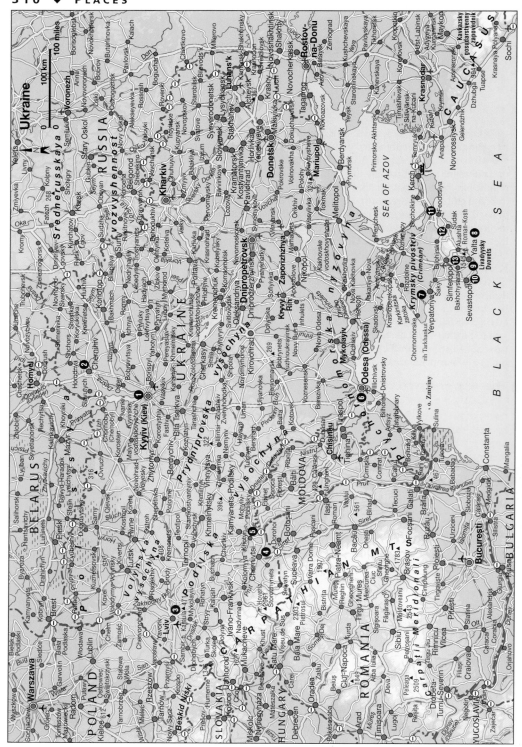

the nomadic Pechenegs. Its Byzantine layout and design, as well as the name taken from the Hagia Sophia in Constantinople, reflect all the authority and prestige that Kievan Rus enjoyed at the time. It was the spiritual heart of the early Rus state and remains a treasure of Eastern Slav civilisation.

The cathedral was restored and enlarged at the end of the 17th century, when many of the external intricacies were added in Ukrainian baroque style. As the models just past the cathedral entrance make clear, the original 11th-century building consisted of the nave and four parallel aisles, each ending in semi-circular apses, its 13 cupolas representing Christ and the Apostles. The striking central mosaic of the Virgin Mary also dates from the 11th century, as do some of the frescoes on the north wall of the nave. The marble tomb of Yaroslav himself lies in the northeast corner.

The exit from St Sophia's is through the 18th-century bell tower, past the grave of Patriarch Volodymyr to your left *(see box on page 314)*, and out across the newly paved square. It was here that the citizens of Kiev turned out in their thousands in 1648 to welcome the Cossack regiments of Bogdan Khmelnitsky after their victory over the Poles. The **statue of Bogdan Khmelnitsky** on horseback in the centre of the square was added only much later, in 1888.

The upper town has been threatened with ruin on many occasions, but in the 20th century a new menace appeared: the Soviet planners. When the Ukrainian SSR joined the Soviet Union in 1922, the Bolsheviks feared that Kiev was too infected with nationalism to be a trustworthy capital, and this honour was granted instead to the eastern city of Kharkiv. By the 1930s Kiev was back in favour, but the authorities still felt that the city was not suitably equipped to house the new generation of Soviet administrators. As a result, they decreed

> **Map on page 312**

On the last weekend in May, the capital celebrates the "Days of Kiev". By this time the chestnuts are in full bloom and the city looks at its best after the long winter.

BELOW: Ukrainian entertainers aboard a cruise ship.

that the entire area from St Sophia's past **Mikhailivska Ploshcha** (St Michael's Square) be cleared to make way for a triumphant new avenue of government buildings. The onset of World War II meant that the plans could not be implemented in full, but this "reprieve" came too late for the 12th-century golden-domed Monastery of St Michael, which was demolished in 1935 and 1936.

Gradually the damage done during the Soviet era is being repaired. The white marble figure of Princess Olha, who privately converted to Christianity 33 years before her grandson Volodymyr the Great, returned to the centre of the square in 1996 after a break of 77 years, flanked by Sts Cyril, Methodius and Andrew. They stand next to the rebuilt bell tower and new golden domes of **Mikhailivsky Sobor ◐** (St Michael's Cathedral). The only reminder of the Soviet plans is the neoclassical bulk at the northwest of the square, built in 1937, which now houses the **Ukrainian Ministry of Foreign Affairs**.

A small exhibition on the history of the Monastery of St Michael – including the Soviet plans for reconstruction of the area – can be seen in the cathedral's new bell tower.

Volodymyr's Town

Beyond the ministry to the left, down **vulitsya Desyatynna**, you move into **Misto Volodymyra ◗** (Volodymyr's Town). It was Volodymyr who first formed the lands of Rus into a coherent political entity in the 10th century, and it was his momentous decision in 988 to adopt Eastern Christianity as its official religion. The **Desyatynna** (Tithe Church), so called because Volodymyr gave up one-tenth of his income to have it built, was the first stone church in Rus. Its foundations are visible in the park across from the end of vulitsya Desyatynna, next to the grey building of the **Ukrainsky Istorychny Muzey ◗** (Museum of Ukrainian History; open Thurs–Tues 10am–5.30pm, closed last Thurs in month). The Tithe Church was founded in 989 and was the burial place of Volodymyr; in

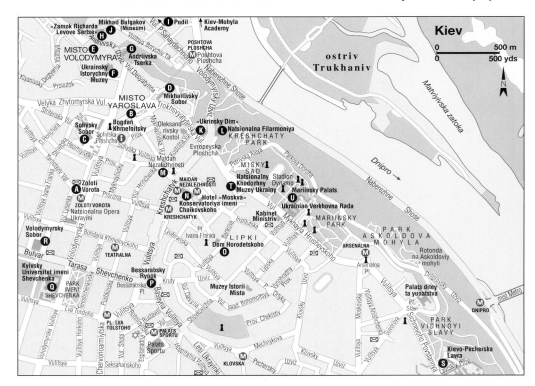

1240 hundreds of Kievans retreated onto its roof to escape Batu Khan. The roof collapsed, and the survivors were left to the mercy of the Tatars.

Andriivska Tserka **G** (St Andrew's Church) provides the perfect antidote to the tales of destruction from early Kiev. Balancing at the top of the hill of the same name, the church was designed with exquisite grace by Rastrelli, the Italian architect who shaped 18th-century St Petersburg. It marks the entrance to one of Kiev's most likeable streets, **Andriivsky Uzviz** (Andrew's Descent), which winds its way down to the Podil region by the river. This is Kiev's Montmartre, full of artists and cafés, and the best place to shop for souvenirs.

Just beyond the 19th-century **Zamok Richarda Levove Sertse** **H** (Castle of Richard The Lion Heart), you can take the wooden steps up to the right to reach an observation platform giving excellent views over the **Podil** **I**. This was traditionally the trading region of Kiev which grew around the main port along the Dnipro (Dnieper). A little further down the street, at No. 13, is a museum dedicated to the writer **Mikhail Bulgakov** **J** (open 10am–6pm, closed Wed in winter and first Mon of month). His novel *The White Guard* remains the best account of the chaos and uncertainty of life in Kiev at the end of World War I. Descending into the Podil, you can return to the upper town by taking the **funicular**, built in 1905, that leaves from the **Poshtova Ploshcha**. You can reach this square by walking to the right along vulitsya Petra Sahaydachnoho, Podil's main street.

The 18th-century St Andrew's Church dominates Kiev's skyline above Podil.

Central Kiev: Kreshchatyk

Vulitsya Kreshchatyk is modern Kiev's central street, famous for the rows of chestnut trees that soften the lines of its post-war architecture. The northern end of the street towards the river is **Evropeyska Ploshcha** (European Square) set against the backdrop of the Soviet arch built in 1982 to celebrate the eternal union of the brother Slavs. The same year also saw the completion of the **Ukrinsky Dim** **K**, formerly the Lenin Museum, now a Ukrainian cultural centre. The view is improved by the reopened **Filarmoniya** **L** (Philharmonia), originally constructed in 1882 as the Kiev Merchant's Association, which holds regular concerts and recitals. The ticket office is down the steps to the left of the building. In 1892 the first electric tram in the Russian Empire trundled past here down the hill towards the Podil.

The city authorities, led by a mayor with a background in the construction business, have tinkered extensively and expensively with Kreshchatyk since the mid 1990s. The six-lane highway was dug up and replaced in 1998 and **Maidan Nezalezhnosti** **M** (Independence Square), next to the distinctive electronic clock tower of the Trades' Union Centre, was remodelled to mark the 10th anniversary of independence in 2001. Above acres of underground shopping, is a rather haphazard collection of national tributes dominated by the huge "Glory to Ukraine" monument. The architectural effect is mixed, but the area retains its life thanks to the crowds of Ukrainians, street entertainers and vendors that gather throughout the year, and to the enlightened city decision to make

BELOW: the hub of modern Kiev, Kreshchatyk.

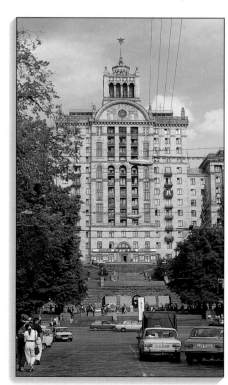

Kreshchatyk a pedestrian zone on weekends and holidays. In the southeast corner of the square you see the columns of the **Konservatoriya imeni Chaikovskoho** (Tchaikovsky State Conservatory).

In the times of Kievan Rus, the Kreshchatyk valley lay outside the city walls and got its name – meaning crossed or crossroads – from the many ravines that marked the hills on either side. Even in the mid-19th century, most of the area on the left-hand side of Kreshchatyk was a country estate belonging to the Mering family. Towards the end of the century it was developed and contains some fine townhouses, as well as the **Dom Horodetskoho** (House of Gargoyles) that now stands opposite the Presidential Administration on vulitsya Bankova.

Bessarabsky Rynok (Bessarabian Market), still under the wary scrutiny of a statue of Lenin opposite, marks the end of Kreshchatyk. Past Vladimir Illych is the tree-lined Bulvar Tarasa Shevchenko, which takes you up in the direction of Kiev's university. Although the first library in Kiev was founded by Yaroslav the Wise in the 11th century, Ukraine had to wait until 1615 before it had its first institute of higher education, the **Kiev-Mohyla Academy** in the Podil. The distinctive red building of the **Kyivsky Universitet imeni Shevchenka** (Kiev State University) appeared in the mid-19th century. Further down the boulevard on the right is another splendid 19th-century addition, the neo-Byzantine **Volodymyrsky Sobor** (St Volodymyr's Cathedral).

The Pechersk Monastery

About 3 km (2 miles) southeast of the town centre is the resplendent **Kievo-Pecherska Lavra** (Kiev Pechersk Monastery), a complex of churches, caves and museums founded in 1051 where you can easily spend a whole day. It is

Hydropark, an island park in the middle of the Dnipro, has Kiev's main beaches and is a great place to see how young Ukrainians spend their summer days and evenings.

BELOW: Monument to the Defence of the Motherland, known locally as the "steel wench".

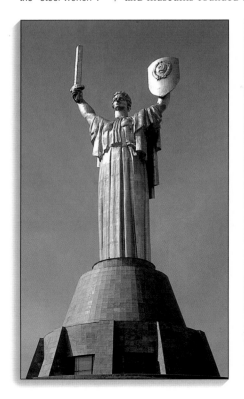

UNORTHODOX RESTING PLACE

As the totalitarian regime started to crumble in the late 1980s, one of the most visible signs of change was the revival of interest in religion. As with most things in Ukraine, this has not been without its moments of controversy. In 1993, members of a cult calling itself the White Brotherhood had to be forcibly prevented from occupying St Sophia's Cathedral. Two years later there was a more dramatic, and tragic, encounter on the same site. Political independence reawakened a split in the Orthodox church in Ukraine between those in favour of a separate Ukrainian branch of Orthodoxy and those giving allegiance to the patriarch in Moscow. When the patriarch of the independent Ukrainian Orthodox church, Volodymyr, died in 1995, his followers wanted to bury him in the grounds of St Sophia's. The cathedral still belonged to the state as a museum, but with the Ukrainian government seemingly unwilling to make a decision the situation was left to escalate out of control when the funeral procession carrying Volodymyr's body was stopped by security forces. During a running battle on St Sophia's Square the patriarch was laid to rest in a hastily-dug hole in the pavement by the bell tower, where his tomb – proclaiming him the patriarch of all Ukraine-Rus – remains to this day.

reached by heading up from **Evropeyska Ploshcha** (European Square) along vulitsya Mykhayla Hrushevskoho, passing the **Natsionalny Khudozhny Muzey Ukrainy** ❶ (Museum of Ukrainian Fine Arts; open Sat–Thurs 10am–6pm) and the white **Kabinet Ministriv** (Cabinet of Ministers) building on the right, and the **Ukrainian Verkhovna Rada** (Supreme Council) on the other side. Set back in a park behind the Rada, is the baroque **Mariinsky Palats** ❶ (Mariinsky Palace), restored in 1868 for the arrival of Tsar Alexander II and Empress Maria (book tours at Muzey Istorii Kieva, vulitsya P. Orlyka 8; tel: 044-293 2485/283 1158; open Sat–Thurs 10am–6pm). At the Arsenalna metro station, the street becomes vulitsya Sichnevoho Povstannya (Street of the January Uprising), which leads to the monastery. Trolleybus No. 20 follows this route from the Kreshchatyk.

The monastery spreads down to the River Dnipro, and the crowd of domes and cupolas poking above the woodland slopes is one of Kiev's most memorable sights. The name "Pechersk" comes from the subterranean passages, chapels and caves *(pechera)* that have been dug into the rock. The monastery barely survived the onslaught of the Tatars in the 13th century, but remained an important site of pilgrimage for Orthodox Christians throughout the Middle Ages. In the 18th century it acquired its present Ukrainian baroque appearance, and under the Soviets it was turned into a museum. Since 1988 most of the monastery has been returned to the Orthodox Church (open Wed–Mon 9.30am–6pm).

The main entrance to the upper part of the monastery is through the elaborately painted **Troitska Nadbramma Tserkva** (Trinity Gate Church), beyond which the interior is dominated by the 96-metre (315-ft) bell tower of the **Uspensky Sobor** (Cathedral of the Assumption). The tower gives a grand perspective over the Dnipro and the left bank, as well as southwards towards the

Bessarabsky Market, at the southern end of Kreshchatyk, presents a colourful show of fruit, flowers and vegetables.

BELOW: Rainbow Arch, Kiev.

Tickets for the main
museums of Pechersk
Monastery, and for the
bell tower and caves
(where you buy a
candle instead of a
ticket) are available
only at the respective
entrances, not at the
main ticket office.

BELOW:
frescoes at the
Kievo-Pecherskaya
Monastery.

rigid features of the huge **Monument to the Defence of the Motherland**, or the "steel wench" as she is known. The magnificent Uspensky Cathedral that once accompanied the bell tower is now being rebuilt. The original was destroyed during World War II. The large golden-striped dome to the east of the tower belongs to the **Trapezna Tserkva Antoniya ta Feodosiya** (Refectory Church of Sts Anthony and Theodosius). The upper monastery includes the **Museum of Historical Treasures** (open for tours; pre-booked hourly tours in English summer only), which has a collection of ancient Scythian jewellery, and the quirky Miniatures Museum featuring such oddities as the world's smallest book.

The lower part of the monastery contains the entrances to the caves. Their origins, and those of the monastery, are linked to the extraordinary life of Anthony of Pechersk, who in 1028 became a monk at the monastery of Esphigmenon on Mount Athos in Greece. He returned to Kiev with the mission to bring the monastic tradition, emphasising asceticism and separation from society, to his native Rus. After settling in a cavern by the Dnipro his fame as a holy man began to attract followers, who in turn started to carve the religious labyrinth into the hillside. When the number of monks reached 15, Anthony retired from the **Dalny Pechera** (Further Caves) and found solitude again in the **Blyzky Pechera** (Nearer Caves). Like the other monks, he is buried underground. In 1051 Kievan Rus ceded the hillside to the monks, and Anthony laid the foundations of the monastery of the caves, the **Kievo-Pecherska Lavra**.

The riches of Chernihiv

One of the richest cities of Kievan Rus, **Chernihiv** ❷ is about 140 km (87 miles) to the northeast of the capital along the main Odessa to St Petersburg

highway. The city was founded in the early 8th century on the River Desna, part of the "water road from the Varangians to the Greeks" that supported its early trading wealth. It reached pre-eminence in the 11th and 12th centuries, and its most valuable sites date from this period. After being sacked by the Tatars in 1239 Chernihiv lost its former importance, and fell to both Lithuanians and Poles before coming under Russian sway in the 17th century.

Approaching Chernihiv from the south you first catch sight of the five golden domes of **Tserkva Sv. Kateryny** (St Catherine's Church). Completed in the 18th century, this church is now a museum of local arts and crafts (open Thurs–Tues 10am–5pm). Behind St Catherine's lies the **Dytynets**, the historic site of ancient Chernihiv. Most of the Dytynets is now included within a park named after Mikhailo Kotsiubinsky, a classic name in Ukrainian modernist writing who lived in Chernihiv from 1898 until his death in 1913.

The **Kotsiubinsky Park** includes two outstanding monuments to the times of Kievan Rus. The **Spaso-Preobraszhensky Sobor** (Spassky Cathedral) dates from 1017, and its two sharp conical towers make it stand out from the more gentle contours that define most Orthodox buildings. It was built at the behest of Prince Mstyslav the Brave, who had challenged his brother Yaroslav the Wise for control of Kievan Rus after Volodymyr's death in 1015. Mstyslav was granted all the lands east of the Dnipro in an attempt to avoid another round of the fratricidal blood-letting that had already cost the lives of three of their brothers. It was only after Mstyslav died in 1036 – he is buried in the cathedral – that Kievan Rus was united to enjoy its "golden age" under the rule of Yaroslav. The 12th-century **Borysohlibsky Sobor** (Cathedral of Sts Boris and Hlib) nearby is slightly younger but retains a much more traditional design. There is, however,

Map on page 310

TIP

If you are planning a day trip to Chernihiv you may wish to take a picnic lunch. There aren't many decent eateries around the town's historic centre.

BELOW: before the start of a church service.

a family connection. Borys and Hlib were two of the three brothers killed in the feuding that followed Volodymyr's death (killed by another brother, Sviatopolk the Damned), and they were later canonised by the Orthodox Church.

The cannons lining the embankments at the southern end of the park point out across the River Desna and its tributary, the Strizhen. Looking out from near the monument to Taras Shevchenko, you can see the Ukrainian baroque outlines of the **Yeletsky Monastery** to the right, and further in the distance the imposing 58-metre (190-ft) bell tower of the **Troyitsky Monastery**. This hill contains the **Pechera Antoniya** (Anthony Caves), named after Anthony of Pechersk; more than 300 metres (984 ft) of underground passages connect five well-lit chapels, most of them constructed before the 14th century.

Lviv and western Ukraine

Travelling west through Ukraine the landscape is gradually transformed as spires and steeples start to appear among the bulbous Orthodox cupolas. These western lands were brought behind the Soviet border only with World War II, and retain many affinities with the central European empires and countries that once held sway here. These are also the parts of Ukraine that feel their national identity most strongly, with Ukrainian spoken as a matter of course.

Lviv ❸ was founded in the 13th century by Prince Danylo of Galicia, and its strategic position controlling the passes across the Carpathian mountains has ensured it a turbulent history. Foreign travel has not been essential for the inhabitants of Lviv; their bitter experience has been that time will bring the foreign countries to visit. A 90-year-old woman who has lived in Lviv all her life would have been born in the Hapsburg Empire, then after a spell in the ephemeral

BELOW: Kievan woman in festive spirit.

Map on page 310

Western Ukrainian Republic after World War I (and a few weeks of Bolshevik rule in 1920) she would have settled down in Poland. In 1939 the Soviets arrived again, only to be driven back by the invading Nazis two years later. From 1941 until 1944 she had to endure the German-controlled General Government of Poland, before again joining the Soviet Union. From 1991 she would have survived to see an independent Ukraine.

The wide boulevard in the centre of Lviv is **prospekt Svobody**, with the **Teatr Opery ta Baletu** (Opera and Ballet Theatre) commanding its northern end. This tree-lined promenade has always been a popular meeting place, and there will often be knots of Ukrainians having earnest and occasionally heated discussions around the **statue of Taras Shevchenko**. The old town is just to the east, and you can reach it by turning left off prospekt Svobody after the monument to the Polish poet **Adam Mickiewicz**. This brings you to Lviv's **Katolytsky Sobor** (Roman Catholic Cathedral), whose tower is one of the city's most distinctive landmarks. Construction began here soon after the city first fell under Polish control in the mid-14th century, although much of the intricate interior work is more recent. The local Catholic population, and indeed the city itself, was given a huge boost in 2001 with the visit of Pope John Paul II, who made Lviv his only other stop in Ukraine after the capital. Be sure to visit also the exquisitely carved **Boyim Chapel**, built by a wealthy Hungarian merchant in the 17th century, just across from the cathedral on the opposite side from the tower. Just past the cathedral you enter the elegant **ploshcha Rynok** (Market Square), with the 19th-century building of the Lviv Town Hall in its centre. Soviet power always sat uneasily in this part of Ukraine, and when controls were relaxed in the 1980s the local authorities in Lviv were at the fore-

For souvenir shopping in Lviv, go to the open-air arts and crafts market in the square behind the Ukrainian Drama Theatre, to the right of the opera house.

BELOW: Opera and Ballet Theatre, Lviv.

Hapsburg influence: Lviv's Grand Hotel.

BELOW: flower sellers in Lviv market.

front of calls for an end to the totalitarian system. The fate of the Lenin statue, invariably a useful barometer of local opinion, is instructive: it had been removed from its perch in front of the Opera already in September 1990, the first such instance in the entire Soviet Union.

To the east of ploshcha Rynok, along vulitsya Ruska, you can see the three-tiered bell tower of **Uspenska Tserkva** (Renaissance Uspensky Church), the traditional focus of the local Orthodox community, with the delicate **Kaplitsya Trox Svyatyteliv** (Three Saints Chapel) clinging to its base. Next door to the north is the dome of **Kostol Dominikana** (Roman Catholic Dominican Church). It was the meeting of these two faiths, when parts of Orthodox Rus came under Polish Catholic control, that produced the hybrid Ukrainian Catholic (known also as Greek Catholic or Uniate) Church in the 16th century. Under the Union of Brest-Litovsk in 1596 parts of the Ukrainian Church agreed to unite with Rome as long as they be allowed to keep their traditional Orthodox rites. The concessions to Rome were bitterly opposed by many Orthodox believers, and as the region came under Russian and then Soviet control, so Ukrainian Catholics were subject to campaigns of forced conversion and persecution. In 1946 a fraudulent synod even proclaimed their formal "union" with Russian Orthodoxy, but priests in western Ukraine continued to minister in secret.

In the autumn of 1989 a quarter of a million Ukrainian Catholics demonstrated in Lviv for the legalisation of their faith, and in 1990 the spiritual centre of Ukrainian Catholicism, **Sobor Svyatoho Yura** (St George's Cathedral) in Lviv, was returned to them. This baroque cathedral is a 20-minute walk to the west of the old town on **ploshcha Svyatoho Yura** (St George's Square).

Lviv is the major city of western Ukraine, but by no means its only attraction,

the Carpathians and the regions to the southwest are fascinating areas to explore. As well as the rich folk cultures of the Carpathians, this is the historic border-land between populations – eastern Slavs, western Slavs, Romanians and Hun-garians – and empires, and every place presents its own mix. The Soviets arrived only with the outbreak of World War II, and towns such as **Uzhhorod** and **Chernivtsi ❹** have kept much of their inheritance from the Hapsburgs, as well as from the inter-war period when they formed part of Czechoslovakia and Romania respectively.

Chernivtsi, the main city of the historic region of Bukovina, was developed by the Austrians after being ceded to them in 1775 by the retreating Ottomans. **Teatr Musyky ta Dramy** (Music and Drama Theatre) was a gift from the Haps-burg monarchy, and designed by the same Viennese architects who had built the opera in Odessa 20 years earlier. The late-19th-century palace, now the main university building, is an intriguing blend of architectural styles. Further to the west, as the road from Chernivtsi to Kamyanets-Podilsky crosses the Dniester river, is the reconstructed fortress at **Khotyn ❺**, the stronghold of local pow-ers from the Kievan Rus principality of Galicia to the Cossacks and the Poles.

Map on page 310

Ukraine's national anthem begins with the rather curious line "Ukraine is not dead yet", only comprehensible in the context of the country's long and difficult history.

The Black Sea port of Odessa

A visit to the southern lands along the Black Sea coast introduces a new cast of characters, including ancient Greeks, Crimean Tatars, Genoese traders and even French noblemen, to the story of Ukraine. **Odessa ❻** and Crimea were not part of the territory of Kievan Rus, and were conquered by the Russian Empire as the armies of Catherine the Great moved south at the end of the 18th century.

In May 1794, the Russian empress moved to consolidate her gains by founding

BELOW: choir in full voice, Armenian Church, Chernivtsi.

a port on the site of a coastal village called Khadzhibei. The new town took its name from the ancient Greek settlement of Odessos, which was wrongly supposed to be nearby, and quickly grew into a thriving commercial centre. Even during the Soviet period Odessa retained the open outlook of a port city, and its natives take credit for the country's funniest jokes and most popular songs. Long stretches of sandy beach (away from the city but accessible by boat or public transport) and plenty of local restaurateurs also make it a very popular place to relax.

A tour of Odessa begins on the majestic terrace of **Prymorsky Bulvar** Ⓐ, by the statue to the city's first governor the **Duke de Richelieu**. It was under his progressive administration that Odessa was transformed in the early 19th century, and after the duke's return to France in 1814 (where he become prime minister after the defeat of Napoleon) the city honoured him with a spot overlooking one of Odessa's most treasured symbols, the **Potyomkinskaya Lestnitsa** Ⓑ (Potemkin Steps). Built between 1837–41 they were immortalised in Eisenstein's classic film about the 1905 Russian Revolution, *The Battleship Potemkin*. The steps are best seen from below, without the discordant backdrop of the modern sea port, and from where the unique tapered design – the bottom step is 9 metres (30 ft) wider than the top – plays tricks with the perspective.

Back at the top of the steps turn left along the boulevard, past the **Hotel Londonska**, towards the **statue of Pushkin** Ⓒ. The Russian poet spent 1823–24 in exile in Odessa, keeping himself busy by working on his epic poem *Evgene Onegin* and also by having an affair with the wife of Count Vorontsov, the new governor. Nearby is a cannon from the British frigate *Tiger*, a trophy from the Crimean War claimed during an Anglo-French naval assault on the city in 1854.

The road heading away from the seafront is **Pushkina vulitsya** and immedi-

TIP

The liveliest beach in Odessa is Arkadiya to the south of the city, a ten-minute taxi ride from the main station. It's full of people and activity all day and night throughout the summer.

Odessa

BLACK SEA

LANZHERON

SHEVCHENKO PARK

0   500 m
0   500 yds

ately on your left you come to the **Muzey Arkheolohii** ⓓ (Museum of Archaeology; open Tues–Sun 10am–5pm), which has a fine collection of relics from the early civilisations that lived around the Black Sea. Opposite, behind the **Muzey Morskoho Flotu** ⓔ (Museum of Maritime History; open Fri–Wed 10am–4pm), is the marvellously ornate late-19th-century **Teatr Opery ta Baletu** ⓕ (Opera and Ballet Theatre), whose style is a blend of Italian Renaissance, Viennese and classical baroque. Music lovers may also like to wander further down Pushkina vulitsya, past the **Muzey Zakhidno-skhidnoho Mistetstva** ⓖ (Museum of Western and Oriental Art; open Thurs–Tues 11am–6pm) to the **Filarmoniya** ⓗ (Philharmonia), where the Odessa Philharmonic Orchestra has been given a new lease of life under the energetic direction of their US conductor, Hobart Earle.

The central street of Odessa, which crosses Pushkina vulitsya past the Opera, is another reminder of French influence over the early city. De Ribas masterminded the military campaign which won this part of the coast from the Turks in the late 18th century, and **Deribasivska vulitsya** ⓘ was named in his honour. The street is one of Odessa's most vibrant, best enjoyed in the summer from one of the many bars and cafés that spill out onto the pavements. From here, vulitsya Ekaterynynska takes you back down towards the Potemkin steps.

Crimea peninsula

The **Crimea peninsula** ❼, jutting out into the Black Sea, contains the most dramatic scenery in Ukraine, where the steppe finally gives way to three parallel ranges of limestone mountains along the rocky southern coast. Its strategic importance for control of the Black Sea has made it a prize that is still disputed,

Maps:
Area 310
City 322

BELOW: Prymorsky Bulvar, Odessa.

Map
on page
310

and generations of settlers and conquerors arriving from all points of the compass have left their mark on the landscape.

Yalta ❽, the main resort of the Crimea, has been the favoured retreat of the Russian élite ever since the imperial family began resting at nearby Livadia in the 1860s. It has a magical reputation across the former Soviet Union for its sunshine, fine wine and fine living, so much so that some locals interpret the very act of arrival as an implicit surrender of the right to get value for money. Nonetheless, it is an exceptional location and an evening stroll along the waterfront remains a wonderfully un-Soviet experience.

Just outside the town to the west is the **Livadyysky Dvovets ❾** (Palace of Livadia; open June–Oct Thurs–Tues 8am–5pm, Nov–May Thurs–Tues 9am–4.30pm), which was built in 1911 for Nicholas II. In February 1945, it hosted the conference of Allied leaders – Stalin, Churchill and Roosevelt – which became synonymous with the post-war division of Europe after Stalin failed to keep a promise to hold free elections in the countries of central and eastern Europe. The ground floor of the palace is devoted to an exhibition about the conference, and upstairs is a series of rooms taking you back to its tsarist past. A little further along the coast is the **Lastochkino Gnezdo** (Swallow's Nest). The castle, balancing on a promontory and now containing an Italian restaurant, is best reached by the regular boat service from Yalta.

The city of **Sevastopol ❿**, which until 1996 was closed to foreigners, offers a completely different set of attractions. Still home to the Russian Black Sea Fleet, which leases bays and infrastructure from the Ukrainians, Sevastopol has a record of heroic resistance to sieges in both the Crimean War and then during World War II, commemorated in various monuments and the vast 115-metre (377-ft) panorama hall Istorichiskii Bulvar (open 9.30am–6pm).

Southwest of the city are the ruins of the ancient Greek colony of **Chersonesus** (1 vulitsya Drevnyaya; open 9am–6pm) founded in 421 BC, and where the Kievan prince Volodymyr the Great is said to have been baptised in 988.

The Greeks were not the only Mediterranean settlers along the shores of the Crimea. Genoa's alliance with Constantinople – the Treaty of Ninfeo of 1261 – opened up the Black Sea area to the Italian city state, and the Genoese set up large trading posts in Kaffa, now **Feodosiya ⓫** and **Sudak ⓬** in eastern Crimea which grew rich on commerce along the Silk Route to China and central Asia. City defences from these times remain, and the walls and towers of the fortress overlooking Sudak have been completely restored.

The fate of the Genoese was sealed in 1453 when Constantinople fell to Mehmed II. Their trade now had to pass through the Turkish-controlled straits, and by 1475 an alliance of Ottoman Turks and Crimean Tatars had squeezed them off the peninsula. The Tatars, settlers who from the times of the Golden Horde, agreed to Ottoman suzerainty and continued to control the Crimea until the Russian conquests of the 18th century. The seat of their khanate was in the town of **Bakhchysaray ⓭** and the Khan's Palace, originally built in 1519, is a poetic reminder of the diversity of Crimean history. ❏

BELOW: Russian Orthodox Church in Yalta, Crimea.
RIGHT: boat trip on the Black Sea.

EXPLORING THE CRIMEAN COAST

Even with its fading tourist infrastructure, the Crimea is still the best choice for seeing the sunnier side of Ukraine

The Crimea has almost everything you could ask for in a tourist destination: dramatic mountains plunging down to the sea, a tropical climate, a remarkable and rich history. The only piece missing has been the tourist industry itself, which adapted very quickly to Western price levels after 1991, but had more problems with delivering similar levels of service and accommodation. This has already begun to change, and a fascinating region is now navigable for the foreign traveller. The naval base of Sevastopol was opened up to foreigners in 1996, and a brief tour along the coast towards Yalta is enough to illustrate the variety of Crimea's attractions.

EXCURSIONS AWAY FROM THE COAST

Just outside Sevastopol, the ruins of the ancient Greek colony of Chersonesus lead on towards the port of Balaklava, in whose defence the Light Brigade was decimated during the Crimean War. Foros, with its nine-domed church high on the cliffs above you, is where Gorbachev was held captive in his *dacha* during the failed putsch of 1991, and from there it is not far across the vineyards to the Russian aristocratic palaces at Alupka and Livadia.

Visitors to Crimea will find that interest is not limited to the coastal areas. Inland, near the Tatar palace at Bakhchysaray, is the cave city of Chufut-Kale, inhabited from the 6th to the mid-19th centuries in turn by Christians, Muslim Tatars and Karaite Jews.

◁ **ANCIENT AND MODERN**
Yalta's 19th-century churches draw their inspiration from past ties with Armenia and the Byzantine Empire.

△ **CRIMEAN TATARS**
The resting place of the former rulers of the Crimea, the Tatar khans, is their "garden palace" at Bakhchysaray.

◁ GREATER YALTA
Hemmed in by the Black Sea and the soaring Crimean mountains, the modern resort town of Yalta now stretches out across the slopes that lead up from the pebbly beaches and the town's seafront.

△ BEACH LIFE
From June until September, Crimea's beaches are packed with Ukrainians and Russians of all ages, shapes and sizes. The best and sandiest beaches can be found around Yevpatoriya and Feodosiya.

▽ SOVIET STYLE
Members of the Soviet élite knew how to relax in style. Brezhnev used to take his holidays in this delightful lodge near Yalta.

▷ FORTIFICATIONS
Feodosiya has long been a fortified city, and parts of the defences from 13th-century Genoese trading posts survive to this day.

▷ HOME COOKING
Some of the best food in Ukraine comes from the family oven and an invitation to dinner should not be refused.

HEADING FOR THE HILLS

The Crimea attracts climbers and hikers from across Europe and beyond, and offers some spectacular trails along its mountainous southern coast. There are some English-language walking guides – Frith Maier's *Trekking in Russia and Central Asia* has a chapter covering Crimea – but it is always worth asking locally for guidance on the most suitable routes and campsites. For day trips around Yalta there is good walking around the Uchansu waterfall and Lake Karagol, both just off the mountain road to Bakhchysaray. For a stroll through a vast variety of Crimean flora, try the Nikitsky Botanical Gardens, accessible by boat and road 5 km (3 miles) to the east of Yalta on the way over towards Hurzuf.

※ INSIGHT GUIDES
TRAVEL TIPS

CONTENTS

Getting Acquainted

The Place.............................330
Time Zones..........................330
Public Holidays 330
Useful Websites 331

Planning the Trip

What to Bring.......................332
Electricity............................332
Money Matters.....................332
Visas and Passports.............332
Getting There 333
Customs 334
Health Regulations 334

Practical Tips

Identity Papers.....................335
Security 335
St Petersburg Police Alert......325
Road Safety 336
Medical Treatment 336
Emergency Numbers.............336
Women Travelling Alone 336
Health Spas 337
Web Information....................337
Newspapers.........................337
Dialling Codes......................337
Postal Services 337
Cables & Telegrams 338
Embassies & Consulates 338
Telephones 338
Business Hours 338
Gay Travellers 338
Travellers with Disabilities.....339
Etiquette 339
Moscow Net Access............. 339
Tipping 339
Religious Services................339
Overseas Missions 339
Airline Offices 340
Chambers of Commerce 340
International Travel Agents 341
Russian Tourist Offices..........341

Getting Around

By Train...............................342
By Car.................................342
Trans-Siberian Railway 342
By Boat...............................344
By Plane 344
City Transport......................344
Tour Operators 345

Where to Stay

Choosing a Hotel..................346
Hotels in Russia 346
Youth Hostels 348
Language Centres.................351
Hotels in Belarus..................352
Hotels in Ukraine..................352

Where to Eat

What to Eat 353
Where to Eat 354
What to Drink........................358

Nightlife

Nightlife in Moscow 359
Nightlife in St Petersburg 359

Shopping

What to Buy 360
Where to Shop 360

Language

Language Tips 362
Transliteration 362
Useful Words & Phrases 363

Further Reading

History.................................367
Politics................................367
Russian Literature................367
Biography/Memoirs...............368
Art 368
Other Insight Guides.............368

Getting Acquainted

RUSSIA

Area 17.1 million sq km (6.6 million sq miles). Land boundaries: 20,139 km (12,514 miles). Coastline: 37,653 km (23,397 miles).
Population 146 million (growth rate –0.001%).
Ethnic mix Russian 81.5%, Tatar 3.8%, Ukrainian 3%, Chuvash 1.2%, Bashkir 0.9%, Belarusian 0.8%, Moldavian 0.7%, others 8.1%.
Major languages Russian.
Government Russia is a federation consisting of 89 regions. New constitution in December 1993.
Capital city Moscow (pop. 9 million).
Communications 893,000 km (555,000 miles) of roads, 145,000 km (90,050 miles) of railways. Number of airports with permanent surface runways: 565.

Climate

Russia spans a range of climatic zones, from the arctic tundra of northern Siberia to the steppes of Central Asia. Almost everywhere is extremely cold in winter, the exception being a small area along the Black Sea coast, where January temperatures remain above freezing. By contrast, most places average around -20°C (-4°F), with the cold intensifying to the northeast. In northeast Siberia, winter temperatures are usually somewhere near -50°C (-57°F), and have been known to plummet as low as -68°C (-90°F). The Pacific coast, European Russia, Belarus and Ukraine are milder; Moscow has January daytime temperatures of around -9°C (16°F), St Petersburg -7°C (19°F).

Most of the country experiences warm summers, the exceptions being the arctic north and the Pacific coasts, where cold ocean currents keep temperatures down. Across much of Siberia summer daytime values are around 20°C (68°F), but can sometimes rise to 38°C (100°F). In Moscow, July daytime temperatures average 23°C (73°F), but vary widely from year to year. Southern Russia and Ukraine have hotter and more humid summers. Most of Russia has a summer maximum of rainfall, with thunderstorms common in early summer. Eastern regions are drier.

Mountain areas include the Carpathian mountains in Western Ukraine and the Caucasus, where the climate is broadly similar to that of the Alps, albeit with colder winters.

Economy

Russia has a free market economic system, but the state still intervenes heavily in the economic system, both officially and unofficially. The former concerns a myriad of onerous decrees regulating every aspect of business, while the latter concerns the enormous corruption that plagues Russia's state bureaucracy and world of business. The Putin administration has promised to wage war on both bureaucracy and corruption, but even the most optimistic forecasts say that significant change will only be seen by the middle of the decade.

In a strange way, Russian organised crime is not as great a problem as in the early 1990s, in large part because criminal groups have established legitimate control over large sectors of the economy, and some figures once known as leading crime bosses are now considered respectable businessmen. These people now crave stability to protect the interests which they may have won through violence, and so it is not surprising that Russia is entering a period of stability.

Industries include the complete range of mining and extractive activities producing coal, oil, gas, chemicals and metals; all forms of machine building from rolling mills to high-performance aircraft and space vehicles; shipbuilding; road and rail transportation equipment; communications equipment; agricultural machinery, tractors, and construction equipment; electric power generating and transmitting equipment; medical and scientific instruments; and consumer durables.

The main agricultural products are grain, sugar beet, sunflower seeds, meat, milk and vegetables.

Religion

In Russia and the eastern region of the Ukraine and Belarus, the Russian Orthodox Church is the

1–5 January (New Year Holidays)
7 January (Orthodox Christmas Day)
23 February (Army Day)
8 March (Women's Day)
1 May (Labour Day)
9 May (Victory Day)
12 June (Independence Day)
4 November (Unity Day)

Time Zones

Russia has eight time zones. Moscow and St Petersburg are three hours ahead of Greenwich Mean Time. Moscow time is adopted nearly everywhere west of the Urals.

When it is 3pm in Moscow, it is 5pm in Yekaterinburg, 7pm in Novosibirsk, 8pm in Irkutsk, 9pm in Chita, and 10pm in Vladivostok.

By then, the inhabitants of Petropavlovsk-Kamchatsky on the far eastern Kamchatka Peninsula have just started a new day and the polar bears on the frozen Chukchi Sea in the far northeast are already an hour into the new day. Moscow time is shown on the station clocks along the Trans–Siberian Railway.

most influential faith. Western regions of Ukraine and Belarus are more influenced by the Roman Catholic Church.

Baptists, Adventists and other Protestant branches are also quite influential, though under attack from nationalist elements in the political and religious establishment.

Islam is the main faith in the Caucasus and among the Tatar population of the lower and middle Volga. Many Jews have emigrated and there are fewer than 100 synagogues. Buddhism is practised by the Buryats near Lake Baikal and the Kalmyks of the lower Volga.

BELARUS

Area 207,600 sq km (80,150 sq miles). Land boundaries: total 3,098 km (1,925 miles). Coastline: none.
Population 10.3 million. Growth rate: -0.15%.
Ethnic mix Belarusian 81.2%, Russian 11.4%, Polish, Ukrainian and other 7.4%.
Major languages Russian, Belarusian.
Government Independent republic. The constitution adopted in 1996 has not been recognised as legitimate by the West.
Capital city Minsk (pop. 1.7 million).
Communications 98,200 km (61,000 miles) of roads, 5,570 km (3,460 miles) of railways.
Climate Mild continental. Average temperatures: January –7°C (19°F); July 17°C (63°F).
Time zone Minsk is GMT plus 2 hours.
Religion Mainly Russian Orthodox.

Economy
Belarus, one of the better developed former Soviet states, has a diverse machine building sector and a healthy agriculture sector. It also serves as a transport link for Russian oil exports to the Baltic states and Eastern and Western Europe. Compared with Russia, there has been very little privatisation and the state still

Useful Websites

www.russiatourism.ru/eng
Great general reference site with lots of useful links
www.russianembassy.org
Information on visas
www.russiatravel.com
Russian tourist office official site
www.travel.spb.ru
St Petersburg tourist information
www.tte.ch
Multi-lingual travel directory with information on Russia, Belarus and Ukraine
www.moscowtimes.ru
Moscow Times
www.times.spb.ru
St Petersburg Times
www.museum.ru
Museums in Russia
www.moscowcity.com
Information about Moscow
www.travel-library.com
Travel information, travelogues

plays a large part in the economy. High inflation was one of the consequences of independence and harsh austerity measures were introduced to combat it. Belarus's principal exports are machinery and transport equipment, chemicals and foodstuffs.

UKRAINE

Area 603,700 sq km (233,100 sq miles). Land boundaries: total 4,558 km (2,832 miles). Coastline: 2,782 km (1,729 miles).
Population 48.4 million. Growth rate: -0.78%
Ethnic mix Ukrainian 73%, Russian 22%, other 5%.
Major languages Ukrainian is the official language; Russian is still widely spoken.
Government Independent republic. A new constitution adopted in 1996.
Capital city Kiev (pop 2.6 million).
Communications 273,700 km (170,000 miles) of roads, 23,350 km (14,500 miles) of railroads.
Climate mild continental, closer to sub-tropical along the southern

and trip reports for Russia, Belarus and Ukraine
www.ru
Russia on the net: directory and links
www.brama.com and
www.infoukes.com
Ukraine portals run from North America
www.kpnews.com
Good source of English-language news in Kiev run by the *Kiev Post*
www.uazone.net
Ukraine portal based in Kiev
www.belarusguide.com
Good range of resources for business and travel
www.waytorussia.net
Comprehensive information on travel and life in Russia.
www.sv-agency.udm.ru
Travel advice and more.
www.destinationrussia.com
Hotels, apartments and travel information.

Crimean coast. Average temperatures: January –7°C (19°F) in the northeast, 4°C (40°F) on the Crimean coast; July 19°C (66°F) in the northeast, 25°C (77°F) on the Crimean coast.
Time zone Kiev is GMT plus 2 hours.

Economy
Ukraine's economy had been second only to Russia's within the former Soviet Union, producing more than three times the output of the next-ranking republic. Its fertile black soil generated more than a quarter of Soviet agricultural output, its farms provided meat, milk, grain and vegetables to other republics, and its diversified heavy industry supplied equipment and raw materials to industrial and mining sites. Following independence, it suffered the same economic cycle as Russia, with high inflation, countered by austerity measures leading to a decline in industrial output. This hampered its intended privatisation programme.

Planning the Trip

What to Bring

Clothing

Today Russia, Belarus and Ukraine are visited by people from many different countries with many different styles of dress. You may dress as you would normally dress at home.

Coming to Russia, Belarus and Ukraine in the cold months (November to March), you should not be surprised to meet temperatures of 25° to 30°C below zero (−13°F to −22°F) and will need to dress accordingly, not forgetting a hat and gloves. It's best to dress in layers of clothing to cope with the variations in temperature between the frozen outdoors and the centrally-heated indoors. Waterproof shoes are a necessity in winter, since the legendary Russian frost is often interrupted by periods of thawing. For business meetings, formal dress is obligatory. The dress code is as rigorously enforced as in the West and compliance is an important matter of status.

Electricity

Electrical current in tourist hotels is normally 220v AC, but don't count on it. In some remote places you will also find 127v. Sockets require a continental-type two-pin plug. It is best to take adaptors with you.

Money Matters

RUSSIA

It used to be the case that most financial transactions undertaken by tourists were made in foreign currencies. This situation has completely changed. It is illegal to make payments in foreign currencies; they should be made in roubles or with credit cards. A new rouble (worth 1,000 old roubles) was introduced in January 1998.

Visas and Passports

Russia

You will need a valid passport, an official application form, hotel reservation (for business travellers and tourists) and three passport photographs, to obtain your visa from a Russian embassy or consulate. If you apply in person, rather than through a travel agency, allow ample time, as it might take a month or so. According to new regulations, this term can be shortened to 48 hours if an applicant is a business traveller, or if he or she has an officially recognised invitation (telex, fax or e-mail are accepted) from a Russian host. Fees for this express service are correspondingly higher.

You are obliged to have your passport and visa registered within three days of arrival – failure to do so may result in a heavy fine upon departure.

There are transit visas (for up to 48 hours), tourist, ordinary and multiple entry visas (for two or more visits). If you go to Russia on the invitation of relatives or friends, you will get a visa for a private journey and no hotel reservation is needed. Independent tourists should organise their trip through an accredited agent or their Russian hosts. They need an itinerary, listing in detail, times, places and overnight reservations.

It is sensible to carry your passport and visa at all times, while you are in Russia since the police have the right to check your identity at will. Without them you may be asked to go to a police station and you might be prohibited from entering your hotel, the embassy of your country and many other places.

There is no limit to the import of hard currency, but the sum must be declared on entry. The amount exported should not exceed the amount declared when entering the country. If you are

Belarus

Visas are issued by Belarusian embassies abroad provided that you can produce evidence of an official invitation or confirmation of booked accommodation through a Belarusian host tourist organisation (that must be licensed by the Belarusian government).

Travellers who do not have a visa cannot register at any hotel Visas are not issued on arrival and airlines have instructions not to board anyone without a visa. Fees fluctuate wildly.

Ukraine

A valid passport and visa are required. Visas are obtained from Ukrainian embassies or consulates worldwide. A letter of invitation from a person, company, or organisation in Ukraine or a tour company voucher is required to obtain a visa, unless you are a citizen of the EU, US, Canada, Japan, Switzerland, Slovakia or Turkey.

Travellers from countries where there is a Ukrainian embassy or consulate cannot obtain visas at airports or border crossings. Travellers must therefore ensure that the proper visa is obtained before arriving in Ukraine. Travellers who intend to visit Russia from Ukraine must also have a Russian visa. All visitors must register on arrival with the local law enforcement authorities.

For those travelling from Kiev to Moscow, it is now possible to pick up transit visas to Russia from the Russian Embassy in Kiev, but it is still advisable to arrange all Russian visas before arriving in Kiev. People have been charged more than $350 for trying to leave Moscow on a Ukrainian visa.

carrying less than US$500 you may enter the country via the Green Corridor at Moscow's Sheremyetovo airport. Unspent roubles should be changed back into hard currency before you leave the country.

The black market has largely disappeared as there are many banks and exchange points. Do compare rates before changing currency, as they vary considerably.

All large hotels have an official exchange counter where you can buy roubles with cash, travellers' cheques and credit cards. You will need your customs declaration form, on which all your money transactions must be recorded. Keep this form as you will need to show it when leaving the country.

ATMS These can be found in major cities on main thoroughfares and at central metro stations.

Credit cards Most tourist-related businesses and restaurants accept major credit cards.

BELARUS

The currency is the Belarusian Rubel (BR), which was re-denominated on 1 January 2000 at one new BR to 2,000 old BRs. In February 2005 there were 2,170 BRs to the US Dollar.

Travellers' cheques are not widely accepted. Most tourist hotels accept either American Express or Visa credit cards. The Planeta Hotel in Minsk provides cash from Visa and credit cards during business hours, but ATMS are not generally in use in Belarus.

UKRAINE

In late 1996, Ukrainians introduced the hryvna to replace a temporary currency – the karbovanets. Despite losing ground after the financial crisis of 1998, the currency has remained relatively stable and in February 2005 was trading at 5.5 UAH to the US Dollar.

Ukraine has a cash economy, but travellers' cheques and credit cards are gaining wider acceptance in larger cities. Use of credit cards is limited to better hotels, tourist-restaurants, international airlines and select stores. Changing US dollars or any other currency is legal only at banks, currency exchange desks at hotels, and at licensed exchange booths.

Getting There

RUSSIA

Until recently, foreigners could only enter Russia through special entry points whose number could be counted on the fingers of one hand. Although today that amount of "doors" is virtually unchanged, all the procedures, including customs formalities, are much simpler.

By Air

More than 30 international airlines connect Moscow's Domodedovo, Sheremetyevo II and Vnukova airport with the rest of the world. Domodedovo is a new modern airport in the south of the city which has taken a lot of business away from Sheremetyevo II. Domodedovo can be reached either by special express train from Paveletsky Vokzal (train station) next to Paveletskaya Metro Station, or by mini bus from outside Domodedovskaya Metro station.

Flights take about 9 to 10 hours from New York, 4 hours from London, Paris and Rome; from Frankfurt it takes 3 hours, 2 from Stockholm, 6 from Delhi and 8 hours from Peking.

In addition to Moscow, some international carriers also fly to Pulkovo–2 in St Petersburg and some are now increasing their coverage to include towns such as Nizhny Novgorod, Saratov and Yekaterinburg.

Aeroflot's destinations include Anchorage, Chicago, London, Los Angeles, Miami, Montreal, New York, San Francisco, Seattle, Shannon (Ireland), Stockholm and Washington DC.

By Sea

Several Russian ports accept international passenger liners. St Petersburg on the Baltic Sea is connected with London, Helsinki, Gothenburg, Stockholm and Oslo. Nakhodka, on the Japan Sea coast, is connected with Yokohama in Japan, Hong Kong, Singapore and Sydney. Additional information about sea routes, schedules and bookings can be obtained from travel agencies, Russian tourist agencies or Morflot.

By Rail

Railways are the most important means of passenger transport within Russia and connect the largest cities (Moscow, St Petersburg, Kiev, Minsk) with Western European capitals. Visitors who have the time can travel in a comfortable first-class sleeping-wagon (SV), the pride of the Russian railways.

Passengers in transit through Belarus to Russia do not need a Belarus visa, but those in transit through Ukraine need a Ukrainian transit visa, which must be obtained before departure. A double-transit visa is needed if the return journey is on the same route.

From Western Europe the train takes two to three days to Moscow, with a change of gauge on reaching Russia.

The most popular rail routes for international traffic are Helsinki to St Petersburg (departing 1pm and arriving at 9pm) and Helsinki to Moscow (departing 5pm and arriving at 9.30am the next morning).

By Road

During the past few years marked changes have taken place in the quality of services along Russian roads. Moscow now has new service and repair stations for non-Russian cars. However, you should still be cautious of travelling through Russia by car. It can be dangerous and road borders take hours to cross due to delays at customs. Outside towns petrol stations are, on average, 100 km (60 miles) apart.

You can bring your own car by sea through St Petersburg, Tallinn in Estonia, Odessa on the Black Sea and Nakhodka in the Far East.

There are no international bus lines direct to Russia, but specially organised bus tours operate from the UK, Germany and Finland.

BELARUS

By Air
Lufthansa fly to Minsk from Frankfurt; Austrian Airlines from Vienna; and Polish Airlines also fly to Minsk. The national carrier, Belarus, flies to most Western European capitals and major US cities.

By Rail
In addition to the traditional rail links with Russia, there is an overnight train from Tallinn, Estonia.

UKRAINE

By Air
Kiev can now be reached through an increasing number of Western airlines. There are flights from most Western European capitals, with Austrian Air, KLM, British Airways and Lufthansa among the regular flyers. Air Ukraine International also has connections to the main European cities.

The main airport, Borispil, is a 40-minute car journey from Kiev city centre. Austrian Air and Lufthansa also fly direct to Odessa.

By Rail
A slower option is to take the train. From Moscow, Kiev is only a night's ride away. In the evening trains depart almost every half–hour from Moscow's Kiev station. From the West, Kiev is on the main train routes from south Central Europe.

By Sea
Odessa on the Black Sea is on the itinerary of liners travelling from many European ports, with the most regular services being to Istanbul.

Customs

When entering Russia you must fill in the customs declaration. It must be returned to the customs office, along with another customs declaration which you fill in on leaving the country.

Russian customs regulations have been revised several times over the past few years. Customs authorities want to find a compromise between conforming to international standards of customs regulations and preventing the export of large batches of cheap goods bought in Russian shops for resale in other countries.

The latest edition of the Russian customs regulations prohibits the import and export of weapons and ammunition (excluding approved hunting tackle), and also drugs and devices for their use. It is prohibited to export antiquities and art objects except for those imported and declared on entry.

As customs regulations change frequently, it is best to check with the Russian consulate or embassy in your home country about restrictions and limitations before travelling.

A 30 percent duty is required to export any personal items worth more than US$10,000. Export duties may be imposed on any items which are determined by customs officials at the point of departure to be of commercial use. Certain items, such as caviar, medications, precious and semi-precious stones or metals, jewellery, and fuel may be exported duty-free in limited amounts only.

Samovars, carpets from central Asia and icons often carry export restrictions requiring you to have them priced by the Ministry of Culture.

Ukraine
In Ukraine, you are exempt from customs formalities if you are carrying less than US$1,000 (or equivalent) and less than US$250 worth of jewellery and valuables. Otherwise you have to fill in a declaration.

Health Regulations

Visitors from the US, Canada, European countries and Japan do not need a health certificate, but vaccinations against tetanus and diphtheria are recommended. It is also advisable to be inoculated against Hepatitis A. Visitors from regions suspected to be infected by yellow fever, especially some African and South American territories, require an international certificate of vaccination against yellow fever.

Belarus
Up to 1000 cigarettes or 1000g of tobacco products, 2 litres of alcohol and other goods up to a value of US$2000 are duty free imports into Belarus. On entering the country, visitors must fill out a customs declaration form, to be handed in when leaving, listing articles imported for personal use, including currency and valuables.

It is prohibited to export weapons, ammunition, precious metals and furs. Works of art and antiques can only be taken out with the permission of the Ministry of Culture. Forbidden imports include narcotics, anti-Belarus propaganda, fruit and vegetables.

Practical Tips

Identity Papers

According to Russian law, everyone should carry their passport (Russians have an internal one) at all times. Foreigners also need to carry a visa. Some visitors choose to carry photocopies, fearing their documents may be stolen, as indeed it is extremely difficult to replace a lost or stolen visa. The snag is that the police don't always accept photocopies as valid proof of identity. Be careful of the police, especially at night, as they often harass citizens and tourists.

Security

Don't carry all your cash in one place, and avoid displaying large sums of money. Be especially careful while buying souvenirs from street vendors – thieves may be watching to see where you keep your money. Tuck your bag and camera firmly under your arm while shopping. The rule to observe is to behave sensibly and be aware that street crime here is as rife as it is in any big city in the world.

Unless you've acquired adequate conversational Russian, it's a good idea to carry a card which says, in Russian, where you are staying and the telephone number. If you get lost, seek assistance in any Western-standard hotel where they are likely to speak English, or hail a taxi and show the driver the card.

When travelling by train, try to book in advance. Never buy tickets from the casual person apparently returning an unwanted ticket at the railway station, and ensure that your ticket reflects your passport details as you will be required to show it to the conductor.

Belarus is safe to visit, although street crime is still a problem especially at night and in or near hotels frequented by foreigners. Be sure to lock your door securely if on an overnight sleeper train.

Corrupt police officers are probably the only major worry a visitor to Russia will have. President Putin recently singled out crooked cops as one of the biggest problems in the country and has vowed to reign them in. Still, it's likely that it will be a while before significant progress is made.

Street crime is not very common in the city centres, except for the pickpockets that work main streets. Violent crime in Russia is mostly connected to conflicts in the rough world of Russian business, and if you are in the country for pleasure, there is little reason to worry about your physical safety.

Women should be aware that most Russian men can be aggressive, have little sense of proper behaviour, tend to see women as sexual objects, and what is considered to be sexual harassment in Anglo-American countries, is considered a normal way to meet a women in Russia.

Russian women tend to be demure and rarely take the initiative to meet a man. If a woman in a restaurant or bar comes across as forward, however, there is a good chance she may be a prostitute, many of whom frequent places that foreigners tend to visit. There are many cases where prostitutes drug and rob their clients.

St Petersburg Police Alert

Crime should be the least of your worries when visiting St Petersburg – according to official statistics, very few crimes are committed against foreigners. The "crime–fighters", however, *are* a cause for concern. A growing number of innocent foreigners have been harassed and beaten by the local police.

In general, Russians accept police brutality as a part of life since there are few controls on the police force, which is a federal ministry, and the local civil rights organisations are still quite weak.

The St Petersburg police force (*militsia*) is considered, even by its own leadership in Moscow, to be one of the most corrupt and inefficient forces in Russia. The problems all begin with a routine document check in the street. According to law, all Russians are required to carry their internal passport with them at all times, while foreigners, too, are supposed to carry their passport. In most cases, those stopped by the police are allowed to go if their documents are in order. If not, or if they are not carrying their passport, or if they are even slightly drunk, then the police can take them to the station. Many of those detained are beaten and robbed.

Practical Advice If you see police walking down the street late at night, cross to the opposite side. If you are stopped, be polite and do what they say. If they wish to detain you, say the word "*konsulat*" (consulate) so that they know you wish to speak with your country's consulate. In most cases, though, the police do not allow people to call. Be polite but firm, insisting that they have to let you go, or they will have big problems when you contact your consulate.

How to Find Help If you are abused by the police, there is almost no recourse, except to complain to the *St Petersburg Times*, tel: (812) 325 9595, 325 6080, which, unfortunately, regularly publishes such stories. If you are the victim of abuse or a crime, it is best first to contact your consulate and ask them to assist in speaking to the police.

Road Safety

Don't assume Russian drivers will stop when you cross the road – they'll expect you to jump out of their way and are likely to hit you if you don't understand this convention. Unfortunately, even drivers who have a licence may not be safe on the roads so when hailing a cab try to stop a registered taxi: in Moscow the taxis are easily recognisable by their bright yellow, New York-style cab colour.

While walking, be aware of a traditional Russian hazard still very much in evidence: the manhole without a cover. And don't expect heavy doors, typical of the underground, to have dampers fitted – they're likely to swing towards you with enough force to knock you off your feet.

Medical Treatment

Apteki (pharmacies) in the major cities are usually well-stocked with domestic and imported medicines, although in times of financial crisis they may be short of foreign medicines. Most pharmacists will understand the English

pronunciation of a drug, not brand names. If you need special medication it is best to bring it with you. Doctors and hospitals often expect immediate cash payment for health services. Medical insurance is essential, preferably with supplementary medical insurance with specific overseas coverage, which includes repatriation.

Pharmacies in Moscow
Drugstore
Sadko Arcade Krasno–gvardeysky Proyezd
tel: (095) 253 9592
Anna Import–Export NV
Priyutsky Per. 3
tel: (095) 978 1073
Dina–Medica
Kashirskoye Shosse 44/1
tel: (095) 323 6510
Diplomatic Polyclinic Drugstore
Dobryninsky 4th Pereulok 4
tel: (095) 237 4034
Eczacibasi Drugstore
ulitsa Maroseyka 2/15
tel: (095) 928 9189, 921 4048
International Pharmacy
ulitsa Kozhevnicheskaya 13
tel: (095) 235 7583
Pharmacy Central Enquiry Office
tel: (095) 927 0561

Emergency Numbers

All Russian cities have unified emergency telephone numbers which can be dialled free from public telephones:

Fire (*Pozharnaya okhrana*)	01
Police (*Militsia*)	02
Ambulance	
(*Skoraya pomoshch*)	03
Gas Emergency	
(*Sluzhba gaza*)	04
Information (*Spravochnaya*)	09

Officials responding to these calls will speak little English, so a knowledge of Russian is needed to make yourself understood.

Take precautions
It is recommended that you wash fruit and vegetables before eating them. You should not drink tap water because a different and unfamiliar mineral composition can easily produce an upset stomach. It is particularly important not to drink St Petersburg's tap water, even in small quantities. Bottled mineral water is available everywhere.

Be careful when buying alcohol from kiosks. It's been known for brand-name bottles to be emptied of their original contents and refilled with homebrew of dubious quality.

Doctors
Your hotel service bureau will find a doctor to come to your hotel room or will refer you to the nearest clinic. Medical standards in Russia are good and in the big cities there are specialists available for every kind of illness. Medicines and hospital treatment must be paid for in roubles.

In Moscow, the following hospitals offer good levels of service:
International Medical Centre
Grokholsky Pereulok, 31, 10th floor
tel: (095) 280 8388
Good service, not too expensive.
European Medical Centre
2-ya Tverskaya-Yamskaya 10
tel: (095) 251 6099, 250 0730.
emergencies (095) 956 7999.
Assit-24, Delta Consulting Group
tel: (095) 229–6536.

Tips for Women Travelling Alone

1 Avoid walking around a city centre alone at night. Russian friends will often insist on walking you either part of the way, or all the way home: refusal could offend.
2 Russian men often behave chivalrously, in a way that some Western women might find offensive. Do not be shocked if they open the door for you, take you by the arm when crossing the street, or stepping off a bus. Again, refusal could offend.
3 Be careful who you smile at. Smiling at a man is often taken to mean that you like him – don't be surprised if he starts following you.
4 If you go anywhere with a man, he will want to pay for you, and any attempt to pay for yourself is a serious insult to his honour.

5 If, at any time, an unpleasant situation does arise in a dark and secluded area, make it clear you are a foreigner, simply by speaking English. Troublemakers take advantage of the fact that Russian women are usually ashamed of violence against them and are unlikely to report a violent incident to the police, but they know that a Western woman is more likely to press for her rights and file charges.
6 In general, be firm and strong with troublemakers, though not rude and aggressive. Most of them are cowards and in some strange way, Russian men have an ingrained respect of women because of their mothers – they respect strong women.

Athens Medical Centre
Michurinsky Prospekt 6
tel: (095) 147 9322.

In St Petersburg:
24-Hour Medical Centre for Foreigners
22 Moskovsky Prospekt
tel: (812) 316 6272.
Although the clinic is open from 8.30am–8pm, it does have a 24-hour emergency ambulance service.
American Medical Center
10 Serpukhovskaya ulitsa
tel: (812) 326 6272.
It is much more expensive than the centre above, so bring a credit card.

Health Spas

The healing properties of the mineral waters in the Mineralnyye Vody Region (Caucasian Spa District) have been known for centuries. This area, and the customs of resort people, were described by the writer Mikhail Lermontov, author of *A Hero of Our Time*, who was killed in a duel in the spa town of Pyatigorsk.

Pyatigorsk mineral waters are still popular and are used to treat bowel complaints, the neural system, dyspepsia, pathological metabolism, and vascular, gynaecological and skin problems. Other spas in this region – Essentuki, Kislovodsk and Zheleznovodsk – are just as famous as Pyatigorsk. However, it's no more safe to venture into the area on your own than it was in Lermontov's time: plane hijacks and kidnappings have been common in recent years, and several tourist groups were abducted and held for ransom in the late 1990s.

Sochi and Matsesta are also in the vicinity of the Kavkazskiye Mineralniye Vody Region, on the Black Sea coast close to the spa of Tskhaltubo.

Newspapers

Foreign-language press
In Moscow, you will find the informative *Moscow News*, and the more recent and authoritative *Moscow Times*. Both are in English,

Web Information

While the rate of change has slowed in the decade after the collapse of the Soviet Union, there is still a greater amount of flux in Russia than in western Europe. For the most up-to-date information, access St Petersburg: The Guide, at www.spbguide.ru or for information about Moscow: www.moscow-guide.ru

and are on sale in most major hotels and at kiosks. The satirical *Exile* bi-weekly carries valuable restaurant and nightlife tips.

When you arrive in Moscow, try to find a copy of the *Moscow Business Telephone Guide*, the city's most detailed telephone directory. Updated on a monthly basis, it is available free of charge at major hotels and restaurants and is on sale throughout the city.

In St Petersburg, the twice-weekly newspaper, *St Petersburg Times*, and the monthly magazine, *Pulse*, will give you important information on local events. If you are staying in the country for some time, a copy of *The Traveller's Yellow Pages*, which can be bought at hotels in Moscow and St Petersburg, is useful.

The English-language newspaper in Kiev, the *Kiev Post*, is an essential guide to Ukrainian life. There is also a weekly listings magazine called *What's On*.

Russian-language press
Izvestya, one of the best-known Russian newspapers in the West, is no longer the "official paper of the Communist party", but owned by a leading capitalist, Vladimir Potanin and his financial-industrial empire, Unexim Group. Most national and local papers are financed by leading financial and industrial corporations. *Argumenty i Facty*, a national weekly newspaper, has a circulation of 20 million. The liberal daily *Komsomolskaya Pravda* has a circulation of more than 12 million. Also popular, but with a smaller circulation are *Kommersant* and

Vedomosti. The most widely read St Petersburg newspaper is the *Sankt–Petersburg Vedomosti* (140,000).

In Ukraine, the better papers are *Den*, *Kievskie Vedemosti* and the weekly *Zerkalo Nedeliy*.

Postal Services

Post offices open Mon–Sat 9am–6pm; they often close at midday for an hour, and are closed on Sundays. Some post offices, however, open only from 9am–3pm or 2–8pm. The mail service in Russia provides an increasing variety and standard of services. Not all post offices accept international mail bigger than a standard letter. International postal delivery can be slow – it may take two or three weeks for a letter from Moscow to reach Western Europe and sometimes even a month or more to reach the US.

Couriers
If you have important documents or packages to send abroad, you should use a courier service. There are a number of international and Russian courier services available.
In Moscow contact:
DHL, 14, 8 Mapta ulitsa , 11/2, tel: (095) 956 1000/961 1000
FEDEX, 17 Gogolevsky bulvar, tel: (095) 787 5555
TNT, Express Worldwide, Denezhny Pereulok 1, tel: (095) 201 2585

Dialling Codes

International codes
Russia – 7
Belarus – 375
Ukraine – 380
City prefixes
Moscow – 095
St Petersburg – 812
Minsk – 017
Kiev – 044
Odessa – 0482
If you are trying to make a call within the CIS, then dial 8 before the city code, and wait for the dial tone.

UPS, Bolshoi Tishinsky Pereulok 8, tel: (095) 961 2211/253 1937
Pony Express, tel: (095) 930 2080
In St Petersburg contact:
DHL, 10 Nevsky prospekt, tel: (812) 326 6400
Westpost, 86 Nevsky prospekt, tel: (812) 327 3092
FEDEX, 16 Griboyedov Canal, tel: (812) 327 0480/299 9071
TNT, 14 Sofiiskaya ulitsa, tel: (812) 118 3330
In Kiev contact:
DHL, 1 Vasylkivska Vyl, tel: (44) 490 2600
TNT, tel: (44) 277 1411
UPS, tel: (44) 290 0000

In Minsk contact:
DHL, 18 ulitsa Brestskaya , tel: (017) 278 1108

Cables & Telegrams

Cables to addresses within Russia can be sent from any post office. The same applies to international cables. It may be simpler, but more expensive, to send a cable from a hotel.

Telephones

The main type of public phone box uses plastic cards, available in units of 5, 10, 20 or 50 at metro stations and kiosks. Insert the card and dial the number. When your call is answered press the # button to complete the connection. Outside Moscow you may find older token call boxes. Tokens can be bought individually. Place a token in the slot on the top of the phone. When answered, depending on the type of telephone, the token may drop by itself (good for 3 minutes – you can place the next token as soon as the first one drops), or press the # button to connect the call.

To dial abroad, go to a post office. This whole process can be complicated and time-consuming. It is simpler but more expensive to phone from your hotel.

Business Hours

Most stores in Russia work 10am to 8pm, though in the centre of major cities it is not difficult to find a 24 hours convenience food store. More and more businesses work the entire day, foregoing closure at lunch time. But some organisations, such as banks, do close for one hour, either between 1–2pm, or 2–3pm. Don't be shocked if service is not courteous, sales personnel are slowly being taught that the customer is most important.

Gay Travellers

Since the change in Russia's legal system in the mid-1990s that abolished Soviet-era prohibitions on homosexuality, Russia's gay community has gained more acceptance. There are several openly gay and lesbian clubs, and society is more tolerant than it was even just 5 years ago.

Travellers with Disabilities

It is strongly recommended that disabled travellers do not travel alone. In general, Russian society is not sympathetic to the plight of the disabled, and has a long way to go to improve their ability to be active members of society.

Embassies and Consulates

Moscow
Canada
Starokonyushenny Peryulok 23
tel: (095) 105 6000
Open 9.30am–5pm
Ukraine
Leontevskiyper
tel: (095) 229 1079
United Kingdom
Sofiyskaya nab. 10
tel: (095) 956 7200
Open 9am–1pm; 2–5pm
United States
Bolshaya Devyatinskiy Per 8
tel: (095) 728 5000

St Petersburg
Canadian Consulate
Malodestkoselskiy prospekt 32
tel: (812) 325 8448
France
nab. Moiki 15
tel: (812) 314 1443, 312 1130
Germany
Furshtatskaya ulitsa
tel: (812) 327 3111
Italy
Teatral'naya pl. 10
tel: (812) 312 3106
Sweden
10th line (VO)
1/3 Malaya Konnushnaya
tel: (812) 329–1430
United Kingdom
Proletarskaya Diktatury 5
tel: (812) 320 3200
Open 10am–5.30pm
weekdays

United States
Furshtatskaya ulitsa 15
tel: (812) 275 1701
emergency after hours: 274 8692
Open 9.30am–5.30pm weekdays

Minsk
France
Pl. Svobody 11
tel: (017) 210 2868
Germany
ulitsa Zakharova 26
tel: (017) 213 3357
United Kingdom
Karla Marxa 37
tel: (017) 210 5920
United States
Starovilenskaya 46
tel: (017) 210 1283
US citizen services 2.30–4.30pm

Kiev
France
Vyl. Reiterska 39
tel: (044) 228 8728
Germany
Vyl. Honchara 84
tel: (044) 216 9583
Russia
Vozdukhnoflotskiy prospekt 27
tel: (044) 244 0961
United Kingdom
Vyl. Desyatinna 9
tel: (044) 462 0011
United States
Vyl. Yuria Kotsyubinskoho 10
tel: (044) 490 4000
Open 9am–6pm weekdays

Russia is quite difficult for disabled travellers to get around, though progress is slowly being made. The Russian Museum in St Petersburg, for example, recently installed equipment to allow those in wheelchairs to go up stairs. But most places do not have the means to accommodate wheelchair users. The transport system also provides no assistance, and it is difficult to rent a car or van that would have facilities for disabled people.

Etiquette

Don't be surprised by Russians' near lack of public manners and rudeness, and don't expect a Russian to apologise if he happens to accidentally bump into you on the

Moscow Net Access

IRPO
ulitsa Chernyakhovskovo 9, #108
tel: (095) 152 7331
Open 9am–9pm
Kuznetski Most Cafe
Kuznetski Most 12
tel: 924-2140.
An hour costs 60 roubles. Open 10am–midnight.
Manezh Shopping Centre
Manezhnaya ploschad (Next to Teatralnaya Metro)
tel: (095) 363 0060
Reportedly the biggest internet cafe in Eastern Europe. Open 24 hours.
Netland
ulitsa Rozhdestvenka 2
tel: (095) 781 0923
Pool tables, bar and table football. Open 9–8am every day except Mon 9am–10pm.
British Council
Nikoloyamskaya ulitsa 1
tel: (095) 234 0201
In the Foreign Literature Library. Not many computers but you can read newspapers in English whilst waiting. Open 9am–5pm.

Internet cafes open and close all the time. These are just a few of the more stable. You'll see them everywhere, especially in the centre.

street. Also, car drivers can be one of the most dangerous encounters for a foot-bound traveller. Even if you have a green light, they may not stop and may hoot and shout at you to get out of the way.

Russians tend to be an unpredictable and emotional people, (though of all Russian cities, the people of St. Petersburg tend to be the most reserved), who sometimes appear to be angry with each other. Often it is just the normal way they speak to each other, and one need not be alarmed. But if a Russian is indeed angry, their mood can just as easily change to joy and laughter.

Despite, their public rudeness, Russians are quite snobbish when it comes to etiquette in the home and at work, and one must be careful not to offend. Russians can also be very kind, sometimes too much so, in the home and on a personal level. Remember to take off your shoes when entering a house and put on the slippers provided. Failure to eat and drink what your host offers will be taken as a grave offence. Russians don't like small talk and don't be surprised if they ask you some questions or make comments most Westerners would find too personal.

Tipping

Though Russia had been socialist for more than 70 years, tipping, one of the capitalist sins, is an accepted practice. Waiters, porters and taxi drivers always appreciate tips; 10 percent is the accepted rule. Porters will take what's acceptable anywhere else in the world. Guides and interpreters also appreciate tips.

Religious Services

Russian Orthodox
Most churches open for services. The main service usually starts around 9 or 10am. Women should always cover their heads. Note that hands in pockets is taken as a sign of disrespect. Observe the etiquette of the locals around you.

It is worth visiting the service at 10am on Sundays at **St Catherine's**,

ulitsa Bolshaya Ordynka 60/2, Moscow, tel: (095) 238 8334, as it is celebrated through English.

Roman Catholic
Chapel of Our Lady of Hope
Kutuzovsky prosp. 7/4, korp. 5, kv. 42, Moscow
tel: (095) 243 9621
Church of the Immaculate Conception
Malaya Gruzinskaya ulitsa 27, Moscow
tel: (095) 252 3911
The Catholic Church
Kovensky Pereulok 7, St Petersburg

Baptist
Seven Day Adventist and Baptist Church
Danilovskaya ulitsa 37, Moscow
tel: (095) 126 8767, 468 6500
The Baptist Church
Bolshaya Ozernaya ulitsa 29a, St Petersburg

Muslim
Vypolzov per. 7, Moscow
tel: (095) 281 3866
Mechel
Kronversky prospekt 7, St Petersburg

Jewish
The Synagogue
Bolshoi Spasoglinischevsky Peryulok 10, Moscow
tel: (095) 924 2424.

Overseas Missions

Russian Missions Abroad
Canada
285 Sharlotta Street, Ottawa
tel: (613) 235 4341;
fax: 236 6342
Visa Department
tel: (613) 236 7220
fax: 238 6158
United Kingdom
5, 13 & 18 Kensington Palace Gardens, London W8 4QG
tel: (020) 7229 3828
Consulate, 58 Melville Street Edinburgh EH3 7HL
tel: (0131) 225 7098
United States
Embassy, Wisconsin Avenue, N.N. Washington DC 200007

tel: (202) 298 5700
fax: 298 5749
Consulate, 9E 91st Street,
New York, NY 10128
tel: (212) 328 0926
fax: 831 9162
Visa Department, 1825 Phelps
Place NW Washington DC
tel: (202) 939 8907
fax: 939 8909

Belarusian Missions Abroad
Canada
130 Albert Street, Suite 600,
Ottawa, Ontario, K1P 5G4 Canada.
tel: (613) 233 99 94
fax: 233 85 00
France
38, Boulevard Suchet, 75016 Paris
tel: (01) 44 14 69 79
fax: 44 14 69 70
Germany
Am Treptower Park 32, 12435
Berlin – Treptow
tel: (0228) 53 63 59 34
fax: 53 63 59 24
United Kingdom
6, Kensington Court, London W85 DL
tel: (020) 7937 3288
fax: 361 0005
United States
1619 New Hampshire Ave., NW,
Washington, DC 20009
tel: (202) 986 1606
fax: 986 1805

Ukrainian Missions Abroad
Canada
331 Metcalfe Street, Ottawa
tel: (613) 230 2961
fax: 230 2400
France
21 Avenue de Saxe, 75007 Paris
tel: (01) 43 06 07 37, 43 06 04 11
fax: 43 06 02 94
Germany
Albrechtstrasse 26,10117 Berlin
tel: (30) 288 87 116
fax: 288 87 163
Consulates in Munich and Dusseldorf
United Kingdom
78 Kensington Park Road,
London W11 2PL
tel: (020) 7229 06 89
fax: 727 35 67
United States
3350 M Street NW
Washington, DC 20007
tel: (202) 333 0606

fax: 333 0817
Also consulates general in Chicago
and New York.

Airline Offices

Moscow
Aeroflot
Leningradsky Avenue 37, bldg 9
tel: 753 5555
fax: 155 6647
www.aeroflot.ru
Air Baltic
Malaya Pirogovskaya Street 18,
bldg 1, office 406
tel: 786 6827
fax: 242 9564
e-mail: airbaltic@continent.ru
www.airbaltic.lv
American Airlines
Sadovaya-Kudrinskaya Street 20,
office 207

Chambers of Commerce

**Russian Chamber of Commerce
and Industry**
6 Ilyinka (Kuybyshev) Street
Moscow 101000
tel: (095) 929 0009
American Chamber of Commerce
7 ulitsa Dolgorukovskaya
14th floor
www.amcham.ru
tel: (095) 961 2141
**Russo-British Chamber of
Commerce**
42 Southwark Street
London SE1 1UN
tel: (020) 7235 2423
Business Centre Dukat II, ulitsa
Gasheka 7, 3rd floor, tel: (095)
961 2161
**French-Russian Chamber of
Commerce**
22 Ave Franklin D. Roosevelt
75008 Paris
tel: (01) 422 59710
Moscow office: Apt. 3, 4
Pokrovsky Blvd, Moscow 101000
tel: (095) 207 3009
**Italian–Russian Chamber of
Commerce**
5 Via San Tomaso, Milan
tel: (2) 481 6725.
Moscow office: 7 Denezhny
Pereulok, Moscow 121002
tel: (095) 241 5729

tel: 234 4074/5
fax: 234 4079
e-mail: talav@comail.ru
www.aa.com
Austrian Airlines
Smolenskaya Street 5
The Golden Ring Hotel
tel: 995 0995
fax: 725 2559
e-mail: auamow@aua.com
www.austrianairlines.ru
British Airways
Sheremetyevo-2 Airport, 6th floor,
office 601
tel: 956 4676
fax: 578 2936
1st Tverskaya-Yamskaya St 23
tel: 363 2525
fax: 363 2505
www.britishairways.com
Delta Airlines
Gogolevskiy blvrd 11, 2nd floor
tel: 937 9090
fax: 937 9091
Finnair
Sheremetyevo-2 Airport, 6th floor,
office 625
tel: 578 2738
fax: 961 2056
www.delta.com
Japan Air
Kuznetsky Most Street 3
tel: 921 6448/6648
fax: 921 3294
www.jal-europe.com
KLM
Usacheva Street 33, bldg 1,
3rd floor
tel: 258 3600
fax: 258 3606
e-mail: klm.russia@klm.com
www.klm.com
LOT (Polish Airlines)
Tverskoy blvrd 26
tel: 229 5771/7388/8525
fax: 229 8829
www.lot.com
Lufthansa
1st Tverskaya-Yamskaya Street 19
Sheraton Palace Hotel
tel: 737 6405
Olimpiysky Avenue 18/1
Renaissance Hotel
tel: 737 6400
fax: 737 6401
e-mail: lufthansa@online.ru
www.lufthansa.ru
SAS (Scandinavia Airlines)
1st Tverskaya-Yamskaya Street 5

tel: 775 4747
fax: 730 4142
e-mail: sas@co.ru
www.scandinavian.net
Swiss Air
Paveletskaya Sq 2, bldg 3
tel: 937 7767
fax: 937 7769
e-mail: moscow.townoffice@
swiss.com
www.swiss.com
TransAero
2nd Smolensky Lane 3/4
Tel: 241 4800/7676
www.transaero.com
Turkish Airlines
Kuznetsky Most Street 1/8
Tel: 292 1667/5121/4345
Fax: 200 2245
e-mail: tkmoscow@turkishline.ru
www.turkishairlines.com.tr

St Petersburg
Austrian Airlines
57 Nevsky prospekt
tel: (812) 325 3260
Open Mon–Fri 9am–5pm
Air France
Pulkovo 2
tel: (812) 104 3433
35 Bolshaya Morskaya Ul
tel: (812) 104 3433
Open Mon–Fri 9am–5pm
British Airways/Deutsche BA
Malaya Konnushnaya 1/3
tel: (812) 325 2565
Open Mon–Fri 9am–5.30pm
Delta Airlines
36 Bol. Morskaya ulitsa
tel: (812) 311 5819/20
Open Mon–Fri 9am–5.30pm
Finnair
44 Kazanskaya ulitsa
tel: (812) 326 1870
KLM
Malaya Morskaya 23, 4th floor
tel: (812) 346 6868
Lufthansa
Voznesensky prospekt 7
tel: (812) 314 4979
SAS
57 Nevsky prospekt
tel: (812) 325 3255
Open Mon–Fri 9am–5pm
Swissair/SAS/Austrian Airlines
57 Nevsky prospekt
tel: (812) 325 3250/55
fax: (812) 164 7873

Swissair
57 Nevsky prospekt
tel: (812) 325 3250
Open Mon–Fri 9am–5pm

Kiev
Air France
Vyl Velyka Zhytomyrska 6/11
tel: (044) 464 1010
British Airways
Yaroslaviv Val. 5
tel: (044) 490 6060
KLM
Vyl Ivana Franka 34/33, 2nd floor
tel: (044) 490 2490
LOT (Polish Airlines)
Vyl Ivana Franka 36
tel: (044) 246 5620
Lufthansa
Vyl. B. Khmelnytskoho 52
tel: (044) 490 3800
Swissair/Austrian Airlines
Vyl. Chervonoarmiiska 9/2
tel: (44) 244 3540/41/42
Transaero
Vyl. Chervonoarmiyska 9/2
tel: (044) 490 6565
Ukraine International
Peremohy prospekt 14
tel: (044) 461 5050

Belarus
Lufthansa
Fanziska Skoriny prospekt 56
tel: (017) 284 7129
fax: (017) 284 3858
Austrian Airlines
Masherova 19
tel: (017) 289 1970
Belavia
Nemiga 14
tel: (017) 210 4100
fax: (017) 229 2383

International Travel Agents

United Kingdom
Andrews Consulting
31 Corsham Street, 2nd floor,
London N1 6DR
tel: (020) 7490 8142
email: london@actravel.com
Asla Ltd
160 High Street, Huntingdon,
Cambridgeshire PE29 3TF
tel: (01480) 433783
email: info@asla.co.uk

Hogg Robinson Business Travel
12 Caxton Street, London SW1H 0QS
tel: (020) 7222 8711
Russia Direct Ltd
39 Palmerston Place
Edinburgh EH12 5AU
email: info@russiadirect.net
tel: (0131) 476 7727
Russian Gateway UK Limited
tel: (07050 803 160)
email: travel@russiangateway.co.uk

Moscow
Incentive Group Inna Travel
ulitsa 2nd Brestskaya 39/4
tel: (095) 926 5556
www.business-travel.ru
Visa House
22 Bolshaya Nikitskaya
Office 18, Moscow
tel: (095) 721 1021
www.visahouse.com
Recommended.

United States
Russian National Group
130 West 42nd Street
Suite 1804
New York, NY 10036
tel: (877) 221 7120 or (212) 575 3431
email: info@rnto.org
Peace Travel Services
1648 Taylor Rd #222
Port Orange, Fl 32128
email: visa@go-russia.com

See also Independent Operators, page 345.

Russian National Tourist Offices

Canada
1801 McGill Avenue, Suite 930,
Montreal, Quebec H3A 2NA
tel: (514) 849 6394
fax: 849 6743
United Kingdom
Russian National Tourist Office
Orchard House,
167–169 Kensington High Street,
London W8 6SH
tel: (020) 7937 7210/7207
fax: (020) 7938 2912
United States
800 Third Avenue, Suite 3101,
New York, NY 10022
tel: (212) 758 1162

Getting Around

With some 145,000 km (90,050 miles), the railway system of Russia is the longest in the world. It is a means of transport used for 4 billion individual trips per year. The busiest lines in European Russia connect Moscow with St Petersburg and Kiev in the Ukraine, where a train leaves almost every hour. You may prefer to travel to St Petersburg and back by train, leaving late at night and arriving the next morning.

There is a daily express train between Moscow and St Petersburg, leaving each city at 6.30am, which takes 4½ hours to reach it's destination. It is much like a commuter train, with seats only and no berths.

In overnight sleeping cars, tea is always served and trains travelling for more than eight hours have a restaurant car attached during the day. Commercial trains running on these lines offer a very comfortable service with food and bed linen included in the price. Economy tickets may not include these services so be prepared to pay extra for your bedding.

Reservations You should make your reservation several days ahead as reserved train seats are in short supply, especially 2nd class tickets, which are cheap but fairly comfortable. You can reserve your seat through a travel agent; at the Intourist counter at the station; or at the Intourtrans Office, Ul. Petrovka 15, Moscow, tel: (095) 929 8743, 929 8848, 921 8968, 929 8741.

There are booking offices in the railway stations of every major city. The ticket must have a cover and a coupon (it is valid only with both these components).

General Inquiries For inquiries about train arrivals and departures from all stations, tel: (095) 266 9000, (095) 266 9333. Ticket booking to all destinations, tel: (095) 266 8333, (095) 262 0319.

In St Petersburg, the telephone number for all inquiries about arrivals and departures of trains is (812) 168 0111.

Car Rental

Western car companies can be found in the major cities and you will find branches at international

This rail link from Europe to the Orient is one of the most exotic train trips in the world, and the longest. Over a period of nine days the train crosses seven time zones from Moscow to Vladivostok, passing through much of the diversity of Siberian Russia. It makes many scheduled stops along the way, but never lingers longer than 15 minutes. If you want to explore further than a few hundred yards from the tracks, you must disembark and rejoin a later train. Stop-offs should be scheduled ahead of time, especially if travelling first class, since you could easily lose your cabin.

The port of Vladivostok was opened to foreign tourists in 1992. It is now possible to begin or end a Trans-Siberian rail trip in Yokohama, near Tokyo in Japan. A two-day cruise connects Vladivostok with Yokohama.

Adding to the network is the Baikal-Amur Mainline (BAM), which connects Tayshet to Komsolmolsk. Located just 66 km (41 miles) from Lake Baikal, Irkutsk is the most popular stopover for Trans-Siberian travellers. A typical Trans-Siberian train trip would include a two-day stop in Irkutsk, from which excursions to Lake Baikal are easily arranged.

Other popular stopovers are Novosibirsk, Listvyanka (on Lake Baikal), Bratsk (by air or train from Irkutsk) and Khabarovsk.

Train accommodation is available in first-class (two-person compartments) and second-class (four-person compartments). Ask the conductor to lock your compartment whenever you leave it, as theft is rampant on Russian trains. Most embassies also recommend that foreign travellers speak as little as possible on the train so as not to attract attention.

The train plying the route, the Rossiya, is of slightly better quality than most Russian trains. The food is also better than normal: soups are usually good, and tea is always available from the conductor at a nominal charge. The best strategy is to do like the Russians: pack your own food and eat it in your own carriage. Bed linen and towels are provided and there is a toilet and wash basin at the end of each carriage.

If nine days on a train doesn't appeal to you, it is possible to disembark somewhere along the route and fly the rest of the way. Taking the train from east to west as far as Irkutsk and connecting to Moscow by air would include the most exotic portion of the train journey and leave time to tour the capital as well.

There are also trans-continental rail routes, such as those from Moscow to Peking in China and Ulan Baatar in Mongolia. They demand an adventurous spirit and a willingness to spend a week in the train contemplating the endless Trans-Siberian landscapes before you.

airports. Cars can also be hired with a driver. Check up-to-date details before you leave, or at hotels, which advertise such companies. Before you hire a car, read the advice printed under "*Routes*" below.

Budget, tel: (095) 915 5237
Eurodollar, tel: (095) 298 6146
Eurocar, tel: (095) 253 1369, 578 3878, 155 0170
Hertz, tel: (095) 578 5646

Routes

If you intend to visit Russia by car you should first contact a specialist tour operator as they have worked out a number of routes that can be easily negotiated with your own vehicle. Road conditions off these routes are very poor.

The ideal route through European Russia means entering the region from Finland, driving via St Petersburg and Moscow to the Caucasus and the Black Sea, ferrying the car across to Yalta or Odessa and then crossing Ukraine

to the Czech and Slovak republics or Poland.
Sovinterautoservice
Institutski per., 2/1, Moscow
tel: (095) 101 496
The specialist for car travel in Russia. It can solve nearly every problem a foreigner may have on Russian roads.

Rules of the Road

Russia is a signatory to the International Traffic Convention. Rules of the road and road signs correspond to international standards. The basic rules, however, are worth mentioning.
1 Vehicles are driven on the right side of the road.
2 It is prohibited to drive a car after consuming any alcohol, even the smallest amount. If you test positive for alcohol, the consequences may be very serious. It is also prohibited to drive a car under the effect of drugs or any powerful medicine.
3 You must have an international driving licence and documents

verifying your right to drive the car (papers must be in Russian and are issued by Intourist). You can obtain a temporary International Driver's Licence from your automobile association at home. In the UK the AA can issue this for a small fee and one passport-size photo.
4 Vehicles, except for Intourist cars, must carry the national registration code and a national licence plate.
5 Using the horn is prohibited within city limits except in emergencies.
6 Seat belts for the driver and front seat passenger are compulsory.
7 The speed limit in populated areas (marked by blue coloured signs indicating "town") is 60 kph (37 mph); on most arterial roads 90 kph (55.5 mph). On highways the limit can differ, so look out for road signs specifying other speeds.
8 You can insure your car in Russia through Ingosstrakh, the national insurance company, or through a private insurance company.

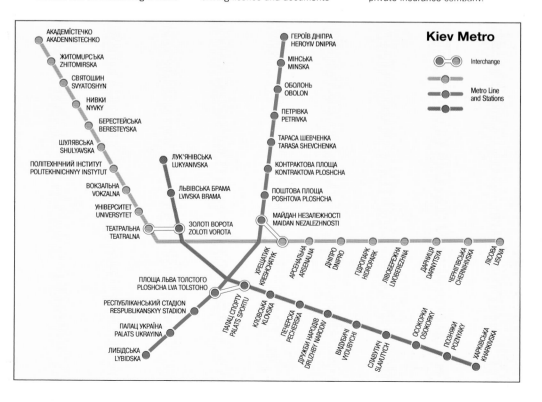

By Boat

Many rivers in European Russia are open to navigation during the spring and autumn. You can travel along the Dnieper, Volga, Oka, Moskva, Don, Dniester, Neva and other rivers. The cities on the banks of the rivers are connected by passenger ships and hydrofoils (Raketa and Kometa Class).

If you plan a trip along one of these routes, you can make a reservation through Intourist or directly at the Moscow River Station (Rechnoy Vokzal).

River Stations

Moscow
Mostourflot
tel: (095) 459 7140
Intourist
tel: (095) 156 8019
Severny Rechnoy Vokzal
Leningradskoe shosse 51
tel: (095) 457 4050.
St Petersburg
Rechnoy Vokzal
Prosp. Obukhovskoy Oborony 195
tel: (812) 262 1318 (information)
262 5511 (booking office)
Kiev
Rechnoy Vokzal
Poshtova Pl
tel: (44) 416 1268

Cruises

Travel agencies offer organised river cruises on comfortable river liners which are relaxing and interesting, but quite expensive. These cruises are offer trips along the Lena, and soon the Ob and the Yenisey will also feature on its programme.

By Plane

Aeroflot, once the world's largest airline, has been broken up, and each republic now runs its own airline. The name Aeroflot is still used by the Russian airline. It flies to many remote and outlying areas, sometimes using helicopters and small hopper planes. Many of its aircraft have been designed primarily for military purposes and lack the comfort of Western carriers, but it has recently bought a fleet of European Airbuses.

The cheapest fares cannot be bought from Aeroflot direct but from consolidators. Fares within Russia can be reasonable and flights have to be booked far in advance since demand exceeds capacity. Check-in starts 1½ hours before departure and ends ½ an hour beforehand. Foreigners pay for their tickets in hard currency and sometimes at grossly unfavourable rates.

In Ukraine and Belarus, the former Soviet fleet now makes up the core of the national airline.

Aeroflot Offices
Moscow
Leningradskiy Prospekt 37, bldg 9
tel: (095) 155 8019; ticket information, tel: (095) 155 5045
St Petersburg
7–9 Nevsky Prospekt
tel: (812) 311 8093 (Russia travel); 315 0072 (international travel)
Khabarovsk
5 Amursky Boulevard
tel: (421) 332 071
Minsk
18–28 Karl Marx Street
tel: (0712) 224 232
Kiev
66 Boulevard Shevchenko
tel: (44) 774 4223

Aeroflot Offices Abroad
London
70 Piccadilly, London W1V 9HH
tel: (020) 7355 2233
New York
235 West 48th Street, NY 10036
tel: (212) 245 1100
Paris
33, Avenue des Champs Elysées
tel: (01) 42 25 43 81, 42 56 19 30

City Transport

MOSCOW

Buses and Trolleybuses

Buses and trolleybuses are slow, because of traffic conditions, but cheap. Most maps show routes,

Minsk Metro

УСХОД
USKHOD

ПУШКІНСКАЯ
PUSKINSKAYA

МАСКОЎСКАЯ
MASKOWSKAYA

ПАРК ЧАЛЮСКІНЦАУ
PARK CHALYUSKINTSAU

МАЛАДЗЁЖНАЯ
MALADZYOZHNAYA

АКАДЭМІЯ НАВУК
AKADEMIYA NAVUK

ФРУНЗЕНСКАЯ
FRUNZYENSKAYA

ПЛОШЧА ЯКУБА КОЛАСА
PLOSHCHA YAKUBA KOLASA

КУПАЛАЎСКАЯ
KUPALAWSKAYA

НЯМІГА
NYAMIHA

ПЛОШЧА ПЕРАМОГІ
PLOSHCHA PYERAMOHI

КАСТРЫЧНІЦКАЯ
KASTRYCHNITSKAYA

ПЕРШАМАЙСКАЯ
PYERSHAMAYSKAYA

ПЛОШЧА НЕЗАЛЕЖНАСЦІ
PLOSHCHA NYEZALYEZHNASTSI

ПРАЛЕТАРСКАЯ
PRALYETARSKAYA

ІНСТЫТУТ КУЛЬТУРЫ
INSTYTUT KULTURY

ТРАКТАРНЫ ЗАВОД
TRAKTARNY ZAVOD

ПАРТЫЗАНСКАЯ
PARTIZANSKAYA

АЎТАЗАВОДСКАЯ
AUTAZAVODSKAYA

Interchange   Metro Line and Stations

МАГІЛЁЎСКАЯ
MOGILYOVSKAYA

City Maps

Particularly recommended for Moscow and St Petersburg are the German Falk plan maps, available from large bookshops.

and bus stops are marked by yellow boards indicating route number and terminus. Buy tickets from the driver.

Taxis

There is a central taxi service and you can book a cab by calling (095) 927 0000, or (095) 923 8052, day or night. Waiting time is about an hour. Never take unlicensed cabs at night. Instead of taking a taxi from the airport, pre-book a transfer with your tour operator.

Taxis usually cost about $100 for this run. A pre-booked taxi should cost around $50. The express mini-bus service can be off-putting for first-timers to Moscow. It is, however, a marked improvement on the city's bus service. It runs past both terminals of Moscow's main airport and is ideal for the economy traveller.

Taxi prices in Moscow are exorbitant if you take a cab from in front of your hotel. Just a couple of blocks away you will probably be able to catch one for half the price, so it's worth walking a short distance. You should be able to get to the city centre for the rouble equivalent of US$5 to $10 and to anywhere in Moscow for $10 to $20 – add an extra couple of dollars at night.

Chauffeur-driven Cars

A chauffeur-driven car can save time and hassle and need not be that expensive, especially if you use one of the private individuals who advertise in the classified columns of the *Moscow Times*. For a more official, possibly more comfortable arrangement, check out:
Intourist, tel: (095) 215 6191
Autosan, tel: (095) 280 3600

The Metro

The Moscow Metro system is famous for its architecture. It is also fast, reliable and cheap and the best

way to travel around Moscow. Buy tickets for 1, 2, 5, 10, 20 rides from the ticket windows in the entry halls or, if you can, buy a monthly pass. Each station, including those which are at the same location but on different lines, has its own name.

ST PETERSBURG

Buses, Trams and Trolleybuses

These run from 6–1am the following morning. To make full use of the system, it is essential to have a special map called *Marshruty Gorodskovo Transporta – Trolleibus, Avtobus i Tramvai* (Town Transport Routes for Trolleybuses, Buses and Trams). Ask your hotel receptionist where to buy a copy.

Stops marked by an "A" sign serve buses, while stops marked "T" serve trolleybuses. The latter are less crowded than buses during rush-hour. Tram signs hang from wires above the middle of the road.

Taxis

Taxis in St Petersburg are cheap. Cabs are pale yellow with a "T" sign. Those which congregate outside hotels inflate their prices considerably, so it is cheaper to flag down a vehicle in the street. Determine the price of a journey before setting out. It's advisable to pre-book a taxi from the airport through your tour operator and should cost about $50.

The Metro

Like St Petersburg's buses and trams, the Metro runs from 6–1am. Famous for its architecture and murals the Metro is the fastest way to get around town, and it is worth trying to get to grips with routes and Cyrillic signs.

KIEV

The Kiev Metro are reliable and cheap. Use of the metro requires *zhetony* (tokens) which are sold from booths by the stations entrance. *See map on page 343.*

MINSK

The Minsk Metro has two lines open between 6–12.30am. *Zhetony* (tokens) can be purchased from attendants at the station. Trolley buses and trams run between 5.30–1am and cover areas that can not be reached by the metro (*see map on page 344*).

Tour Operators

Intourist, the former state travel agency, was privatised at the beginning of 1993. It offers services in all the large Russian cities, but it no longer has the monopoly on the Russian travel business. Tours, which include cruises from Moscow to St Petersburg, city breaks, business trips and conferences, can still be booked through Intourist offices in main cities.

Intourist Offices
London
Intourist House, 219 Marsh Wall, London E14 9FJ
tel: (020) 7538 8600/5961
fax: (020) 7538 5967
e-mail: info@intourus.demon.co.uk
www.intourist.co.uk
New York
630 Fifth Avenue, Suite 868
tel: (212) 757 3884
Paris
7, Boulevard de Capucines
tel: (01) 47 42 47 40
Sydney
Underwood House, 37–49 Pitt Street
tel: (02) 277 652

Independent Operators
United Kingdom
Voyages Jules Verne
21 Dorset Square, London NW1 6QG
tel: (020) 7616 1000
www.vjv.co.uk
Offers cruises and more expensive, specialist tours.
Noble Caledonia
11 Charles Street, London W1X 8LE
tel: (020) 7409 0376
Offers cruises.
Cox & Kings Travel
Gordon House, 10 Greencoat Place, London SW1P 1PH
tel: (020) 7873 5000

Arranges luxury train journeys throughout Russia on the Bolshoi Express.

Regent Holidays
15 John Street, Bristol BS1 2HR
tel: (0117) 921 1711
www.regent-holidays.co.uk
Provides cheap flights, bespoke tours, trips on the Trans-Siberian Railway and will book hotels all over Russia.

The Russia Experience
Research House, Fraser Road, Perivale, Middx UB6 7AQ
tel: (0181) 566 8846
fax: (0181) 566 8843
e-mail: russ–exp@compuserve.com
www.trans-siberian.co.uk
Organises informal trips for individuals featuring family stays, trans-Siberian trips and trekking.

United States

Russiatours
13312 North 56th Street, Suite 102, Tampa, Florida 33617
tel: (813) 987 2477
fax: (813) 988 6420
e-mail: Russiatour@aol.com
Aims to provide clients with American–style service.

Australia

Passport Travel
Suite 11A, 401 St Kilda Road, Melbourne 3004
tel: (3) 9867 3019
fax: (3) 9867 1055
e-mail: passport@werple.net.au
www.travelcentre.com.au
Arranges homestays in Russia; Trans-Siberian, Trans-Manchurian and Trans-Mongolian rail journeys; and individual tours through China.

Where to Stay

Choosing a Hotel

Accommodation is improving, in particularly Moscow and St Petersburg. Foreign-run hotels and joint ventures between Russian and Canadian and Finnish operators in particular are helping to push up standards. A number of grand old hotels and wonderful Art Nouveau establishments have been lavishly restored, but these tend to be expensive. Intourist-run hotels can usually be relied upon to provide a fairly consistent, though not necessarily inspiring service. At the budget end of the price spectrum, facilities are basic.

Price Guide

Prices are based on the cost of a room for two, including breakfast.
$$$$ Luxury over: US$280
$$$ Expensive: US$150–280
$$ Moderate: US$35–150
$ Budget: US$10–35

Russia

Some hotels discount rooms to attract foreign visitors. Others offer more favourable rates for group tour bookings. It is worth checking what's on offer with a reliable tour operator before booking.

MOSCOW

Luxury

Baltschug Kempinski Moskau
Balchug ulitsa 1
tel: (095) 230 6500
www.kempinski-moscow.ru
www.kempinski-moscow.com

Located just across the river from the Kremlin, this hotel has a superb view. Kempinski is a well-known chain of German luxury hotels. $$$$

Marriott Grand Hotel
Tverskaya ulitsa 26
tel: (095) 935 8500
www.marriott.com
Former US President, Bill Clinton, stayed here on a visit to Moscow. $$$$

Metropol
Teatralny Proyezd 1–4
tel: (095) 927 6000
e-mail: metropol@metmos.ru
This is the place to stay if you can possibly afford it. Beautifully renovated, elegant and luxurious. $$$$

Expensive

Aerostar
37 Leningradsky prospekt
tel: (095) 213 9000
A Canadian-Russian hotel with an excellent seafood restaurant. A 15-minute journey from the city centre. $$$

Arbat
Plotnikov Pereulok 12
tel: (095) 244 7635
In New York parlance this hotel is in a "downtown off-Broadway" location. $$$

Art Sport
ulitsa Peshchannaya 3rd 2
tel: (095) 955 2300
e-mail: artsport@glasnet.ru
Located in a quiet area, relatively close to the centre. $$$

Le Meridien
Nakhabino Moscow Country Club
tel: (095) 926 5911
www.lemeridien-mcc.ru
Some 30 km (19 miles) from Moscow; reasonable long-stay rates. $$$

Mir
Novy Arbat ulitsa 36/9
tel: (095) 290 9518/04
Next door to the US Embassy. $$$

Novotel
Sheremetyevo II Airport
tel: (095) 926 5900
A fine hotel, useful for the airport, but quite a way from the city. $$$

Radisson Slavyanskaya
Berezhkovskaya nab. 2

tel: (095) 941 8020
www.radissonsas.com
Luxury hotel with several fine
restaurants and a cinema that
shows English-language films. Good
view of the river. Avoid the Kievsky
railway terminal area next door. A
three-stop metro ride into the city
centre may be much quicker than
an expensive hotel cab in the rush
hour. **$$$**

Renaissance Moscow
Olimpiysky prospekt 18/1
tel: (095) 931 9000/9833
Good service; English-language
cinema; some distance from the
centre. **$$$**

Sheraton Palace Hotel
ulitsa Tverskaya–Yamskaya 1st 19
tel: (095) 931 9700
e-mail: palacehotel.admin@co.ru
www.sheraton.com
Western-style hotel on Moscow's
main thoroughfare. **$$$**

Sofitel Hotel Iris
Korovinskoye Shosse 10
tel: (095) 488 8000
e-mail: sofitel.iris.moscow@co.ru
www.sofitel.com
Quality Western-style hotel, a long
way from the city centre. **$$$**

Tverskaya
ulitsa Tverskaya-Yamskaya 1st 34
tel: (095) 290 9900, 258 3000
www.marriott.com
In the city centre; recently
renovated. **$$$**

Moderate

Cosmos
Prospect Mira 150
tel: (095) 215 6791, 234 1587
Tourist-grade hotel 20-minutes from
the city centre. **$$**

Mezhdunarodnaya
Krasnopresnenskaya Nab 12
tel: (095) 253 1391/2103
Good service, but a 20-minute
journey from the city centre. **$$**

Rossiya
ulitsa Varvarka 6
tel: (095) 232 5000
Lingering Soviet flavour, right next
to the Kremlin and Red Square. **$$**

Ukraina
Kutuzovsky Prospekt 2/1
tel: (095) 243 2596/3030
One of Moscow's "wedding cake"
buildings, with a superb river view. **$$**

Budget

Belgrad
ulitsa Smolenskaya 8
tel: (095) 248 1643
Good service, but a bit out-of-the-
way. **$**

Budapest
Petrovskiye Linii 2/18
tel: (095) 924 8820/921 1060
In a nice downtown location. **$**

Izmaylovo
Izmaylovo 71
tel: (095) 166 3627/2763
A modern hotel, 15 minutes by
metro from the city centre, with
friendly English-speaking staff.
There is a flea market next door
which attracts souvenir-hunters.
$

ST PETERSBURG

Luxury

Astoria
39 ulitsa Bolshaya Morskaya
tel: (812) 313 5757
e-mail: reserv@astoria.spb.ru
www.rfhotels.com
A grand and luxurious hotel
opposite St Isaac's Cathedral. The
old wing retains its Art Nouveau
features. **$$$$**

Grand Hotel Europe
1–7 ulitsa Mikhailovskaya
tel: (812) 329 6000
e-mail: res@ghe.spb.ru
www.grand-hotel-europe.com
Another upmarket option, nicely
restored and centrally located.
$$$$

Corinthian Nevsky Palace
57 Nevsky prospekt
tel: (812) 275 2001
e-mail: bc@sheratonnevskij.ru
Centrally located and upmarket with
first-class restaurants. **$$$$**

Expensive

Angleterre
39 Bolshaya Morskaya ulitsa
tel: (812) 313 5666/5009
e-mail: reserv@astoria.spb.ru
www.rfhotels.com
Owned by the same company as
the Astoria, and in an adjacent
building, but cheaper. Centrally
located on St Isaac's Square.
$$$

Moderate

Pulkovskaya
1 ploshchad Pobedy
tel: (812) 123 5732
e-mail: sale@pulkovskaya.ru
A long way from the centre, on the
road to the airport. Comfortable and
often used by tourist groups. **$$**

St Petersburg (formerly Leningrad)
5/2 Pirogovskaya Naberezhnaya
tel: (812) 542 9411
e-mail: postmaster@spbhotel.spb.su
A short metro ride away from the
centre, overlooking the cruiser
Aurora and the Neva River, with
adequate rooms. **$$**

Moskva
2 ploshchad Alexandra Nevskovo
tel: (812) 274 0022
e-mail: business@hotel-moscow.ru
www.hotel-moscow.ru
Centrally located opposite the
Alexander Nevsky Monastery, which
compensates for the poorly
maintained rooms. **$$**

Sovietskaya
43 Prospekt Lermontovo
tel: (812) 329 0182
e-mail: hotel@sovetskaya.com
www.sovetskaya.com
A joint Finnish-Russian venture, only
a short bus ride from the centre
along the Fontanka River. **$$**

Karelia
27/2 ulitsa Marshala
Tukhachevskaya
tel: (812) 226 3515
Inexpensive hotel used by Intourist,
10 km (6 miles) from the centre. **$$**

Pribaltiiskaya Hotel
14 ulitsa Korabelstroiteli
tel: (812) 356 0263
e-mail: market@pribaltiyskaya.ru
www.pribaltiyskaya.ru
Great view of the Gulf of Finland,
but far from the city centre. **$$**

Deson Ladoga
26 prospekt Shaumyana
tel: (812) 528 5202
e-mail: dladoga@bcltele.com
www.deson.lek.ru
Across the river from Smolny
Cathedral, this hotel is inconvenient
if you don't have a car. **$$**

Budget

Cheaper options, where the
standard will be basic, go for about
US$10–$30 a night. These include:

Hotel Druzhba
4 ulitsa Chapygina
tel: (812) 234 1844 **$**
Dvorets Molodyozhy
47 ulitsa Professor Popov
tel: (812) 234 3278 **$**
Vyborgskaya
3 ulitsa Torzhkovskaya
tel: (812) 246 9141 **$**
Hotel Sputnik
34 prospekt Morisa Toreza
tel: (812) 552 5632/356 8504 **$**
Matisov Domik
3/1 reki Pryazhki Naberezhnaya
tel: (812) 219 5445 **$**

Private Accommodation

Pulford Real Estate
tel: (812) 325 6277
e-mail: pulford@mail.wplus.net
www.pulford.com
A room in an apartment costs
about US$80 per room per night.
Perhaps the most affordable
option in the city for a fine level of
comfort.
Rand House Bed and Breakfast
11 ulitsa Grivtsova; apt 83
tel: (812) 310 7005
www.randhouse.ru
Well-run, clean and efficient, US-
owned B&B in the city centre off the
Griboyedov Canal, costing US$50–70
per double a night (4 rooms).

Alina Suslova
81 Chaikovskaya
tel: (812) 296 1865
e-mail: suslova@mail.ru
www.hotelspb.narod.ru
Three-room private apartment in
the city centre near the Tauride
Palace.

THE GOLDEN RING

Kostroma
Ipatevskaya Sloboda
ulitsa Beregova 3A
Tel: (0942) 577179/626791
Lovely little hotel just outside the
monastery of St Ipatev with
comfortable and tasteful wood-
panelled rooms. Has a separate
isba that can fit groups of friends
with a tighter budget.
$$** or **$ for *isba*.
Hotel Complex Rus
ulitsa Yunosheskaya 1
tel: (0942) 546163/543320
Soviet venue with cheap, large but
drab rooms and a restaurant
serving mediocre food. **$**

Rostov
Dom na Pogrebakh
tel: (08353) 61244
Small hotel inside the Kremlin with
clean wood-panelled rooms. Two
rooms have private bathrooms. **$**

Sergiev Posad
Aristocrat
ulitsa Sergievskaya 1A
tel: (254) 725 94
Central hotel with a great view on
the monastery. Sauna. **$$**

Suzdal
Pokrovskaya
tel: (09231) 20908/21837
Small timber hotel inside the
Intercession Convent with wood-
panelled rooms in traditional
Russian style. Call Tourcentre to
book rooms. **$$**
Sokol
Torgovaya ploshchad 2A
tel: (09231) 20088
Friendly and comfortable hotel
recently opened in an old building
right in the centre. **$$**
Tourcentre, Hotel Suzdal
tel: (09231) 20908
Unattractive complex 3 km (2 miles)
from the centre with Western-style,
comfortable rooms, sauna,
swimming pool, bar, gym and
decent restaurant. **$$**

Yaroslavl
Yubileinaya
Kotoroslnaya naberezhnaya 26
tel: (0852) 309259
The usual Soviet concrete slab but
rooms are comfortable with internet
access and a good view of either

Youth Hostels

The non-profit making national
Russian Youth Hostel Association
(also known as Hostelling Russia,
Russian Youth Hostels and RYH)
was founded in 1992. In addition
to building a network of budget
accommodation within Russia
itself, Russian Youth Hostels also
has close ties to many Hostelling
International national associations.
    Through this large network of
associations, it is now possible to
stay in youth hostels in all the
countries situated by the Baltic Sea.

Moscow
Heritage Hostel
Kosmonavtov ul, 2
tel: (095) 286 0536 **$**

Travellers Guest House
Bolshaya Pereyaslavskaya 50,
10th floor
tel: (095) 631 4059 **$**
G&R International Asia
Zelenodolskaya ulitsa 3/2
tel: (095) 378 0001 **$**

St Petersburg
St Petersburg International Hostel
3rd Sovetskaya ulitsa, 28,
St Petersburg, 193036
tel: (812) 329 8018
www.ryh.ru
e-mail: ryh@ryh.spb.su
Postal address (to Russia via
Finnish post): St Petersburg
International Hostel, PO Box 8,
SF–53501, Lappeenranta, Finland.

This is a Russian-American joint
project with English-speaking
staff. The renovated 19th-century
building contains a cybercafé
and shows nightly movies. **$**
Summer Hostel
Baltiyskaya ulitsa 26
tel: (812) 252 5381, 252 7563
Bunk goes for around $12. **$**

Novgorod
Roza Vetrov
Novoluchanskaya ulitsa 27A
tel: (8162) 772033 **$**

Irkutsk
Baikalhostel
Lermontova ulitsa 136
tel: (3952) 527798 **$**

Price Guide

Prices are based on the cost of a room for two, including breakfast.

$$$$ Luxury over: US$280
$$$ Expensive: US$150–280
$$ Moderate: US$35–150
$ Budget: US$10–35

the river or the city; business centre, sauna, fitness room, two bars, and a restaurant with decent food. Central location. **$$**

Kotorosl
Bolshaya Oktyabrskaya ulitsa 87
tel: (0852) 212415
A modern five-storey hotel with restaurant, sauna and gym, two tram stops from the city centre. **$$**

Vladimir

Vladimir Hotel
Bolshaya Moskovskaya ulitsa 74
tel: (0922) 327239
Small Western-standard hotel in the centre near the train and bus stations. **$**

Zolotoye Koltso
Chaikovskovo ulitsa 27
tel: (0922) 248807
Modern tourist complex with space for 380 and a sauna, acupuncturist, lawyer, dentist and faith-healer. **$$**

THE EUROPEAN NORTH

For those travelling under their own steam, finding Western-standard hotels is not possible, so you have to take what is on offer. The best option is to stay in one of the larger urban centres and journey out from there. An alternative option, if possible, is to stay in one of the monasteries, such as Solovetsky.

Arkhangelsk

Belomorskaya
3 ulitsa Timme
tel: (8182) 661660
www.belhotel.ru
Modern, nine-storey hotel with 190 rooms. Located in city centre. **$$**

Best Eastern Purnavolok
88 Severnaya Dvini Naberezhnaya
tel: (8182) 655827

Centrally located with fine river views. It has 78 rooms, a sauna and a restaurant, where dinner costs about US$8. **$**

Polina
ulitsa Chumbarovo-Luchinskovo 37
tel: (8182) 268300
A nice wooden hotel in one of the city's most beautiful streets. **$$**

Murmansk

Arctica
82 ulitsa Lenina
tel: (8152) 457988
Soviet-style with slight improvements. **$$**

Polarnizori
ulitsa Knipovicha 17
tel: (8152) 289500
www.russlandia.ru
Considered the best and most modern hotel in town. **$$**

Vologda

Spasskaya
25 ulitsa Oktyabrisky
tel: (8172) 20145
A modern hotel with 738 rooms. **$$**

Vyborg

Druzhba
5 Zheleznodorozhnaya ulitsa
tel: (278) 22411/24942
Modern hotel with a restaurant with Russian cuisine. **$$**

Novgorod

Beresta Palace
Rajon 3, Studentscheskaja ulitsa 2a
tel: (8162) 158010/2
www.novtour.ru
Located centrally on the east of the river: a luxury hotel with 202 rooms, swimming pool, tennis

Northern Cruising

If you are on a cruise around the European north of Russia you will not require a hotel or a restaurant. The Western-run tour boats have excellent facilities, while the Russian ones are also pleasant, if limited on the choice of food. Both provide evening entertainment, a dance in the café, or a dubbed US film.

courts and facilities for the disabled. **$$$**

Intourist
ulitsa Velikaya 16
tel: (8162) 74236
On the west of the river just north of the Kremlin. **$$**

Volkhov
24 ulitsa Predtechhenskaya
tel: (8162) 115505
Close to the Kremlin and 5 minutes from the bus and train stations. Has a bar and a casino. **$$**

Petrozavodsk

Hotel Severnaya
21 prospekt Lenina
tel: (8142) 762080
Three-storey modernised hotel built by the Finns in 1937. Located in the city centre, about 700 metres (a quarter mile) from the railway station. Comprises 189 rooms, a restaurant and café. **$$**

Karelian Tourist Centre
2 Naberezhanya Gyllinga
tel: (81422) 553113/557358
In the city centre on the shores of Lake Onega, 2 km (1¼ miles) from the railway station. The 10–storey centre was built in 1978 with 280 beds in single or triple rooms. **$$**

Pskov

Oktyabrskaya
Oktyabrskaya prospekt 36
tel: (8112) 164246
Modern Soviet-style hotel. **$$.**

Rizhskaya
25 Rizhsky prospekt
tel: (8112) 462223
fax: (8112) 462301
Modest but quite adequate hotel west of the Velikaya River. **$$**

Vyborg

Sadko Hotel
16 ulitsa Gagarina
tel; (8162) 661807
Comfortable hotel with a good location and a nice restaurant **$–$$**

SOUTHWESTERN RUSSIA

Kursk

Kursk
ulitsa Lenina
near corner of ulitsa Mozhayskovo

tel: (0712) 26980
Has a decent restaurant. **$$**
Tsentralnaya
Lenina ulitsa 2
tel: (0712) 569048
An old hotel with a reasonable
restaurant. **$**

Orel
Russ Hotel
Gorky ulitsa 37 near ploshchad
Lenina
If you are desperate for someone
to speak English to you, rather
than Russian, this is the hotel to
try. The food is satisfactory. **$$**

Bryansk
Bryansk
100 prospekt Lenina, north end
tel: (0832) 666844.
Standard and deluxe rooms; two
bars and a restaurant. **$$**
Desna
Lenina prospekt 39
tel: (0832) 740135
A moderately priced hotel without a
restaurant. **$$**

Smolensk
Rossia
23/2 ulitsa Dzerzhinskovo
tel: (0812) 655970
Smolensk's most modern hotel. **$$**
Tsentralnaya
ulitsa Lenina 2/1
tel: (0812) 223604
Decent restaurant. **$**

ALONG THE VOLGA

Kazan
Tatarstan
ulitsa Pushkina 4
tel: (8432) 388379
Not the city's most centrally located
hotel, but a better-quality service
makes it the most attractive. **$$**

Samara
National
ulitsa Frunze 91/37
tel: (8462) 337695
A second-rate intourist hotel that is
reasonably priced. **$$**
Rossia
ulitsa Maxima Gorkogo 82
tel: (8462) 390311

Both the Rossia and National are
Intourist hotels. The National is the
better of the two and more
expensive but neither is
extortionate. **$$**

Saratov
Slovakia
ulitsa Lermontova 30
tel: (8452) 280883/289501
A three-star Intourist hotel not far
from the Volga embankment. **$$**
Volga
Nemetskaya ulitsa 34
tel: (8452) 243645/35
A less expensive hotel. **$–$$**

Astrakhan
Lotus
ulitsa Krimlovskaya 4
tel: (8512) 229500
This local Intourist hotel is still
the best place in town to stay.
$$

Price Guide

Prices are based on the cost of a
room for two, including
breakfast.
$$$$ Luxury over: US$280
$$$ Expensive: US$150–280
$$ Moderate: US$35–150
$ Budget: US$10–35

Volgograd
Hotel Volgograd
12 Mira ulitsa
tel: (8442) 408030
A big hotel without much
atmosphere. **$$**
Intourist
ulitsa Mira 14
tel: (8442) 337713
A good a choice as any. **$$**

THE URALS

Yekaterinburg
Magister
8-Marta ulitsa 50
tel: (343) 257 4206
Excellent and unobtrusive service
at a very reasonable price. Big
single rooms, well equipped and
centrally located. Great breakfast.
$$

Oktyabrskaya
ulitsa S. Kovalevskoi 17
tel: (343) 374 5146
Finnish-built former Communist
Party hotel. One of the best in town.
With 69 pleasant, clean rooms all
with well-kept bathrooms. Situated
in a quiet environment just outside
the centre, a few blocks from the
Urals State Technical University. **$$**
Ural
8-Marta ulitsa 45
tel: (343) 371 1333
Just down the road from the
Magister, slightly more expensive
and in a more Soviet style. **$$$**

Perm
Almaz Urala
58 ulitsa Lenina
tel: (3422) 906220
Includes a health centre and,
incongruously, a variety of different
bars. Located in the city centre.
$$$
Hotel Ural
ulitsa Lenina 58
tel: (3422) 344417/906220
The city's best hotel. **$$**

THE EUROPEAN SOUTH

Sochi
Sochi has a huge variety of
accommodation on offer, from
private flats (try the bureau by the
station) to large hotels.

Expensive
Primorskaya
Sokolova 1
tel: (8622) 925743
fax: (8622) 924006
Well-situated seafront hotel with
great views of the Black Sea. It has
a bar and restaurants. **$$$**
Radisson SAS Lazurnaya
Kurortniy prospekt 103
tel: (095) 411 7777
fax: (095) 745 7705
e-mail: res@lazurnaya.ru
A 10-minute drive from the centre of
Sochi and 20 minutes from the
airport. Suites and villas in addition
to rooms. Three restaurants, a
fitness centre and an outdoor pool.
Weekend deals are often available
out of season and if you can't

afford to stay, splash out on breakfast and spend the day by the pool. **$$$**

Radisson Lazurnaya Peak Hotel
77 Zaschitnikov Kavkaza Street
Tel: (095) 411 7766
Fax: (095) 745 7706
e-mail: resp@lazurnaya.ru
In the heart of the Caucasian mountains; 10 villas, a family cottage and a "presidential villa". A 50-minute drive from the Black Sea Coast. Spa, fitness centre, outdoor and indoor swimming pools. **$$$**

Moderate

Zhemchuzhina
Chernomorskaya 3
tel: (8622) 661188
fax: (8622) 928797
Three-star hotel, 27 km (17 miles) from the airport, on the seafront in town centre. Sea-water swimming pools, tennis courts and sauna. **$$**

Budget

Vstrecha
Leningradskaya 7
tel: (8622) 521441
Located 18 km (11 miles) from the town centre and 45 km (28 miles) from the airport. Comprises three hotels – the Dagomys, Olimpiiskaya and Meridian (motel). With indoor and outdoor pools, sauna, fitness room, restaurants and bars. **$–$$**

SIBERIA

Bratsk
Taiga
ulitsa Mira 35
tel: (3953) 413979
This simple, Intourist-run, 2-star hotel provides an adequate base for touring the region. **$$**

Irkutsk
Angara
ulitsa Sukhe–Batora 7
tel: (3952) 255105/6
Centrally located. **$$**
Intourist
ulitsa Gagarina 44
tel: (3952) 250167
Situated by the Angara River, a short walk from the centre of town. **$$**

Krasnoyarsk
Oktyabrskaya Hotel
Prospekt Mira 15
A favourite haunt of Communist Party guests in the Soviet era. Prices here are generally higher than those elsewhere in Siberia. **$$**
Sun Hotel
295 Baykalsyaka Street
tel: (3952) 255910
fax: (3952) 255912
e-mail: sunhotel@xemi.com
Probably the city's top hotel. **$$$**

Lake Baikal
Baikal
Listvyanka
tel: (3952) 250391
The only hotel on the lake. Has splendid views and a good restaurant – the local perch is delicious. Even if you're staying in Irkutsk, it's worth visiting the restaurant. **$$**

Novosibirsk
Sibir
ulitsa Lenina 21
tel: (3832) 230203
Modern, Intourist-run Sibir is the best hotel in Novosibirsk. **$$**

Ulan-Ude
Geser
ulitsa Ranzhurova 11
tel: (30122) 28151
fax: (30122) 25925
Centrally located, with good business services and a sauna. **$$**

Vladivostok
Amursky Zaliv
ulitsa Naberezhnaya 9
tel: (4232) 225520
The best hotel in town is this maze-like, huge, Soviet-style hotel. Its great location on Amur Bay makes up for the architecture. **$$**
Hotel Vladivostok
ulitsa Naberezhnaya 10
tel: (4232) 412808
e-mail:
vladhotl@fastmail.vladivostok.ru
www.vladhotel.vl.ru
Opposite the Amursky Zaliv with views of the bay. Be warned: both hotels are overrun with prostitutes who may knock on your door at any time of the night. **$$**

Yakutsk
Ontario
Vilyuisky trakt 6
tel: (4112) 422066
The best hotel in Yakutsk, 6 km (3½ miles) north of town, in the style of a Yakut log building. **$$**
Sterkh
Prospekt Lenina 8
tel: (4112) 242701
For the comforts of inner-city life try the 3-star Intourist-run Sterkh. **$$**

ALTAY REPUBLIC

Barnaul
Sibir
Sotsialisticheskiy Prospekt 116
tel: (3852) 255170

Language Centres

A relatively inexpensive way to visit Russia is through institutes that run Russian language courses. Among these are the Lomonosov and Lumumba universities and the Pushkin Institute of Russian Language in Moscow, the University of St Petersburg, the Shevchenko University in Kiev and other universities and linguistic co-operatives.They are all able to arrange visas and inexpensive accommodation during the study period.

To communicate directly with the universities you should contact the cultural attaché of the Russian embassy or consulate. It is rather more difficult to make contact with the co-operatives since they are not represented abroad.

When selecting courses, care should be taken to ensure that the teaching is on a professional level. It is also worth contacting the Russian departments of universities at home. Many are now running short (one- or two-week) overseas study tours (which includes flights, accommodation and transport within Russia, and tuition fees) for the general public.

Built in 1967 in the centre of Barnaul, near the railway terminal and 30 minutes from the airport. It has five floors and 156 rooms. **$**

Belokurikha
Altaisky Krai, Belokurikha
tel: (38577) 23712
Includes three sanatoria, Belokurikha, Siberia and Katun. Guests can make use of the medical facilities or simply enjoy the surrounding beauty and fresh air. **$**

Belarus

Hotel accommodation in Belarus has changed little from Soviet times, and Western notions of service have yet to appear. The following are the best available. The prices are calculated at the official exchange rate.

Minsk

Belarus
15 Starazaevskaya vulitsa
tel: (017) 234 8252
A comfortable hotel. Some rooms overlook the lake. Friendly staff. **$$**

IBB
Gazety Pravda 11
tel: (017) 270 3996
A little out of the centre to the southwest, this modern hotel is attached to the Minsk International Education Centre. **$$**

Jubileinaya
Masherova prospekt 19
tel: (017) 226 9120
Fairly central, reasonably priced hotel.

Orbita
39 Pushkina
tel: (017) 252 3933
This hotel offers a rent-a-car service, hairdressers and other conveniences. **$$**

Planeta
Masharova prospekt 31
tel: (017) 226 7853
Modern hotel; nothing special, however. **$$**

Tourist
31 Partizanskiy
tel: (017) 245 4004
Near one of the city's biggest parks and a well-stocked supermarket. **$$**

Yubileinaya Hotel
19 prospekt Masherova
tel: (017) 226 9024

One of the two main Intourist hotels in the capital. **$$**

Brest

Belarus
6 Shevchenko Bulvar
tel: (0162) 221646
Located in the centre of the city, right on the river bank. **$–$$**

Intourist
Maskovskaya 15
tel: (0162) 252082
www.brest-intourist.com
This is the main hotel for foreign guests to the city. **$$**

Ukraine

Kiev

Business Hotels

Bratislava
1 Andriya Malyshka vulitsa
tel: (044) 537 3975
www.bratislava.com.ua
Modern hotel with facilities for businessmen.

Dnipro
Khreshchatyk 1/2
tel: (44) 291 8450
Centrally located and one of the better of the Soviet-era hotels. **$$–$$$**

Khreschatyk
Khreschatyk 14
tel: (44) 229 7339
Centrally located just off the main square. A cheaper hotel, though far from picturesque. **$$**

Premier Palace
5 Bulvar Shevchenko
tel: (44) 244 1201
The old Ukraina hotel has been reborn as Kiev's newest and plushest. **$$$**

President Hotel Kyivsky
Hospitalna 12
tel: (44) 220 4144
A former Intourist hotel that has been renovated. Pricey. **$$$**

Hotels in Kiev

Kiev has lagged behind in upgrading the variety and quality of its places to stay. The business hotels in the city centre still tend to be overpriced and the tourist hotels rather basic.

Rus
Gospitalna 4
tel: (44) 220 4226
Situated just down the hill from the Kyivska, but costing around $50 less per room. **$$**

Tourist Class

Andriivskyi Complex
Vozdvizhenska 60
In the courtyard just off Andriivskyi Uzviz 24
tel: (44) 416 2256
Well-placed but erratic. Check for booking fees. **$$**

Dniprovskiy Ship Hotel
Dnipro River
River terminal
Prichal 2
tel: (44) 490 9055
A ship hotel with rooms from standard to luxury. **$$–$$$$**

Domus
Yaroslavskaya vulitsa 19
tel: (044) 417 0000
Good hotel, near the centre. More expensive than average.

Impressa
21 Sagaidachnogo Street
tel: (044) 239 2939
www.impressa.com.ua
Good hotel, right in the centre. Quite expensive, but with a good reputation.

Kozatsky
1/3 vulitsa Mykhailivska
tel: (44) 229 4925/228 2786
Close to the centre. Rooms comfortable enough. **$$**

Lybid
1 Peremohy ploshchad
tel: (44) 274 0063
In the city centre, within walking distance of the circus. **$$**

St Petersburg
Shevchenko Blvd. 4
tel: (44) 225 7101
Vyl. Volodymyrska 36
tel: (44) 229 5943
One of Kiev's oldest hotels. **$$**

Other tourist hotels with basic rooms can be found on the left bank of the river.

Private Accommodation

Sherborne Apartments
4 vulitsa Staronavodnitskaya #43
tel: (44) 295 8832

Price Guide

Prices are based on the cost of a room for two, including breakfast.
$$$$ Luxury over: US$280
$$$ Expensive: US$150–280
$$ Moderate: US$35–150
$ Budget: US$10–35

European standard apartments in the centre of the city. Quite good value. **$$–$$$**

Odessa
Chorne More Hotel
59 Rishelevska
tel: (0482) 240028
Large Intourist hotel; reliable. **$$**
Grand Moscow
Vyl. Deribasivska 29
tel: (0482) 224016
There are a number of slightly decrepit but worthwhile places along this street, of which the Hotel Grand Moscow is the most notable. **$$**
Kempinski Odessa
6 Primorskaya Morvokzal
tel: (0487) 294808
Down the Potemkin steps to this hotel towering above the harbour. **$$$**
Krasnaya
Vyl. Pushkina 15
tel: (0482) 227220
The substantial Krasnaya is the best of the rest of the hotels. **$$$**
Londonskaya
15 Primorskaya Boulevard
tel: (0482) 210510
Grand old hotel in picturesque part of Odessa, best rooms face out towards the sea. **$$$**

Lviv
Dniestr
Vyl. Mateika 6
tel: (0322) 720 783
More austere than the George but with better plumbing **$$**
George
1 Mickiewicz Square
tel: (0322) 725 952
A former Intourist hotel, which was built by an Englishman at the end of the 19th century. **$$**

Grand
Pr. Svobody 13
tel: (0322) 724 042
Features Hapsburg architecture and a good Ukrainian restaurant. **$$$**

Chernivtsi
Cheremosh
13a Komarova
tel: (03722) 48777
The best tourist hotel in town, 3.5 km (2 miles) from the centre. **$$**

THE CRIMEA

The southern Crimean coast has plenty of tourist rooms, but little has been done since 1991 to upgrade them or promote them to visitors.

Yalta
Oreanda
Lenin Embankment 35/2
tel: (0654) 328336
The Oreanda, at the western end of the Lenin Embankment, is the best place to stay in Yalta. **$$–$$$**
Palas
Chekhova 8
tel: (0654) 324380
The Palas is a smaller and more pleasant place near the centre. **$–$$**
Yalta
Vyl. Dryazhinskoho 50
tel: (0654) 350150
With more than 2,000 beds, it dominates the other end of the town. **$$**

Sevastopol
Sevastopol
Nakhimova 8
tel: (0692) 523671
Hotels in Sevastopol are limited, but this is a reasonable bet. **$**
Yard
Astana Kesaeva vulitsa 9
Private hotel close to the city beaches. **$$**

Sudak
Horyzont
Vyl. Turistikoyu
tel: (06566) 334882
Situated behind the fortress, this hotel is worth trying. **$**

Where to Eat

What to Eat

Most of the different ethnic groups populating the CIS pretend to have their own national cuisine, and some of them genuinely do have. Within this diversity, Russian, Georgian and Ukrainian cuisines are said to be the best.

Russian
The most famous dishes are beef Stroganov and Beluga caviar. Russian cuisine includes dishes like *bliny* (pancakes with butter and sour cream, caviar, meat, jam etc), *shchi* (sour cabbage soup with meat and mustard), *pelmeny* (boiled dumplings with meat) and *kasha* (a type of porridge made of different grains).

Georgian
Georgian food has always been popular in Russia, and several Georgian restaurants have recently opened in Moscow to compete with the venerable but Soviet-style monopolist Aragvi on Tverskaya and the Tbilisi in St Petersburg. Georgian cuisine is famous for its *shashlik*, *tsyplyata tabaka* (chicken fried under pressure), *basturma* (spicy salted and smoked meat), *suluguni* (salted cheese), green and red *lobio* (beans), specially cooked aubergines, and *satsyvi* (chicken). It can be served with *lavash* (a special kind of bread), or with *khachapuri* (a roll stuffed with cheese) flavoured with various spices such as *tkemali* or with a delicious *bazha* sauce.

Ukrainian
Ukrainians have traditionally been known to have vast appetites – but their cuisine is also tasty. Specialities include *borshch* (beetroot soup with cabbage,

meat, mushrooms and other ingredients), *galushky* (small boiled dumplings) and *varenyky zvyshneyu* (curd dumplings with red cherries served with sugar and sour cream). Known and served around the world is chicken Kiev (or Kiev cutlet), prepared with different spices and garlic.

Loved by everyone in the Ukraine is *salo* (salted raw lard spiced with garlic) served with black bread. Also very popular is *kolbasa* (assorted smoked sausages).

Where to Eat

Inevitably the following list of restaurants concentrates on Moscow and St Petersburg where choice is continually expanding. In other cities and towns, it is often best to ask around when you arrive.

MOSCOW

All national cuisines are well represented, with the big hotels accommodating several excellent restaurants. Booking is not usually necessary. However, unlike ten years ago, there are hundreds of fine restaurants to choose from – check out the *Moscow Business Telephone Guide* and *Exile*.

Russian
Bochka ("Barrel")
ulitsa 1905 Goda
tel: (095) 252 3041
Open round the clock. The barbecue is as hot as things got here in 1905 and, indeed, 1993. **$$$**
Izba Rybalka
48 ulitsa Baumanskaya
tel: (095) 267 6308
Specialising in fish dishes. **$**
Mefisto
Shmitovsky Proyezd 10
tel: (095) 259 6497
Open 10–6am. Mefisto is a fashionable "cellar" restaurant serving tasty, not always strictly Russian, meat and seafood dishes. You can watch your pork ribs or a mutton leg being grilled as you work on the appetisers. **$$**

Moo-Moo
26 Komsomolsky prospekt
tel: (095) 245 7820
Cheap, delicious food that has a homemade feel to it. Can get very crowded. **$**
Oblomov
1 Monetchikovsky Per 5
tel: 953 6828
Good Russian food. **$$$**
PIROGI
19 Nikolskaya ulitsa
tel: (095) 921 5827
A popular student hangout with a bookshop. **$**
Praga
Arbatskaya ploshchad
tel: (095) 290 6171
Open noon–3pm and 6pm–4am. Probably Moscow's most famous restaurant since the 19th century. **$$$**
Red Square
1 Red Square (Krasny ploshad)
tel: (095) 925 3600
Noble Russian dishes of the 18th and 19th centuries. **$$**
Russky Pogrebok
26 ulitsa Tverskaya
tel: (095) 937 0028
In a restored wine cellar. **$$**
Samovar
ulitsa Myasnitskaya 13
tel: (095) 924 4688
Open noon–11pm.
A quiet, elegant restaurant. Check out the *pelmeny*; the orthodox *pelmeni* mix should contain beef, pork and mutton; there are plenty of kinds to choose from. **$$$**
U Yuzefa
ulitsa Dubininskaya 11/17
tel: (095) 238 4646.
Open noon–midnight.
A Jewish restaurant with a Russian touch. **$$$**
Yama
10 Stoleshnikov Pereluk
tel: (095) 292 0115
Follow signs and the sound of music to find it. It's behind the shop fronts. Tasty food and cheap beer. Beer garden. Unobtrusive live music. **$**
Zhiguli
Novy Arbat 11
tel: (095) 291 4144
A restaurant designed in Soviet style. The prices are, however, decidedly Russian. **$$**

Georgian
Guria
Komsomolsky prospekt 7/3
tel: (095) 246 0378
Open 7–11am, noon–2.30pm, and 5.30–10.30pm.
(see Mama Zoya) **$**
Mama Zoya
Sechenovsky Pereulok 18
tel: (095) 201 7743
Open noon–10pm.
Both Guria and Mama Zoya serve excellent *khachapuri*, *satsivi*, *shahlik*, *lobio* and aubergine. Service may be a little sloppy but the atmosphere is warm, friendly and gregariously Georgian. Be prepared for some really loud live ethnic music. **$**
Suliko
Bolshaya Polyanka 42/2
tel: (095) 238 1027
Open noon–midnight.
Serves great *shashlik* and aubergine. Tasteful live music. **$$**
Tiflis
Ostozhenka 32
tel: (095) 290 2897
Open noon–midnight.
A wide variety of Georgian dishes.
U Pirosmani
Novodevichy Proyezd 4
tel: (095) 247 1926
Open noon–11pm (kitchen until 10pm)
Named after a famous Georgian painter, this is probably the finest (and most expensive) Caucasian restaurant in town. It has a beautiful interior and a good view. Quiet live music. **$$$**
Wine note: You will find authentic Georgian wine at Pirosmani, Suliko and Tiflis.

European
The following Western-style restaurants are expensive, but provide good service and most offer Russian cuisine.
Café des Artistes
5/6 Kamergersky Pereulok
tel: (095) 292 0673
Small French bistro. **$**
CDL
50 ulitsa Povarskaya
tel: (095) 291 1515
Russian and French cuisine; expensive but in élite surroundings. **$$$**

Crab House
6 Tverskaya ulitsa
tel: (095) 202 1312
Mediterranean, Asian and European
seafood. **$$**

Cutty Sark
12/1 Novinsky boulevar
tel: (095) 385 0185
Italian and Mediterranean cuisine.
$$$

Mekhano Bankso
9/1 Smolenskaya ploschad
tel: (095) 241 3132
Very tasty, filling Bulgarian food.
Good atmosphere and service.
Recommended. **$$**

American

American Bar and Grill
ulitsa Tverskaya–Yamskaya 32/1
tel: (095) 251 7999
Open round the clock. **$$**

B.B. King
ulitsa Sadovaya–Samotyochnaya 4/2
tel: (095) 299 8206
Open noon–midnight.
Features live blues and other music,
with American Cajun cuisine. **$$**

Moosehead
ulitsa Bolshaya Polyanka 54
tel: (095) 230 7333
Open noon–5am. **$**

Papa John's
ulitsa Myasnitskaya 22
tel: (095) 755 9554
Open 6pm–morning. **$**

Starlite Diner
ulitsa Bolshaya Sadovaya 16
tel: (095) 290 9638
Korovy Val 9
tel: (095) 959 8919
Open round the clock. **$$**

Other

Cous Cous
11 ulitsa Novoslobodskaya
tel: 973 5174
Middle Eastern and vegetarian food.
$$

Djagannat
ulitsa Kuznetsky Most 11
tel: (095) 928 3580
One of Moscow's very few
vegetarian restaurants. Including a
takeaway section and food shop. **$$**

Hola Mexico
7/5 Pushechnaya ulitsa
tel: (095) 925 8251
Mexican food. **$$**

Goa
8/2 Myasnitskaya ulitsa
tel: (095) 504 4031
Modern restaurant decorated in a
psychedelic Indian style. Flies in
DJ's from all over the world. Indian
and French cuisine. Recorded
jungle sounds in the toilets. **$$**

Moscow–Berlin
Ploschad Zastava 52
tel: (095) 251 2282
A 24-hour cosy café/restaurant, with
good, but unobtrusive DJs. **$–$$**

Tandoor
ulitsa Tverskaya 30
tel: (095) 299 5925
Serves Indian and Chinese food.
Nice atmosphere. Well-prepared
food. Good for vegetarians. **$$**

Taras Bulba
ulitsa Petrokva 30/7
tel: (095) 284 3019
Specialising in Ukrainian food,
named after the hero of Gogol's
novel of the same name. **$–$$**

Tibet-Himalaya
ulitsa Pokrovka 19
tel: (095) 125 1196
Tibetan food in relaxed
surroundings. Worth a visit. **$$**

Yakatoria
16 ulitsa Petrovka
tel: (095) 924 0609
A chain sushi bar. Good value and
service. Highly recommended for
sushi lovers. **$$**

Yaponsky Gorodsky
Gnezdnikovsky Per 9
tel: (095) 229 2108
A good sushi restaurant. **$$–$$$**

St Petersburg

The city has a wide selection of
restaurants representing most of
the world's major cuisines.

Russian

1913
13/2 Voznesensky prospekt,
tel: (812) 315 5148
Perhaps the finest Russian cuisine
for the price. **$$$**

Admiralty
Nevskij Palace Hotel
57 Nevsky prospekt
tel: (812) 275 2001
Russian and seafood specialities
served in a maritime setting. **$$**

Aquarelle
On a boat moored to Bizhevoi
Bridge on the Petrograd side.
tel: (812) 320 8600
Features a fusion of cuisines from all
over the world. Delicious food, but
pricey. **$$$**

Austeria
Peter and Paul Fortress
tel: (812) 238 4262
Atmosphere of early St Petersburg,
with fine Russian and European
cuisine. **$$$**

Bliny Domik
8 Kolokolnaya ulitsa
tel: (812) 315 9915
Cheap, great Russian food with arty
atmosphere. **$**

Da Vinci,
15 Malaya Morskaya
tel: (812) 311 0173
Russian cuisine in flashy, neon
club. **$$$**

Europa
Grand Hotel Europe, Nevsky prospekt
tel: (812) 329 6000
Leading Russian and continental
gourmet restaurant with a striking
Art Nouveau setting. **$$**

Kameya
21 2nd Sovetskaya
tel: (812) 277 5542
Russian cuisine in elegant atmo-
sphere, off the beaten track. **$$$**

Masha i Medved
1 Malaya Sadovaya
tel: (812) 310 4631
Authentic, traditional Russian
cuisine. Themed on the Russian
fairy tale of the same name. A bear
greets you as you enter. **$–$$**

Na Zdorovye
13 Bolshoi prospekt
tel: (812) 232 4039
Fine Russian country cooking in
folky atmosphere. **$$$**

Price of a Meal

The following restaurant
categories are based on the
price of a meal for one. They
serve as a guide only, due to
fluctuations in the rouble-dollar
exchange rate.
$$$ Expensive: more than US$50
$$ Moderate: US$20–$50
$ Budget: less than US$20

Old Customs House
1 Tamozheny Pereulok
tel: (812) 327 8980
Fine Russian and European cuisine
in a historic interior. **$$$$**

Polonaise
45 Bolshaya Morskaya ulitsa
tel: (812) 315 0319
Russian cuisine in a historic 18th-
century building. **$$**

Restoran
2 Pereulok Tamozheny
tel: (812) 327 8979
Chic decor and fine Russian
cuisine. **$$$**

Svir
Hotelship Peterhof, Makarov Emb
tel: (812) 325 8888
An elegant restaurant on the Neva
serving international, Russian and
seafood. Live music. **$$$**

Troika
27/21 Zagorodny prospekt
tel: (812) 113 5343
Russian cuisine and folk show,
catering to tourists. **$$$**

Valhalla
22 Nevsky prospekt
tel: (812) 311 0024
A hearty Russian dinner on Nevsky
prospekt for those looking for a
rowdy night out. **$$$**

European

Bistro Garcon
95 Nevsky prospekt
tel: (812) 277 2467
Fine French cuisine in cosy Parisian-
style setting. **$$$**

Borsalino
39 Bolshaya Morskaya
tel: (812) 313 5115
Considered to be the finest
European cuisine in St Petersburg
in the Anglettere Hotel. **$$$**

Brasserie
Grand Hotel Europe
ulitsa Mikhailovskaya 1–7
tel: (812) 329 6000
Elegant Italian restaurant. **$$**

Il Grappola
Belinskovo ulitsa 5
tel: (812) 273 4904
Excellent Italian food – the chef is
from Italy. Sometimes has art
exhibitions. **$$$**

Nikolai
52 Bolshaya Morskaya
tel: (812) 311 1402

Next to St Isaac's Square, Nikolai
serves European cuisine with
salmon specialities from Finland. **$$**

Red Lion
Alexandrovsky Park 4
tel: (812) 233 9391
The city's only English bar/
restaurant. Has an outside terrace
which is good for summer nights.
Open 24 hours, 365 days a year. **$$**

Price of a Meal

The following restaurant
categories are based on the
price of a meal for one. They
serve as a guide only, due to
fluctuations in the rouble-dollar
exchange rate.
$$$ Expensive: more than US$50
$$ Moderate: US$20–$50
$ Budget: less than US$20

Other

Brasilia
24 Kazanskaya Street
tel: (812) 320 8777
Dishes are something between
Latin and Russian, but be certain
its good. **$$$**

Cafe Idiot
82 Naberezhnaya Moika
tel: (812) 315 1675
The pseudo-bohemian decor and
atmosphere is popular with tourists
and ex-pats. **$**

La Cucaracha
39 Naberezhnaya Reki Fontanki
tel: (812) 110 4006
One of the few genuine Mexican
restaurants in town; centrally located
just off of Nevsky prospekt. **$**

Golden Dragon
62 Dekabristov ulitsa
Near the Mariinsky Theatre
tel: (812) 114 8441
Chinese and Southeast Asian
cuisine. **$–$$**

Mollie's Irish Bar
36 Rubinshteina ulitsa
tel: (812) 319 9768
Open 11–3am.
Guinness on tap and hearty pub
food; live music. **$$**

Tandoor
2 Voznesensky prospekt
Near St Isaac's Cathedral
tel: (812) 312 3886

Indian food with a good, varied
vegetarian selection. **$$**

Tinkov's
7 Kazanskaya ulitsa
tel: (812) 314 8485
Centrally located restaurant; one of
the coolest and largest in town.
Serves sushi, pizza, and US-style
salads, and has its own micro-
brewery. **$–$$**

Russkaya Ribalka
Primorsky Park Pobeda
2nd South Pond
tel: (812) 235 2395
One of the city's most enjoyable
piscine venues. You catch the fish
in the pond, and they cook it for
you. **$$$**

Staroe Cafe
108 Fontanka Embankment
tel: (812) 316 5111
Cosy, with four tables, and live
piano music in evenings. **$$**

Sholk
Malaya Konushennaya 4/2
tel: (812) 311 5078
Good Japanese food. Interior in a
minimalist style. Quite
expensive. **$$$**

THE GOLDEN RING

Kostroma

Parus
ulitsa Skvortsova 4
tel: (0942) 324133
Serves tasty fare at reasonable
prices and is worth a peep just for
its unbelievably kitsch Art Nouveau
interior.

Yellow Submarine
ulitsa Sovietskaya 79/73
tel: (0942) 577639
Atmospheric bar with trendy
submarine-themed interior and
great, cheap food. Close to Hotel
Rus and a helpful alternative to its
mediocre restaurant.

Rostov-Veliky

Trapeznaya Palata
tel: (08353) 62871
Cosy restaurant inside the Kremlin
serving delicious Russian cuisine.

Suzdal

Trapeznaya
tel: (09231) 20908

Inside the Intercession Convent. Serves good Russian cuisine in a historical but rather sober interior.

Vladimir
Zolotoye Koltso
ulitsa Chaikovskovo 27
tel: (0922) 248807
Popular with tourists and serves very nice pancakes. **$$**

Yaroslavl
Kotorosl
ulitsa Bolshaya Oktyabrskaya 87
tel: (0852) 212415
Good hotel restaurant.
Spasskie Palaty
Bogoyavlenskaya ploshchad 25
tel: (0852) 304807
A popular venue inside the monastery gates with medieval décor and delicious Russian cuisine.

THE EUROPEAN NORTH

Arkhangelsk
Yubileiny
52 Troitsky prospekt
tel: (8182) 432 880

Murmansk
Thanks to the number of foreign sailors in town, restaurants here are better than might be expected.
Darya Morya
26/9 prospekt Lenina
tel: (8152) 72335
Good venue for seafood. **$**

Novgorod
Fortress
The best place to eat is in the fortress itself, which provides warming sustenance in winter and has an open veranda for hot summer days. **$**
Intourist Hotel
16 ulitsa Velikaya
tel: (8162) 94288
On the bank of the river. Russian and European cuisine. **$–$$**
Sadko Restaurant
ulitsa Fyodorovsky 16
tel: (8162) 663004
The walls of the restaurant are painted with mythical sea creatures from local legends. Good filling food. Credit cards not accepted. **$$**

Pskov
Kavkaz
10 Oktyabrisky prospeckt
tel: (8112) 21637
Tasty Georgian food. **$**
Rus
7 Vlasevskaya Bashnya
tel: (8112) 720090
Inside the Kremlin. Candlelit tables and fresh, tasty beer from the tap. **$**

Vologda
Saigon
12 ulitsa Chekova
tel: (8172) 250576
Good Vietnamese food and pop music. Worth a visit. **$**
Spasskiy
25 ulitsa Oktyabrisky
tel: (8172) 760138
Traditional Russian food and disco. **$**

Vyborg
Even though this is a small town, you can eat your heart out in a variety of grill bars and restaurants.
Hotel Druzhba
ulitsa Zheleznodorozhnaya 5
tel: (278) 94464 **$$**

SOUTHWEST RUSSIA

Kursk
Grim Restaurant
For simple fare, try this unfortunately named restaurant near Hotel Kursk. **$**
Kursk
ulitsa Lenina
near corner of ulitsa Mozhayskovo
tel: (0712) 26980. **$$**
Tsentralnaya
ulitsa Lenina 2
tel: (0712) 569048. **$**

Bryansk
Hotel Bryansk
Prospekt Lenina
tel: (0832) 466844
Worth trying. **$$**

Orel
Café Aktyor
Ploshchad Lenina
Southeast of Turgenev Theatre. Standard Russian café fare – bread, cakes, biscuits and hotpots. **$**

Smolensk
Farfalle
7 ulitsa Oktyabriskaya Revolutsia
The choice for Italian food in Smolensk. **$**
Lapatinski Sad
Ploshchad Lenina
Good for a basic, filling meal. **$$**

THE URALS

Yekaterinburg
Bulvar Blues
1 ulitsa Krasnoarmeiskaya
tel: (3432) 564535
The jazz music centre of the city. Good European cuisine. **$–$$**
Hotel Oktyabrskaya
ulitsa S. Kovalevskoi 17
tel: (3432) 445146
The best option for eating out. **$**

THE EUROPEAN SOUTH

Most hotels have restaurants priced according to the level of the hotel.

Sochi
Kanyon
Kazachii Brod
tel: (8622) 448189
A good traditional Greek restaurant. **$**
Kavkavskiye Aul
tel: (8622) 970817
Near the Agurskie waterfalls. Excellent Caucasian food. **$$**
Lubava
Hotel Zhemchuzhina
Chernomorskaya 3
tel: (8622) 992976
Russian food. **$$**

SIBERIA AND THE FAR EAST

Irkutsk
Arktika
ulitsa Marksa 26
Good seafood, especially perch, fresh from Lake Baikal. **$–$$**
Havana
18 ulitsa Suhe-Batora
tel: (3952) 334384
Cuban cuisine, good service, filling food. At weekends from noon to

4pm every child gets a gift and they show cartoons on a big screen. **$**

Intourist
ulitsa Gagarina 44
tel: (3952) 290167/290273
The hotel offers a choice of restaurants. The second-floor restaurant is the best in town, though the music is too loud and the menu irregular. The menu diminishes as the night goes on, so arrive early. The Peking restaurant (**$–$$**) serves a dreadful imitation of Chinese food. However, on the fourth floor of the hotel there is a delightful little tea shop that serves caviar blinis.

Tsentralny
ulitsa Litvinova 17
tel: (3952) 344149
Russian specialities. **$**

Yakutsk
Ontario
Vilyushkyy Trakt
tel: (4112) 422066
A joint venture; Yakutsk's best. **$$**

UKRAINE

Ukraine is famous for several dishes: chicken Kiev and *borshch* being best known. The first – the white meat of chicken stuffed with garlic and butter – is almost invisible on the menus of the cities' restaurants. The second, a cabbage, beetroot and potato soup, is available everywhere and often the best thing on the menu. Also good are *vereniki*, small dumplings

Some of the best places to eat in Yalta are along the Lenin Embankment. In summer open-air restaurants and bars line both sides of the walkway, and some good food is available all the way along, from the Oreanda hotel at one end to the Cactus Club specialising in Mexican fare at the other.

Oreanda Hotel
Lenin Embankment 35/2
tel: (0654) 328166
Good value. **$$**

filled with meat potatoes, vegetables, or fruit.

Kiev
Apollo
15 Khreschatyk St
tel: (044) 229 0437
One of the first of the new restaurants to emerge since 1991 and still one of the best. **$$$**

Edelweiss
21 Sahaydachnogo St
tel: (044) 416 0213
Bavaria's finest. **$$**

Khutorets
Naberezhno-Khrechatytska St
tel: (044) 416 8039
Excellent Ukrainian food in a river boat on the Dnipr. **$$$**

Kozak Mamay
Prorizna 4
tel: (044) 228 4273
Traditional Ukrainian cuisine. Beer garden in summer time. Good food for reasonable prices. **$–$$**

San Tori
41 Sahaydachnoho St
tel: (044) 462 4994
Excellent sushi and Thai food. **$$$**

Shchekavytsya
Konstyantynivska 46/52
tel: (095) 417 1472
Ukrainian cuisine. Homemade vodka (*samogon*) available. **$$$**

Tequila House
8 Spaska St
tel: (044) 417 0358
Good Mexican food. **$$**

Lviv
Amadaus
Kathedralna Sq. 7
tel: (0322) 978022
Good food; live jazz. **$**

Grand Hotel
Prosp. Svobody 13
tel: (0322) 722936
The restaurant in the Grand Hotel has traditional Ukrainian dishes at very reasonable prices. **$$–$$$**

Kolyba
14, Burdenka St
Lviv-Briukhovychi
tel: (0322) 593141
Out of town, but well worth it for some traditional Ukrainian dishes. **$**

Vienna Coffeehouse
Prosp, Svobody 12
tel: (0322) 722021

The following restaurant categories are based on the price of a meal for one. They serve as a guide only, due to fluctuations in the rouble-dollar exchange rate.
$$$ Expensive: more than US$50
$$ Moderate: US$20–$50
$ Budget: less than US$20

Re-visit the Lviv of Austrian times; sit outside in the summer. **$**

Odessa
Hotel Kempinski
tel: (0487) 294808
Good range of food and views, especially from the top floor Black Pearl bar/restaurant. **$$$**

Londonskaya Hotel
Prymorsky Blvd
tel: (0482) 210510
This hotel has a wonderful courtyard for summer lunches and dinners.

Pivdenna Palmira
tel: (0482) 684477
If you are down at Arcadia beach, it's worth stopping here.

Steakhouse
20 Deribasivska.
tel: (0482) 348782
A good bet on Odessa's bustling main street. **$**

Other
Himalaya
Khreshatyk 23 phone
tel: (044) 462 0437
Indian cuisine. Friendly service. Ask if you want it spicy, as the food is somewhat adapted to local tastes. **$$**

Yakitoria
Lesi Ukrainky 27
tel: (044) 295 8161
Good-value tasty sushi. **$–$$**

Everyone knows what they drink in Russia: vodka, and tea from the samovar. This is only half the truth. There are many other drinks that accompany different cuisines. And Russians are drinking more and more beer, owing to the country's booming beer industry.

The Ukrainian traditional alcoholic drink is *horilka* which resembles vodka. But more popular, and more refined, is *horilka z pertsem*, i.e. gorilka with a small red pepper. The traditional non-alcoholic drink is *uzvar* (made of stewed fruit). Georgians drink different dry and semi-dry wines, such as *Adzhaleshi*, *Kindzmarauli*, *Akhasheni*, *Tsinandali*, *Mukuzani*, *Kinzmarauli*, *Alazan Valley*, and *Tvishi* (reported to have been the favourite wine of Stalin). Non-alcoholic drinks from Georgia are represented by the best in Russian mineral water such as *Borzhomi* and *vody Lagidze* (mineral water with various syrup mixtures).

In summer Russians prefer to drink *kvas*, a refreshing drink prepared from bread fermented with water and yeast.

Nightlife

Moscow

Nightclubs

Alexander Blok
Krasnopresnenskaya Naberezhnaya
tel: (095) 255 9284/78
In a boat by the Mezhdunarodnaya Hotel. Includes a casino.

Arbat Blues Club
Filippovsky Pereulok 11
Building 2
tel: (095) 291 1546

Bilingua
Krivokoleny Per 10
Metro: Chistiye Prudy
tel: (095) 923 9660
Art café; nice atmosphere.

Night Flight
ulitsa Tverskaya 17
tel: (095) 229 4165

Pariskaya Zhizn' (Paris Life)
ulitsa Karetniy Per 3
Metro: Pushkinskaya
tel: (095) 209 4524
Straightforward disco.

Piro .G.I
ulitsa Nikolskaya 19
Metro: Lubyanka
tel: (095) 921 5827
Good bar/bookshop. Very crowded at weekends.

Propaganda
Bolshaya Zlatoustinsky Per 7
Metro: Kitai Gorod
tel: (095) 924 5732
Flies in DJs from Britain and the US.

Music

Moscow's best venues for live jazz, reggae and rock concerts:

DOM
24 Bolshoi Ovchinnikovsky Perelok
tel: (095) 953 7236/34
Unusual concerts, for example, festivals of Tuvan throat singing. Sometimes completely empty, sometimes crowded. Call in advance. English spoken.

Kitaisky Lyotchik Dzhao Da
25 Lubyansky Proyezd
tel: (095) 924 5611
Popular venue with a good café. Open 22 hours a day. Concerts at night.

Projek OGI
8/12 Potapovsky Perulok
(enter through the courtyard)
tel: (095) 927 5776
Good live music. Good café as well.

Treti Put
4 Pyatnitskaya ulitsa
tel: (095) 951 8734
Alternative music venue in a former *komunalka*.

Vermel
Raushskaya Naberezhnaya 4/5
tel: (095) 231 7895
Popular among students and ex-pats. Film screenings shown occasionally.

Casinos

Casino Arbat
Arbat restaurant
ulitsa Novy Arbat 21
tel: (095) 291 1134

Casino Metropole
Metropole Hotel
Teatralny Proyezd 1/4
tel: (095) 927 6950
Open round the clock.

Cherry Casino (Metelitsa)
Novy Arbat 21
tel: (095) 291 1170

St Petersburg

Nightclubs

Akvatoria
61 Vyborgskaya Embankment
tel: (812) 245 2030
Top city disco, including bowling and billiards; cover charge of around $10.

Captain Morgan
61 Bolshoi prospekt (PS)
tel: (812) 230 7151
Casino and club for young, wealthy crowd.

Decadence
12 Admiralteisky Embankment
tel: (812) 312 3944
Small, cosy, top-notch club for glamorous youth; tough face-control for Russians while almost no problem for foreigners.

Dostoevsky Art Bar
15 Vladimirsky prospekt
tel: (812) 310 6164
Rocking club with live music.

Fish Fabrique
Pushkinskaya ulitsa 10
tel: (812) 164 4857
www.fishfabrique.spb.ru
Legendary Petersburg club/music
venue that is very popular with
students and local artists.

Griboedov
Voronezhskaya ulitsa 2a
tel; (812) 164 4355
www.griboedovclub.ru
In an old underground bomb
shelter. Big queues at weekends.

Konyushney Dvor
5 Griboedov Canal
tel: (812) 315 7607
Swinging scene for students and
yuppies; strip shows daily; cover
charge.

London
41 Chorny Rechki Embankment
tel: (812) 327 1567
Sophisticated dance club for
upscale crowd.

Luna
46 Voznesensky prospekt
tel: (812) 310 3628
Upscale, rich crowd, with cover of
about $20.

Moloko
Perekupnoi Perulok 12
tel: (812) 274 9467
Popular venue for live punk, reggae.

Plaza
2 Admiral Makarov Embankment
tel: (812) 323 9090
City's top club; for the glamorous
crowd; cover charge.

Sinners (Greshniki)
28 Griboedyov Canal
tel: (812) 318 4291
St Petersburg's gay club.

Jazz clubs

Since Soviet times, St Petersburg
has had Russia's most vibrant jazz
scene.

Jazz Philharmonic Hall
27 Zagorodny Prospect
tel: (812) 164 8565

JFC Jazz Club
33 Shpalernaya ulitsa
tel: (812) 272 9850

Jimi Hendrix Club
33 Liteiny prospekt
tel: (812) 279 8813

Quadrat
83 (Petrograd Side) Bolshoi prospekt
tel: (812) 315 9046

Shopping

What to Buy

Goods are plentiful throughout the
CIS, except in times of financial
crisis, and many Western chains
have opened stores in Moscow and
St Petersburg. Apart from at
markets, bargaining does not take
place.

In the large cities, shopping
hours are more in line with those of
the West, especially in the large
malls. Standard opening hours
elsewhere are Mon–Sat
10am–7pm. Many smaller shops
take a lunch break from 2–3pm.

Souvenirs

Inexpensive souvenirs, toys and
other knick-knacks abound on
Russian streets.

The "must see" street in
Moscow is the Arbat, where
Moscow painters and woodcarvers
sell their works. Prices are quite
high, so don't be in a hurry to buy a
set of Russian *matryoshkas* (the
wooden dolls which fit inside one
another) – the same set may be
found much cheaper somewhere
else. The Izmailovo market in the
city's northeastern suburb (metro
Izmailovsky Park) is worth a trip.

There are places similar to Arbat
in St Petersburg (Ostrovsky
ploshchad), in Kiev (on October
Revolution Square) and in other big
cities. More upmarket souvenirs
can be bought in specialist shops,
art-salons and curio shops. But
beware of the problems waiting at
customs: according to recent
Russian regulations, antiquities,
precious metals and artworks may
not be exported without prior
approval. The risk of confiscation is
real. Customs officials are
particularly strict about antique

icons. Permits can be obtained
from the government offices on
Neglinnaya Street 8–10, 2nd floor,
room 29, Moscow, tel: (095) 921
3258. Many art galleries will
provide the necessary
documentation. *For further
information on Customs, see page
334.*

Outside Moscow and St
Petersburg, look out for lace,
jewellery (Veliky Ustiug), painted
wooden objects (Archangelsk) and
carved ivory (especially in the
village of Lomonsovo, near
Archangelsk).

Russian and Ukrainian crafts and
traditional goods are similar.
Therefore, items common to both
countries, such as fur hats, can just
as easily be bought in Kiev. A
particularly good place to buy is the
huge weekend market at the central
Republican Stadium.

Ukraine's crafts include painted
wooden boxes, plates and spoons,
earthenware pottery, embroidered
cloths and linen and woollen rugs.
Though souvenir shops are quite
common in Kiev, the best selection
is available at Andriivsky Uzviz.

Where to Shop

MOSCOW

Department stores

GUM (State Department Store)
Krasnaya ploshchad 3 (Red Square)
This famous arcade has been
commandeered by branches of
foreign stores, and you won't find
many Russian goods here although
there are some Russian handicrafts
and souvenirs. Foreign-made goods
will probably be more expensive
than at home. However, it is worth
visiting, if only for the fabulous
decor.

Detsky Mir (Children's World)
Teatralny Proyezd 5
This store sells everything from
toys and clothing to buggies.

TsUM (Central Department Store)
ulitsa Petrovka 2
You'll find plenty of kitsch here in
addition to traditional Russian
goods, such as amber and coral
jewellery, samovars, rugs and furs.

Petrovsky Passage
ulitsa Petrovka 10
Another magnificent arcade. It is as
expensive as GUM.

Fur Shops
Ars
ulitsa Malaya Bronnaya 4
Alina Salon
Prospekt Vernadskogo 39
Bogumin
Zheleznodorozhny Proyezd 6
Claude Litz
ulitsa Kuznetsky Most 14
Salon Ekaterina
ulitsa Bolshaya Dmitrovka 1
Furs and Leather Shop
Chistoprudny Boulevard 21
Gornostai
Aptekarsky Pereulok 10A
Intermekh
ulitsa Petrovka 2
Russian Fur
ulitsa Dokukina 10
Sovmehkastoria
ulitsa Bolshaya Dorogomilovskaya
14

Speciality shops
Russkiye Souveniry
Kutuzovsky Prospekt 9
This is the place to do your
shopping if you are interested in
buying upmarket souvenirs, such as

lacquer boxes, silverware and
ethnic costumes.

Jewellery shops
Afran
National Hotel, ulitsa Mokhovaya
15/1
Almaz
Komsomolsky Prospekt 49
Centre Yuvelir #1
ulitsa Petrovka 24/1
Check the *Moscow Business Guide*
for other Centre Yuvelirs.
Imperator
Berezhkovskaya Naberezhnaya 2
Jewels
ulitsa Pushechnaya 7/5
Russian Gold
ulitsa Lesnaya 43

Antiques shops
Aktsia
ulitsa Bolshaya Nikitskaya 21/
18;
Raritet
ulitsa Arbat 31
Starina
ulitsa Petrovka 24

ST PETERSBURG

One of the best places to buy
souvenirs is at the three bridges,

Photography

Photographic equipment is easily
obtainable in Moscow, St
Petersburg and Kiev and quick
film-developing services are
available. Generally speaking,
taking photographs in galleries,
museums and exhibitions is
permitted, but visitors should
take care not to take
photographs of military
installations or anything else
that might be seen as a threat
to security.

next to the cathedral of Our Saviour
on the Blood, right on Kanal
Griboyedova.

Department stores
Gostinny Dvor
35 Nevsky prospekt
Most famous of St Petersburg's
department stores.
Passage
48 Nevksy prospekt
Another big department store.

Books, maps and music
Bukinist
59 Liteiny prospekt
Secondhand books.

Moscow's Food Shops

Food shops abound in Moscow.
You will find dozens of stores
selling a variety of domestic and
imported comestibles on every
street. Caviar is stocked by all the
major food outlets.
Here is a selection:

Yeliseyevsky Gastronom
Unitsa Tverskaya 14
Novoarbatsky Food Store
Ulitsa Novy Arbat 11
Food Island
Leningradsky prospekt 50
Foodland
Krasnopresnenskaya
Naberezhnaya 9
Global USA
Ulitsa Tverskaya 6
Sovhispan S.A.
Novinsky Boulevard 7/1

Expo-EM
Ulitsa Fersmana 9
Gastronoom No. 20
Ulitsa Bolshaya Lubyanka 14
Good for chocolates and
champagne.
Eldorado
1 Bolshaya Polyanka
Global USA
112 Leningradskoe Schosse
Manege Shopping Mall
Three-floor underground shopping
mall directly under Manezhnaya
ploshchad. Accessible from
Oxotny Ryad metro.
Perekriostok
Sukharovskaya ploshchad 1
Ramstore
Sheremetevskaya ulitsa 60a
Seventh Continent
12 Bolshaya Lubyanka

Language

Linguistic History

Russian belongs to the Slavonic branch of the Indo-European family of languages. English, German, French, Spanish and Hindi are its relatives.

It is important when speaking Russian that you reproduce the accent (marked here before each stressed vowel with the sign ') correctly to be understood well.

Historically Russian can be called a comparatively young language. The evolution of the language to its present form on the basis of the spoken language of Eastern Slavs and the Church-Slavonic written language is thought to have occurred between the 11th and 14th centuries.

Modern Russian has absorbed a considerable number of foreign words. Very few tourists will be puzzled by Russian words such as *telefon, televizor, teatr, otel, restoran, kafe, taxi, metro, aeroport.*

What intimidates people making their first acquaintance with Russian is the Cyrillic alphabet. In fact the alphabet can be remembered easily after a few repetitions and the difference with the Latin alphabet is only minimal. An understanding of the Russian alphabet permits one to make out the names of the streets and the shop signs.

The Russian (or Cyrillic) alphabet was created by two brothers, philosophers and public figures Constantine (St Cyril) and Methodius, both born in Solun (now Thessaloniki in Greece). Their purpose was to facilitate the spread of Greek liturgical books to Slavonic speaking countries. Today the Cyrillic alphabet with different modifications is used in the Ukrainian, Belarusian, Bulgarian and Serbian languages, among others.

Transliteration

There are four systems of transliteration of Russian words into English (*see The Transliteration of Modern Russian for English Language Publications* by J.T. Shaw, the University of Wisconsin Press, 1967). If necessary, the systems can be combined so that one letter or a group of letters is transliterated according to one system and the other according to another. To transliterate some Russian letters, English letter combinations are used:

ж = zh, x = kh, ц = ts, ч = ch, ш =sh, щ = shch, ю = yu, я = ya, ё = yo. The Russian letter combination кс is transliterated both as *ks* and as *x* Russian letters are transliterated (with a few exceptions) in a similar way: й, ы = y, e, ё = e.

To transliterate the Russian soft sign between the consonants and before no-vowel, the apostrophe is used, or the soft sign is ignored, as before vowels. The transliteration of nominal inflections has a number of peculiarities: ый, ий = y, ие, ье = ie, ия = ia.

If the traditional English spelling in names differs from their letter-by-letter transliteration they are mostly translated in their English form: Moscow (city), but river Moskva.

The Genetive inflections in the names of streets and other objects are translated according to their pronunciation, and not their spelling: площадь Горького, (*ploshchad' Gór'kogo*) = pl. Gorkovo in this book. The transliteration in this section shows the way to pronounce Russian words and therefore does not correspond exactly with their spelling.

The city maps and their captions use Russian words and abbreviations: ul. (*úlitsa*) means street; per. (*pereúlok*) – lane; prosp. (*prospékt*) – avenue; pl. (*plóshchad'*) – square; *alléya* – alley; *bul'vár* – boulevard; *magistrál* – main line; *proézd* – passage; *shossé* – highway; *spusk* – slope.

The Russian system of writing out house numbers is as follows *prosp. Kalinina 28* (*28 Kalinin Avenue*).

The Alphabet

The first two columns show the printed letter in Russian upper and lower case. The third column shows how the Russian letters sound and the fourth column shows the name of the letter in Russian.

А	а	**a**, archaeology **a**	
Б	б	**b**, buddy **be**	
В	в	**v**, vow **v**	
Г	г	**g**, glad **ge**	
Д	д	**d**, dot (the tip of the tongue close to the teeth, not the alveoli) **de**	
Е	е	**e**, get **ye**	
Ё	ё	**yo**, yoke **yo**	
Ж	ж	**zh**, composure **zhe**	
З	з	**z**, zest **ze**	
И	и	**i**, ink **i**	
Й	й	**j**, yes **jot**	
К	к	**k**, kind **ka**	
Л	л	**l**, life (but a bit harder) **el'**	
М	м	**m**, memory **em**	
Н	н	**n**, nut **en**	
О	о	**o**, optimum **o**	
П	п	**p**, party **pe**	
Р	р	**r** (rumbling – as in Italian, the tip of the tongue is vibrating) **er**	
С	с	**s**, sound **es**	
Т	т	**t**, title (the tip of the tongue close to the teeth) **te**	
У	у	**u**, nook **u**	
Ф	ф	**f**, flower **ef**	
Х	х	**kh**, hawk **ha**	
Ц	ц	**ts**, (pronounced conjointly) **tse**	
Ч	ч	**ch**, charter **che**	
Ш	ш	**sh**, shy **sha**	
Щ	щ	**shch**, (pronounced conjointly) **shcha**	
ъ		(the hard sign)	
Ы	ы	**y** (pronounced with the same position of a tongue as when pronouncing G, K) **y**	
ь		(the soft sign)	
Э	э	**e**, ensign **e**	
Ю	ю	**yu**, you **yu**	
Я	я	**ya**, yard **ya**	

Useful Words and Phrases

Numbers

1	adín	один
2	dva	два
3	tri	три
4	chityrі	четыре
5	pyat'	пят́
6	shes't'	шесть
7	sem	семь
8	vósim	восемь
9	d'évit'	девять
10	d'ésit'	десять
11	adínatsat'	одиннадцать
12	dvinátsat'	двенадцать
13	trinátsat'	тринадцать
14	chityrnatsat'	четырнадцать
15	pitnátsat'	пятнадцат́
16	shysnátsat'	шестнадцать
17	simnátsat'	семнадцать
18	vasimnátsat'	восемнадцать
19	divitnátsat'	девятнадцать
20	dvátsat'	двадцать
21	dvatsat' adin	двадцать один
30	trítsat'	тридцать
40	sórak	сорок
50	pidisyat	пятьдесят
60	shyz'disyat	шестьдесят
70	s'émdisyat	семьдесят
80	vósimdisyat	восемьдесят
90	divinósta	девяносто
100	sto	сто
200	dv'és'ti	двести
300	trísta	триста
400	chityrista	четыреста
500	pitsót	пятьсот
600	shyssót	шестьсот
700	simsót	семьсот
800	vasimsót	восемьсот
900	divitsót	девятьсот
1,000	tysicha	тысяча
2,000	dve tysichi	две тысячи и
10,000	d'ésit' tysich	десятьтысяч
100,000	sto tysich	сто тысяч
1,000,000	milión	миллион
1,000,000,000	miliárd	миллиард

Pronouns

I/we
ya/my
Я/мы

You
ty (singular, informal)/
vy (plural, or formal singular)
ты/вы

He/she/they
on/aná/aní
он/она/они

My/mine
moj (object masculine)/
mayá (object feminine)/
mayó (neutral or without marking
the gender)/
maí (plural)
мой/моя/моё/мои

Our/ours
nash/násha/náshe/náshy (resp.)
наш/наша/наше/наши

Your/yours
tvoj etc. (see My)
vash etc. (see Our)
твой/ваш

His/her, hers/their, theirs
jivó/jiyó/ikh
его/её/их

Who?
khto?
Кто?

What?
shto?
Что?

Greetings & Acquaintance

Hello!
zdrástvuti (neutral, and often
accompanied by shaking hands, but
this is not necessary)
Здравствуйте!

zdrástvuj (to one person, informal)
Здравствуй!

alo! (by telephone only)
Алло!

priv'ét! (informal)
Привет!

Good afternoon/Good evening
dóbry den'/dobry véchir
Добрый день/Добрый вечер

Good morning/Good night
dobrae útra/dobraj nóchi (= Sleep
well)
Доброе утро/Доброй ночи

Goodbye
dasvidán'ye (neutral)
До свиданья

ciao! (informal)
Чао!

paká! (informal, literally "until")
Пока!

Good luck to you!
shchislíva!
Счастливо!

Terms of Address

Modern Russian has no
established and universally used
forms of salutation. The old
revolutionary form "tavárishch"
(comrade), still used among
some party members, lacks
popularity among the rest of the
population. Alternatives include:
"Izviníti, skazhíte pozhálsta..."
(Excuse me, tell me, please...) or
"Izviníti, mózhna sprasít...") or "I
ozhálst" (Excuse me, can I ask
you...).

If you want to sound original
and show your understanding of
the history of courteous forms
of greeting, you can address a
man as gospodin (sir), and a
woman as gospozha (madam).
Many people want to restore
these pre-Revolutionary forms
of address in modern Russian
society.

If you know the name of the
father of the person you are
talking to, the best and the most
neutral way of addressing them
is to use either
gospodin/gospozha together with
the relevant paternal name.
English forms of address –
Mister/Sir or Madam/Miss – are
also acceptable.

You will hear the common
parlance forms Maladói
chelavék! (Young man!) and
Dévushka! (Girl!) directed toward
a person of any age, and also
Zhénshchina! (Woman!) to
women in the bus, in the shop or
at the market. These forms should
be avoided in conversation.

What is your name?
kak vas (tibya) zavút?/kak váshe ímya ótchistva? (the second is formal)
Как вас (тебя) зовут?/Как ваше имя иотчество?

My name is.../I am...
minya zavut.../ya...
Меня зовут.. Я...

It's a pleasure
óchin' priyatna
Очень приятно

Good/excellent
kharashó/privaskhódna
хорошо/отлично

Do you speak English?
vy gavaríti pa anglíski?
Вы говорите по-английски?

I don't understand/I didn't understand
ya ni panimáyu/ya ni pónyal
Я не понимаю/Я не понял

Repeat, please
pavtaríti pazhálsta
Повторите, пожалуйста

What do you call this?
kak vy éta nazyváiti?
Как вы это называете?

How do you say...?
kak vy gavaríti...?
Как вы говорите...?

Please/Thank you (very much)
pazhálsta/(bal'shóe) spasíba
Пожалуйста/(большое) спасибо

Excuse me
izviníti
Извините

Getting Around

Where is the...?
gd'e (nakhóditsa)...?
Где находится...?

beach
plyazh
...пляж

bathroom
vánnaya
...ванная

bus station
aftóbusnaya stántsyja/aftavakzál
...автобусная станция/автовокзал

bus stop
astanófka aftóbusa
...остановка автобуса

airport
airapórt
...аэропорт

railway station
vakzál/stántsyja (in small towns)
...вокзал/станция

post office
póchta
...почта

police station
milítsyja
...милиция

ticket office
bil'étnaya kássa
...билетная касса

market place
rynak/bazár
...рынок/базар

embassy/consulate
pasól'stva/kónsul'stva
...посольство/консульство

Where is there a...?
gd'e z'd'es'...?
Где здесь...?

currency exchange
abm'én val'úty
...обмен валюты

pharmacy
apt'éka
...аптека

(good) hotel
(kharóshyj) atél'/(kharoshaya) gastínitsa
...(хороший) отель/(хорошая) гостиница

restaurant
ristarán
...ресторан

bar
bar
...бар

taxi stand
stayanka taxí
...стоянка такси

subway station
mitró
...метро

service station
aftazaprávachnaya stantsyja/aftasárvis
...автозаправочная станция

news stand
gaz'étnyj kiósk
...газетный киоск

public telephone
tilifón
...телефон

hard currency shop
val'útnyj magazín
...валютный магазин

supermarket
univirsám
...универсам

department store
univirmák
...универмаг

hairdresser
parikmákhirskaya
...парикмахерская

jeweller
yuvilírnyj magazin
...ювелирный магазин

hospital
bal'nítsa
...больница

Do you have...?
u vas jes't'...?
У вас есть...?

I (don't) want...
ya (ni) khachyu...
Я (не) хочу...

I want to buy...
ya khachyu kupít'...
Я хочу купить...

Where can I buy...
gd'e ya magú kupít'...
Где я могу купить...

cigarettes
sigaréty
...сигареты

wine
vinó
...вино

film
fotoplyonku
...фотоплёнку

a ticket for...
bilét na...
...билет на...

this
éta
...это

postcards/envelopes
atkrytki/kanv'érty
...открытки/конверты

a pen/a pencil
rúchku/karandásh
...ручку/карандаш

soap/shampoo
myla/shampún'
...мыло/шампунь

aspirin
aspirn
...аспирин

I need...
mn'e núzhna...
Мне нужно...

I need a doctor/a mechanic
mn'e núzhyn dóktar/aftamikhánik
Мне нужен доктор/автомеханик

I need help
mn'e nuzhná pómashch'
Мне нужна помощь

Car/plane/trains/ship
mashyna/samal'yot/póist/karábl'
машина/самолёт/поезд/корабль

A ticket to...
bil'ét do...
билет до...

How can I get to...
kak ya magu dabrátsa do...
Как я могу добраться до...

Please, take me to...
pazhalsta atvizíti minya...
Пожалуйста, отвезите меня...

What is this place called?
kak nazyváitsa eta m'ésta?
Как называется это место?

Where are we?
gd'e my?
Где мы?

Stop here
astanavíti z'd'es'
Остановите здесь

Please wait
padazhdíti pazhalsta
Подождите, пожалуйста

When does the train [plane] leave?
kagdá atpravl'yaitsa poist [samalyot]?
Когда отправляется поезд (самолёт)?

I want to check my luggage
ya khachyu prav'érit' bagázh
Я хочу проверить багаж

Where does this bus go?
kudá id'yot état aftóbus?
Куда идёт этот автобус?

Shopping

How much does it cost?
skól'ka eta stóit?
Сколько это стоит?

That's very expensive
eta óchin' dóraga
Это очень дорого

A lot, many/A little, few
mnóga/mála
много/мало

It (doesn't) fits me
eta mn'e (ni) padkhódit
Это мне (не) подходит

At the Hotel

I have a reservation
u minya zakázana m'esta
У меня заказана комната

I want to make a reservation
ya khachyu zakazát' m'esta
Я хочу заказать место

A single (double) room
adnam'éstnuyu (dvukhmestnuyu) kómnatu
одноместную (двухместную) комнату

I want to see the room
ya khachyu pasmatrét' nómer
Я хочу посмотреть номер

Key/suitcase/bag
klyuch/chimadán/súmka
ключ/чемодан/сумка

Eating Out

Waiter/menu
afitsyánt/minyu
официант/меню

I want to order...
ya khachyu zakazat'...
Я хочу заказать

Breakfast/lunch/supper
záftrak/ab'ét/úzhyn
завтрак/обед/ужин

the house speciality
fírminnaya blyuda
фирменное блюдо

Mineral water/juice
minirál'naya vadá/sok
минеральная вода/сок

Coffee/tea/beer
kófe/chai/píva
кофе/ чай/пиво

What do you have to drink (alcoholic)?
shto u vas jes't' vypit'?
Что у вас есть выпить?

Ice/fruit/dessert
marózhynaya/frúkty/disért
мороженое/фрукты/десерт

Salt/pepper/sugar
sol'/périts/sákhar
соль/перец/сахар

Beef/pork/chicken/fish/shrimp
gavyadina/svinína/kúritsa/ryba/kriv'étki
говядина/свинина/курица/рыба/креветки

Vegetables/rice/potatoes
óvashchi/ris/kartófil'
овощи/рис/картофель

Bread/butter/eggs
khleb/másla/yajtsa
хлеб/масло/яйца

Soup/salad/sandwich/pizza
sup/salát/butyrbrót/pitsa
суп/салат/бутерброд/пицца

A plate/a glass/a cup/a napkin
tar'élka/stakán/cháshka/salf'étka
тарелка/стакан/чашка/салфетка

The bill, please
shchyot pazhalsta
Счёт, пожалуйста

Delicious/Not so good
fkúsna/ták sibe
вкусно/так себе

I want my change, please
zdáchu pazhalsta
Сдачу, пожалуйста

Money

I want to exchange currency (money)
ya khachyu abmin'át' val'yutu (d'én'gi)
Я хочу обменять валюту (деньги)

Do you accept credit cards?
vy prinimáiti kridítnyi kártachki?
Вы принимаете кредитные карточки?

Can you cash a traveller's cheque?
vy mózhyti razminyat' darózhnyj chek?
Вы можете разменять дорожный чек?

What is the exchange rate?
kakój kurs?
Какой курс?

Time

What time is it?
katóryj chas?
Который час?

Just a moment, please
adnú minútachku
Одну минуточку

How long does it take?
skól'ka vrémini eta zanimáit?
Сколько времени это занимает?

Hour/day/week/month
chas/den'/nid'élya/m'ésits
час/день/неделя/месяц

At what time?
f kakóe vrémya?
В какое время?

This (last, next) week
eta (próshlaya, sl'édujshchiya) nid'elya
эта (прошлая, следующая) неделя

Yesterday/today/tomorrow
fchirá/sivód'nya/záftra
вчера/сегодня/завтра

Sunday
vaskris'én'je
воскресенье

Monday
panid'él'nik
понедельник

Tuesday
ftórnik
вторник

Wednesday
sridá
среда

Thursday
chitv'érk
четверг

Friday
pyatnitsa
пятница

Saturday
subóta
суббота

The weekend
vykhadnyi dni
выходные дни

Signs & Inscriptions

вход/выход/входа нет
fkhot/vykhat/fkhóda n'et
Entrance/exit/no entrance

туалет/уборная
tual'ét/ubórnaya
Lavatory

Ж (З)/М (М)
dlya zhén'shchin/dlya mushchín
Ladies/gentlemen

зал ожидания
zal azhidán'ya
Waiting hall

занято/свободно
zánita/svabódna
Occupied/free

касса
kassa
booking office/cash desk

медпункт
medpúnkt
Medical services

справочное бюро
správachnae bzuro
Information

вода для питья
vadá dlya pit'ya
Drinking water

вокзал
vakzál
Terminal/railway station

открыто/закрыто
atkryta/zakryta
Open Closed

запрещается/опасно
zaprishchyaitsa/apásna
Prohibited/danger

продукты/гастроном
pradúkty/gastranóm
Grocery

булочная/кондитерская
búlachnaya/kan'dítirskaya
Bakery/confectionery

закусочная/столовая
zakúsachnaya/stalóvaya
Refreshment room/canteen

самообслуживание
samaapslúzhivan'je
Self-service

баня/прачечная/химчистка
bánya/práchichnaya/khimchístka
Bath-house/laundry/dry cleaning

книги/культтовары
knígi/kul'taváry
Books/stationery

мясо/птица
m'ása/ptítsa
Meat/poultry

овощи/фрукты
óvashchi/frúkty
Green-grocery/fruits

универмаг/универсам
univirmák/univirsám
Department store/supermarket

Further Reading

History

The Blackwell Encyclopaedia of the Russian Revolution, edited by H. Shukman (Blackwell, 1989).
Catherine the Great, by J.T. Alexander (Oxford University Press, 1989).
Comrades 1917 – Russia in Revolution, by Brian Moynahan (Hutchinson, 1992).
History of Soviet Russia, by EH Carr (Pelican). In three volumes, first published 1953.
A History of the Soviet Union, by GA Hosking (Fontana/Collins, 1990).
A History of Twentieth Century Russia, by Robert Service (Harvard University Press, 1997).
The Icon and the Axe, by James Billington (Vintage US).
The Last Tsar, by Edvard Radzinsky (Hodder & Stoughton, 1992).

Russian Literature

And Quiet Flows the Don and **The Don Flows Home to the Sea**, by Mikhail Sholokhov.
Anthology, by Daniil Kharms.
Blue Lard, by Vladimir Sorokin (1999).
Children of the Arbat, by Anatoli Rybakov (Hutchinson, 1988).
Crime and Punishment, The Brothers Karamazov, The Devils, by Fyodor Dostoyevsky. Penguin.
Dead Souls Diary of a Madman and Other Stories, by Nikolai Gogol.
Doctor Zhivago, by Boris Pasternak (Penguin).
Eugene Onegin, by Alexander Pushkin (Penguin).
Fathers and Sons, On The Eve, A Hero of Our Time, by Mikhail Lermontov (Penguin).
Lady with Lapdog and Other Stories, by Anton Chekhov (Penguin).
The Life of Insects, by Victor Pelevin (Faber and Faber, 1999).
The Master and Margarita, by Mikhail Bulgakov.
The Penguin Book of Russian Short Stories, edited by David Richards (Penguin, 1981).
Red Cavalry and Other Stories, by Isaac Babel.
Soviet Russian Literature: Writers and Problems and **The Epic of Russian Literature**, by Mare Slonim.
Sportsman's Sketches, by Ivan Turgenev (Penguin).
We, by Evgeny Zamyatin (Penguin).
War and Peace, Anna Karenina and **The Death of Ivan Ilyich and Other Stories**, by Leo Tolstoy (Penguin).

The Making of Modern Russia, by L Kochan and R Abraham (Penguin, 1983).
A People's Tragedy, by Orlando Figes (Pimlico).
Nicholas II: Emperor of all the Russians, by Dominic Lieven (John Murray, 1993).
Paul I of Russia, by Roderick E McGrew (Oxford, 1993).
Peter the Great: His Life and Work, by Robert K Massie (Abacus).
Soviet Colossus: History of the USSR, by Michael Kort (M.E. Sharp, 1993).
Stalin, Man of Contradiction, by KN Cameron (Strong Oak Press, 1989).
Stalinism and After: Road to Gorbachev, by Alec Nove (Routledge, 1993).

Politics

Glasnost in Action, by A Nove (Unwin Hyman, 1989).
Lenin's Tomb, by David Remnick (Viking, 1993).
The Other Russia, by Michael Glenny and Norman Stone (Faber and Faber, 1990).
Voices of Glasnost, by S Cohen and K. van den Heuvel (Norton, 1989).

Biography/Memoirs

Black Earth, by Charlotte Hobson (Granta, 2002).
An English Lady at the Court of Catherine the Great, edited by AG Gross (Crest Publications, 1989).
The Gulag Archipelago, by Alexander Solzhenitsyn (Collins Harvill, 1988).
The House by the Dvina, by Eugenie Fraser (Corgi, 1986).
In the Beginning, by Irina Ratushinskaya (Hodder & Stoughton, 1990).
Into the Whirlwind; Within the Whirlwind, by Eugenia Ginzburg (Collins Harvill, 1989).
The Making of Andrei Sakharov, by G Bailey (Penguin, 1990).
On the Estate: Memoirs of Russia Before the Revolution, edited by Olga Davydoff Bax (Thames & Hudson, 1986).
Russia: Despatches from the Guardian Correspondent in Moscow, by Martin Walker (Abacus, 1989).
Ten Days that Shook the World, by John Reed (Penguin, first published 1919).

Art

Folk Art in the Soviet Union (Abrams/Aurora, 1990).
The Hermitage (Aurora, 1987).
History of Russian Painting, by A Bird (Phaidon, 1987).
The Irony Tower, by Andrew Solomon (Knopf).
The Kremlin and its Treasures, by Rodimzeva, Rachmanov and Raimann (Phaidon, 1989).
Masterworks of Russian Painting in Soviet Museums (Aurora, 1989).
New Worlds: Russian Art and Society 1900–3, by D Elliott (Thames & Hudson, 1986).
Russian Art of the Avant Garde, by JE Bowlt (Thames & Hudson, 1988).
Russian Art from Neoclassicism to the Avant Garde, by DV Sarabianov (Thames & Hudson, 1990).
Street Art of the Revolution, Tolstoy, VI Bibikova and C Cooke (Thames & Hudson), 1990.
Travel and Natural History Among the Russians, by Colin Thubron (Penguin, first published 1983).

Atlas of Russia and the Soviet Union, by R. Millner–Gulland, with N. Dejevsky (Phaidon, 1989).
The Big Red Train Ride, by Eric Newby (Picador, 1989).
Caucasian Journey, by Negley Farson (Penguin, first published 1951).
Epics of Everyday Life, by Susan Richards (Penguin, 1991).
First Russia, Then Tibet, by Robert Byron (Penguin, first published 1933).
The Food and Cooking of Russia, by Lesley Chamberlain (Penguin, 1982).
Imperial Splendour, by George Galitzine (Viking, I991).
Journey into Russia, by Laurens van der Post (Penguin, first published 1964).
The Natural History of the USSR, by Algirdas Kynstautas (Century Hutchinson, 1987).
The Nature of the Russia, by John Massey Stewart (Boxtree, 1992).
The New Russians, by Hedrick Smith (Vintage, I990).
Portrait of the Soviet Union, by Fitzroy Maclean (Weidenfeld and Nicolson, 1988).
Russia (Bracken Books, 1989).
Russia, with Tehran, Port Arthur and Peking, by Karl Baedeker (I914).
Sailing to Leningrad, by Roger Foxall (Grafton, 1990).
The Taming of the Eagles: Exploring the New Russia, by Imogen Edwards-Jones. Photographs by Joth Shakerley (Weidenfeld & Nicolson, 1993).
The Trans–Siberian Rail Guide, by Robert Strauss (Compass, 1993).
Ustinov in Russia, by Peter Ustinov. (Michael O Mara Books, 1987).

Travel

Lost Cosmonaut, by Daniel Humphries (Faber and Faber, 2006).
Imperium, Ryszard Kapuscinski (Random House, 1994).
Born out of Necessity, by Vladimir Arkhipov (Typolygon, 2003).
Hope against Hope, by Nadezhda Mandelstam (Harvil Press, 1971).

Other Insight Guides

Among the 200-plus-title Insight Guide series are two companion volumes to the present book. **Insight Guide: Moscow** and **Insight Guide: St Petersburg** cover Russia's two major cities.

Insight Pocket Guides

Insight Pocket Guides to **Moscow** and **St Petersburg** are designed for visitors keen to make the most of a short stay. Each book comes with a full-size fold-out map.

Insight Compact Guides

Insight Compact Guides to **Moscow** and **St Petersburg** are the perfect on-the-spot reference guides. This low-price series packs an astonishing amount of information into a portable format, with text, photographs and maps all carefully cross-referenced.

Feedback

We do our best to ensure the information in our books is as accurate and up-to-date as possible. The books are updated on a regular basis, using local contacts, who painstakingly add, amend and correct as required. However, some mistakes and omissions are inevitable and we are ultimately reliant on our readers to put us in the picture.

We would welcome your feedback on any details related to your experiences using the book "on the road". The more details you can give us (particularly with regard to addresses, e-mails and telephone numbers), the better.

Please write to us at:
Insight Guides
PO Box 7910
London SE1 1WE
United Kingdom
Or send e-mail to:
insight@apaguide.demon.co.uk

ART & PHOTO CREDITS

Picture Spreads

INSIGHT GUIDE
RUSSIA

Cartographic Editor **Zoë Goodwin**
Design Consultants
Carlotta Junger, Graham Mitchener
Picture Research **Hilary Genin**

Maps Geodata

© 2005 Apa Publications GmbH & Co.
Verlag KG (Singapore branch)

Index

Numbers in italics refer to photographs

a

Abramtsevo Estate 101, *176*
Artists' Colony 101, 176
Museum of Literature and Art 176
Abrau-Dyurso 249
Russian champagne 249
accommodation
see also **health resorts and spas**
Grand Hotel (Lviv, Ukraine) 320
Grand Hotel Europe (St Petersburg) 199, 347
Hotel Londonskaya (Odessa, Ukraine) 322
Hotel Moskva (Kiev) 313
hotel ships at Odessa 322
listings 346–53
Metropol Hotel (Moscow) 157, 346
National Hotel (Moscow) 158, 346
Pekin Hotel (Moscow) 160
Rossiya Hotel (Moscow) 152, 347
in Suzdal 177
"tourist" pricing 244
youth hostels 348
Adams, Henry 15
agriculture 55, 293–4, 332
collective farms 55, 293
crops of the Northern Caucasus 249
airline offices 340–41
air travel 333
Aivazovsky, Ivan 101
The Wave 101
Akhamatova, Anna 111, 112
Muzei Anni Akhmatovoi (Anna Akhmatova Museum, St Petersburg) 201
Requiem 112
Aksyonov 113
Alexander I 47
Alexander II 48–9, 190
burial place 190
Alexander III 49
Altay Mountains 265–6
Alyabev, Alexander 117
Andropov, Yuri 57
Arakcheyev, Count 47
Aral Sea 20
Arctic, The 19, 259, 261

Arkhangelsk 215–6
accommodation 349
eating out 357
art 97–104
see also **galleries**
see also individual artists' names
Abramtsevo Estate artists' colony 101
Blue Rose Group 102
Constructivism 103
Knave of Diamonds group 102
The Mother of God of Vladimir 98
Moscow Conceptualism 104
Moscow metro art 168–9
New Academy of Arts (St Petersburg) 104
Rayism 102
religious art 97
secular art 99–100
Socialist Realism 103–4
Society for Travelling Art Exhibitions (the Wanderers) 100
Sots Art 104
Stroganov Masters 214–5
Suprematism 102
World of Art magazine 101
Artemov, Eduard 122
Artemova, Vyacheslav 122
arts, the 70
see also **music and dance**
Alexandriinsky Dramatichesky Teatr (Alexander Theatre of Drama, St Petersburg) 200
Ballets Russes 102, 119
Bolshoy Teatr (Moscow) 121, 157
Detsky Teatr (Central Children's Theatre, Moscow) 157
Dom-muzei Stanislavskogo (Stanislavsky Museum, Moscow) 161–2
Filarmoniya (Philharmonia, Kiev) 313
Filarmoniya (Philharmonia, Odessa, Ukraine) 323
Irkutsk Dramatichesky Teatr (Drama Theatre, Irkutsk) 268–9
Irkutsk Filarmoniya (Philharmonic, Irkutsk) 269
International Tchaikovsky Competition 121, 160
Kiev Opera and Ballet Theatre 309
Kirov *see* Mariinsky
Kolonny Zal (Hall of the

Columns) concert hall (Moscow) 158
Konservatoriya imeni Chaikovskoho (Tchaikovsky State Conservatory, Kiev) 314
Konservatoriya imeni Chaikovskogo (Moscow Conservatory of Music) 161
Kontsertny zal imeni Chaykovskogo (Tchaikovsky Concert Hall, Moscow) 160
Maly Teatr (Moscow) 157
Maly Teatr imeni Musorgskogo (Small Musorgsky Theatre of Opera and Ballet, St Petersburg) 199
Mariinsky Theatre (St Petersburg) 122, 196, 197
miniature theatre (Ostankino) 117
Stanislavsky Theatre (Moscow) 158
Teatr imeni Gorkogo (Drama Theatre, Samara) 230
Teatr Musyky ta Dramy (Music and Drama Theatre, Chernivtsi, Ukraine) 321
Teatr Operi i Balleta (Opera and Ballet Theatre, Saratov) 231
Teatr Opery ta Baletu (Opera and Ballet Theatre, Lviv, Ukraine) *319*
Teatr Opery ta Baletu (Opera and Ballet Theatre, Odessa, Ukraine) 323
Teatr Volkov (Yaroslavl) 177
Vaganova Ballet School (St Petersburg) 200
Ashkenazy, Vladimir 122
Astrakhan *233*, 233–5
accommodation 350
Belaya Mechet (White Mosque) 235
boat trips of Volga delta reserve 235
Chernaya Mechet (Black Mosque) 235
City Technical School 234
Demidov Homestead 234
Department for the Supervision of the Kalmyk People 234–4
Ioann Zlatoust (St John Chrysostom) church 234
Kartinnaya Galereya B.M.

Kustodieva (Kustodiev Art Gallery) 235
Katolicheskaya Tserkov (Roman Catholic church) 235
Kirillovskaya Chasovnya (Chapel) 234
Kremlin 234
Preobrazhensky Monastyr (Transfiguration Monastery) 234
Troitsky Sobor (Trinity Cathedral) 234
Uspensky Sobor (Cathedral of the Assumption) 234
Aurora Borealis
see **Northern Lights**

b

Babel, Isaak 112
Odessa Tales 112
Red Cavalry 112
Baikal Lake 18, 20, 261, *264*, 266–7, 272–3, 124
accommodation 351
beaches 267
climate 267
ecology 267
Olkhon Island 267, 273
Port Baikal 267
Bakhchysaray Tatar Palace (Ukraine) 324, 326
Bakst, Leon 101–2
Balabanov, Alexei 123
Brother 123
Balakirevin, Mily 118
Balaklava 326
Barents Sea 218
Barnaul 266
accommodation 352
Altaisky Krayevoi Muzei Istorii (Altay Museum of Regional Studies and History) 266
Gosudarstvenny Khudozhestvenny Muzei Altaiskogo Kraya (Altay State Art Museum) 266
Batu Khan 33–4, 309, 313
beaurocracy 65
Belarus 18, 279–305, 331
see also place names
economy 291–3, 296–7, 331
getting there 334
independence 291–2
money matters 333
politics 291–3
visas and passports 332
Belokurikha 266
Belomorsk 218

boat trips to Solovetsky Islands 218
Belovezhskaya Pushcha Nature Reserve (Belarus) 301, 305
Belozersk 214
fortress remains 214
Preobrazhensky Sobor (Cathedral of the Transfiguration) 214
Uspensky Sobor (Church of the Assumption) 214
Vsemilostivogo Spasa (Church of the Most Merciful Saviour) 214
Berezovsky, Boris 69, 73, 78
Berezovsky, Maksim 117
Bering Strait 261
Big Diomede island 261
Black Sea 249–52, 321, *324*, 327
beaches 250–1
contamination 249
marine life 249–50
Blok, Alexander 101, 111, 188
The Twelve 188
Bobritsky, Alexei 43
Bodpad Kivach (Kivach waterfall) 217
Bodrov, Sergei 123
Prisoner of the Mountains 123
Bolsheviks 53, 185, 202, 302, 311
Bolshoi Akhun Mountain 253
Agurskiye vodopady (Agur waterfalls) 253
Borodin, Alexander 118
Prince Igor 118
Bortnyansky, Dmitri 117
Bratsk 265
accommodation 351
hydroelectric station 265
Otkryty Muzei Etnografii (open-air museum) 265
Brener, Alexander 104
Brest 301
accommodation 352
fortress *303*
World War II memorial *301*
Brezhnev, Leonid 57, 92, 327
Brodsky, Joseph 112
Bryansk 227
accommodation 350
eating out 357
Partizanskaya Polyana (Partisan Field) and museum 227
Svensky Monastyr (Sven Monastery) 227

Uspensky Sobor (Assumption Cathedral) 227
Bryullov, Karl 100
Last Day of Pompeii 100
Bulatov, Erik 104
Bulgakov, Mikhail 112, 313
Mikhail Bulgakov museum (Kiev) 313
The Master and Margarita 112, 163
The White Guard 313
bus services see **transport**
Business hours 338

c

cables and telegrams 338
calendar 70
Gregorian 90, 189
Julian 70, 90, 189
Cape Dezhnev 20
Caspian Sea 20, 229, 233, 249
Catherine the Great 43–4, 75, 207
Caucasus Mountains 249–54
see also individual place names
Caucasian State Preserve 253
Chaadayev, Peter 112
Chagall, Marc 103
Chaliapin 102, 119
Chaliapin Museum (St Petersburg) 102
chambers of commerce 341
Chancellor, Sir Richard 37, 211
Chechnya 58
Chekhov, Anton 111
burial place 166
Chelyabinsk 245
Chelyabinsk-65 nuclear installation 18, 245
Geologichesky Muzei (Geology Museum) 245
Kartinnaya Galereya (Picture Gallery) 245
Muzei Prikladnykh Iskusstv (Applied Art Museum) 245
nuclear accidents 245
Chernenko, Konstantin 57
Chernihiv (Ukraine) 316–8
Borysohlihsky Sobor (Cathedral of Sainst Borys and Hlib) 317
Dytynets area 317
Mikhailo Kotsiubinsky park 317
Museum of arts and crafts 317
Pechera Antoniya (Anthony

Caves) 318
Spaso-Preobraszhensky Sobor
(Spassky Cathedral) 317
Chernivtsi 321
accommodation 353
Teatre Musyky ta Dramy (Music
and Drama Theatre) 321
Chernobyl disaster 18, 287,
294, 305
Chernomyrdin, Victor 69
Chernyshevsky, Nikolai 191
What is to be Done? 191
Chufut-Kale cave city (Ukraine)
326
Chukotsky peninsula 20
Chukrai, Pavel 123
The Thief 123
churches and cathedrals
see also **monasteries**
Andriivska Tserka
(St Andrew's, Kiev) 313
Arkhangelskoe Sobor
(Cathedral of the Archangel
Michael, Nizhny Novgorod)
231
Arkhangelsky Sobor
(Archangel Cathedral,
Moscow) 144
Barysahlyebskaya (Saints
Barys and Hlyeb, Hrodno,
Belarus) 301–2
Blagoveshchensky Sobor
(Cathedral of the
Annunciation, Moscow) 144
Blagoveshenchsky Sobor
(Annunciation Cathedral,
Solvychedgodsk) 215
Blagovshensky (Annunciation,
Kargopol) 215
Bogoyavlenia (Incarnation,
Yaroslavl) 176
Bogoyavlensky Sobor (Mani-
festation, Moscow) 151
Bogoyavlensky Cathedral
(Smolensk) *226*
Borysohlihsky Sobor
(Cathedral of Sainst Borys
and Hlib, Chernihiv,
Ukraine) 317
Desyatynna (Tithe Church,
Kiev, Ukraine) 312
Dmitrievsky Sobor (Cathedral
of St Dmitry, Vladimir) 178
Donskoy (Moscow) 163
Farny Sabor (Farny Cathedral,
Hrodno, Belarus) 302
Ilyi Proroka (Church of Elijah
the Prophet) and museum
(Yaroslavl) 176–7

Ioann Zlatoust (St John
Chrysostom, Astrakhan)
234
Isaakiyevsky Sobor
(St Isaac's Cathedral,
St Petersburg) 195
Katolicheskaya (Roman
Catholic church, Astrakhan)
235
Katolytsky Sobor (Roman
Catholic Cathedral, Lviv,
Ukraine) 319
Kazansky Sobor (Kazan
Cathedral, St Petersburg)
199
Khram Khrista Spasitelya
(Cathedral of Christ the
Saviour, Moscow) 165–6
Khram Spasa na Krovi
(Resurrection,
St Petersburg) 199
Kirillovskaya Chasovnya
(Astrakhan) 234
Kostol Dominikana (Roman
Catholic Dominican Church,
Lviv, Ukraine) 320
Lyudovika (St Ludovic's,
Moscow) 155
Mikhaila Arkhangela
(Archangel Gabriel,
Moscow) 154
Mikhailivsky Sobor
(St Michael's Cathedral,
Kiev, Ukraine) 312
Nikolsky Morskoy Sobor
(Cathedral of St Nicholas,
St Petersburg) 196–7
Odigitrii (Icon of the Hodigitria,
Rostov Veliky) 176
Petra Mitropolita (Peter the
Metropolitan, Pereyaslavl-
Zalessky) 175
Petropavlovsky Sobor (Peter
and Paul Cathedral,
St Petersburg) 190
Pokrovskaya (Protection of
the Virgin, Krasnoyarsk) 264
Preobrazhenskaya
(Transfiguration, Kizhi
island) *216*, 218
Preobrazhensky Sobor
(Cathedral of the Trans-
figuration, Belozersk) 214
Preobrazhensky Sobor
(Cathedral of the
Transfiguration, Valaam
Islands) 217
Rispolozheniya (Deposition of
the Robe, Moscow) 145

Rozhdestvensky Sobor
(Cathedral of the Nativity of
the Virgin, Suzdal) 178
Russian Orthodox church
(Yalta, Ukraine) *324*
Saphiyskyy Sabor (Cathedral
of St Sophia, Polatsk,
Belarus) 305
Simeona Stolpnika (Simeon
the Styline, Veliky Ustyug)
214
Smolny Sobor (Smolny
Cathedral, St Petersburg)
202
Sobor Svyatoho Yura (St
George's Cathedral, Lviv,
Ukraine) 320
Sobor Svyatoi Troitsi (Trinity
Cathedral, Saratov) 231
Sobor Vasiliya Blazhennogo
(St Basil's Cathedral,
Moscow) 147–8
Sofiysky Sobor (St Sophia's
Cathedral, Kiev, Ukraine)
308, 309, 311
Sofiysky Sobor (Cathedral of
St Sophia, Novgorod) 221
Sofiysky Sobor (Cathedral of
St Sophia, Vologda) 213
Spas-na-Senyakh (Saviour
over the Galleries, Rostov
Veliky) 176
Spasskaya (Our Saviour,
Irkutsk) 268
Spaso-Preobraszhensky Sobor
(Spassky Cathedral,
Chernihiv, Ukraine) 317
Spasopreobrazhensky Sobor
(Cathedral of the
Transfiguration of the
Saviour, Pereyaslavl-
Zalessky) 175
Spaso-Preobrazhensky Sobor
(Cathedral of the
Transfiguration, Pskov)
222
Stary Sobor (Old Cathedral,
Saratov) 231
Svyatikh Konstantin i Yelena
(SS Constantine and Helen,
Vologda) 213
Trapeznaya Tserkov St Sergei
(Refectory Church of St
Sergei, Sergiev Posad)
173-4
Troitsky Sobor (Trinity
Cathedral, Astrakhan) 234
Troitsky Sobor (Trinity
Cathedral, Pskov) 222

Troitsky Sobor (Trinity
Cathedral, Sergeyev Posad)
173
Uspenska Tserkva
(Renaissance Uspensky
Church, Lviv, Ukraine) 320
Uspenskaya Sobor (Cathedral
of the Assumption, Kirillov)
214
Uspensky Sobor (Cathedral of
the Assumption, Astrakhan)
234
Uspensky Sobor (Church of
the Assumption, Belozersk)
214
Uspensky Sobor (Assumption
Cathedral, Bryansk) 227
Uspensky Sobor (Cathedral of
the Assumption, Moscow)
144
Uspensky Sobor (Cathedral of
the Assumption, Pechory)
222
Uspensky Sobor (Assumption
Cathedral, Rostov Veliky)
176
Uspensky Sobor (Assumption
Cathedral, Sergeyev Posad)
174
Uspensky Sobor (Assumption
Cathedral, Smolensk) 226
Uspensky Sobor (Cathedral of
the Assumption, Veliky
Ustyug) 214
Uspensky Sobor (Assumption
Cathedral, Vladimir) 178
Vsemilostivogo Spasa
(Church of the Most
Merciful Saviour, Belozersk)
214
Zachatiya Anny (Conception of
St Anne, Moscow) 152
Zhawn-Mironosets (Holy
Women, Veliky Ustyug) 214
Churchill, Sir Winston 15
cinema see **film industry**
climate 330, 331
clothing 332
Cossacks 39, 232, 249, 261,
270, *284*, 311
**Commonwealth of Independent
States (CIS)** 305
courier services 338
crime
government corruption 69, 78
corruption in the police 79
gangs 79
"New Russians" 79
personal security 335–6

pick-pockets 79
Russian mafia 72, 78–9
St Petersburg Police Alert 335
Crimea, The (Ukraine) 17, 297,
321, 358
see also place names
Crimean Coast 326–7
Crimean Mountains 327
Crimean peninsula 323–4
Crimean War 48, *285*, 326,
322
Charge of the Light Brigade
285, 326
Florence Nightingale 285
Cui, César 118
currency 303, 332–3
see also **money matters**
customs 334

d

dachas 70, 219, 294
Dagomys 249
tea plantations 249
Daniil 112
Dargomizhsky 118
Dashkov, Catherine 75
Decembrists 47
Deineka 104
Denisov, Edison 122
Diaghilev 102, 119
Ballets Russes 102, 119
Dionisius 99, 214
Dmitry, Grand Prince 35, 144
Dobrotvorsky, Sergei 123
documents 262
see also **visas and passports**
Dolgoruky, Prince Yuri 30, 141
Dostoyevsky, Fyodor 71, 110,
188, 191, 262
The Brothers Karamazov 110
burial place 202
Crime and Punishment 110,
200
The Devils 110
Dostoyevsky Museum
(Staraya Russa) 221
Dostoyevsky Museum (St
Petersburg) 201
driving 342–3
Dzerzhinsk (Belarus) 303
Dzerzhinsky, Felix 302–3

e

Earle, Hobart 323
eating out
listings 353–8
ecology 18

see also **pollution**
of Baikal Lake 267, 272–3
deforestation 217, 265
economy 54, 57, 58, 71–2,
291–3, 332, 333
capitalism 58
cost of living 71–2
first Five-Year-Plan 55, 92,
169, 244, 261, 286
New Economic Policy (NEP) 54
education 69–70, 295–6
12 Kollegi (Twelve Colleges,
St Petersburg) 197
Akademgorodok (Academic
Town, Novosibirsk) 263
Akademiya Khudozhestv
(Academy of Arts,
St Petersburg) 197
Akademiya Nauk (Academy of
Sciences, St Petersburg)
197–8
City Technical School
(Astrakhan) 234
Kazan university 229
language centres 351
Moscow university 158
Smolny Institut
(St Petersburg) 202
Uralsky Gosudarstvenny
Tekhnichesky Universitet
(Urals State Technical Uni-
versity, Yekaterinburg) *243*
Eisenstein 222, 322
Alexander Nevsky 222
The Battleship Potemkin 322
electrical current 332
Elton Lake 231
embassies and consulates 338
emergency telephone numbers
336
Enlightenment 44
Etiquette 339
European North 211–22
see also *individual place
names*
European South 249–54
see also *place names*
climate 249
crops 249

f

Falik, Yuri 122
Fedotov, Pavel 100
Feodosia 101
Ivan Aivazovsky museum 101
Feodosiyn (Ukraine) 324
**Ferapontov Monastyr (St
Therapont Monastery)** 99, 214

Rozhdestvensky Sobor
(Cathedral of the Nativity of
the Virgin) 214
festivals and events 70
Days of Kiev celebration
311
Easter 70
international film festival
(Sochi) 251
International Women's Day
70
International Tchaikovsky
Competition (Moscow) 121,
160
New Year 70
"old New Year" 70
Revolution Day 70
Victory Day 70
white nights festival (St
Petersburg) 17, 186, 190,
194
film industry 123
see also directors' names
Gorky Film Studio (Moscow)
123
international film festival
(Sochi) 251
Lenfilm 123
Mosfilm 123
NTV-Profit (Moscow) 123
STV Film Studio
(St Petersburg) 123
Filonov, Pavel 104
Firsova, Elena 122
folklore
see **literature**
Fomin, Yevstignei 117
food and drink 82–5, 178,
353–4, 358
Armenian cognac 84
Asian 83–4
Caucasus specialities
251
caviar 85
champagne 84, 249
European influence 82
Filippov Bakery (Moscow)
160
kvas 84
medovuka 84
nalivka 84
nastoika 84
sbiten 84
tea 84, 249
traditional Russian cuisine
82, 84
vodka 84
wine 84, 249
forests 19, 20, 217

Foros (Ukraine) 326
further reading 367–8
Fyodor, Prince 39

g

Gadai, Leonid 123
Diamond Arm 123
A Woman in Captivity in the
Caucasus 123
Gagarin, Yuri 245
Galich, Alexander 113
galleries
Gosudarstvennaya Kartinnaya
Galereya (State Picture
Gallery, Perm) 245
Gosudarstvenny
Khudozhestvenny Muzei
Altaiskogo Kraya (Altay State
Art Museum, Barnaul) 266
Istoriko Krevedchesky Muzei
(Museum of Peasant Life
and Art Gallery, Omsk) 263
Kartinnaya Galereya (Picture
Gallery, Chelyabinsk) 245
Kartinnaya Galereya B.M.
Kustodieva (Kustodiev Art
Gallery, Astrakhan) 235
Kartinnaya Galereya (Art
Gallery, Smolensk) 226
Khudozhestvenny Muzei (Art
Museum, Nizhny Novgorod)
231
Muzei Iskusstva (Art Museum,
Yekaterinburg) 243
Muzei Iskusstv Imeni
Radishcheva (Art Museum,
Saratov) 231
Muzei Izkusstv Imeni
Sukhacheva (Art Museum,
Irkutsk) 268
Muzei Izobrazitelnykh
Iskusstv (Sochi Art Gallery)
251
Muzei Izobrazitelnykh
Iskusstv (Fine Arts
Museum, Volgograd) 233
Musei Izobrazitelnikh Iskusstv
imeni Pushkina (Pushkin
Fine Arts Museum,
Moscow) 165
Muzei S.T. Konenkova
(Sculpture Museum,
Smolensk) 226
Muzei Prikladnykh Iskusstv
(Applied Art Museum,
Chelyabinsk) 245
Muzey Zakhidno-skhidnolio
Mistetstva (Museum of

Western and Oriental Art,
Odessa, Ukraine) 323
National Portrait Gallery
(St Petersburg) 194
Natsionalny Khudozhny
Musey Ukrainy (Museum of
Ukrainian Fine Arts, Kiev)
314
Novaya Tretyakovskaya (New
Tretyakov, Moscow) 162
Novgorodsky Gosudarstvenny
Muzei-Zapovednik
(Novgorod State Museum)
221
Tretyakov Gallery (Moscow)
97, 98, 99, 100, 103,
162, 163
gambling 359
Gatchino Palace 204
Gay travellers 338
geography 17–20
getting around 342–6
by boat 344
by car 342–3
by plane 344
by train 342
Trans-Siberian Railway 342
getting there 333–4
Ghengis Khan 30, 33
glasnost 57–8, 122
Glazunov, Alexander 119
Glinka, Mikhail 116, 117
burial place 202
A Life for the Tsar 117
Ruslan and Lyudmila 117
Gobi Desert 124, 125
Gogol, Nikolai 109–10, 198
Dead Souls 110, 198
The Government Inspector 110
The Nose 109–10
The Overcoat 109–10
The Two Ivans 109–10
Godunov, Boris 39, 144, 177
burial place 174
Godunov family 177
Golden Ring 173
see also place names
Goncharova, Natalia 102
Gora Elbrus mountain 254
Gorbachev, Mikhail 25, 57, 93,
287, 326
Gorky, Maxim 111, 191, 231
Childhood, Apprenticeship
and My Universities 111
The Lower Depths 111
Gubaidulina, Sofia 122
Gumilev, Nikolai 112
Gusinsky, Vladimir 73

h

health
see also **health resorts and spas**
banya (sauna) 69
medical treatment 336–7
pharmacies 336
pollution-related problems 240
regulations for visitors 334
Spa Research Institute (Pyatigorsk) 254
health resorts and spas 337
Belokurikha 266
Mineralnyye Vody region 254, 337
Khosta 253
Kislovodsk 254
Matsesta 253
Pyatigorsk 254
Sochi 251
Solvychedgodsk 215
Yessentuki 254
Zheleznovodsk 254
history 27–58, 141, 185–9, 226, 239, 261, 283–7, 309, 367
Cold War 57, 245
conference of Allied leaders in 1945 324
Crimean War 48, 285, 326
Cuban Missile Crisis 56–7
Decembrist uprising 47
early settlers 27–30
Field of Kulikovo 35
glasnost 57–8, 122
Great Terror 55
Mongols *see* Tatars
Napoleonic War 47
peasant revolt of 1773 44
perestroika 57–8, 77, 93, 104
Revolution 50, 53–4
Russian Empire 284–5
Siege of Leningrad 188–9
Soviet era 53–8, 65
Tatars 27, 33–5, 97, 141, 309, 324
tsars 37–50
Viking conquest 27
World War I 185, 285, 301
World War II (Great Patriotic War) 55–6, 67, 76, 185, 188–9, 202, 218, 227, 231, 232–3, 239, 301, 303–4
Hrodno (Belarus) 301
accommodation 351
Barysahlyebskaya Tserkva (Church of Saints Barys and Hlyeb) 301–2
castle 302
Farny Sabor (Farny Cathedral) 302
Hrushevsky, Mykhailo 291
History of Ukraine-Rus 291

i

Ilf 112
Ilmen Lake 221
industry *see* **trade and industry**
international travel agents 341
internet access 339
internet cafés in Moscow 339
Irkutsk 125, 267–9
accommodation 351
boat trips on Lake Baikal 273
central market 268
Dom Volkonskhyx Decembrists museum 267
eating out 357
hydroelectric station 272
Irkutsk Dramatichesky Teatr (Drama Theatre) 268–9
Irkutsk Filarmoniya (Philharmonic) 269
Krayevedchesky Muzei (Local History Museum) *266*, 268
Muzei Izkusstv Imeni Sukhacheva (Art Museum) 268
riverside park 268
Spasskaya Tserkov (Church of our Saviour) 268
Iset River 240
Ivan III (the Great) 37, 116, 141
Ivan IV (The Terrible) 37, 38, 213, 214, 220
Ivanov, Alexander 100
Christ's Appearance before the People 100
Ivanova 177

k

Kabakov, Ilya 104
Kalita, Grand Prince Ivan 141
Kama River 229
Kamchatka peninsula 20
Kandinsky, Wassily 102
Karagol Lake (Ukraine) 327
Kareliya 217–8
see also *place names*
Karetnikov, Nikolai 122
Kargopol 215
Blagovshensky Tserkov (Church of the Annunciation) 215
Kavkazskiye Mineralniye Vody 254
Kazan 229
accommodation 350
Kremlin 229
Spasskaya Bashnya (Tower) 229
Suyumbiki (Tower) 229
Tainitskaya (Tower) 229
university 229
Kemerovo 264
coal mine visits 264
Kemerovsky Istoriko-Arkhitekurny Muzei Krasnaya Gorka (Regional Museum of Nature, History, Architecture and Ethnology) 264
train trips to zapovednik nature preserve 264
Khabarovsk 125
Khachaturian, Aram 121
Khamar-Daban mountains 273
Kharkiv 311
Khatyn (Belarus) 304
Khmelnitsky, Bogdan 284
Khosta 253
beaches 253
forest preserve 243
Khotyn fortress (Ukraine) 321
Khrennikov, Tikhon 121
Khrushchev, Nikita 56–7, 92, 250, 295
burial place 166
Kiev (Ukraine) 30, 309–16
accommodation 352–3
Andriivska Tserka (St Andrew's Church) 313
Andriivsky Uzviz (Andrew's Descent) 313
beaches 314
Bessarabsky Rynok (Bessarabian Market) 314, 315
Days of Kiev celebration 311
Desyatynna (Tithe Church) 312
Dim Horodetskoho (House of Gargoyles) 314
eating out 358
Filarmoniya (Philharmonia) 313
funicular 313
Hotel Moskva 313
Hydropark 314
Kiev Opera and Ballet Theatre 309
Kievo-Pecherska Lavra (Kiev Pechersk Monastery) 314–5
Kyivsky Universitet imeni

Shevchenka (Kiev State
University) 314
Konservatoriya imeni
Chaikovskoho (Tchaikovsky
State Conservatory) 314
Kreshchatyk 313
Maidan Nozalezhnosti
(Independence Square) 313
Mariinsky Palats (Mariinsky
Palace) 315
metro 345
Mikhail Bulgakov museum
313
Mikhailivska Ploshcha (St
Michael's Square) 312
Mikhailivsky Sobor (St
Michael's Cathedral) 312
Monument to the Defence of
the Motherland ("steel
wench") 314, 315
Museum of Historical
Treasures 316
Natsionalny Khudozhny
Musey Ukrainy (Museum of
Ukrainian Fine Arts) 314
Podil 313
shopping 313
Sofiysky Sobor (St Sophia's
Cathedral) 308, 309, 311
statue of Khmelnitsky 311
Ukrainsky Istorychny Musey
(Museum of Ukrainian
History) 312
Ukrinsky Dim cultural centre
313
Volodymyr's Town 312
Volodymyrsky Sobor
(St Volodymyr's Cathedral)
314
Yaroslav's Town 309
Zamok Richarda Levove
Sertse (Castle of Richard
the Lion Heart) 313
Zoloti Vorota (Golden Gate)
and museum 309
Kievian Rus 283–4
Kiprensky, Orest 100
Kirillov 213–4
St. Kirill-Belozersky Monastyr
213
Uspenskaya Sobor (Cathedral
of the Assumption) 214
Kislovodsk 254
Zamok Kovarstva i Lyubvi rock
formation 254
Zamok restaurant
(Kislovodsk) 254
Kizhi island 217–8
museum of wooden

architecture 217–8
Preobrazhenskaya Tserkov
(Church of the
Transfiguration) 216, 218
Knaifel, Alexander 122
Kollontai, Alexandra 76
Komar 104
Korsakov 270
Kostroma 177
Godunov family 177
Ipatevsky Monastyr
(Monastery) 177
Romanov family 177
Kovalevskaya, Sofia 75
Kozhina, Vassilisa 75
Krasnaya Polyana 252
Caucasian State Preserve 253
Krasnodar 249
Krasnoyarsk 125, 264
boat trips 265
Krasnoyarsky Kulturnno-
istorichesky Tsentr i
Muzeiny Kompleks
(Krasnoyarsk Cultural and
Historical Centre and
Museum Complex) 264
Krasnoyarskiye Stolby
(Krasnoyarsk Pillars) 265
Muzei-usadba V.I. Surikova 265
Pokrovskaya Tserkov (Church
of the Protection of the
Virgin) 264
the St Nikolai 264–5
Kravchuk, Leonid 292–3, 305
Kremer, Gidon 121
**Krutinskiye Ozera (Steep
Lakes)** 263
Kuchma, Leonid 293
Kulik, Oleg 104
Kunashir island 271
Kurile Islands 270–1
Kursk 227
accommodation 350
eating out 357
museum of the Battle of
Kursk 227
Kustodiev, Boris 102, 235
Chaliapin 102
Kustodiev Art Gallery
(Astrakhan) 235
Kuznetsov, Pavel 102

I

Ladoga Lake 189, 218, 219
lakes
Baikal 18, 20, 261, 264,
266–7, 272–3
Elton 231

Ilmen 221
Karagol (Ukraine) 327
Krutinskiye Ozera 263
Ladoga 189, 218, 219
Ozero (Onega) 217
Seliger 229
Siverskoye 213
Tambukanskoye 254
language 65, 294–5, 362–367
language centres 351
Larionov, Mikhail 102
Lenin, Vladimir 53
Apartment Museum (Moscow)
145
birthplace 229
mausoleum (Moscow) 147
museum (Moscow) 149
Lermontov, Mikhail 109, 253,
338
A Hero of Our Time 109, 253,
338
Lermontov Museum-Reserve
(Pyatigorsk) 253
Listvyanka 267
Muzei Baikolovedeniya
Limnologicheskogo
Instituta (Baikal
Limnological Institute) 267,
273
Listyev, Vladislav 78
literature 109–13, 368
see also individual writers
and poets names
The Acmeists 111
dissidents 112
folklore 77, 109
The Futurists 111
after glasnost 113
samizdat 113
Slovo o polku Igoreve (The
Lay of Igor's Host) 109,
177
The Symbolists 111
under the Soviets 112
The Thaw 112–3
Lukashenka, Alexandr 292
Luzhkov, Yuri 123, 165
Lviv (Ukraine) 318–21
accommodation 353
eating out 358
Grand Hotel 320
Katolytsky Sobor (Roman
Catholic Cathedral) 319
Kostol Dominikana (Roman
Catholic Dominican Church)
320
open-air arts and crafts
market 319
Sobor Svyatoho Yura

(St George's Cathedral) 320
Teatr Opery ta Baletu (Opera
  and Ballet Theatre) *319*
Uspenska Tserkva
  (Renaissance Uspensky
  Church) 320
Lyadov, Anatoli 119
Lyavlya 216
  Muzei-zapovednik
  Derevyanova (Wooden
  Architecture Museum
  Reserve) 216

m

Magadan 271
Magnitogorsk 244–5
Maier, Frith 327
  *Trekking in Russia and
  Central Asia* 327
de Maistre, Joseph 65
Malevich, Kazimir 102
  Black Square 102
Mamontov, Savva 101
Mandelshtam, Osip 112
maps 345
Martinov, Vladimir 122
matryoshka dolls 226, 360
Matsesta 253
Mayakovsky, Vladimir 103, 112
  Mayakovsky Museum
  (Moscow) 152
media 70, 73
  foreign-language newspapers
  73, 201, 337
  freedom of speech 73
  magazines 73
  newspapers 73, 337
  NTV (Independent Television)
  73
  ORT (Public Russian
  Television) 73
  television 70, 73
Medical help *see* **Health**
Medvedev, Roy 112
Melamid 104
Melnikov, Konstantin 164
Mikhalkov, Nikita 123
  Burnt by the Sun 123
Minsk (Belarus) 303
  accommodation 352
  Bernardzinskaya Tsarkva
  (Orthodox cathedral of the
  Bernadine monastery) 303,
  305
  Muzey Historii Byalikay
  Aychynnay Vayny (Museum
  of the Great Patriotic War)
  303–4

Troitskaya Naberezhna (Trinity
  Embankment) 303
Mir (Belarus) 302
monasteries and convents
  Alexander Nevsky Lavra
  (St Petersburg) 201
  Bernardzinskaya (Minsk,
  Belarus) 303, *305*
  Ferapontov (St Therapont) 99,
  214
  Goritsky (Pereyaslavl-
  Zalessky) 175
  Ipatevsky (Kostroma) 177
  Kievo-Pecherska Lavra (Kiev
  Pechersk Monastery, Kiev)
  309, 314–5
  Kirillov-Belozersky 213
  Knyaginin (Princess Convent,
  Vladimir) 178
  Mikhailo-Arkhangelsky
  (Archangel Michael, Veliky
  Ustyug) 214
  Mirozhsky (Pskov) 222
  Novodevichy (New Convent of
  the Maiden, Moscow) 166
  of the North 213–4
  Pokrovsky (Intercession
  Convent, Suzdal) 178
  Preobrazhensky
  (Transfiguration, Astrakhan)
  234
  Pskovo-Pcherskaya Lavra
  (Monastery of the Caves,
  Pechory) 222
  Rizopolozhensky (Deposition
  of the Virgin's Robe,
  Suzdal) 178
  Sergeyev Posad 91
  Solovetsky 216
  Spaso-Preobrazhensky
  (Yaroslavl) 177
  Spaso-Prilutsky (Monastery of
  the Saviour on the Bend)
  213
  Spaso Yefimiyevsky (Lament
  of Christ, Suzdal) 178
  Svensky (Sven, Bryansk) 227
  Svyato-Danilovsky (Danilov,
  Moscow) 163
  Svyatogorsky (Pushkinskiye
  Gory) 222
  Troitse-Sergiyevsky Lavra
  (Trinity Monastery of
  St Sergius, Sergeyev
  Posad) 91, 173
  Valaamsky (Valaam Islands)
  217
  Yavleniya Bogorodtsib
  (Monastery of the

Presentation of the Virgin,
  Solvychedgodsk) 215
  Yuriev (St George, Novgorod)
  221
  Znamensky (Monastery of the
  Sign, Moscow) 152
money matters 332–3
Moscow 34–5, 37, 141–66
  accommodation 346–7
  Alexandrovsky Gardens 146
  Arkhangelsky Sobor
  (Archangel Cathedral) 144
  Arsenal 143
  Batashev Dvorets (Palace)
  154
  Blagoveshchensky Sobor
  (Cathedral of the
  Annunciation) 144
  Bogoyavlensky Sobor (Church
  of the Manifestation) 151
  Bolshoi Kremlyovsky Dvorets
  (Great Kremlin Palace) 145
  Bolshoy Teatr (Theatre) 157
  Borovitsky Bashnya (Tower)
  144
  buses *see* transport
  climate 145
  Detsky Mir children's store
  156, 360
  Detsky Teatr (Central
  Children's Theatre) 157
  Dom Melnikov (Melnikov
  house) 164
  Dom-muzei Stanislavskogo
  (Stanislavsky Museum)
  161–2
  Dom Pashkov (Palace) 158–9
  Dom Soyuzov (House of Trade
  Unions) 158
  Donskoy Monastery 163
  Dvorets Syezdov (Palace of
  Congress) 143
  eating out 354–5
  Ekaterina Romanovna
  Vorontsova Dvorets
  (Palace) 161
  Filippov Bakery 160
  Gorky Park 158, 163
  Gostiny Dvor (Old Merchant
  Arcade) 151
  Gosudarstvenny Istorichesky
  Muzei (Historical Museum)
  146
  Granovitaya Palata (Palace of
  the Facets) 144–5
  Great Fire of Moscow 147
  Grenadiers monument 154
  GUM department store 149,
  360

International Tchaikovsky
  Competition 121, 160
Khram Khrista Spasitelya
  (Cathedral of Christ the
  Saviour) 165–6
Kitai-Gorod wall 150
Kolokolnya Ivana Velikogo
  (Bell Tower of Ivan the
  Great) 144
Kolonny Zal (Hall of the
  Columns) concert hall 158
Konservatoriya imeni
  Chaikovskogo (Moscow
  Conservatory of Music) 161
Kontsertny zal imeni
  Chaykovskogo (Tchaikovsky
  Concert Hall) 160
Krasnaya Ploshchad (Red
  Square) 146
Kremlin 141–6
Lenin Museum 149
Lubyanka prison 156
Maly Teatr (Maly Theatre) 157
Manege 158
markets 151, 156, 158
Marshal Georgy Zhukov
  statue 149
Mavzolei Lenina (Lenin
  Mausoleum) 147
Mayakovsky Museum 152
Menshikov Dvorets (Palace)
  161
metro 168–9
Metropol Hotel 157
Ministerstvo Inostrannykh Del
  (Foreign Ministry) 165–5
Mogila Neizvestnogo Soldata
  (Tomb of the Unknown
  Soldier) 146
Moskva Hotel 157
Muzei Istorii i Rekonstrukstii
  Moskvy (Museum of the
  History and Reconstruction
  of Moscow) 154
Musei Izobrazitelnikh Iskusstv
  imeni Pushkina (Pushkin
  Fine Arts Museum) 165
muzei-kvartira (Lenin
  Apartment Museum) 145
Muzei Palaty v Zaryadie 153
Muzei Sovremennoi Istorii
  Rossii (Museum of the
  Modern History of Russia)
  158
Musei V Tropinina (Tropinin
  Museum) 163
National Hotel 158
Neskuchny Garden 163
nightlife 359

Novaya Tretyakovskaya
  Galereya (New Tretyakov
  Gallery) 162
Novodevichy Monastyr (New
  Convent of the Maiden) 166
Novy Arbat 163
Okhotny Ryad market 158
Old Arbat 163–4
Orlov Dvorets (Palace) 161
Oruzheinaya Bashnya (Arsenal
  Tower) 143
Oruzheinaya Palata (State
  Armoury museum) 143–4
Patriarshiye Prudy (Patriarchs'
  Ponds) 163
Pekin Hotel 160
Politekhnichesky Muzei
  (Polytechnic Museum) 154,
  155
public baths 156
Pushkin Monument 160
Red Square see Krasnaya
  Ploshchad Rossiya Hotel
  152
Russkaya Gosdarstvennaya
  Biblioteka (Russian State
  Library) 158, 159
sculpture in the city 165
shopping 151, 156, 158,
  160, 360-1
Sobor Vasiliya Blazhennogo
  (St Basil's Cathedral)
  147–8
Spasskaya Vorota (Saviour's
  Gate) 143
Spasskaya Bashnya
  (Saviour's Tower) 146
Stanislavsky Theatre
  (Moscow) 158
Svyato-Danilovsky Monastyr
  (Danilov Monastery) 163
taxis see transport
Taynitskaya Bashnya (Tower
  of Secrets) 145
Teremnoy Dvorets (Terem or
  Belvedere Palace) 145
transport 143, 168–9, 344–5
Tretyakov Gallery 97, 98, 99,
  100, 103, 162, 163
Troitskaya Bashnya (Trinity
  Tower) 141
Tsar Cannon 148
Tsentralny farmers' market
  156
Tserkov Lyudovika
  (St Ludovic's church) 155
Tserkov Mikhaila Arkhangela
  (Church of the Archangel
  Gabriel) 154

Tserkov Rispolozheniya
  (Church of the Deposition
  of the Robe) 145
Tserkov Zachatiya Anny
  (Church of the Conception
  of St Anne) 152
TsUM department store 156,
  360
Tverskaya 157, 159–60
underground city 150
university 158
Uspensky Sobor (Cathedral of
  the Assumption) 144
Voskresenskiye Vorota
  (Resurrection Gate) 149
Yeliseyevsky Gastronom
  supermarket 160
Yushkov Dvorets (Palace) 155
Zamoskvorechye district 163
Znamensky Monastyr
  (Monastery of the Sign) 152
Mossolov, Alexander 120
The Iron Foundry 120
motoring *see* **getting around**
mountains
  Altay 265–6
  Altynnaya 230
  Bolshoi Akhun 253
  Carpathian 320, 332
  Caucasus 249, 332
  Crimean 327
  Gora Elbrus 254
  Khamar-Daban 273
  Lysaya 230
  Mashuk 254
  Mount Bolshevik 271
  Udokan 269
  Urals 17–18, 239–45
  Uvekskaya 230
  Verkhoyansky 269
Mravinksy 121
Mstyslav the Brave 317
Murmansk 17, 218
  accommodation 349
  eating out 357
  Muzei Militarny Severnogo
    Morskogo Flota (Museum
    of the North Sea Fleet) 218
museums
  Altaisky Krayevoi Muzei Istorii
    (Altay Museum of Regional
    Studies and History)
    (Barnaul) 266
  Chaliapin Museum
    (St Petersburg) 102
  Domik Petra Velikogo (Peter
    the Great's Wooden Cabin)
    museum (St Petersburg)
    191–2

Dom-muzei Stanislavskogo (Stanislavsky Museum, Moscow) 161–2
Dom Volkonskhyx Decembrists museum (Irkutsk) 267
Dostoevstovo Muzei (Dostoevsky Museum, Staraya Russa) 222
Etnografichsky Muzei (Ethnographic Architecture Museum, Perm) 245
Geological Research Institute and Karelian Science Centre (Petrozavodsk) 217
Geologichesky Muzei (Geology Museum, Chelyabinsk) 245
Geologichesky Muzei (Geological Museum, Yekaterinburg) 243
Goritsky Monastery and museum (Pereyaslavl-Zalessky) 175
Gosudarstvenny Istorichesky Muzei (Historical Museum, Moscow) 146
Hermitage Museum (St Petersburg) 193, 206–7
Istorichesky Muzei (Local History Museum, Novosibirsk) 263
Istorichesky Muzei (Regional History Museum, Yekaterinburg) 242
Istoriko Krevedchesky Muzei (Museum of Peasant Life, Omsk) 263
Ivan Aivazovsky museum (Feodosia) 101
Kemerovsky Istoriko-Arkhitekurny Muzei Krasnaya Gorka (Regional Museum of Nature, History, Architecture and Ethnology, Kemerovo) 264
Krasnoyarsky Kulturnno-istorichesky Tsentr i Muzeiny Kompleks (Krasnoyarsk Cultural and Historical Centre and Museum Complex, Krasnoyarsk) 264
Krayevedchesky Muzei (Local History Museum, Irkutsk) *266*, 268
Kunstkamera (Chamber of Curiosities, St Petersburg) 198
Lenin Museum (Moscow) 149

Ludwig Museum 194
Mayakovsky Museum (Moscow) 152
Menshikovsky Dvorets (Menshikov Palace) Museum (St Petersburg) 197
Museum of Architecture and Ancient Monuments (Novgorod) 97
Museum of arts and crafts (Chernihiv, Ukraine) 317
Museum of Historical Treasures (Kiev) 316
Museum of literature and art (Abramtsevo Estate) 176
Museum of the Battle of Kursk (Kursk) 227
Museum of Music and Time (Yaroslavl) 176
Museum of wooden architecture (Kizhi island) 217–8
Museum of Wooden Architecture and Peasant Life (Suzdal) 176
museum (Solvychedgodsk) 215
museum (Spasskoe Lutovinova) 227
Muzei Anni Akhmatovoi (Anna Akhmatova Museum, St Petersburg) 201
Muzey Arkheolohli (Museum of Archaeology, Odessa, Ukraine) 323
Muzei Baikolovedeniya Limnologicheskogo Instituta (Baikal Limnological Institute, Listvyanka) 267, 273
Muzey Belkarushka Knihadrukavanni(Museum of Historical Books and Printing, Polatsk, Belarus) 305
Muzei Botika ("Little Boat" Museum, Pereyaslavl-Zalessky) 175
Muzei Derevyannovo Harodnovo Zogchestvo Vitoslavits (Vitoslavitsky Museum of Wooden Architecture) 221
Muzei F.M. Dostyevskovo (Dostoyevsky Museum, St Petersburg) 201
Muzey Historii Byalikay Aychynnay Vayny (Museum of the Great Patriotic War, Minsk, Belarus) 303–4
Muzei Istorii Goroda-kurorta Sochi (History Museum, Sochi) 252
Muzei Istorii i Kultury Narodov Sevena imeni Yaroslavskovo (Museum of North Peoples, Yakutsk) 270
Muzei Istorii Moskvy (Museum of the History and Reconstruction of Moscow, Moscow) 154
Muzei Kraiyevedeniya (Museum of Local Lore, Saratov) 231
Muzei-kvartira (Lenin Apartment Museum, Moscow) 145
Muzei Militarny Severnogo Morskogo Flota (Museum of the North Sea Fleet, Murmansk) 218
Muzei Molodyozhi (Youth Museum, Yekaterinburg) 242
Muzey Morskoho Flotu (Museum of Maritime History, Odessa, Ukraine) 323
Muzei Palaty v Zaryadie (Moscow) 153
Muzei Pisatelya Nikolaya Ostrovskogo (Ostrovsky Literary Museum, Sochi) 252
Muzei A.D. Sakharova (Andrey Sakharov Museum, Nizhny Novgorod) 231
Muzei Sovremennoi Istorii Rossii (Museum of the Modern History of Russia) 158
Musei V Tropinina (Tropinin Museum, Moscow) 163
Muzei-usadba V.I. Surikova (Krasnoyarsk) 265
Muzei Yestestvoznaniya (Museum of Natural History, Yuzhno-Kurilsk) 271
Muzei-zapovednik Derevyanova (Wooden Architecture Museum Reserve, Lyavlya) 216
Muzei Zodchestva i Etnografii (Museum of Wooden Architecture and Ethnography, Taltsy) 267

Novgorodsky Gosudarstvenny
Muzei-Zapovednik
(Novgorod State Museum)
221
Oruzheinaya Palata (State
Armoury museum,
Moscow) 143–4
Otkryty Muzei Etnografii
(open-air museum, Bratsk)
265
Partizanskaya Polyana
(Partisan Field) and
museum (Bryansk) 227
Politekhnichesky Muzei
(Polytechnic Museum,
Moscow) 154, 155
Pushkin's study (Pushkinskiye
Gory) 222
Russky Muzei (Russian
Museum, St Petersburg)
100, 101, 103, 199
Trinity School museum
(Sergeyev Posad) 174
Trubetskoy Bastion museum
(St Petersburg) 191
Ukrainsky Istorychny Musey
(Museum of Ukrainian
History, Kiev, Ukraine) 312
Voyenno-Morskoi Muzei
(Central Naval Museum,
St Petersburg) 198
Zoloti Vorota (Golden Gate)
and museum (Kiev,
Ukraine) 309
Zoological Museum
(St Petersburg) 198
music and dance 116–22
see also individual composers
and musicians names
see also the arts; festivals
and events; nightlife
Association of Contemporary
Music 120
bards 113
church music 116
Congress of Composers 121
Conservatoire (St Petersburg)
118
folk music 116
Free School of Music 118
Konservatoriya imeni
Chaikovskoho (Tchaikovsky
State Conservatory, Kiev)
314
Konservatoriya imeni
Chaikovskogo (Moscow
Conservatory of Music)
161
Kontsertny zal imeni

Chaykovskogo (Tchaikovsky
Concert Hall, Moscow) 160
Odessa Philharmonic
Orchestra 323
Rimsky-Korsakov
Conservatory
(St Petersburg) 196
rock and pop music 122, 194
Russian Association of
Proletarian Musicians 120
Russian Musical Society 118
Sankt Peterburzhskaya
Filarmoniya (St Petersburg
Philharmonia) 199
skomoroki 116
Socialist Realism 120
traditional instruments 116
Union of Soviet Composers
120
Musorgsky, Modest 118
Boris Godunov 118, 196
burial place 202
Myaskovsky, Nikolai 120, 121
Mylnikov, Andrey 104

n

Nakhodka 270
Napoleon 143, 148, 285
Narva-Ivangorod 220
**national parks and nature
reserves**
Belovezhskaya Pushcha
Nature Reserve (Belarus)
301, 305
Caucasian State Preserve
(Krasnaya Polyana) 253
Kareliya nature reserve 217
Khosta forest preserve 253
Volga delta reserve 235
zapovednik nature preserve
(Siberia) 264
Nevsky, Alexander 201, 222
Nevsky, Prince Daniel 163
newspapers see **media**
Nicholas I 47–8, 100
Nicholas II 50, 185, 190, 222,
242
abdication 222
execution and burial at
Yekaterinburg 241, 242
final burial place
(St Petersburg) 190
nightlife 359
Nikon, Patriarch 90–1
Nizhny Novgorod 231
Arkhangelskoe Sobor
(Cathedral of the Archangel
Michael) 231

Gorky Avto Zavod GAZ (Gorky
Car Plant) 231
Khudozhestvenny Muzei (Art
Museum) 231
Kremlin 231
MiG aircraft factory 231
Muzei A.D. Sakharova (Andrey
Sakharov Museum) 231
Njasvich (Belarus) 302
Northern Lights 218
Novgorod 39, 220–1
accommodation 349
Battle of the Novgorodians
with the Suzdalians 97
eating out 357
Novikov, Timur 104
Novocherkassk 250
Triumphal Arch 250
Novorossisk 250
Novosibirsk 263
accommodation 351
Akademgorodok (Academic
Town) 263
Istorichesky Muzei (Local
History Museum) 263

o

Odessa (Ukraine) 321–3
accommodation 353
beach 322, 323
eating out 358
Filharmoniya (Philharmonia)
323
Hotel Londonska 322
Muzey Arkheolohli (Museum
of Archaeology) 323
Muzey Morskoho Flotu
(Museum of Maritime
History) 323
Muzey Zakhidno-skhidnolio
Mistetstva (Museum of
Western and Oriental Art)
323
Potemkin Steps 322
Prymorsky Bulvar 322
Pushkin statue 322
Teatr Opery ta Baletu (Opera
and Ballet Theatre) 323
Vulitsyn Deribasivska 323
Oimyakon 270
Oistradk, David 121
Oistrakh, Igor 121
Okoujava, Bulat 113
Old Izborsk 222
Olga, Princess, of Kiev 29
Omsk 262–3
excursions from 263
Katonsky Ostrov (Katon

Island) 262
Muzei Izobrazitelnykh Izkusstv
(Museum of Fine Art) 263
Novy Krepost (New Fort) 263
Stary Krepost (Old Fort) 262
Onezhskoe Ozero (Lake Onega)
217
Oranienbaum Palace 203
Orel
accommodation 350
eating out 357
Orenburg 245
atomic bomb testing 245
Orlov, Grigory 43
Ostankino 117
miniature theatre 117
Ostrovsky, Nikolai 252
overseas missions 340
Ovstug 227

p

palaces
Bakhchysaray Tatar Palace
(Ukraine) 324, 326
Batashev (Moscow) 154
Beloselskikh-Belozerskikh
(St Petersburg) 201
Bolshoi Kremlyovsky (Great
Kremlin Palace, Moscow)
145
Bolshoi Yekaterinsky
(Catherine Palace)
(Pushkin) 203
Dom Pashkov (Moscow)
158–9
Ekaterina Romanovna
Vorontsova (Moscow) 161
Emir of Bukhara's palace
(Zheleznovodsk) 254
Gatchino 204
Granovitaya Palata (Palace of
the Facets, Moscow) 144–5
Iosifa Zolotovo (Joseph the
Golden, Vologda) 213
Kikiny (St Petersburg) 202
Letny (Summer Palace,
St Petersburg) 192
Livadyysky (Palace of Livadia,
Yalta, Ukraine) 324
Mariinsky (Kiev) 315
Mariinsky (St Petersburg)
196
Menshikov (Moscow) 161
Menshikovsky (St Petersburg)
197
Mramorny (Marble Palace,
St Petersburg) 194
Oranienbaum 203

Orlov (Moscow) 161
Pavlovsk *204*
Petrodvorets *202*, 202–3
Sheremetyevykh
(St Petersburg) 201
Tavrichesky (St Petersburg)
202
Teremnoy Dvorets (Terem or
Belvedere, Moscow) 145
Yushkov (Moscow) 155
Yusupovsky (St Petersburg)
196
parks and gardens
Alexandrovsky Gardens
(Moscow) 146
Botanical Garden (Tomsk) 264
Drendrariy Park botanical
garden (Sochi) 251
Gorky Park (Moscow) 158, 163
Letny Sad (Summer Garden,
St Petersburg) 192
Mikhailo Kotsiubinsky park
(Chernihiv, Ukraine) 317
Neskuchny Garden (Moscow)
163
Nikitsky Botanical Gardens
(Yalta, Ukraine) 327
Riviera Park (Sochi) 251
Pashkov, Peter 159
Pasternak, Boris 111, 112
Pavlovsk Palace *204*
Pechory 222
Pskovo-Pcherskaya Lavra
(Monastery of the Caves) 222
Uspensky Sobor (Cathedral of
the Assumption) 222
people 65–72, 75–7, 249, 286
Buryat culture 269
Magyars 29
"New Russians" 72
Slavs 27–9, 283, 297
Tatars 33–5, 326
Varangians 27, 283
women of Russia 75–7
perestroika 57–8, 77, 93, 10-4
Pereyaslavl-Zalessky 175
Goritsky Monastyr (Monastery)
and museum 175
Kremlin 175
Muzei Botika ("Little Boat"
Museum) 175
Spasopreobrazhensky Sobor
(Cathedral of the
Transfiguration of the
Saviour) 175
Tserkov Petra Mitropolita
(Church of Peter the
Metropolitan) 175
Perm 245

Etnografichsky Muzei
(Ethnographic Architecture
Museum) 245
Gosudarstvennaya Kartinnaya
Galereya (State Picture
Gallery) 245
Perov, Vasily 100
Peter the Great 39, 41–3, 99,
116, 185
burial place 190
Wooden Cabin Museum
(St Petersburg) 191–2
Petrodvorets Palace *202*, 202–3
Petrokrepost 219
krepost (fortress) 219
Petrov 112
Twelve Chairs 112
Petrov-Vodkin, Kuzma 103
The Bathing of the Red Horse
103
Petrozavodsk 217
accommodation 349
Geological Research Institute
and Karelian Science
Centre 217
Kruglaya Ploshchad (Round
Square) 217
photography 361
Polatsk (Belarus) 305
Muzey Belkarushka
Knihadrukavanni (Museum
of Historical Books and
Printing) 305
Saphiyskyy Sabor (Cathedral
of St Sophia) 305
politics 53–8, 291–3
Bolsheviks 53, 185, 202,
302, 311
Communism 65, 185
Communist Party 68
corruption in government 69,
78
The Duma (Russian
parliament) 68
Muzei Molodyozhi museum of
Soviet history
(Yekaterinburg) 242
pollution 18, 20, 240, 244,
245, 269
acid rain 18
atomic bomb testing
(Orenburg) 245
Chernobyl disaster 18, 287,
294
nuclear accidents 245, 287
radiation poisoning 18, 245,
287, 304
in Siberia 261
toxic waste 18, 20

Polzunov, Ivan 266
Port Baikal 267
postal services 337–8
Potanin, Vladimir 73
Potemkin, Grigory 43, 202
Povolzhye 229–35
Powers, Gary 240
 U2 spy plane incident 240
Prigozhin, Lucian 122
Prokofiev, Sergei 119, 121
Pskov 222
 accommodation 349
 eating out 357
 Kremlin 222
 Kutekrom Bashnya (Tower)
  222
 Mirozhsky Monastyr 222
 Spaso-Preobrazhensky Sobor
  (Cathedral of the
  Transfiguration) 222
 Troitsky Sobor (Trinity
  Cathedral) 222
public holidays 331
Pugachev, Emelian 44
Pushkin 203–4, 222
 Amber Room mystery 203
 Bolshoi Yekaterinsky Dvorets
  (Catherine Palace) *203*
Pushkin, Alexander 109,
 187–8, 322
 Boris Godunov 222
 The Bronze Horseman 109,
  188
 Evgeny Onegin 109, 188,
  222, 322
Pushkinskiye Gory 222
 Mikhailovskoye estate 222
 Petrovskoye estate 222
 Pushkin's study 222
 Svyatogorsky Monastyr 222
 Trigorskoye estate 222
Putin, Vladimir 25, 58, 68-73,
 93, 104, 187, 293-5, 335
Pyatigorsk 253, 254
 Lermontovskaya Galereya
  (Lermontov Gallery) 254
 Lermontov Museum-Reserve
  253
 Mount Mashuk 254
 Spa Research Institute 254

r

Rachmaninov, Sergei 119
Radishchev, Alexander 112, 191
 *Journey from St Petersburg to
  Moscow* 112, 191
Radziwill family 302
Radziwill, Barbara 302

rail services *see* **transport**
Rasputin 196
Ratushinskaya, Irina 112
Razin, Stepan 39, 148
Reed, John 147
 *Ten Days That Shook the
  World* 147
religion 29, 89–93, 330–1
 Baptists 93, 339
 Buddhism 93, 268
 Christianity 29, 89–93
 Islam 29, 93, 339
 Judaism 29, 303, 305, 339
 "Living Church" 92
 miracles 98
 monasticism 91
 Mormon 93
 Moscow as "the Third Rome"
  90, 97
 Museum of the History of
  Religion (St Petersburg) 199
 "Old Believers" 91, 99, 259
 oppression under
  Communism 57, 91–3
 Pentecostal 93
 Protestant 93
 religious services 339
 Roman Catholic 90, 93, 339
 Russian Orthodox Church 34,
  89, 339
 "Uniate" (Greek Catholic)
  Church 284, 320
Repin, Ilya 100
 The Volga Bargehaulers 100
 *The Caporozhie Cossacks
  Writing a Mocking Letter to
  the Turkish Sultan* 100
revolution of 1905 50
revolution of 1917 50, 53
Richter, Svyatoslav 121
Rimsky-Korsakov, Nikolai 118,
 119
 burial place 202
rivers 20, 344
 Angara 261, 273
 cruises 344
 Desna 316
 Dnieper (Dnipro) 28, 29, 226,
  283
 Dniester 321
 Dvina 211, 214, 283, 305
 Iset 240
 Kama 229
 Kamenka 178
 Klyazma 178
 Kola 218
 Lena 20, 259, 261, 269–70
 Moika 196
 Moskva 141

 Neva 189, 191
 Ob 20, 259, 266
 Onega 215
 Samara 230
 Selenga 269
 Sochi 250
 Sukhona 211
 Svislach 303
 travelling by passenger boat
  344
 Tsaritsyn 232
 Volkhov 221
 Volga 28, 229–35
 Vologda 213
 Yenisei 20, 259, 261, 264
Rodchenko, Alexander 103
Roerick, Nikolay 102
Rogozhkin, Alexander 123
 *Peculiarities of the National
  Hunt* 123
Romanov dynasty 39, 177, 190
 Alexander I 47
 Alexander II 48–9, 190
 Alexander III 49
 Alexei 39, 191
 Catherine the Great *24,*
  43–4, 75, 207
 fall of dynasty 50
 Mikhail 39, 145, 177
 Nicholas I 47–8, 100
 Nicholas II 50, 185, 190,
  222, 242
 Paul I 44
 Peter the Great 39, 41–3, 99,
  116, 185
 Sophia 41–3
Roslavets, Nikolai 120
Rostov Veliky 175–6
 Kremlin 176
 Tserkov Odigitrii (Church of
  the Icon of the Hodigitria)
  176
 Tserkov Spas-na-Senyakh
  (Church of the Saviour over
  the Galleries) 176
 Uspensky Sobor (Assumption
  Cathedral) 176
Rostropovich, Mstislav 121, 122
Rozhdestvensky, Gennady 121
Rubinstein, Anton 118
Rubinstein, Nikolai 118
Rublyov, Andrei 98–9
Russian national tourist offices
 344
Rust, Matthias 152
Rybakov, Anatoly 113
 Children of the Arbat 113

S

St Elizabeth Feodorovna 93
St Petersburg 17, 42–3, 185–204
see also **Petrodvorets, Oranienbaum, Pushkin, Pavlovsk** and **Gatchino**
12 Kollegi (Twelve Colleges) 197
accommodation 347–8
Admiralteistvo (Admiralty) 195, 196
Akademiya Khudozhestv (Academy of Arts) 197
Akademiya Nauk (Academy of Sciences) 197–8
Alexander Nevsky Lavra monastery 201
Alexandriinsky Dramatichesky Teatr (Alexander Theatre of Drama) 200
Alexandrovskaya Kolonna (Alexander Column) 193, boat tours to Kareliya 217
Bolshevik headquarters 185
buses see transport
Chaliapin Museum 102
climate 186
Conservatoire 118
Domik Petra Velikogo (Peter the Great's Wooden Cabin) museum 191–2
Dvorets Beloselskikh-Belozerskikh (Beloselsky-Belozersky Palace) 201
Dvorets Sheremetyevykh (Sheremetyev Palace) 201
Dvorets Yunikh Pionerov (Palace of Young Pioneers) 201
Dvortsovaya Ploshchad (Palace Square) 193–5
eating out 355–6
Generalny Shtab (General Staff Building) 194
getting around 189
Gostiny Dvor department store 200, 361
Grand Hotel Europe 199
Hermitage Museum 206–7
Inzhenerny Zamok (Engineer's Castle a.k.a. St Michail Castle) 193
Isaakiyevsky Sobor (St Isaac's Cathedral) 196,
Kazansky Sobor (Kazan Cathedral) 199

KGB headquarters 191
Khram Spasa na Krovi (Church of the Resurrection) 187, 199
Kikiny Palati (Kikin Palace) 202
Kommandantsky Dom (Commandant's House) 189
Kreyser Avrora (Aurora) battleship 192
Kunstkamera (Chamber of Curiosities) 198
Lazarus Cemetery 201
Letny Dvorets (Summer Palace) 192
Letny Sad (Summer Garden) 192
Maly Teatr Operi i Baleta imeni Mussorgskogo (Small Musorgsky Theatre of Opera and Ballet) 199
Mariinsky Dvorets (Mariinsky Palace) 196
Mariinsky Theatre 122, 197
Marsovoye Pole (Field of Mars) 194
Mechet Troitskaya Ploshchad (mosque) 182
Medny Vsadnik (The Bronze Horseman) 188, 195
Menshikovsky Dvorets (Menshikov Palace) Museum 197
metro see transport
Mramorny Dvorets (Marble Palace) 194
Muzei Anni Akhmatovoi (Anna Akhmatova Museum) 201
Muzei F.M. Dostyevskovo (Dostoyevsky Museum) 201
Muzei Istoriya Religii (Museum of the History of Religion) 199
Nakhimovskoye Uchilishche (Nakhimov Naval Academy) 192
Nevsky Prospekt 198
New Academy of Arts 104
Nikolskaya Ploshchad (St Nicholas Square) 196
Nikolsky Morskoy Sobor (Cathedral of St Nicholas) 196–7
Petropavlovskaya Krepost (Peter and Paul Fortress) 189, 189–91
Petropavlovsky Sobor (Saviour on the Blood Cathedral) 190

Petrovskiye Vorota (Peter Gate) 190
Piskarovskoye Memorial Cemetery 189
Ploshchad Dekabristov (Decembrists Square) 195
Ploshchad Ostrovskogo (Ostrovsky Square) 200
police brutality 335
Rimsky-Korsakov Conservatory 196
Rossiskaya Natsionalnaya Biblioteka (Russian National Library) 200
Russky Muzei (Russian Museum) 100, 101, 103, 199
Sankt Peterburzhskaya Filarmoniya (St Petersburg Philharmonia) 199
Senat i Sinod (The Senate and the Synod) 195
Sennaya Ploshchad (Hay Square) 200
shopping 361
Smolny Institut 202
Smolny Sobor (Smolny Cathedral) 202
Taleon Club 199
Tavrichesky Dvorets (Tauride Palace) 202
taxis see transport
Teatralnaya Ploshchad (Theatre Square) 196
Tikvin Cemetery 202
transport 187, 203, 235
Trubetskoy Bastion Museum 191
Vaganova Ballet School 200
Vasilievsky Ostrov (Basil's Island) 197
Vitebsk Station 203
Vokhov Cemetery 202
Voyenno-Morskoi Muzei (Central Naval Museum) 198
white nights festival 17, 186, 190, 194
Yusupovsky Dvorets (Yusupov Palace) 196
Zayachy Ostrov (Hare Island) 189
Zoological Museum 198
St Sergium of Radonezh 91
Sakhalin island 271
Sakharov, Andrei 58, 112
Sakurov, Alexander 123
Mother and Son 123
Samara 230

accommodation 350
Teatr imeni Gorkogo (Drama
 Theatre) 230
Samokhvalov 104
Saratov 230–31
 accommodation 350
 Muzei Iskusstv imeni
 Radishcheva (Art Museum)
 231
 Muzei Kraiyevedeniya
 (Museum of Local Lore) 231
 Sobor Svyatoi Troitsi (Trinity
 Cathedral) 231
 Stary Sobor (Old Cathedral)
 231
 Teatr Operi i Baleta (Opera
 and Ballet Theatre) 231
Schnittke, Alfred 122
Scriabin, Alexander 119
 burial place 166
secret police
 Cheka 53, 302
 KGB 57, 156, 268, 304
 NKVD 55, 304
 oprichnina 38–9
Seliger Lake 229
Sergei, Patriarch 92
Sergeyev Posad 173–4
 Trapeznaya Tserkov St Sergei
 (Refectory Church of
 St Sergei) 174
 Trinity School museum 173–4
 Troitse-Sergiyevsky Lavra
 (Trinity Monastery of St
 Sergius) 91, 173
 Troitsky Sobor (Trinity
 Cathedral) 173
 Uspensky Sobor (Assumption
 Cathedral) 174
Serov, Valentin 101
 Ida Rubinstein 101
Sevastopol (Ukraine) 324, 326
 accommodation 353
 Chersonesus ruins 324, 326
Severodvinsk 215
Sheremetev, Count 117
Shikotan island 271
Shinrikyo, Aum 93
Sholokhov 112
 And Quiet Flows the Don 112
shopping 360–61
 Detsky Mir children's store
 (Moscow) 156, 360
 Gostiny Dvor department
 store (St Petersburg) 200,
 361
 GUM (Moscow) 149, 360
 in Kiev 313
 in Moscow 156, 160, 360

in St Petersburg 361
open-air arts and crafts
 market (Lviv, Ukraine) 319
Tsentralny farmers' market
 (Moscow) 156
TSUM department store
 (Moscow) 156, 360
Yeliseyevsky Gastronom
 supermarket (Moscow) 160
Shostakovich, Dmitri 119, 120–1
 Fifth Symphony 120
 First Symphony 120
 Fourth Symphony 120
 Lady Macbeth of Mtsensk 120
 The Nose 120
 Tenth Symphony 121
Shushkevich 305
Siberia 259–71
 *see also individual place
 names*
 geography 259
 getting around 262
Sinyavsky 112
Skaryna, Frantsysk 305
Slonimsky, Sergei 122
Smirnov, Dmitry 122
Smolensk 226
 accommodation 350
 Bogoyavlensky Cathedral 226
 city wall 226, *227*
 eating out 357
 Kartinnaya Galereya (Art
 Gallery) 226
 Muzei S.T. Konenkova
 (Sculpture Museum) 226
 Uspensky Sobor (Assumption
 Cathedral) 226
Smolenksy, Alexander 73
Sochi 250–51, *252*
 accommodation 350–1
 climate 250
 Derevo Druzhby (Tree of
 Friendship) 251
 Drendariy Park botanical
 garden 251
 eating out 357
 international film festival 251
 Kurortny Prospekt 251
 Muzei Istori Goroda-kurorta
 Sochi (Sochi History
 Museum) 252
 Muzei Izobrazitelnykh Iskusstv
 (Sochi Art Gallery) 251
 Muzei Pisatelya Nikolaya
 Ostrovskogo (Ostrovsky
 Literary Museum) 252
 Riviera Park 251
Solovetsky Islands 216
 Anzersky Island 216

boat trips 216, 218
Solovetsky Monastyr
 (Solovetsky Monastery) 216
Solovetsky Special Purpose
 Camp 216
Solvychedgodsk 215
 Blagoveshenchsky Sobor
 (Annunciation Cathedral) 215
 museum 215
 Yavleniya Bogorodtsib
 (Monastery of the Pre-
 sentation of the Virgin) 215
Solzhenitsyn, Alexander 112–3
 Cancer Ward 112
 First Circle 112
 The Gulag Archipelago 112
 *One Day in the Life of Ivan
 Denisovich* 112–3
Somov, Konstantin 102
Sosnovy Bor 220
 nuclear power station 220
souvenirs 313, 360
 see also **customs**
**Spaso-Prilutsky Monastyr
 (Monastery of the Saviour on
 the Bend)** 213
Spasskoe Lutovinova 227
 museum 227
sport and recreation 70
 climbing 266, 327
 cross-country skiing 219
 Dynamo Kiev 297
 fishing 259, 273
 football 297
 hiking 253, 263, 266, 273,
 327
 horseriding 273
 hunting 259, 265
 river rafting 266
 skating 273
 skiing 253, 266
 snow-mobiling 259
 trekking 266, 327
 troika rides 273
 winter sports 70
Stalin, Joseph 54
Stanislavsky 162
Staraya Ladoga 219
Staraya Russa 221–2
 Dostoevstovo Muzei
 (Dostoevsky Museum) 222
steppe 19, 20
Sterligov, Vladimir 104
Stolypin, Peter 49
Stravinsky, Igor 119, 121
 The Firebird 119
 Petrushka 119
 Rite of Spring 119
Stroganov family 214–5

Sudak 324
  accommodation 353
Surikov, Vasily 100, 265
  Muzei-usadba V.I. Surikova
    (Krasnoyarsk) 265
Suzdal 176, *177*, 177–8
  accommodation 349
  eating out 178, 357
  Museum of Wooden
    Architecture and Peasant
    Life 176
  Pokrovsky Monastyr
    (Intercession Convent)
    178
  Rizopolozhensky Monastyr
    (Monastery of the Deposition
    of the Virgin's Robe) 178
  Rozhdestvensky Sobor
    (Cathedral of the Nativity of
    the Virgin) 178
  Spaso Yefimiyevsky Monastyr
    (Monastery of the Lament
    of Christ) 178
Svetlanov 121
Sviridova, Giorgi 122

t

taiga 19, 20, *261*
Taltsy 267
  Muzei Zodchestva i Etnografii
    (Museum of Wooden
    Architecture and
    Ethnography) 267
Tambukanskoye Lake 254
Tanyeyev, Sergei 119
Tara 263
Tataria 229
  see also place names
Tatlin, Vladimir 103
taxis *see* **transport**
Tchaikovsky, Boris 122
Tchaikovsky, Pyotr 118, 198
  burial place 202
  Eugene Onegin 118
  The Queen of Spades 118
  Sleeping Beauty 196
telephone 338
  dialling codes 337
Tennyson, Alfred Lord 285
  Charge of the Light Brigade
    285
Tereshkova, Valentina 75
Theofan "the Greek" 97, 98
Tikhon, Patriarch 91
Tikhvin 219–20
time zones 261, 330
tipping 339
Tishchenko, Boris 122

Tolstoy, Leo 110
  Anna Karenina 110, 188
  War and Peace 110–11, 188
Tolyatti 230
  Volzhsky Avtozavod (Volga Car
    Factory) 230
Tomsk 263–4
  Botanical Garden 264
Totma 214
tourist information 341
tour operators 345–6
trade and industry 330
  coal (Kuzbass region, Siberia)
    264
  coal mine visits (Kemerovo)
    264
  GAZ/Gorky Car Plant (Nizhny
    Novgorod) 231
  Hanseatic League 98, 220
  industrialisation under Stalin
    55
  MiG aircraft factory (Nizhny
    Novgorod) 231
  oil 261
  in Siberia 261, 264
  trade routes 226, 230,
    262
  in the Urals 239–45
  the Silk Route 324
  Uralsky Mashinostroitelny
    Zavod (Urals Factory of
    Heavy Machine
    Construction, Yekaterinburg)
    243
  Volzhsky Avtozavod (Volga Car
    Factory) 230
transport
  Moscow 162
  taxis 263
Trans-Mongolian railway 124
Trans-Siberian railway 49,
    124–5, 259, 261–2, *263*,
    267, 270, 342
Travellers with disabilities
    339
Trotsky, Lev 50, 54
  Diary in Exile 54
  *History of the Russian
    Revolution* 54
  Stalin 54
Tsereteli, Zurab 165
Tsvetaeva, Marina 113
Tuapse 250
tundra 19, 270
Turgenev, Ivan 110, 226, 227
  Fathers and Sons 110, 227
  Hunter's Sketches 110
  A Nest of Gentlefolk 227
Tyutchev, Fyodor 15, 227

u

Uchansu Waterfall (Ukraine)
    327
Ugarov, Boris 104
Ukraine 17–18, 279, 283–97,
    309–12, 331
  see also place names
  economy 291–3, 296–7, 331
  getting there 334
  independence 291–2
  money matters 333
  National Anthem 321
  politics 291–3
  Treaty of Riga 286
  Ukrainian National Republic
    285
  visas and passports 332
  Western Ukrainian National
    Republic 285
Ulan-Ude 268, 269
  accommodation 351
  Ivolginsk Datsan Buddhist
    temple 268
Ulyanov, Alexander 191, 219
Ulyanovsk 229
Ural mountains 17–18,
    239–45
Urmany bog 261
USSR
  disintigration of 58, 67, 185,
    287, 305
  formation of 53, 286
Ustvolskaya, Galina 122

v

Valaam Islands 217
  Preobrazhensky Sobor
    (Cathedral of the
    Transfiguration) 217
  Valaamsky Monastyr (Valaam
    Monastery) 217
**Valdaiskaya Vozvyshennost
  (Valdai Hills)** 229
Vasily III 214
Vasnetsov, Viktor 100
Veliky Ustyug 214
  Dom Shilova (Shilov House)
    214
  Mikhailo-Arkhangelsky
    Monastyr (Monastery of the
    Archangel Michael) 214
  Tserov Simeona Stolpnika
    (Church of Simeon the
    Styline) 214
  Uspensky Sobor (Cathedral of
    the Assumption) 214
  Tsrekov Zhawn-Mironosets

(Church of the Holy
Women) 214
Venetsianov, Alexei 100
Harvest Time: Summer 100
Vereshchagin, Vasily 100
Verstovsky, Alexei 117
visas and passports 332
rail passengers in transit 332
Vladimir 178
accommodation 349
Church of the Intercession
178
Dmitrievsky Sobor (Cathedral
of St Dmitry) 178
eating out 356–7
Knyaginin Monastyr (Princess
Convent) 178
Uspensky Sobor (Assumption
Cathedral) 178
Zolotiye Vorota (Golden Gate)
178
Vladivostok 124–5, 270
accommodation 351
boat trips to Kurile Islands 270
Voinovich, Vladimir 112
Volga Region 229–35
see also place names
Volga River 229–35
Volgograd 231–3
accommodation 350
Battle of Stalingrad 232
Mamaev Kurgan (Mamaev
Mound) memorial 232
Muzei Izobrazitelnykh Iskusstv
(Fine Arts Museum) 233
Planetary (Planetarium) 233
Volkov, Fyodor 177
Volodymyr (Vladimir), Prince
29–30, 309, 311, 313, 324
Vologda 213
accommodation 349
Dom Admirala Barsha (Barsh
Mansion) 213
Dom Levashova (Levashov
House) 213
Dom Zasetskikh (Zasetsky
House) 213
eating out 357
Kremlin 213
Palati Iosifa Zolotovo (Palace
of Joseph the Golden) 213
Skliabinskaya Bogadelnaya
(Skuliabin Almshouse) 213
Sofiysky Sobor (Cathedral of
St Sophia) 213
Tserkov Svyatikh Konstantin i
Yelena (Church of SS
Constantine and Helen) 213
Vorontsova, Ekaterina

Romanovna 161
Voznesensky, Andrei 113
Vrubel, Mikhail 101
Vyborg 219
accommodation 349
eating out 357
Vyborgsky Zamok (Vyborg
Castle) 219
Vysotsky, Vladimir 113

W

White Sea 216
wildlife 19
see also national parks and
nature reserves
women
equality 76, 77
in folklore 77
Ravnopravki (women for equal
rights) 76
role in World War II 76
of Russia 75–7
travelling alone 336

Y

Yakutia 17, 20
diamonds 20
Yakutsk 270
accommodation 352
boat trips 270
Derevnya Yakutsk (old village)
270
eating out 358
Lenskiye Stolby (Lena Pillars)
270
Muzei Istorii i Kultury
Severnikh Narodov
(Museum of North Peoples)
270
Yalta (Ukraine) *297*, 324, 326,
327
accommodation 353
boat trips 327
eating out 358
Lastochkino Gnezdo
(Swallow's Nest) castle
278, 324
Livadyysky Dvorets (Palace of
Livadia) 324
Nikitsky Botanical Gardens
327
Russian Orthodox church *324*
Yaroslavl 125, 176–7
accommodation 348
eating out 356
Spaso-Preobrazhensky
Monastyr (Monastery) 177

Teatr Volkhova 177
Tserkov Bogoyavlenia (Church
of the Incarnation) 176
Tserkov Ilyi Proroka (Church of
Elijah the Prophet) and
museum 176–7
Yaroslav the Wise 176, 309, 317
Yekaterinburg 125, *238*, *239*,
240–44
accommodation 350
climate 240
Dom Gorodskogo Pravitelstva
(City Hall) 243
Dom Ipatyeva (Ipatyev
House), site of 243
eating out 357
execution of Tsar Nicholas II
241
Istorichesky Muzei (Regional
History Museum) 242
Muzei Iskusstva (Art
Museum) 243
Ploshchad 1905 (1905
Square) 243
Uralsky Gosudarstvenny
Tekhnichesky Universitet
(Urals State Technical
University) *243*
Uralsky Mashinostroitelny
Zavod (Urals Factory of
Heavy Machine
Construction) 243
Yeltsin, Boris 58, 69, 93,
241–2, 243, 305
Yesenin, Sergei 111, 112
Yessentuki 254
Yevtushenko, Yevgeny 15, 113
Yuzhno-Kurilsk 271
boat trips to Shikotan island
271
Muzei Yestestvoznaniya
(Museum of Natural
History) 271
Yuzhno-Sakhalinsk 271
Mount Bolshevik 271

Z

Zamyatin, Evgeny 112
The Cavemen 188
Zheleznovodsk 254
Emir of Bukhara's palace 254
Ostrovsky Baths 254
permafrost caves 254
Zhiguli Hills 229–30
Zinoviev 113
Zoshchenko 112